Equity Derivatives

Neil C Schofield

Equity Derivatives

Corporate and Institutional Applications

Neil C Schofield
Verwood, Dorset, United Kingdom

ISBN 978-0-230-39106-2   ISBN 978-0-230-39107-9   (eBook)
DOI 10.1057/978-0-230-39107-9

Library of Congress Control Number: 2016958283

This Palgrave Macmillan imprint is published by Springer Nature
The registered company is Macmillan Publishers Ltd.
The registered company address is: The Campus, 4 Crinan Street, London, N1 9XW, United Kingdom

Acknowledgements

Like the vast majority of authors, I have been able to benefit from the insights of many people while writing this book.

First and foremost, I must thank my friend and fellow trainer, David Oakes of Dauphin Financial Training. On more occasions than he cares to remember David has kindly answered my queries in his normal cheerful manner. If you ever have a question on finance, I can assure you that David will know the answer! I must also thank Yolanda Clatworthy who spent a significant amount of time reviewing chapter three. Her insights have added enormous value to the chapter. Stuart Urquhart arranged for me to have access to Barclays Live and the quality of the data and screenshots has added significant value to the text. Over the years that I have known Stuart he has been a great supporter of all my writing and training activities often when the benefit to himself is marginal. A true gentleman. Many thanks to Doug Christensen who gave permission for the Barclays Live data to be used.

Aaron Brask and Frans DeWeert both critiqued the original text proposal and made a number of useful pointers as to how the scope could be improved. Although I had to drop some of the suggestions due to time and space constraints, their contributions were significant and gladly received. Also thanks to Matt Deakin of Morgan Stanley who helped clarify some equity swap settlement conventions. Troy Bowler was an invaluable sounding board in relation to a number of topics.

Thanks also go to the many participants who have attended my classroom sessions over the years. The immediacy of the feedback that participants provide is invaluable in helping me deepen my understanding of a topic.

Finally, a word of thanks to my family who have always been supportive of everything that I have done. A special word of thanks to Nicki who never complains even when I work late. "V".

Although many people helped to shape the book any mistakes are entirely my responsibility. I would always be interested to hear any comments about the text and so please feel free to contact me at neil.schofield@fmarketstraining.com or via my website www.fmarketstraining.com.

PS. Alan and Roger—once again, two slices of white toast and a cuppa for me!

Contents

List of Figures

List of Tables

1

Equity Derivatives: The Fundamentals

1.1 Chapter Overview

The objective of this chapter is to provide the reader with an overview of the main concepts and terminology of the 'cash' equity market that is directly relevant to the equity derivatives market.[1] Although the products covered in this chapter will reappear throughout the text, certain variants (e.g. dividend and variance swaps) will be described in the chapters where they feature most prominently. The products and concepts covered in this chapter are as follows:

- 'Cash' equity markets
- Equity derivative products
- Market participants

1.2 Fundamental Concepts

1.2.1 Corporate Capital Structures

In general terms there are three ways in which a company can borrow money:

- Bank loans
- Bond issuance
- Equity issuance

---

[1] For readers looking for more detail one suggested reference is Chisholm, A (2009) 'An introduction to capital markets' John Wiley and Sons.

© The Author(s) 2017
N. Schofield, *Equity Derivatives*, DOI 10.1057/978-0-230-39107-9_1

These borrowings are shown on a company's financial statements as liabilities since they represent monies owed to other entities and can be used to finance the purchase of assets, that is, items owned by the company. Collectively, these three sources of funds are loosely referred to as 'capital' and taken collectively represent a company's capital structure. In an ideal world the assets purchased by these liabilities should generate sufficient income to finance the return to the different providers of capital. The interest on bank loans and bonds will be contractual interest, typically variable for bank loans and fixed for the issued bonds. Equities will pay a discretionary dividend whose magnitude should reflect the fact that in the event of the company going out of business, shareholders will be the last to be repaid.

1.2.2 Types of Equity

As in many aspects of finance it is common to use many different terms to describe the same concept. For example, equities can also be referred to interchangeably as either 'shares' or 'stock'.

There are several different types of equity:

- *Ordinary shares*—holders of these shares have the right to vote on certain company-related issues at the annual general meeting (AGM) and will also receive any dividends announced by the company. There is something of an urban myth which suggests that shareholders 'own' the company, whereas in reality this is not the case.[2]
- *Preferred shares*—this class of equity sits above ordinary shares for bankruptcy purposes and holders will typically receive a fixed dividend payment before any ordinary shareholders are repaid.
- *Cumulative preference shares*—these are a version of preferred shares where if the company does not have sufficient cash flow to pay the dividend in any given year it must be paid in the following year or whenever the company has generated sufficient profits. Any dividend arrears must be paid off before dividends can be paid to the ordinary shareholders.
- *Treasury stock*—this is not really a type of share but Treasury stock represents a situation where a company has decided to repurchase some of its own shares in the market. The shares are not cancelled but are held on the balance sheet. A company may decide to repurchase its own shares if they felt they were undervalued.

---

[2] See for example: 'Is it meaningful to talk about the ownership of companies' on www.johnkay.com

1.2.3 Equity Indices

Introduction

An equity index is a numerical representation of the way an equity market has performed relative to some base reference date. The index is assigned an arbitrary initial value of, say, 100 or 1000. For example, the UK FTSE 100 share index was launched on 3rd January 1984 with a base value of 1000.

They are also widely used as a benchmark for fund management performance; a fund that has generated a 5 % return would need to have its performance judged within some context. If 'the market', as defined by some agreed index, has returned 7 %, then at a very simple level the fund has underperformed.

Each of the indices will be compiled according to a different set of rules that would govern such aspects as follows:

- What constitutes an eligible security for inclusion in the index?
- How often are the constituent members reviewed?
- What criteria will lead to a share being removed from or added to the index?
- How are new issues, mergers and restructurings reflected within the index?

Reference is sometimes made to 'investable indices', which refers to those indices where it is possible for market participants to purchase the constituent shares in the same proportions as the index without concerns over liquidity or without incurring significant transaction costs.

Index Construction

Generally speaking, there are two ways in which an index can be constructed. The simplest form of index construction uses the concept of price weighting. The value of the index is basically the sum of all the security prices divided by the total number of constituents. All the shares are equally weighted with no account taken of the relative size of the company. This type of method is rarely used but it does form the basis of how the Dow Jones Industrial Average is constructed.

The most commonly used method is market-value weighting which is based on the market capitalization of each share. This technique weights each of the constituent shares by the number of shares in issue so the relative size of the company will determine the impact on the index of a change in the share price. The market capitalization of a company is calculated based on the company's 'free float'. This is the number of shares that are freely available to purchase. So if a company were to issue new shares but wished to retain ownership of a certain proportion, only those available to the public would be included within the index calculation.

Index Divisor

To understand how market-value weighted indices work, it is important to understand the concept of the index divisor. The main role of the divisor is to act as a scaling factor. To illustrate this concept, consider Eq. 1.1.

$$\text{Index level} = \frac{\sum_i P_i Q_i}{\text{Divisor}} \qquad (1.1)$$

Where:
P_i = the price of the ith stock within the index
Q_i = the number of shares for the ith stock used in the calculation

The numerator of Eq. 1.1 would return a very large value and so the divisor scales the result down to a more meaningful level. To illustrate how this works, consider the following simplified example based on four shares detailed in Table 1.1.

Suppose that this market is about to start trading for the very first time. The index provider has decided that the initial opening value of the index will be set at a level of 1000. By establishing this value, it is possible to determine from the principles of Eq. 1.1 the initial level of the index divisor.

$$\text{Index level} = \frac{(\$10 \times 100) + (\$20 \times 20) + (\$3 \times 300) + (\$8 \times 80)}{\text{Divisor}}$$

$$1000 = \frac{\$2,940}{\text{Divisor}} \qquad (1.2)$$

$$\text{Divisor} = 2.94$$

By the end of the day assume that the company A's share price has increased to $11 but everything else is unchanged. This means the overall market capitalization has increased by $100 to $3040. The original divisor can now be used to calculate the closing index value, which would be 1034 ($3040/2.94).

Table 1.1 Hypothetical constituents of an equity index

	Price (P)	Number of shares (Q)	Market capitalization (P × Q)	Market capitalization weighting (%)
A	$10	100	$1000	34.0
B	$20	20	$400	13.6
C	$3	300	$900	30.6
D	$8	80	$640	21.8
Total			$2940	100

Although the divisor does scale the market capitalization, it is also used to ensure that the index displays continuity when there is a change to the constituent stocks. This might result from shares entering or leaving the index in accordance with the provider's rules or perhaps as a result of something like a corporate action which results in a merger or acquisition.

To illustrate this aspect of the divisor, suppose that after the close of the market on day #1 stock D leaves the index for some reason and is replaced with stock E. This stock is valued at $15 and has 50 shares in issue. The key to understanding the role of the divisor is that the following day the market must open at the previous day's close, that is 1034. So using the same principles illustrated in Eq. 1.2 the divisor must now change to 3.046.

$$\text{Index level} = \frac{(\$11 \times 100) + (\$20 \times 20) + (\$3 \times 300) + (\$15 \times 50)}{\text{Divisor}}$$

$$1,034 = \frac{\$3,150}{\text{Divisor}} \tag{1.3}$$

$$\text{Divisor} = 3.046$$

Price Versus Total Return Indices

Indices can be published as either a price return or as a total return. A price return index (such as the FTSE 100) only reflects movements in the price, whereas a total return index (such as the DAX) will reflect both the change in price of the shares as well as any dividend that is paid. The dividend income is assumed to be reinvested in the overall index rather than in the specific stock that paid the dividend.

There are a number of steps needed to calculate a total return index.

The first step is to calculate the cash value of the dividends paid on a daily basis:

$$\text{Total daily dividend} = \sum_i \text{Dividend}_i \times \text{Shares}_i \tag{1.4}$$

Where:
Dividend$_i$ = the dividend per share paid on a particular date
Shares$_i$ = the number of shares to which the dividend is applied
This is then converted to an index number by dividing by the applicable divisor

$$\text{Dividend in index points} = \frac{\text{Total daily dividend}}{\text{Divisor}} \qquad (1.5)$$

From this it is possible to calculate a daily total return value expressed as a decimal:

$$\text{Daily total return}_t = \frac{\text{Index level}_t + \text{Index dividend}_t}{\text{Index level}_{t-1}} - 1 \qquad (1.6)$$

The index level in period 't' is calculated in the same manner as the previous market capitalization example.

The final step is to use the result of (Eq. 1.6) to calculate the level of the total return index:

$$\text{Total return index level}_t = \text{Total return index level}_{t-1} \\ \times \left(1 + \text{Daily total return}_t \right) \qquad (1.7)$$

Index Ratios

It is also very common for each index to publish comparable equity ratios.[3] Equity ratios are used to assess the value and performance of an individual stock or the market as a whole. For example, they may be useful for comparing

- the level and trend in a stock's ratios relative to those of the market index;
- the ratios on one index with similar ratios in other domestic equity indices—for instance, ratios on a 'headline' index comprising the main components of a particular market against those on 'second-line' stocks;
- the ratios in one national equity market with similar ratios from other markets. This may not, however, be an exact science due to national differences in accounting practice;
- equity index ratios against comparable ratios from related asset classes such as bonds;

One popular measure relates a company's profits ('earnings') to the number of shares in issue. This is the earnings per share or EPS. To calculate the value for all of the index constituents the formula is

---

[3] Equity ratios will be analysed in greater depth in Chap. 3.

$$\text{EPS for index} = \frac{\sum_i \text{EPS}_i \times \text{shares}_i}{\text{Divisor}} \qquad (1.8)$$

The numerator of Eq. 1.8 returns the sum of the monetary value of the announced earnings on a per share basis with the denominator converting this into an index equivalent. Another measure is the price—earnings ratio (PE) which returns the ratio of the share price to the EPS. This in effect is a form of payback calculation; how many years of earnings will it take before I am repaid my initial investment? From an index perspective it is calculated as

$$\text{PE for the index} \frac{\dfrac{\sum_i P_i \times \text{shares}_i}{\text{Divisor}}}{\dfrac{\sum_i \text{EPS}_i \times \text{shares}_i}{\text{Divisor}}} \qquad (1.9)$$

The same general approach can be used to calculate other key ratios of interest to the investor.

1.2.4 Volume-Weighted Average Price

A common theme in finance is whether a purchase or sale of an asset has been done at a fair market price. The concept of the Volume-Weighted Average Price (VWAP) has become a popular benchmark price against which the relative success of a transaction could be judged.

VWAP is the weighted average price per share over a predefined period, where the weight is the volume of shares traded. VWAP trading is the buying and selling of shares at a price that tracks the VWAP. VWAP trading strategies could be used for large orders where the client is concerned that the size of the transaction may cause the market to move significantly. Very often investment banks will use computerized algorithms to execute a VWAP trade.

Consider the following trades executed over some time horizon:

- 10,000 shares @ 2.35
- 12,000 shares @ 2.33
- 15,000 shares @ 2.34
- 11,000 shares @ 2.36

The VWAP is calculated as:

$$= \frac{(10,000 \times 2.35) + (12,000 \times 2.33) + (15,000 \times 2.34) + (11,000 \times 2.36)}{10,000 + 12,000 + 15,000 + 11,000}$$

$$= \frac{112,520}{48,000}$$

$$= 2.344167 \tag{1.10}$$

1.2.5 Share Price Dilution

The issue of share price dilution arises in many different contexts within both the cash and derivative equity markets. The concept relates to how shareholders may experience a transfer of wealth and an erosion of control either by the actions of an issuer or indeed by the investors themselves. To illustrate the concept, consider the following simple example. You decide to set up a company with a friend and decide to inject a total of £10,000, with the shareholding agreed as a 70/30 split in your favour. You decide to issue 10,000 shares meaning that each share is worth £1. A few months later you decide to borrow some more money from a new investor who offers you £5000 but demands a 50 % stake in the company. In order for the new investor to own 50 % of the company you would need to issue a further 10,000 shares such that the total number of shares outstanding is 20,000. Since the new investor's offer infers a value of £10,000 for the whole company the share price must be £0.50 (20,000 shares valued at £10,000). Not only have the original owners seen their stake fall to 35 % and 15 % (an example of control or percentage dilution) but the value of their holding fall by half (an example of share price dilution).

Another way of illustrating the issues of dilution is to consider a rights issue, which is a technique used by companies to raise new funds. In some countries the concept of pre-emption rights provides for the protection of existing shareholders as the principle requires companies to first offer existing shareholders the right but not the obligation to purchase more shares in the company. Pre-emption rights are designed to protect existing shareholders from share price dilution. However, pre-emption rights are not universal (e.g. the UK has pre-emption rights, while the USA does not).

The new shares that are offered as part of a rights issue will be priced at a discount to the current share price. If the offer price were higher than the existing share price, there would be little incentive to participate in the issue as it would be cheaper to buy them in the underlying market.

The terms of the rights issue will involve setting a ratio for the rights, which establishes the number of new shares on offer for each share held. Some types of rights issues allow the rights to be sold in the marketplace thereby transferring the opportunity to purchase additional shares to another market participant. As a result, the rights have a value which is separate from the value of the underlying shares as they allow the holder to buy the shares at a discount to their current price. Existing shareholders will then have to choose between

- taking up the rights;
- selling the rights (if the transaction allows);
- doing nothing.

This choice will be time-bounded and the offer document will outline the deadline by which the owners must make their decision.

In a rights issue shares will trade 'ex-rights' (without the rights) or 'cum rights' (with the rights). The theoretical ex-rights price (TERP) is the price at which the shares should trade after the exercise of the rights on offer. It can be estimated using the following formula:

$$\frac{\left(\text{Existing shares} \times \text{cum rights price}\right) + \left(\text{new shares} \times \text{offer price}\right)}{\text{Existing shares} + \text{new shares}} \quad (1.11)$$

The cum-rights price is defined as the share price immediately before the shares start to trade ex-rights.

Suppose there is a '1 for 2' rights issue at 90p (1 new share for every 2 held). If the cum-rights price is 100p the TERP is

$$\left[\left(100 \times 2\right) + \left(90 \times 1\right)\right]/3 = 96.66\text{p}$$

The value of the right would therefore be the difference between the TERP and the price at which the new shares would be offered. In this case it would be 6.66p per share.

To illustrate the concept of share price dilution, consider the following example.[4] Suppose a company announces a 1 for 1 rights issue at an offer price of €1.05, where the cum-rights price was €2.55. We will assume that the investor holds a position of 1000 shares, which for ease of illustration we will

---

[4] This example is based on 'Understanding rights issues' Lee and Taylor (2009), Barclays Capital Research.

Table 1.2 Illustration of impact of rights issue depending on whether the rights are taken up or not

	Rights not taken up	Rights taken up
Initial value of shareholding	€2550	€2550
TERP	€1.80	€1.80
Value of the rights	€0.75	€0.75
Proceeds from selling the rights	€750	Not applicable
Amount subscribed to rights issue	Not applicable	€1050
Shares held post rights issue	1000	2000
Value of shares post issue	€1800	€3600
Total value received	€2550	€2550
Percentage shareholding post rights issue	2.5 %	5.0 %

assume represents a shareholding of 5 %. Table 1.2 shows the position of the investor depending on whether the rights are taken up or not.

The TERP and the value of the rights are calculated using the same method as described earlier in the section. The line entitled 'total value received' can be interpreted as follows:

• *Rights not taken up*—this is the sum of the proceeds received from selling the rights plus the value of the shares after the rights issue.
• *Rights taken up*—this is the value of the shares post issue minus the subscription amount.

Note that whether the rights are taken up or not the value to the investor is the same €2550. However, the example shows that unless the investor subscribes to the new shares they will suffer dilution of their percentage holding. If the issue of new shares were not offered to existing shareholders, then their existing shareholding would reduce in both percentage and value terms.

1.2.6 Stock Lending and Equity Repo

Stock Lending
Stock lending can be thought of as the temporary transfer of securities on a collateralized basis. According to the Securities Lending Association[5] it 'describes the market practice by which for a fee, securities are transferred temporarily from one party, the lender, to another, the borrower; the borrower is obliged to return them either on demand or at the end of any agreed term'.

---

[5] www.isla.co.uk

To an extent the use of the word 'lending' is misleading. Legally, the transaction will require the absolute transfer of title against an undertaking to return equivalent securities. The transfer of title is important as it allows the borrower to either sell or lend the securities. Equivalence means that the securities returned must have the same International Securities Identification Number.

The transaction will be collateralized by the borrower with cash or securities of equal or greater value than the securities that have been loaned. This will protect the lender of the securities against the default of the borrower. Inevitably given there seems to be an exception to everything in finance, it is also possible for the entity that initially delivers cash to apply a substantial 'haircut' to the proceeds. This means that the amount of cash forwarded would be less than the market value of the securities and anecdotal stories of 40 % haircuts during the height of the financial crisis were recounted to the author.

The loan can be for a specified term or open (sometimes referred to as 'at call'). An open trade does not have a fixed maturity but allows the lender of the security to recall the equity at short notice (e.g. 24 h).

The supply of securities comes mainly from the portfolios of large institutional investors such as pension funds, insurance companies and unit trusts/mutual funds. The underlying demand to borrow securities comes from investment banks and hedge funds.

There are a number of reasons why an entity would wish to borrow an equity. The most common reason to borrow a security is to cover a short or sold position and so the borrowed security is used to facilitate the settlement of the transaction. It is common for the popular press to describe short sales as 'selling something that you don't own'. This is an inaccurate description—selling something you don't own is called theft! To be able to deliver a security the seller will need to have taken full title, which is achieved by borrowing the asset in the securities lending market.

Another popular motivation for short selling is to express a view that the price of an underlying asset is expected to fall. The bank or hedge fund will borrow the asset, re-register it, sell it and then wait for the price to fall. After some designated period, the asset is repurchased asset and then redelivered back to the original lender. The profit to the short seller is simply the difference between the funds received from the initial sale less the cost of repurchasing the asset. However, this profit is reduced as the lender of the security will charge the borrower a fee. Other motivations for borrowing securities will include:

• *Pairs trading*—the simultaneous purchase and sale of two shares whose prices are considered to be trading away from some notion of theoretical value.

- *Merger arbitrage*—this strategy involves the purchase and sale of shares of companies who are in the process of a potential merger.
- *Convertible bond arbitrage*—this will involve the purchase of a convertible bond and the short selling of the underlying equity to exploit the volatility of the issuer's share price.
- *Index arbitrage*—this involves the selling (buying) shares and buying (selling) index futures to exploit a perceived mispricing of the futures contract.

We will consider some of these strategies in subsequent sections of the book.

The motivations for lending securities include:

- *Fee income*—the lender of the security will be able to charge a fee for the loan of the securities.
- *Collateralized loan*—some hedge funds use the mechanism as a way of borrowing money. For example, they may approach a bank and offer to lend a portfolio of equities in return for cash. In this case the bank may apply a very significant 'haircut' to the loaned funds. Anecdotally this may mean that for every $100 of securities lent the bank may only forward $30—$40 of cash.

There are many conventions that have evolved in the securities lending market. For example, the lender of the equity will lose title to the share but will retain the economic benefits. Although the company borrowing the asset will be able to vote at the company's AGM since they are the registered owner, the lender will often exercise their right to recall the security at short notice if they wish to vote. If the share is subject to any corporate action during the loan this will be received by the borrower but the benefit must be passed onto the lender. Examples of corporate actions include regular dividends, special dividends and bonus issues. If the borrowing entity has sold or on-lent the asset when, say, a dividend is paid, although the borrower of the share will not receive the cash they are still required to forward a sum of money to the lender under the terms of the loan agreement. In this case they will simply have to borrow the requisite amount of cash and forward it to the lender; this is referred to as a 'manufactured' dividend.

The lender will also retain all of the price exposure. If the price of the share has moved up or down since the start of the loan the lender receives back a share at its prevailing value. If the underlying share issuer becomes bankrupt,

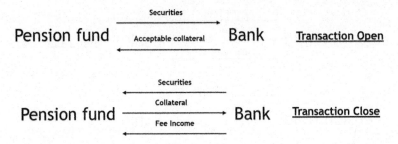

Fig. 1.1 Movements of securities and collateral: non-cash securities lending trade (*Source*: author)

then the borrower simply returns the now defaulted asset and receives back any collateral that has been forwarded as part of the loan.

Securities lending transactions can be executed in two forms, the difference relating to the nature of the collateral exchanged in the transaction. In a non-cash trade (see Fig. 1.1) the lender of the security simultaneously accepts collateral in the form of, say, bonds or perhaps a letter of credit.[6] As was previously pointed out, distributions such as dividends paid during the course of the transactions will need to be remitted to the lender irrespective of whether the borrower still retains the shares.

By convention the value of the collateral taken by the lender is greater than the value of the loaned security. As a rule of thumb in 'normal' the market value of the collateral will be in the region of 102–105 % of the market value of the loaned security. However, during the financial crisis of the late 'noughties' these collateral 'haircuts' increased substantially due to concerns over counterparty credit worthiness.

At the termination of the trade the lender will repay any collateral to the borrower and will receive a fee based on the market value of loaned securities (e.g. 0.15 % p.a.).

A cash transaction (Fig. 1.2) will have many similarities with the non-cash trade with the major difference being the way in which the lender earns their fee. At the opening of the transaction the borrower will remit cash to the lender, again in excess of the market value of the underlying position. The lender will have use of these funds for the term of the loan and so will probably reinvest the cash to earn a rate of return. At the transaction close the borrowing bank will return the asset and receive a cash rebate from the lender. At first glance this appears to be inconsistent with the market practice of a non-cash trade; the borrower has had use of the asset and has seemingly earned

---

[6] A letter of credit is a third party documentary guarantee.

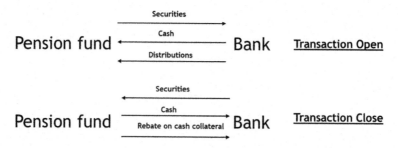

Fig. 1.2 Movements of securities and collateral: cash securities lending trade (*Source*: author)

a rate of return. However, the level of the cash rebate is slightly lower than the interest rate that the lender will be earning on the funds they have been investing. So if the lender was able to reinvest the cash collateral at, say, 3 % they may agree a rebate of perhaps 2.85 % earning, a return of 0.15 % p.a. for lending the securities. So in theory, the difference between the interest earned by the lender on the cash collateral minus the agreed rebate to the borrower will be equal to the fees that would be charged on a non-cash transaction.

One of the topical issues relating to securities lending is what would happen if the borrower of the asset were to default? Pre-emptively, lenders try and avoid this problem by ensuring that the value of the collateral that they have taken exceeds the value of the loaned equities. The value of the collateral with respect to the loaned securities will be reviewed regularly, probably on a daily basis. This process is referred to as 'marking to market'. If the value of the collateral were to fall below a pre-agreed threshold, then the lender would request more collateral from the borrower. Equally, a borrower of securities may request the repayment of collateral if the value of their borrowed asset exceeds the value of the collateral by some pre-agreed amount.

In the event of a counterparty defaulting the first step is for the non-defaulting entity to calculate their net exposure. This is calculated as the difference between the value of the collateral and the value of the loaned securities. The non-defaulting counterparty has right of set off; for example, a lender can liquidate the collateral they possess and use the proceeds to repurchase their loaned securities in the open market. In this example, if the lender had applied the normal level of haircuts to the transaction, had marked the position to market on a daily basis and had exchanged collateral to ensure the deal remained within acceptable valuation parameters, they would actually have a net liability to the defaulting counterparty. This sum would then be payable to the bankruptcy administrators of the defaulting company. Notice that in this case the lender would not have any right to file a claim for a return of the securities. This is due to the fact that the transaction is a legally binding true sale. The only claim they may have is the net difference between the loaned securities and the value of any collateral that is held.

One other point of note is the concept of 'specialness'. In some circumstances a particular equity or class of equities may be in high demand for a particular reason. For example, during the financial crisis a popular trade was to short sell the equity of Spanish banks. In this case the fees charged to borrow the stock rose substantially; if the transactions were collateralized with cash this would mean that the interest amount rebated to the borrower would be very low.

Equity Repo
A repurchase agreement (or 'repo' for short) is a well-established mechanism in the fixed income market and is used by market participants whose motivations are similar to those outlined in the stock lending section.

A repo is an agreement whereby an institution:

- Agrees to sell securities for spot settlement in exchange for their current market value.
- Simultaneously agrees to repurchase the same securities from the buyer at a later date, repaying the original sum of money plus an agreed interest rate for the fact they have had use of the cash over the term of the transaction.

Within the fixed income world, the interest rate payable by the entity that has the use of cash for the duration of the transaction is referred to as the repo rate. But annoyingly, the equity world tends to define this term in a different manner. According to Combescot (2013) the beneficial owner of the security (i.e. the pension fund in Fig. 1.2) will pay interest on the cash posted; this is effectively the rebate rate. The borrower 'pays repo' to the beneficial owner. This is essentially the difference between the rate at which the pension fund can reinvest the cash and the agreed rebate. In normal markets the beneficial owner's reinvestment rate is higher than the rebate rate and so the market terms this a 'positive repo rate', that is, the return the pension fund earns for lending out the security.

Combescot (2013) argues that this repo rate is positive when there is demand for a particular security. So in the earlier Spanish bank trade this would be a situation where lending fees on non-cash trades would increase significantly and rebate rates on cash transactions would fall. He goes on to argue that the equity repo rate can become negative when there is significant demand to borrow cash using equities as security. In this case market participants are willing to pay another entity to hold the stock for a period. Banks lending cash will charge increasing rebate rates as the demand to borrow cash increases. It is quite plausible for this rebate rate to be higher than the reinvestment rate, resulting in 'negative fees', that is, negative repo rates.

1.3   Equity Derivatives

1.3.1   Forwards and Futures

A forward transaction is a legally binding over-the-counter (OTC) commitment to fix the price today for delivery of an asset at some future date. A futures transaction is economically identical but will be traded on an organized exchange. Forwards or futures on single stocks can either be physically-settled or cash-settled. Physical settlement of the transaction would involve the delivery of the asset in exchange for the pre-agreed fixed price. Cash-settlement of the forward will require the buyer to pay the pre-agreed fixed price at the settlement date in return for the prevailing spot price. The two different methods will ensure that the two types of settlement methodology will be economically identical, although at first glance this is not altogether apparent.

Consider a pension fund that is concerned that the value of a share currently trading at $27.00 is expected to increase over the next 3 months. They will not be able to buy the share until then and so agree to buy the asset for forward delivery at a fixed price of, say, $26.90. Suppose that in 3 months' time the share price has fallen to $25.00. If the pension fund were to physically receive the share to satisfy the forward commitment it would hand over $26.90 and receive the share in return. With hindsight their view of the share price movement was wrong and the forward purchase has cost them $1.90 more than if they had done nothing.

A cash-settled forward would not involve the physical delivery of the share but would require them to exchange cash flows with their counterparty. Under the terms of the cash-settled forward they would receive a sum equal to the final value of the share ($25.00) and pay the pre-agreed fixed price ($26.90). Since the two cash flows coincide in terms of their timing the pension fund would pay $1.90 and would then have to go into the cash market and buy the share at $25.00 meaning the total cost of acquiring the share is $26.90. This is the same cost as the physically-settled transaction. If the share price had actually risen over the life of the contract, the result would be unchanged—the pension fund would deliver the $26.90 of cash and receive the share. If the price had risen to say $30, then the cash-settled transaction would require the pension fund to receive $3.10 from their counterparty which could be used to offset the higher purchase of the share. However, on a net basis the purchase cost is still $26.90.

Exchange-traded equity futures are referenced to either single stocks or indices. Consider the contract specification for the cash-settled FTSE 100 index futures contract.

Unit of trading	Contract valued at £10 per index point
Delivery months	March, June, September and December (nearest four available for trading)
Quotation	Index points
Minimum price movement	0.5 index points (£5.00)
Last trading day	Third Friday in the delivery month
Delivery day	First business day after the last trading day

Source: ICE

Equity futures can be used to protect the value of a portfolio against an adverse movement in share prices or to express views on expected market movements. As is common with most futures very few of the contracts are ever held to maturity with the position being terminated early. If held to maturity, the contracts are also cash-settled as it would be awkward operationally for the seller of the index to acquire the requisite number of shares in the right proportions to deliver to the seller. The cash-settlement will be based on the spot price of the share or index at the maturity of the futures contract.

As a result of this cash-settlement convention the exchanges need to 'monetize' the index value. For the FTSE 100 future each half index point has been assigned an arbitrary value of £5. This 'index multiplier' will vary between different index futures; for example, the S&P 500 futures will have a value of $250 per index point. However, a more popular contract that references this index is the E-mini S&P 500 whose index multiplier is $50. So if the FTSE 100 index future is purchased at a level of, say, 6000 index points, the buyer is deemed to have a long exposure to the UK equity markets equal to £60,000 per contract. One of the features of these index futures is that the exchanges do not require the participants to pay the market value of the contract upfront. Instead the exchange requires them to pay only a small percentage amount, referred to as initial margin, which acts as collateral in case of their default. As a rule of thumb this value will be in the region of about 5 % of the initial market value of the contract. Applying this principle to the previous example would mean that both participants would be required to pay £3000. One consequence of the initial margin process means that the contract offers the investor leverage, which is the ability to use a small amount of money (£3000) to control a much larger exposure (£60,000); this implies a leverage factor of 20. This initial margin is returned to the participants when the position is closed out subject to them performing according to the conditions of the contract.

Another feature of the futures market is that profits and losses are remitted to the participants on a daily basis. This is referred to as the variation margin process, and similar to the initial margin, the main purpose of this process is to lower the risk of a counterparty defaulting.

Suppose that the day after executing the transaction the futures contract rises in value by 50 index points to 6050. The long futures position is now worth £60,500 and so a profit of £500 is remitted to the buyer. Conversely the seller will now have to make good their loss of £500. A hedge fund wishing to trade a futures contract would need to have the transaction executed by a prime broker. One definition of this function is (BIS 2013): 'Institutions (usually large and highly rated banks) facilitating trades for their clients (often institutional funds, hedge funds and other proprietary trading firms). Prime brokers enable their clients to conduct trades, subject to credit limits, with a group of predetermined third-party banks in the prime broker's name. This may also involve granting the client access to electronic platforms that are traditionally available only to large dealers.' Typically, the client trade is normally 'given up' to the hedge fund's clearing prime broker. The clearing broker will in turn deal directly with the central clearing counterparty attached to the exchange that now becomes the counterparty to both legs of the trade. All margin payments to and from the hedge fund will pass via their broker to the central clearing house who are now the buyer to every seller and the seller to every buyer. If one of the counterparties to the trade were to default, their positions would be unwound and any shortfall would be made up by the exchange. There are three ways in which the exchanges can offer this assurance:

1. The collection of initial margin from both buyer and seller.
2. The operation of a default fund which comprises of contributions from clearing members based on the level of initial margin deposited at the exchange.

3. The central clearing houses are typically owned by the member banks that make use of them and so are very well capitalized.

It is believed that these provisions should allow the exchange to cover the default of one or two of their clearing members.[7]

The final value for the futures contract will be based on the Exchange Delivery Settlement Price (EDSP) on the last trading day of the contract. This value is based on the underlying cash market as the mechanics of a future mean that expiry of the cash and futures market will have converged.[8]

Although this section has focused on the collateralization of exchange-traded transactions, most banks will apply similar techniques to forward contracts executed on an OTC basis.

1.3.2 Equity Swaps

Swap transactions are characterized as an exchange of cash flows, where one is fixed and the other is floating. Equity swaps, however, are normally traded as either total return or price return transactions, referenced to either a single stock or an index. A total return swap will involve the payment by one entity of a cash flow referenced to the change in price in the underlying share or index over a predefined period plus any announced dividends. A price return swap will reference only the change in the price of the share or index. This component of the swap is sometimes referred to as the 'return leg'. Subsequent chapters will consider equity swaps in greater detail (Chap. 10), and also dividend swaps (Chap. 13), variance swaps (Chap. 14) and correlation swaps (Chap. 15). Swaps are traded on the basis of an agreed notional amount which establishes the size of the trade and the magnitude of the subsequent cash flows. It does not, however, represent an actual cash flow as they are traded on the basis of a notional amount or in terms of index units. The offsetting cash flow will also be variable and will be referenced to an interest rate index such as the London Interbank Offered Rate (LIBOR) or for some US transactions the Fed Funds rate. This is sometimes referred to as the 'funding leg'. An example of an equity swap is shown in Fig. 1.3.

In order to finance the index leg payment, the bank will typically buy and hold the underlying asset. The funding cash flow is offset with a money market transaction.

---

[7] 'Blow your clearing house down' Risk Magazine October 2011.
[8] See Sect. 4.3.

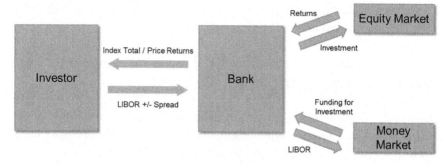

Fig. 1.3 Example of an equity swap (*Source*: author)

1.3.3 Equity Options

Similar to forwards, futures and swaps, options can be referenced to single stocks, indices and dividends and are essentially a variation of forward and futures. Recall that forwards and futures represent a binding commitment to buy or sell an asset at a pre-agreed price. In the previous section on forwards we considered how a pension fund could use a forward transaction to fix the future value of an equity position. In the example we illustrated that the forward would ensure that the pension fund would not suffer a loss in value in the case where share prices have increased. It was also illustrated that they were not able to benefit if the share price fell.

The option contract overcomes this drawback of the forward and allows the buyer to enjoy the best of both worlds, albeit at a fee, which is termed the premium. The formal definition of an option is a contract that allows the buyer the right but not the obligation to buy or sell an underlying asset. From this definition it is possible to infer that the buyer of the option has the right to do something, while the seller of the option has the obligation to perform if required by the buyer.

A call option gives the holder the right but not the obligation to buy the underlying asset. A put option allows the buyer to sell the underlying. Selling a call option means that the seller must make delivery of the underlying asset if the option is exercised by the buyer. Selling a put will require the seller to take delivery of the underlying asset.

The price at which the two parties will trade is referred to as either the strike price or the exercise price. A distinction is made between options that can be exercised at any time during their life ('American') and those that can only be exercised at maturity ('European'). A semi-American option (also sometimes referred to as a Bermudan option) incorporates features of both; that is, it can be exercised according to a pre-agreed schedule. Although some North

America readers may disagree, the argument goes that Bermuda lies half way between the Americas and Europe and therefore a Bermudan option will incorporate features of both markets.

The value of options is often expressed in terms of whether the position is likely to be exercised. An in-the-money (ITM) option is where the strike price is more favourable than the underlying price. An out-of-the money (OTM) option is where the strike price is less favourable than the underlying price. An at-the-money (ATM) option is where the strike price is equal to the underlying price.

Let us consider an ATM equity option written on Morgan Stanley. The option will have a maturity of 3 months, a strike price of $25.00 and a premium of $0.90. The buyer of the call will exercise the option if the underlying share price at the maturity of the option is greater than $25.00 although the position will not break even until the price has risen sufficiently to recoup the premium (i.e. $25.90). If at expiry the price of the option is less than $25.00, the strike rate is less favourable than the underlying price and so the option buyer would simply forfeit the premium and walk away. The option expires OTM as the option buyer could purchase the share at a lower price in the underlying market price. The buyer of a put option with the same features would exercise the option if the price were below the strike price; having the ability to sell the asset above the prevailing market price would be attractive. On the other hand, the option buyer would allow the transaction to lapse if the underlying price were higher than the strike rate. The breakeven on the purchased put option would be the strike price minus the premium (i.e. $24.10). However, note that for both the call and put note the definition of an ITM and OTM option does not take into account the option premium. It merely considers the advantage of the strike over the underlying price. This means that the option will be exercised if it is ITM even if it has not broken even—the option holder will be attempting to recoup their losses. The profit and loss profiles of the different types of option are shown in Fig. 1.4.

Note that the payoffs for the option sellers are the mirror image of the option buyers. Where the buyer loses the seller gains and vice versa. A common trap that some people fall into is the belief that the opposite of a purchased call is actually a short put. However, a cursory glance at Fig. 1.4 should hopefully dispel this myth! The opposite of a purchased call is a sold call.

The diagram also illustrates that the profit for buying positions is unlimited while the losses are limited. The sellers are faced with limited profits and potentially unlimited losses. Some readers may see that for put options the losses/profits are actually limited given that it is impossible to have negative share prices.[9]

---

[9] Negative prices for commodities have been empirically observed in markets such as natural gas and electricity. This is largely due to oversupply and the producers decide it is economically more viable to pay people to take it off their hands!

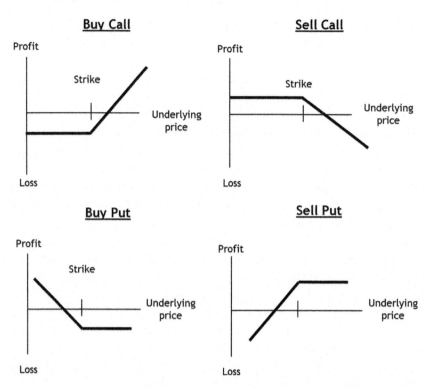

Fig. 1.4 Profit and loss profiles for the four main option building blocks (*Source*: author)

Options can either be cash or physically-settled. A physically-settled option trade will consist of the exchange of the asset for cash. So a buyer of a call option will deliver the cash value of the strike price and receive the underlying asset, while the buyer of a put will deliver the asset and receive the strike price. Cash-settled transactions will not involve the movement of the asset but will ensure equivalence with a physically-settled transaction. The settlement amounts will be:

$$\text{Value of a long call option}: \text{MAX}(\text{underlying price} - \text{strike}, 0)$$
$$\text{Value of a long put option}: \text{MAX}(\text{strike} - \text{underlying price}, 0)$$

Where MAX is interpreted to mean 'the maximum of'.

To illustrate the equivalence between cash and physical settlement, recall the previous example of options on Morgan Stanley. If the underlying share price at expiry is $27.00, the owner of a physically-settled call option contract exercises his right to buy by delivering $25 and taking delivery of a share that is now worth $2.00 more than he paid for it. His net profit is $1.10 after taking into account the $0.90 premium. A cash-settled transaction will see the holder being paid $2.00 based on the settlement convention noted above:

$$\text{Value of a long call option} : \text{MAX}\left(\$27 - \$25, 0\right)$$

Once the premium is taken into account the net profit will be $1.10—the same as that experienced by the buyer of the physically-settled option.

1.3.4 Exotic Equity Options

Along with the Foreign Exchange market, equity derivatives have arguably been at the forefront of developments in the exotic options area. In this section we will briefly introduce two of the main exotic structures while other products will be analysed in subsequent chapters.[10]

Barrier options are one of the most popular forms of exotic option and can be classified as being 'knock ins' or 'knock outs'. A knock in option is where the holder is granted a regular European-style option that is only activated if a predefined barrier is traded. A knock out option is where the holder starts with a European option that is terminated if a predetermined barrier is traded. The next distinction relates to the placement of the barrier. A regular barrier option has the barrier placed in the OTM region, while a barrier placed in the ITM region is referred to as a reverse barrier.

Initially, the different barrier permutations can be confusing so an example may be useful. Using the ATM option on Morgan Stanley introduced earlier, a regular knock in call option would have a strike of $25.00 and a barrier of, say, $23.00. The underlying price will need to fall before the holder of the option is granted an option, which will now be OTM by $2.00. A knock out version of the same option would mean that the holder of the option would see the contract disappear when the price falls by $2.00. In the latter example this is not necessarily a bad thing as the buyer does not need protection in this area. They will, however, have no protection if the underlying price were to subsequently rise. A call with a strike of $25 and a barrier at $27.00 means the option would be described as a reverse knock in/out. A reverse knock out means that the holder of the option will only be able to enjoy $2.00 worth of

---

[10] An excellent standalone reference for exotic options is 'Exotic options trading' by Frans De Weert John Wiley and Sons Ltd (2008).

profit before the option terminates. A reverse knock in structure means that the holder is granted the option to buy the share at $25.00 only when $27.00 trades; the option is born with $2 of value.

Based on these different permutations the market has developed the following colloquial terms to describe the main barrier building blocks:

- Regular knock out call—down and out
- Regular knock out put—up and out
- Regular knock in call—down and in
- Regular knock in put—up and in
- Reverse knock out call—up and out
- Reverse knock out put—down and out
- Reverse knock in call—up and in
- Reverse knock in put—down and in

An example of reverse knock in and out call options is shown in Fig. 1.5.

The other popular type of option is the binary option. In some ways this is a very simple structure. The buyer of a binary call will receive a fixed amount of money when the underlying price rises above a given strike price. The payout is fixed and is not a function of the magnitude of the rise in the underlying price. Similarly, the binary put pays out a fixed amount if the price falls below an agreed strike. There are variations on this structure, notably a 'no touch' structure which will pay out only if the strike is not touched. Examples of binary calls and puts are shown in Fig. 1.6.

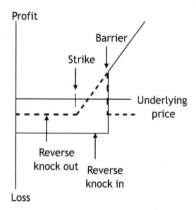

Fig. 1.5 Example of expiry payoffs for reverse knock in and out options (*Source:* author)

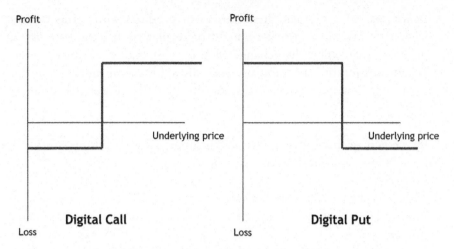

Fig. 1.6   At expiry payoffs for digital calls and puts (*Source*: author)

1.4   Overview of Secondary Equity Markets

1.4.1   Institutional Investors

As with many financial markets it is possible for participants to compete in either one or more segments of the market. To illustrate the different types of equity-related businesses consider the Aviva group. According to their financial statements they provide 'around 43 million customers with long-term insurance and fund management products and services'. They split their business into three main segments:

- Life insurance and savings business
- General insurance and health insurance
- Fund management

Within the life insurance and savings business they offer the following types of products:

- *Pensions*—a means of providing an income in retirement
- *Annuities*—a policy that pays out regular amounts of benefit for the remainder of a person's life. A person's pension savings could be converted to an annuity at the point of retirement.
- *Insurances*—these are designed to offer protection against death or ill health.

- *Bonds and savings*—there are a variety of products within this category where the investor can make one-off or regular contributions to savings products that will either change in line with market prices or offer a guaranteed return. The company also offers a range of mutual fund/unit trust style investments that will considered in more detail later in the chapter.

In the general insurance and health insurance line of business they offer different varieties of protection:

- *Personal*—motor, household, travel
- *Commercial*—fleet car insurance, professional liabilities and commercial property
- *Health insurances*—private health insurance, income protection and personal accident insurance

The third line of business is the fund management business which 'provides fund management services to Aviva's long-term insurance and savings and general insurance operations as well as to a growing number of third party investors'.

What is perhaps most pertinent for this text is the description of how the company generates the investment returns. 'We invest our policyholders' funds and our own funds in order to generate a return for both policyholders and shareholders ....Our aim is to match the investments held to support a line of business to the nature of the underlying liabilities, while at the same time considering local regulatory requirements, the level of risk inherent within different investments and the desire to generate superior investment returns.' The annual report further outlines how their investment approach varies between business lines. For the long-term insurance and saving business the company has tended to emphasize equities and real estate. Where the policy offers some form of guaranteed payment the company prefers to invest in fixed income securities and mortgage loans. For the mutual fund/unit trust business the investment policy will follow the guidelines set out in the terms of each of the contracts. The general insurance and health insurance business tends to have shorter-term liabilities and since the success of the company's investment activities in this area will be borne by the shareholders Aviva have chosen to invest a higher proportion of these proceeds into fixed income securities.

1.4.2 Pension Funds

Pension plans are investment pools that aim to provide income to individuals on their retirement. Although the regulations surrounding pensions is complex and will vary between countries, it is possible to distinguish between private and company pensions. Private pensions will be taken out by the individual with a provider such as Aviva. Corporate pensions will usually be offered as part of a benefits package for an employee. These will be set up for individuals by the plan 'sponsor', typically the employer who may contribute money to the fund. There are two main types of sponsored plan: defined benefit or defined contribution. A defined benefit scheme, also sometimes referred to as a 'final salary' scheme, will base the pension payment on the individual's final salary at retirement and the number of years worked at the company. Consider the following simple example. Suppose an individual were to retire on a final salary of $18,000 after 10 years of service. The company offers a final salary scheme where it pays 1/60th of the individual's final salary. This will result in a pension payment that will be $3000 per annum ($18,000 × 10/60). It may well also be the case that the pension plan will increase this annual retirement payment in line with inflation but such issues as this as well as the longevity assumptions that are built into the calculation are beyond the scope of the text.

Since many of these pension schemes are for larger companies they are often run by volunteer employee trustees. The role of a trustee is to make decisions on where the monies should be invested for the sole interest of the beneficiaries. However, the trustees will often take advice from independent external investment advisors. Additionally, it would be typical for a third-party fund-management company (again think of Aviva) to be contracted to manage the assets. With this type of pension plan it is the employer's responsibility to make sure that there is sufficient investment money to cover all of the fund's liabilities. However, this type of pension fund has fallen out of favour in recent years as many employers have found the burden of financing such a benefit simply too expensive.

In a defined contribution (DC) pension plan the individual decides where to invest the monies usually based on a selection of funds offered by a third-party asset-management company which is chosen by trustees. The sponsor's obligation is limited to how much they are willing to pay into the designated investment funds with the contribution usually defined as a percentage of the employee's gross salary. In this type of scheme, the sponsor makes no promises as to the level of future income at retirement. The proceeds available at retirement will be determined exclusively by the performance of the investment funds chosen by the employee. Depending on local regulations the pension proceeds can usually be taken as some combination of cash and annuity.

1.4.3 Unit Trusts/Mutual Funds

A unit trust or mutual fund structure is an investment product traditionally marketed to the retail sector. For the purposes of this text the two terms will be used interchangeably. Fund management companies offering these types of investment will set up individual funds with a distinct set of investment objectives and permitted instruments. Examples of this may be a fund investing in a developed market such as the USA, emerging markets or smaller companies within a particular country. Investors' funds are pooled and used to purchase assets that conform to the rules upon which the fund is based. The pool of assets is then split up into a series of units, which is ultimately what is bought or sold by the investor; they do not buy or sell the underlying shares directly, that is the role of the fund manager.

The value of the units is directly linked to the value of the underlying assets and unit-linked investments are priced on a daily basis. They are also sometimes referred to as open-ended investments as the fund manager can purchase new assets and create new units based on investor demand. Equally, units can be cancelled and assets sold if demand for the investments declines. Typically, unit-linked structures are not allowed to borrow money to boost their investment proceeds and are often restricted in their use of derivatives.

1.4.4 Investment Trusts

An investment trust is essentially a limited company quoted on a stock exchange whose role is to invest in a range of assets. Similar to unit-linked structures investment trusts will invest according to a specific theme. Investors buy and sell shares in the investment trust company whose value should rise and fall in line with the underlying investments. However, they are referred to as closed-end funds as the number of shares in issue of the investment trust is fixed. Since the investment trust is a limited company then it is possible for the board to authorize the issue of new shares but this is not as common as a fund manager issuing new units in a mutual fund/unit trust. As a result of their closed-end nature it is possible for the shares to trade at premium or a discount to the value of the net assets held by the trust. A fund is said to be trading at premium when the share price is greater than the value of the underlying assets and at a discount when the share price is less than the value of the underlying assets. Although the price of an investment trust's shares will be driven by the performance of the underlying assets because the number of shares available to investors is fixed it is possible for the two values to diverge and hence the emergence of premiums and discounts. It is tempting to think that investment trusts trading at a discount (premium) are trading cheap ('rich') to their fair value. However, casual empiricism would suggest that it is possible for these premiums and discounts to exist for long periods and sometimes may even become more pronounced.

1.4.5 Hedge Funds

Similar to a mutual fund/unit trust a hedge fund is another example of how a pool of client money can be invested collectively by a fund manager. Generally speaking, hedge funds will be targeted more towards the high net worth individual, semi-professional or institutional investor rather than the retail market. Depending on the type and location of the hedge fund an investor will either become a partner within the structure or buy shares if the entity is set up as a limited company.

There are a range of strategies offered by hedge funds some of which will be considered as part of the text as they relate to the world of equity derivatives such as volatility, dividend and dispersion strategies. The essence of hedge funds is that they are designed to offer higher return strategies with perhaps a higher degree of risk than that seen in a retail-focussed vehicle.

There are other structural differences that are also pertinent to the equity world. For example, mutual funds/unit trusts cannot take short positions in an equity or an index; they may be restricted in their use of derivatives and they usually cannot borrow money. Borrowing to boost the available investment proceeds is referred to commonly as 'leverage'. This creates a liability for the fund that at some stage will need to be repaid. As such the investment manager must be confident that the return on their assets will be greater than the interest paid on the borrowed money. Indeed, if the asset defaults it does not excuse the fund from having to repay their debts.

1.4.6 Exchange-Traded Funds

An exchange-traded fund (ETF) is an exchange-traded share whose value tracks a basket of underlying assets rather than the performance of the issuing company. There are a number of key roles within an ETF structure:

- Issuing company
- The sponsor

- The underlying index or asset
- The Trustee
- Custodian
- Approved applicants/approved participants
- The Stock Exchange

Gold Bullion Securities (GBS—the issuing company) Limited is a limited company that was incorporated in Jersey, one of the UK Channel Islands. GBS is a special purpose vehicle in that it has no prior operating history and no employees; it was set up by ETF Securities Limited (the sponsor) for the sole purpose of issuing Gold Bullion Securities. Since the issuing company does not employ anybody the plan sponsor contracts a third-party company (ETFS Management Company (Jersey) Limited) to administer the structure.

Each share is denominated in USD and has a nominal face value of USD 0.00001. The securities are backed by physical gold bars which are held in the name of the trustee (in this instance the Law Debenture Trust Corporation plc). The physical metal is held in secure vaults and segregated from other gold holdings by a custodian (HSBC plc). GBS are listed on the London Stock Exchange and will trade in the same manner as other shares. There will typically be a number of companies who will agree to make a market in the securities. The price of the share is:

$$0.10\text{oz of Gold} \times \text{Gold spot price less a management fee}$$

Legally the securities represent direct and unconditional obligations of GBS, although each share grants to the holder an entitlement to the gold that backs the security. However, this entitlement is reduced daily by a management fee, which is charged at a rate of 0.40 % per annum.

Since the issuing company does not have any employees, the management company will appoint a number of 'approved applicants' (sometimes referred to as approved participants) who will buy the underlying asset, handle the associated cash flows and take delivery of newly created securities. A new security is created when an approved applicant delivers sufficient physical gold relative to the number of securities requested. This process ensures that that there is a direct relationship between the number of GBS securities in issue and the amount of gold held at the Trustee's account at the custodian. Typically, the approved applicants are a mix of investment banks and hedge funds.

If the ETF were to reference an equity index the approved applicants would purchase the requisite number of shares which would be delivered to the nominated custodian. In conjunction with the issuing company the custodian will then issue what is referred to as a creation unit to the authorized participant. The receipt of the creation unit allows the authorized participant to issue ETF shares which can then be bought and sold by the end investors.

According to the prospectus: 'A Gold Bullion Security will only be issued once the subscription price equal to the market value of the Per Security Entitlement to Gold at the time of subscription has been paid by an Applicant to the Company, such payment to be satisfied by the deposit of gold equal to the Per Security Entitlement to Gold into the Subscription Unallocated Account.'

Suppose that an approved applicant wishes to create 1,000,000 GBS securities. The prospectus outlines the per share entitlement, which as of mid-2012, was 96.75 % of one troy ounce of gold. For ease of illustration let us assume that gold is trading at $2000/troy ounce so one-tenth of this is $200; 96.75 % of this value is $193.50. So to issue 1 m securities the approved applicant would need to deliver $193.5 m worth of gold into the Trustee's account at the custodian. It is also possible for an investor to redeem their securities into either cash or gold by essentially reversing this process. If the holder wished to take delivery of gold, then the metal will be transferred to a bullion account.

It is important to make a distinction between redemption and transferability. If an investor wishes to dispose of the security it is not a requirement for them to redeem the security. Since GBS trades like a share it is freely transferable and so there will be a secondary market for the security, similar to any share traded on a stock exchange.

One interesting question is how the company or the sponsor makes money from this activity. This is done by reducing each share's entitlement to gold on a daily basis at a rate of 0.4 % per annum. When GBS was set up in 2005 the per share entitlement was approximately 99.55 % of one-tenth of a troy ounce. The prospectus estimates that an investor's per share entitlement by 2014 will be 95.95 %. They are in a sense being paid in gold and so even if all the securities were redeemed there would still be gold left over which would belong to the issuing company.

Some ETFs will generate their return synthetically. This means that the return on the ETF is not generated by a basket of shares but by a derivative such as a total return swap.

1.5 Overview of the Equity Derivative Markets

One of the themes of the book is to help the reader understand how activity in one part of the equity derivative market may have an impact elsewhere. Figure 1.7 illustrates some of the linkages that exist between the different market participants as well as a number of popular strategies. These include:

Equity products—this includes products such as pension funds or unit trusts/mutual fund structures.

Equities, convertibles and warrants—these represent financing instruments for the issuers but for secondary market participants will represent a series of trading opportunities. For example, a classic hedge fund strategy is to buy a convertible bond and separate it into its component parts (fixed income, credit, equity volatility) and then express views on some or all of these components.

Synthetic replication—this catch-all could encompass a variety of different strategies. The phrase suggests that a derivative has been used to generate a cash flow that should be similar to that achieved from trading the underlying asset. For example, an asset manager may decide to buy an index future rather than buying the individual shares. The index future should generate the same profit or loss as a purchase of the underlying shares but is operationally easier

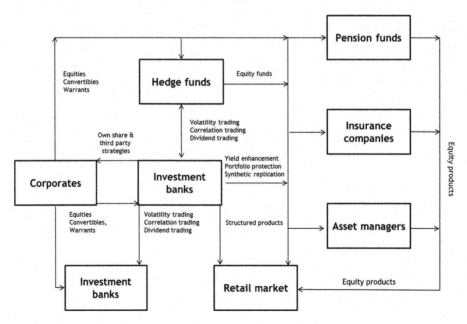

Fig. 1.7 Overview of equity market interrelationship (*Source*: author)

to execute. Another example in the same vein is referred to as 'access trades'. In this example an investor wishes to take exposure to a particular equity market but perhaps face legal or regulatory restrictions. However, they may be able to enter into an equity swap which references this particular market without the need or requirement to invest directly.

Correlation/dispersion trading—this type of activity arises from the risks generated from the sale of structured products. One popular structured equity investment is where the investor has a capital protected investment combined with a long position in a basket option. One of the valuation parameters for a basket option is the price correlation for the constituent components. Basket options will be analysed in Chap. 8, where it will be argued that such options result in an exposure to equity price correlation. Correlation trading (Chap. 15) is a technique that is used to mitigate this risk.

Dividend trading—another popular equity investment that offers an investor some degree of yield enhancement is the reverse convertible. This product will be considered in greater detail in Chap. 14 but in essence an investor deposits money with a bank and sells a put option on a "blue chip" name. Since the bank is long a put option they will suffer losses if dividends were to fall (see Sect. 4.5.2.5). It is because of products such as reverse convertibles that a number of dividend-based structures have evolved (see Chap. 13).

2

Corporate Actions

2.1   Introduction

'Corporate actions' is an umbrella term that describes the distribution of benefits to shareholders (Simmons (2002)). Corporate actions might include:

- Dividend payments
- Bonus issues
- Stock splits
- Reverse stock splits
- Rights issues
- Demergers, mergers and takeovers

Since some of these corporate actions will have an impact on an investor's holdings or the share price or both, it will have a material impact on the terms of any associated derivative contract.

The following descriptions are based on the methodology used by ICE Futures Europe outlined in their Corporate Actions Policy (2016) guide. Broadly speaking, there are two techniques that are used to change the terms of the derivative to reflect the impact of a corporate action: the ratio method and the package method. The aim is to ensure that the economics of the transaction move in line with the corporate action such that the holder of the derivative is neither advantaged nor disadvantaged.

© The Author(s) 2017   **35**
N. Schofield, *Equity Derivatives*, DOI 10.1057/978-0-230-39107-9_2

2.2   The Ratio Method

The terms of the contract (e.g. transaction size, the strike price of an option) can be restated using the concept of an adjustment ratio. In general terms, this is calculated as:

$$\text{Adjustment ratio} = \frac{\textit{Ex}\text{-entitlement holding}}{\textit{Cum}\text{-entitlement holding}} \qquad (2.1)$$

The ex-entitlement holding is a share position that does not have the right to the benefit, while a cum-entitlement holding means that the share position does have the right to the benefit. So using an equity option as an example, this technique means that the exercise price would move in line with the theoretical value of the underlying shares and there would be a change in transaction size to ensure that the monetary value of the deal remains the same.

A more detailed formula for the adjustment ratio is:

$$\text{Ratio} = \frac{\left(SP_{cum} - V\right) \times \left(\dfrac{A_{cum}}{A_{ex}}\right)}{SP_{cum}} \qquad (2.2)$$

Where:
SP_{cum} = Closing price of the cum-entitlement share
V = value of entitlement on a per share basis
A_{cum} = cum amount of shares
A_{ex} = ex amount of shares

For bonus issues, stock splits and reverse stock splits the equation reduces further:

$$\text{Ratio} = \frac{A_{cum}}{A_{ex}} \qquad (2.3)$$

For certain transactions such as rights issues, the corporate action will have some value to the investor, that is the value of the right (see Sect. 2.10). This value is represented by 'V' in Eq. (2.2). This value can be calculated as follows:

$$V = \frac{SP_{cum} - DIV - Sub}{\left(\dfrac{A_{Elig}}{A_{New}} + 1\right)} \qquad (2.4)$$

DIV = any dividend to which the new shares are not entitled
Sub = subscription price of new share
A_{Elig} = Number of shares eligible for the entitlement
A_{New} = number of new shares to be issued for eligible shares

For rights issues the adjustment ratio becomes:

$$\text{Ratio} = \frac{SP_{cum} - V}{SP_{cum}} \qquad (2.5)$$

2.3 Mergers

Suppose company A has made an all-share merger offer for a rival, company B. Under the terms of the transaction, shareholders in company B will be offered two new shares in company A for every share they currently own. If derivatives on both entities exist and if the takeover is successful, contracts in company B will cease to exist. If an investor has traded, say, a future or option on company B, this will be redesignated as a contract in company A.

In the example given, the ex-entitlement position would be one share, while the cum-entitlement is two shares; this gives an adjustment ratio of 0.5. To illustrate the concept, suppose an investor has bought 10,000 call options[1] on company B with an ATM strike rate of $9.00. The monetary value of this exposure is $90,000. For every 1 cent increase in the underlying price before the merger, a call option on company B would show an 'at maturity' profit of $100 (i.e. $0.01 × 10,000). To readjust for the takeover offer then the strike on the redesignated contract is readjusted downwards to $4.50 (i.e. the strike is multiplied by the adjustment ratio) while the transaction size is increased to 20,000 (i.e. the transaction size is divided by the adjustment ratio). This means that the monetary value of the exposure is still $90,000. A 1 cent change in the underlying price would now generate an 'at maturity' profit of $200, which is twice the amount earned before the merger. However, this is logical as the merger 'rewards' the investor with twice as many shares.

---

[1] One call option is assumed to be written on one underlying asset.

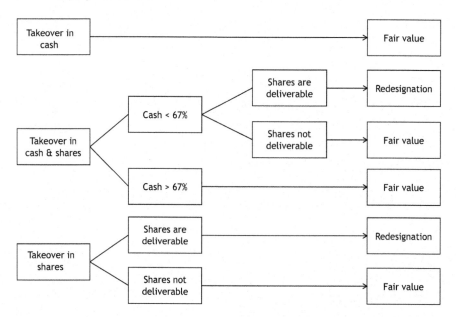

Fig. 2.1 Techniques applied to equity derivative positions dependent on the type of takeover activity (*Source*: ICE Futures Europe, Author)

An interesting variation on this theme is where the takeover is a straight cash offer. That is, the acquiring company will offer existing shareholders in company B cash with no other alternative. In this instance, one possibility is to simply terminate the derivative contract immediately by calculating the position's mark to market. The investor for whom the contract is in the money would receive a cash settlement amount. This is sometimes referred to as the 'fair value' approach. This technique will also be used in circumstances where there is an all-share offer but the shares cannot be delivered into the domestic exchange.

In instances where the offer is a mix of cash and shares, the adjustments to the position are more involved but will involve one or other of the techniques described above. The scenarios and the resulting action are summarized in Fig. 2.1.

2.4   Special Dividend

Most derivative contracts do not adjust their terms for regular dividend payments as these are often factored into their respective valuation models. Although the payment of a dividend may lead theoretically to a fall in the company's share price (although in actuality it may not), the payments are to an extent known and anticipated by the market. By their very nature special dividends are payable by companies on a one-off basis in addition to their regular dividend and as a result it is more likely that the share price will fall to reflect this.

Special dividends may be motivated for a variety of reasons. The company could be holding excess cash balances for which they cannot find a useful purpose or perhaps have a cash windfall as a result of the sale of an asset.

A version of the ratio method is used to determine the ratio amount:

$$\text{Ratio} = \frac{Cum\text{-event share price} - \text{ordinary dividend paid} - \text{special dividend}}{cum\text{-event share price}} \quad (2.6)$$

The 'cum-event price' is the price of a share that is entitled to receive the special dividend. If the company pays an ordinary dividend at exactly the same time as the special dividend, this amount is also included in the formula.

Amended transaction sizes for both futures and options are derived by dividing by the ratio while option exercise prices will be multiplied by the ratio. Ryan Air, the Irish low-cost airline, announced a special dividend of €0.34 per share for their investors in November 2012. Suppose that the cum-event share price was €4.94 and no ordinary dividend was paid. This would generate a ratio value of 0.9312. An investor with 10,000 ATM calls would now have a redesignated position of 10,739 options with a strike rate of €4.60. The lower strike is reflective of the fact that theoretically the price of the share should drop by the amount of the special dividend. The monetary value of the original option exposure is €49,400, which is maintained after the adjustment ratio has been applied (i.e. 10,739 × €4.60).

2.5   Restructuring

This could encompass a variety of different motivations including:

- *Reclassifying shares from one type to another*—for instance, preference shares into ordinary shares.
- *Corporate reorganization*—an example would be the creation of a new holding company that will be the owner of the operational components of a group of components.

If these reorganizations involve a 1 for 1 ratio, then no adjustments are necessary. Typically, transactions are redesignated as contracts based on the new shares.

2.6   Spin-offs

In October 2012, Kraft Foods completed the spin-off of Mondelez. Kraft Foods Group was the new name of the North American grocery business while Mondelez operated the global snacks and confectionary business. Under the terms of the deal, shareholders of the 'old' Kraft Foods Company received one share of Mondelez and one-third of a share of the 'new' Kraft Foods Group.

Adjustments to derivatives on Kraft were subject to what is sometimes referred to as the 'package' method. This method entails substituting the underlying shares with a package that consists of the ex-entitlement shares and the proportionate number of entitlements. So for our example outstanding derivative contracts would become a package of one Mondelez International Inc. share and 0.3333333333 Kraft Foods Group Inc. shares. Once these contracts have expired investors would be able to trade options on each individual name.

2.7   Return of Capital

A return of capital occurs when a company decides to repay part or all of a shareholder's investment. Although at first glance it may appear to be a dividend payment it is executed by reducing the amount of equity held on the balance sheet.

In 2012 Telenet Group announced a return of capital of €3.25 per share. Derivative futures and options were subject to the adjustment using the ratio method. The closing price of eligible shares prior to the corporate action was €34.40. The ratio was calculated using the principles of Eq. (2.6) as 0.90552 (€34.40—€3.25/€34.40). Transaction sizes for futures and options were divided by the ratio and option strike prices were multiplied by the ratio.

2.8   Stock Split

In August 2012, Coca-Cola announced a share split whereby each existing share was divided into two new shares. This is often done by a company whose share price has appreciated significantly and they are concerned that a high price may dissuade potential investors who perhaps would consider the asset overpriced. The impact would initially be neutral for Coca-Cola investors—they would own twice as many shares but the price would fall by half all other things being equal. In this case, the ratio method would apply with a value of 0.5. Transaction sizes would double while option strikes would halve.

2.9   Reverse Stock Split

A reverse stock split occurs when there is a consolidation of ordinary shares. In mid-2012, Royal Bank of Scotland executed a reverse stock split where they consolidated ten shares into one. This is often done to optically increase the share price but similar to stock splits, an investor is no better or worse off. They will see the share price rise but will own proportionally fewer shares. The ratio method returns a value of 10 with transaction sizes being divided by the ratio, while option strike prices would be multiplied by 10.

2.10 Rights Issues

The rationale for rights issues was introduced in Sect. 1.2.5. In early 2012 Peugeot, the French car maker, announced that shareholders would have the right to purchase 16 new shares at a price of €8.27 per share for every 31 shares held. The cum-event price was €13.21 and so derivative contracts were adjusted using a two-step method based on the principles of Eq. (2.4). The first step was to determine the value of the entitlement per share, which was calculated as:

$$\text{Value of entitlement per share} = \frac{\text{Cum-event price} - €8.27}{31\!\!\diagup\!\!_{16} + 1}$$

$$= \frac{€13.21 - €8.27}{31\!\!\diagup\!\!_{16} + 1}$$

$$= €1.6817$$

The ratio method was then applied in a slightly adjusted manner

$$\text{Ratio} = \frac{\text{Cum-event price} - \text{value of entitlement per share}}{\text{Cum-event price}}$$

$$= \frac{€13.21 - €1.6817}{€13.21}$$

$$= 0.87269$$

To accommodate this corporate action transaction sizes were divided by the ratio, while exercise prices for options were multiplied by the ratio.

2.11 Bonus Issue

A bonus issue is where a company issues new shares to existing shareholders for free in proportion to their existing shareholdings. However, the use of the word 'bonus' in this case is perhaps somewhat misleading as the share price will fall in proportion to the new shares issued. In some ways, this will look very similar to a stock split but there is a subtle difference. When companies make profits they can choose either to pay them out as dividends to the shareholders or to retain them on the balance sheet. Retained earnings are shown in a reserve account on the shareholders' equity portion of the balance sheet as they still belong to investors. At some future date, a bonus issue essentially converts this reserve into shares. The overall size of the balance sheet remains the same as retained earnings will fall but issued share capital will increase by the same amount.

To calculate the ratio adjustment for a bonus issue the number of shares held by the investor before the issue is divided by the total number of shares held after the issue. So if a company were to issue one new share for every seven shares currently held the ratio would be 0.875 (seven shares held before the issue divided by eight shares held after the issue). Transaction sizes would be divided by the ratio while option strikes will be multiplied by the ratio.

2.12 Share Buybacks

Reasons for buying back shares include:

- The company believes the market undervalues their own shares.
- The shares are needed to fulfil a commitment to deliver shares under an employee share option scheme.

In 2011, Bouygues announced an offer for its own shares where shareholders would be allowed to sell their shares at a price of €30.00 per share. The company was prepared to repurchase a maximum of 41,666,666 shares. To calculate the adjustment ratio, the following formula was applied:

$$\text{Ratio} = \frac{((O-S)-(41{,}666{,}666 \times €30.00)) \times \big/ (O-41{,}666{,}666)}{O-S}$$

Where:
O = number of shares outstanding
S = Cum-event price

Inputting the market data that prevailed at the time yields a ratio of 0.98665:

$$\text{Ratio} = \frac{\left((356{,}535{,}356 \times €27.25) - (41{,}666{,}666 \times €30.00)\right) \times 356{,}535{,}356 \big/ (356{,}535{,}356 - 41{,}666{,}666)}{356{,}535{,}356 \times €27.25}$$

$$= 0.98665$$

2.13 Summary

The chapter started with a general definition of a corporate action before considering how these activities might impact the value of a derivative position. There are two ways in which the terms of an existing derivative can be changed to ensure that the contract reflects the economics of the corporate action: the ratio method and the package method. The remaining part of the chapter considered a number of worked examples to illustrate the key principles.

3

Equity Valuation

3.1 Introduction

One thing that has struck me over the 25 years I have spent teaching derivatives is the way in which new participants often obsess over the technical details of financial products. Perhaps this is as a result of their formal education background which places a premium on academic rigour? However, a casual glance at an equity research report or a walk around a dealing floor reveals a very different picture—traders and sales people will be more interested in a company's *story*. This should not be taken to mean that the products are irrelevant—indeed that is the main reason I have chosen to write the book. However, like all things a wider context needs to be considered; products are only a means to express some view on expected market movements or to hedge a specific exposure.

This chapter will focus on the issue of equity valuation. The main thing to realize, which to an extent is stating the blindingly obvious, is that ultimately the price of a share is determined by demand and supply. The implications of this statement mean that there is simply no model that will tell you the 'right' price of an asset. A model will, however, help an analyst assess the value of the share relative to its quoted price.

The chapter breaks down into three broad themes: a review of basic accounting concepts and the multitude of associated terms, the use of discounted cash flows techniques to derive a fair value of the asset and then how comparable analysis ('comps') can be used for relative valuation purposes. The coverage within the chapter is not meant to be exhaustive; my goal is to arm the reader with sufficient understanding of how the fundamental performance of

© The Author(s) 2017
N. Schofield, *Equity Derivatives*, DOI 10.1057/978-0-230-39107-9_3

a company can enhance their understanding of the equity derivatives world. The intention is that a reader should be able to pick up a research report or have a meaningful discussion with a colleague and understand the significance of terms such as EBITDA or EPS. Readers interested in a more detailed coverage of equity valuation are referred to alternative sources such as Pinto et al. (2010) and Viebig et al. (2008).

3.2   Financial Statements

One of the main challenges in writing this section was to try and highlight the main accounting principles without unnecessarily regurgitating what has been documented elsewhere. The aims are to provide a concise coverage of the principles, to refer interested readers to alternative sources for those who require a more in-depth analysis, to define and interpret the key terminology associated with analysing equities and to reconcile the many conflicting terms that are used in different accounting jurisdictions. The book is not intended to be a comprehensive accounting guide as principles will change regularly.

In one sense a company's financial records provide an evaluation of four main aspects of management performance:

- How able they are to complete the operating cycle of the business and manage the company's asset investment in order to generate maximum sales revenue.
- Effective management of how assets are financed in order to minimize risk to creditors.
- Their ability to manage the company's operations and costs in order to generate profits.
- The ability of the company to generate cash. It is possible to have a profitable company but the main reason companies go out of business is that they simply run out of cash.

A company's main financial records have four main components:

- *The balance sheet*—a record of what a company owns (e.g. its assets) and what it owes (e.g. its liabilities). After the collapse of Lehman Brothers in 2008, a popular joke in the London financial markets was along the lines of *there are two sides of a balance sheet, left & right (assets and liabilities, respectively): the problem with the Lehman balance sheet is that on the right side there is nothing right, and on the left side there is nothing left.*

- *The income statement*—alternatively referred to as the 'profit and loss account' or 'statement of operations'. This component shows the company's income, expenditure and profit for the year.
- *Cash flow statement*—this documents the evolution of a company's cash position over the course of the financial year showing the inflows and outflows.
- *Statement of changes in shareholders' equity*—provides greater detail of activity within the shareholders' equity part of the balance sheet, which includes things like retained profit and share issuance.

3.2.1 The Balance Sheet

A company's balance sheet provides a snapshot of their assets and liabilities at a specific point in time. Although the formats will differ between jurisdictions, a simplified balance sheet structure may look as follows:

<u>ASSETS</u>
Cash and cash equivalents
Plus inventory
Plus accounts receivable
Plus land and buildings
Plus plant, property and equipment
Plus intangible assets
Plus investments
Plus others
Equals Total Assets
<u>LIABILITIES</u>
Accounts payable
Plus short-term debt
Plus long-term debt
Plus Taxation
Plus others
Equals Total Liabilities
Plus shareholders' funds

So in simple terms, what a company owns or is owed (the assets) is financed by 'external' sources of funds (current liabilities, long-term loans and creditors) and 'internal' sources (funds provided by the shareholders). Another way of thinking about it is that the liabilities are invested in the assets.

Shareholders' funds will often be described using the following inter-changeable phrases:

- Shareholders' equity
- Share capital and reserves
- Equity

This section of the balance sheet comprises a number of items with the following being relevant to our analysis:

- *Common and preferred stock*—sometimes termed 'ordinary shares' and 'preference shares', respectively.
- *Treasury stock*—shares that have been repurchased by the company but have not been retired.
- *Retained earnings*—represent the accumulated earnings from previous years that have not yet been paid out as dividends. Since they have not been paid out, they are being used by management to invest in the business. They are recorded as a liability as they are viewed as belonging to the shareholders.

This gives us the basic accounting equation, that is, that the balance sheet must balance:

$$\text{Assets} = \text{Liabilities} + \text{Shareholders'funds}$$

This identity also shows that shareholders' funds represent the net assets (i.e. assets minus liabilities) available after all liabilities have been paid.

Take as an example Apple Inc.; their 2015 annual report shows the following balance sheet, an abbreviated version being shown in Table 3.1.

Table 3.1 2015 Balance sheet for Apple Inc.

Current assets (e.g. cash, short-term marketable securities, accounts receivable, inventories)	$89,378
Other assets (long-term marketable securities, property, intangible assets)	$201,101
Total assets	*$290,479*
Current Liabilities (e.g. accounts payable)	$80,610
Other liabilities	$90,514
Total liabilities	*$171,124*
Shareholders' equity (e.g. issued common stock, retained earnings)	$119,355
Total liabilities and shareholders' equity	*$290,479*

Figures in millions (Source: www.apple.com)

3.2.1.1 Asset Conversion Cycle

The asset conversion cycle (Fig. 3.1) is a useful way of visualizing the different components of the balance sheet. It is also sometimes referred to as the working capital cycle.

In a general sense the production cycle of a company could involve five continuous steps:

- Raw materials are acquired and paid for in cash and accounts payable (money owed to other entities) are created. For example, the company may not have to pay for the raw materials for 30 days.
- The raw materials become 'work in progress', where value is added and accrued expenses (such as salaries) are now incurred.
- Finished goods are now completed and additional expenses incurred.
- The finished goods are now sold and 'sales, general and administrative expenses' (SG&A) are incurred (e.g. advertising, delivery expenses) and

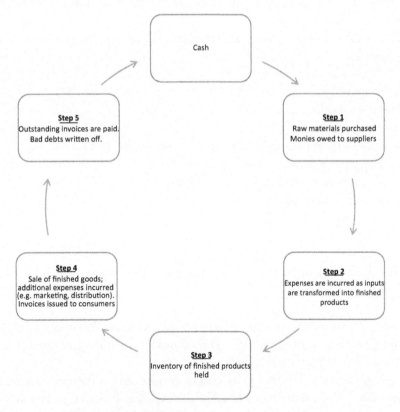

Fig. 3.1 The asset conversion cycle

accounts receivables are created (i.e. monies owed to the company, perhaps becoming due 30 days after the sale date).
- Accounts receivable are collected which translates back into a cash payment.

There is an implication within this simple description that the company does not require any external financing. In a perfect world it would be ideal if the company were able to receive cash from the sale of its product before it was liable to pay for the purchased inventory and expenses. Since this is unlikely, a new company would probably need some form of external finance such as the owners' own funds or a bank loan.

3.2.2 The Income Statement

The income statement of a company is often the main focus of equity analysis with the emphasis on 'earnings' (or 'profits' if you prefer). We will see however, that both of these terms are often used ambiguously as there are different measures (e.g. gross, net, retained) used at different points of the income statement's construction.

A generalized form of income statement will be constructed in the following manner:

Sales revenue
Minus cost of sales
Equals gross profit
Minus sales and general administrative expenses ('SG&A')
Equals operating profit
Plus/minus interest receivable and payable
Equals profit before taxation
Less provision for taxation
Equals net income

The different components of the income statement are broadly defined as follows:

- *Sales revenue* (also variously referred to as 'net sales', 'turnover', 'revenues', 'total revenues', 'net revenue'). This relates to revenues generated from the sale of a company's products.
- *Cost of sales* (also referred to as 'cost of goods sold') is then subtracted from turnover. These costs relate to all of the expenses incurred to buy and convert the required production inputs. Although the components included

within this category may vary from company to company, they represent those costs that can be directly linked to the revenues earned from the sale of the company's production. This results in the following relationship:

Revenue from sales minus cost of sales = gross profit

- If the company reports a gross profit it will then subtract from this measure a series of other operating expenses most commonly called *selling, general and administrative expenses*. This may include items such as salaries, advertising and rent. Within this entry there is also a value for asset depreciation. Depreciation is a measure of how the value of asset will decline over time (e.g. as it becomes worn out) and is spread over its life. Consider the £1,500 laptop on which this manuscript is being written. When it was purchased the company's balance sheet showed a decrease in cash balances and an increase in fixed assets. However, the impact of this purchase on the income statement is spread over the usable life of the machine, which we will say for the sake of argument is 3 years. So in very simple terms—as there are different ways of depreciating assets—the value of the fixed asset on the balance sheet is reduced every year by 1/3rd (i.e. £500). In addition, within the income statement there will be an offsetting entry of equal value recorded in the SGA expenses account as a cost which reduces the company's profit. It is important to realize that this depreciation cost does not represent a movement in cash. The depreciation amount is not stated explicitly in the income statement but is usually detailed in the notes to the accounts. A related concept is amortization which relates to how intangible assets are expensed. An example of an intangible asset is the concept of goodwill. This is extra amount paid by a company in excess of its market value when acquiring another entity.

One important aspect of depreciation and amortization is the way in which a change of policy may impact net income. If the company decided to increase what they consider to be the useful life of an asset, the value of the asset on the balance sheet will not decline as rapidly, SGA expenses will be lower and operating profit will be higher.

At this point in our analysis of the income statement we can outline the following relationship:

Gross profit minus other operating expenses = operating profit

Operating profit may be termed different things such as 'Net operating profit', 'Operating income' or 'Earnings before interest' (EBIT).

- After operating profit (i.e. EBIT) has been calculated the company will take into account *interest income and expense*. Interest expense arises from long-term and short-term debt shown on the balance sheet. Since this is regarded as a business cost it is regarded as a pre-tax expense; that is a company's taxable income is reduced by this amount. It is feasible that the company may have received some form of financial income perhaps in the form of dividends from shareholdings in other companies as well as any interest income from their investment portfolio. This income will be related to the cash and cash entries shown on the asset side of the balance sheet.
- At this point we have reached a company's *income before tax* and so unsurprisingly the next stage is to record a *provision for taxation*. The end result is referred to as either the company's *net income* or *profit after tax*. It is from this amount that the company can choose to pay dividends or simply retain the earnings. Retained earnings are shown in the shareholders' equity portion of the balance sheet.

Apple's income statement ('statement of operations') for 2015 was (Table 3.2):

Table 3.2 2015 Income statement for Apple Inc.

Net sales	$233,715
Cost of sales	$140,089
Gross margin	$93,626
Operating expenses (research and development; selling, general and administrative)	$22,396
Operating income (gross margin less operating expenses)	$71,230
Other income and expense	$1285
Income before provision for income taxes (operating income *plus* other income and expense)	$72,516
Provision for income taxes	$19,121
Net income	$53,394

Figures in millions (Source: www.Apple.com)

3.2.3 Cash Flow Statement

The cash flow statement is designed to show the company's cash inflows and outflows over the course of the financial year. Companies go bust not because of a lack of profit but because they run out of cash to pay their bills. As has been already suggested a company's profit figure is based on a number of accounting practices that might not involve the movement of cash—depreciation being one example. Equally, accounting practice allows for companies to accrue for income and expenses. So, for example, if the author were to deliver a training course today and issue an invoice requiring payment within 30 days, this could be recognized on the company's income statement immediately and hence a profit would be recorded even though no cash has been received.

The cash flow statement comprises of three main elements:

- Cash used by and generated from a company's operating activities (e.g. cash collected from customers, interest expense and income, dividends received from investments, salaries paid to employees)
- Cash flows from investing activities (e.g. outgoing cash flows related to the purchase of an asset or incoming cash flows from the sale of an asset)
- Cash flows from financing activities (e.g. cash inflows from issuing debt or equity, cash outflows from debt repayment, dividends paid to shareholders)

The 2015 Apple Inc. annual report shows the following cash flow figures, which have been summarized. (Table 3.3):

Table 3.3 Abbreviated 2015 statement of cash flows for Apple Inc.

Cash and cash equivalents, beginning of the year	$13,844
Cash generated by operating activities	$81,266
Cash used in investing activities	($56,274)
Cash used in financing activities	($17,716)
Cash and cash equivalents, end of the year	$21,120

Figures in millions (Source: www.Apple.com)

So although Apple generated $81,266 m of cash it consumed $73,990 m and so their cash resources increased by $7,276 m.

Having presented the most common financial information, we will see how it is used to analyse the value of shares relative to their quoted price.

3.3 Valuation Techniques

Kay (2009) points out there are broadly two approaches to valuing any asset:

- The value of an asset is what someone will pay for it.
- The value of an asset is a function of the cash flows it will generate over its life.

Blake (1990) points out that valuing bond cash flows is relatively straight forward. Bond coupons are generally fixed, the contractual obligation to pay interest means that their timing is predetermined and the final redemption cash flow is also known. Arguably the difficulty in valuing bond cash flows lies in trying to determine the appropriate discount factor.[1] When trying to adapt the same valuation technique for equities, the analyst is required to make a number of judgements:

- What is the most appropriate methodology? Cash flow analysis? Comparable analysis? A proprietary model?
- Which cash flows should be used? Dividends? Cash?
- How do we overcome the uncertainty of estimating future cash flows since they are discretionary and dependent on economic conditions?
- Since shares have no maturity, how far into the future do we need to forecast and how do we cope with the lack of a final redemption payment?
- Since equities are the last liabilities to be repaid in the event of a company's bankruptcy and therefore have the highest degree of credit risk, how is this reflected in the discount rate used to present value of the cash flows?

Given these uncertainties it is not surprising that different models have evolved to address these issues. However, this takes us back to one of our assertions—the model may provide some insight into a company's value but does not represent an absolute truth, that is, a 'right' price. Indeed, cash flow based models that require some subjective assumptions will sometimes generate nonsense values. This suggests that equity value focuses less on a model approach and more on trends in a company's performance and in particular its profitability. Hence it may be more meaningful to use alternatives such as comparable analysis.

Despite some drawbacks, a short review of the main models is still useful in understanding some of the 'drivers' of value for an equity.

3.3.1 Dividend Discount Model

In its simplest form the model states:

$$\text{Share price}_0 = \sum_{t=1}^{\infty} \frac{\text{Dividend payments}_t}{\left(1 + \text{credit adjusted interest rate}\right)^t} \qquad (3.1)$$

---

[1] See for example Schofield and Bowler (2011).

The main difference between the fixed income and equity approach is that the dividend discount model ignores the impact of any redemption payment, since shares do not offer this feature.

From Eq. 3.1 we can see that there are a number of shortcomings. For example, the equation assumes that:

- All future dividend payments are known in terms of their magnitude and timing.
- The impact of the very long dated cash flows on the price will decline due to the mathematics of discounting.
- The credit adjusted interest rate used to present value the cash flows is known and is constant for all future maturities. This rate is also referred to the required return on equity (ROE) as an investor will base a purchase decision based on the returns of the security relative to that of alternative equivalent assets.

In order to solve the issue of unknown future dividend levels, one approach is to make some assumptions about how they are expected to grow. One of the models used in this respect is the Gordon growth model, which has become the standard dividend discounting model largely due to its simplicity:

$$\text{Share price}_0 = \frac{\text{Dividend payment}_1}{\left(\text{required return on equity} - \text{dividend growth rate}\right)}$$

$$SP_0 = \frac{DP_1}{RROE - DGR} \tag{3.2}$$

where :

$$DP_1 = DP_0 \times \left(1 + DGR\right)$$

This equation states that the current fair value of the share can be derived from the next dividend payment divided by a constant. The next dividend payment is simply the current dividend payment multiplied by some assumed growth rate. The constant is the required ROE less the expected growth in dividends. Recall that the phrase 'required return on equity' is synonymous with the term 'credit adjusted interest rate' used earlier.

Readers who are mathematically inclined may notice that the equation is only meaningful if the required return is greater than the dividend growth rate. This suggests that the method would be appropriate if the company pays dividends and that the growth in the dividends is expected to be stable. To illustrate the application of the formula and some of its other applications, let us make some simple assumptions about a fictitious share:

- Current share price = $7
- Current dividend = $1 per share
- Dividend growth rate = 5 %
- Required ROE = 20 %

$$SP_0 = \frac{DP_1}{RROE - DGR}$$

$$\$7 = \frac{\$1 \times (1 + 0.05)}{0.20 - 0.05} \tag{3.3}$$

For example, since the price of the share is observable and there is some consensus for the expected dividend growth rate, it is possible to rearrange the formula to calculate the required return on the equity.

$$RROE = DGR + \frac{DP_0 \times (1 + DGR)}{SP_0}$$

$$20\% = 0.05 + \frac{\$1 \times (1 + 0.05)}{\$7} \tag{3.4}$$

A similar approach could also be taken to calculate the dividend growth rate implied by the market for a given share price and required return.

$$DGR = \frac{(SP_0 \times RROE) - DP_0}{SP_0 + DP_0}$$

$$5\% = \frac{(\$7 \times 0.20) - \$1}{\$7 + \$1} \tag{3.5}$$

However, if we were to use the equation to calculate the fair value of a stock we would need to generate some estimate of the unknown parameters on the right hand side of Eq. 3.3.

- The dividend growth rate can be based on how the dividend has evolved historically but clearly any future expectations will inevitably include some element of subjectivity. One approach is to forecast a company's future financial statements and derive the expected dividend from these numbers. A common "sanity check" that is often used is to ensure that the future dividend growth does not exceed the growth rate of the economy as a whole as measured by the Gross Domestic Product (GDP).

- The required ROE can be calculated using the Capital Asset Pricing Model (CAPM), which is considered later in this chapter (Sect. 3.3.4).

The approach so far assumes that dividends will grow at one single constant rate. Multistage models allow for different growth rates in dividends in two or three stages as the company grows and matures. Interested readers are referred to Pinto et al. (2010) for further information on these models.

3.3.2 Free Cash Flow Approaches

One of the most popular approaches to valuing a company's equity is the use of free cash flow (FCF) techniques. This builds on the dividend discount approach in that it treats the share as the present value of the future cash flows but specifically defines what those cash flows are, introduces a technique to overcome the lack of a final redemption payment and uses a separate model to define the appropriate discount rate.

A dividend discount model looks at the cash flows that are paid out to investors, while the FCF approaches consider the cash flows that are available for distribution to a variety of stakeholders. FCF can be calculated at two different levels. Free cash flow to the firm (FCFF) considers the amount of cash available to all providers of capital, which widens the discussion to include debt financing. Free cash flow to equity (FCFE) focuses on the cash flows available to shareholders only.

The FCF approach to valuing an equity is probably the most popular equity valuation method. The technique values the equity of a company based on its ability to generate future cash flows typically over a 5- to 10-year period, which are then present valued. The strength of the process is that cash flows cannot be easily manipulated by accounting policies. On the other hand, the FCF forecasting method relies on a number of subjective assumptions, which can of course be open to debate.

A brief overview of a single period FCF calculation is shown below:

Calculation	Explanation
Operating profit ('Earnings before interest and taxation'- EBIT)	This represents the profit generated from the operational assets
Minus tax on operating profit ('Net operating profit less adjusted tax'—NOPLAT)	The tax figure is not that reported on the income statement. The taxation figure used is the corporate rate multiplied by the EBIT
Plus depreciation and tax-deductible amortization	This converts the EBIT into a cash flow amount by adding back non-cash expenses
Plus/minus the change in working capital	This captures the cash consumed or generated during the asset conversion cycle
Minus capital expenditure	This represents the new investment in fixed assets needed to support future activity
Plus/minus change in other operational assets and liabilities	This may include long-term assets or liabilities needed to support the company's future activity
= Free cash flow to the firm (FCFF)	This represents the cash flows generated by the business after required investment. It is available to pay out to both debt and equity holders

If interest costs associated with any debt are deducted from this final value, the result is sometimes referred to as the Free Cash Flow to Equity (FCFE).

There are some additional points worthy of note:

- Earlier EBIT was defined as a measure of earnings that incorporated all of a company's operating costs such as cost of sales and SGA expenses. However, it was pointed out that depreciation and amortization were included within these operating costs. These were non-cash flow accounting entries that influenced the level of a company's EBIT. Since we are trying to calculate the cash flow component of EBIT we need to ADD these back (i.e. the earnings would be greater without these expenses). The resultant figure that is derived is referred to as EBITDA and is a popular measure of pre-tax corporate profitability. It is popular since it gives a measure of earnings that can be compared to other companies without having to worry about different depreciation policies or taxation regimes.
- Expenditure on fixed assets ('Capital expenditure' or 'capex') is seen as a necessary expense in order for the company to be able to generate sales revenues. It is common to distinguish between maintenance and growth capex. The former is required simply to keep a business running and can be thought of as the need to replace worn out assets. Growth capex is designed to grow the business and could represent a substantial drain on cash.
- Working capital is defined as current assets minus current liabilities. If working capital increases, it represents a drain on cash, whereas a decrease

in it represents an increase in cash. This can be seen in relation to the asset conversion cycle shown in Fig. 3.1. If accounts receivable or inventory increases (both current assets) this will absorb cash. In contrast, if account payable increases (a current liability) this increases the firm's funding as it is a cash inflow. The level of a company's working capital will generally increase with an increase in sales volumes. For example, if a company's sales were to double, inventories will also increase. Although some of the inventory purchased could be financed from internal sources such as retained profits, the expansion may require the use of external sources of finance such as bank borrowing.

- The calculation of the taxation rate is a subject of great debate. Should an analyst use the company's marginal corporation tax rate? Is it more appropriate to use the average tax rate paid by the company on the basis that they may have been able to take advantage of different rules? Since the tax sum may not be payable until sometime in the future, what about the timing of the tax payment? Such issues are outside the scope of this text.

To illustrate how the numbers could be derived consider Apple's 2015 financial statements to calculate a single period FCFF value:

Operating profit ('EBIT')	$71,230
Minus tax on operating profit	$18,520
Plus depreciation and amortization	$11,257
Minus Net change in working capital	$3,595
Minus Capital Expenditure	$11,247
Equals Free Cash Flow to the Firm	$49,125

For ease of illustration a tax rate of 26 % was used in the calculation. This rate was based on the amount of tax actually paid by Apple as stated in their accounts.

Gray et al. (2004) argue that there are five key drivers of FCF and therefore company value:

- Sales growth rates
- EBIT margins (operating profit relative to sales i.e. how much of a company's sales translate into operating profit).
- Tax rates
- Capital expenditure
- Working capital requirements

A full FCF calculation is made up of the following steps:

- Determine the length of the forecast period (typically 5–10 years).
- Collect all of the required data from a company's current financial records.
- Forecast the future cash flow values based on expectations of how the FCF components are expected to evolve.
- Calculate a 'terminal value' for the company at the end of the forecast period. This is covered in Sect. 3.3.3.
- Discount all the cash flows at an appropriate interest rate (the weighted average cost of capital—WACC) and sum their value. WACC is covered in Sect. 3.3.4.

$$\text{Value of the firm} = \sum_{t=1}^{n} \frac{\text{FCFF}_n}{(1+\text{WACC})^n} \qquad (3.6)$$

Where:

WACC = Weighted average cost of capital

- The final step is to subtract the market value of the net debt to determine the implied equity value of the company.
- The implied equity value is then divided by the number of shares to return the theoretical value of the share.

3.3.3 Calculating the Terminal Value

The terminal value of a company represents its value at the end of the forecast period. In one sense it represents the value of the company from that point until perpetuity. There are different techniques in how this should be calculated but a popular technique is referred to as the perpetuity method. This assumes that the business will continue to operate normally and that free cash flow will continue to grow at some perpetual growth rate.

The formula to calculate the terminal value using the perpetuity approach is:

$$\text{Terminal value} = \frac{\text{Free cash flow in final forecast year} \times (1+\text{growth rate})}{(\text{Weighted average cost of capital} - \text{growth rate})} \qquad (3.7)$$

The choice of growth rate poses a problem for the analyst but it should reflect economic conditions. For example, it may be considered unrealistic for the company to grow faster than the GDP of the country in which it is based.

3.3.4 Calculating the Weighted Average Cost of Capital

Once all of the free cash flows and the terminal value of the company have been estimated, their present values are calculated using an appropriate discount rate. The generally accepted approach is to use an interest rate that reflects the cost of the different components used to finance the company. These components are then weighted by their proportion within the funding mix.

The formula used to calculate the WACC is:

$$\text{WACC} = \left[C_{equity} \times \frac{\text{MV}_{equity}}{\text{MV}_{equity} + \text{MV}_{debt}} \right] + \left[C_{debt} \times \frac{\text{MV}_{debt}}{\text{MV}_{equity} + \text{MV}_{debt}} \right] \quad (3.8)$$

C_{equity} = Cost of equity
C_{debt} = After-tax cost of debt
After-tax cost of debt = Gross yield on debt × (1—Corporate tax rate)
MV_{equity} = Market value of equity in financing mix (number of shares outstanding × share price)
MV_{debt} = Market value of debt in financing mix

The first step in solving the equation is to solve for the cost of equity. This is defined as the annual rate of return that an investor expects to earn when investing in a company. Return within an equity context will comprise of both dividends and price change. One of the techniques used to calculate this return uses the concept of the CAPM.

The relationship can be stated as:

$$R = R_f + \beta \times (R_m - R_f) \quad (3.9)$$

Where:
R = Expected return on the security
R_F = The return on a risk-free security
R_M = The estimated return on a market portfolio of stocks

β = The stock's beta (the percentage change in the return on a stock for a 1 % change in the market return). This measures the riskiness of the asset's returns relative to the risk on a market portfolio

Let us consider each of the components within this relationship. The risk-free rate is defined as the return on a default free instrument. However, modern finance now questions whether such a rate exists. One of the more popular rates in recent times has been the use of an overnight index swap (OIS) rate.[2] The next issue faced by the analyst is to determine which maturity should be selected. The most common practice is to pick a rate that matches the maturity of the forecasted cash flows.

Beta measures the market risk of the share relative to the risk of the market. It can be interpreted as the percentage change in the price of the stock that corresponds to a 1 % move in the market as a whole. A value of 1 indicates that the market risk of the asset is equal to the risk of the market, while a value of less (more) than 1 indicates that the asset is less (more) volatile than the market.

The R_m—R_f component of Eq. 3.9 is referred to as the equity risk premium (ERP). It is defined as the extra return over and above risk-free rates that an equity investor demands for investing in the riskier equity market. The ERP has always been a relatively difficult number to assess with any accuracy and is sensitive to the way in which it is measured. One of the techniques used is to take the earnings yield of an index (the inverse of the P/E ratio) and subtract the yield to maturity of a government bond of a certain maturity (although there is no agreement on what this maturity should be). In their Equity—Gilt Study Barclays Capital (2016) a 10-year annualized measure for the USA of the ERP showed that the measure turned negative in 2008 reaching a level of about −7 % and by early 2016 was +0.3 %. Other measurements have suggested that for the USA the value has averaged 2.45 % from January 1881 to end of September 2011.[3]

Traditional valuation approaches suggest that a company's cost of debt can be derived by adding a credit spread to a risk-free yield to maturity. However, the problem with this approach is that the term 'credit spread' is a relatively ambiguous phrase. Traditional approaches to bond pricing take a corporate bond yield to maturity and then simply subtract a risk-free rate to determine the credit spread. However, this approach ignored other factors that may be

---

[2] See Schofield and Bowler (2011) for a discussion of the use of OIS rates as a risk-free proxy.

[3] See 'What the equity risk premium tells us today' Financial Times Fund Management supplement, 7 November 2011.

embedded within this value. For example, if the bond was considered to be illiquid investors would demand a premium to hold the issue and so this would overinflate the value of the so-called credit component. There is no single solution to this problem but a popular measure used in assessing the credit of cash bonds is the z spread. This is the fixed number of basis points that has to be added to the risk-free zero coupon curve such that the theoretical value of the bond matches the observed market price. A fuller discussion of this technique can be found in Schofield and Bowler (2011).

The WACC equation suggests that the market values of the debt and equity should be used. Although this may be relatively easy to determine for equity, the lack of liquid bond prices often means that the analysts choose to use the nominal value instead.

The WACC calculation also requires the use of the after-tax cost of debt. The after-tax cost of debt is:

$$Pre-tax \ cost \ of \ debt \times (1 - corporate \ tax \ rate)$$

As was noted previously, interest expense incurred from borrowing money comes before tax is deducted. The higher the interest expense, the lower the profit and so the lower the tax rate. This benefit is sometimes referred to as the tax shield.

3.4   Comparable Company Analysis

Anyone looking to sell a car will probably start off by trying to judge the value of their vehicle relative to similar versions being sold in the market. Perhaps the seller will look at the models being offered on dealer forecourts or buy a trade magazine that lists second hand values based on mileage, model or engine size. From these values it is possible to determine a benchmark from which their car could be valued as the vehicle to be sold relative to a number of chosen criteria. The seller may determine that since their vehicle has fewer miles than the benchmark listing it may have a greater value.

One of the issues of assessing performance within an equity context is whether a given level of, say, net income is 'good' or 'bad'. Since no two companies are identical, trying to compare absolute values of some financial statement component can be a meaningless exercise. This suggests that performance needs to be assessed relative to something—perhaps a benchmark or another company. As a result, the use of ratios or comparable company analysis ('comps') is a fundamental part of the equity analysis. The technique is also sometimes referred to as 'multiple analysis' as once an appropriate benchmark metric has been established companies can be compared using a multiple of the measure.

One of the key issues of this type of analysis is determining what constitutes a comparable company. Again there is no agreement on how this issue should be approached but common criteria include:

- Similar product markets
- Geographical coverage
- Equivalent business risk
- Same stage of development
- Comparable capital structures
- Ownership structure (e.g. quoted company vs. privately owned)
- Revenue or profits

Comparable analysis can be performed at two levels.

- *Equity price analysis*—the analysis is carried out by relating the company's share price to some other measure within the financial statements.
- *Enterprise level metrics*—this perspective uses an adjusted market capitalization value for a company's, which is commonly referred to as 'enterprise value' (sometimes also referred to as 'firm value' or 'asset value').

$$\text{Enterprise value}\left(\text{EV}\right) = \text{market capitalisation of equity} + \text{net debt}$$

Where:
Market capitalization = share price multiplied by the number of shares outstanding
Net debt = total debt less cash

By incorporating the two main sources of borrowing (debt and equity), enterprise value (EV) represents a broader valuation of a company rather than the somewhat narrower focus of equity market capitalization.

As Pinto et al. (2010) point out the rationale for using ratios based on the price of the share is that it allows an investor to consider "what a share buys in terms of per-share earnings, net assets, cash flow or some other measure of value". Extending the argument to the enterprise level, they go on to point out: "The intuition behind EV multiples is similar; investors evaluate the market value of an entire enterprise relative to the amount of earnings before interest and taxes (EBIT), sales, or operating cash flow it generates."

When constructing the measures, the analyst must take care to note whether the metric is being illustrated using 'trailing' (i.e. historical) or projected future values.

In the sections that follow, the numerical examples that are used are based on the numbers reported in Apple's 2015 financial statements and for simplicity, the 'headline' figures have been used. Some analysts may choose to make subtle adjustments to the published numbers but these issues are outside the scope of the text. Unless stated otherwise the values are shown in millions.

3.4.1 Profitability Ratios

The Return on Equity

Since shareholders inject their own cash into a company it is not unreasonable for them to want to know what return they are earning on their investment. The ROE would be calculated as net income divided by shareholders' funds. It can be instructive to decompose ROE into three key drivers: profitability, efficiency and leverage.

$$\frac{\text{Net income}}{\text{Sales}} \times \frac{\text{Sales}}{\text{Total assets}} \times \frac{\text{Total assets}}{\text{Shareholders' funds}} \tag{3.10}$$

The 'sales' and 'total assets' will cancel out leaving the single ROE ratio. The first component (profitability) of the decomposed ROE equation looks at how each unit of a company's sales is being transformed into net income. The second component (efficiency) looks at how many units of sales are created from the total resources available to the company. The final component (leverage) illustrates what proportion of the resources are financed by 'internal' sources of funds (i.e. shareholders' funds) rather than external borrowings, which at some stage will need to be repaid. This measure shows whether the shareholders or debt holders bear the risk of the company defaulting. The greater the proportion of debt in the company's capital structure the greater the interest expense, which in a recession could cause a strain on cash flow.[4]

The figures for Apple are:

---

[4] In general terms interest expense is tax deductible and so debt can be cheaper than equity. A full discussion of optimal capital structures is outside the scope of the text.

$$= \frac{\text{Net income}}{\text{Sales}} \times \frac{\text{Sales}}{\text{Total assets}} \times \frac{\text{Total assets}}{\text{Shareholders' funds}}$$

$$= \frac{\$53,394}{\$233,715} \times \frac{\$233,715}{\$290,479} \times \frac{\$290,479}{\$119,335}$$

$$= 44.74\%$$

3.4.2 Margin Ratios

The use of margin ratios has proved to be a popular technique over the years and is an attempt to illustrate the profitability of a company. The analyst will usually select some measure of profit or earnings (gross, operating profit, net income) and relate them to the sales revenues earned by the company. The aim is to identify how much revenue from selling the product is transformed into profit.

3.4.3 Share Price Ratios

Earnings Per Share
Earnings per share (EPS) is defined as net income less dividends paid on preference shares divided by the average number of shares in issue during the period. Some entities will report a diluted measure that takes into account that certain outstanding instruments may impact the number of shares in issue such as employee share option schemes, convertible bonds and warrants.

Looking at a worked example for Apple with net income shown as a full value:

$$= \frac{\text{Net income}}{\text{Number of shares in issue}}$$

$$= \frac{\$53,394,000,000}{5,753,421,000}$$

$$= \$9.28$$

P/E Ratio

Within the context of equity analysis arguably the most commonly quoted ratio is the Price-Earnings (P/E) ratio.

This is calculated as:

$$\frac{\text{Share price}}{\text{Earnings per share}} \qquad (3.11)$$

This tells us how much it will cost to buy a unit of the company's earnings. It can also be thought of as a payback ratio. For example, a value of 10 would suggest it would take a decade of earnings before the investment is repaid.

Suppose we have two very similar companies. Company A has a P/E of 20 while company B has a P/E of 10. At a very simple level company A would be described as being expensive relative to company B since investors are paying twice as much per unit of earnings.

The P/E ratio can also be calculated for a sector or indeed the overall market index based on the values for each component share weighted by the market capitalization.

The P/E ratio is also sometimes seen as an indicator of the market's outlook for a company's earnings growth. A company that has a track record of strong earnings growth may trade at a 'high' P/E ratio; conversely, low growth companies may trade at lower ratios. During the Dot Com boom many technology companies were trading on very high P/E ratios. This implied that current earnings were low but the share price was moving upwards. An investor would only logically pay very high multiples of current earnings if they had an expectation that earnings were going to increase substantially and their initial investment would be recouped faster than the payback period implied by the P/E ratio. However, this is not the same as saying that high P/E ratios are always a good thing, for example, has the growth come from new projects that will be able to generate returns on a sustainable basis? As history showed us many Dot Com businesses went bust as investors' expectations of future earnings were unrealistic. As perhaps as a rule of thumb it might be reasonable to say that an investor may be interested in a company with a lower rather than a higher P/E ratio. One of the more popular ways of applying the P/E ratio is to compare the current value with its historical average. In some sense this is saying that the absolute level of the ratio is less important than its value relative to a comparable company and how it has performed relative to historical experience. Both of these approaches it does assume some reversion to the mean and has to be used with some degree of caution:

- If the companies under comparison are at different points at the corporate 'lifecycle' they may be experiencing different expected growth rates. So in this case a new entrant to a market should perhaps not be compared to a relatively mature market participant.
- It cannot easily be used to compare two companies with very different capital structures. This is because the EPS figure used in the denominator is after interest has been paid. To illustrate how this may impact the figure, consider the following simple example. Suppose we have two companies A and B whose pre-tax EBIT is $100 for both companies. Company A has no debt while company B has $20 of interest expense; their taxable profits are therefore 100 and 80, respectively. If we assume that both companies pay corporation tax at 10 %, then A's post-tax profit is $90, while company B's profits are $72. So even though their pre-tax earnings were comparable the impact of B's capital structure would impact their post-tax earnings.
- It is important to ensure that the earnings measures used in both companies are consistent. Examples of this include situations where the comparable company is subject to different accounting practices as well as ensuring that all one-off sources of income or expense are removed from the calculation.
- The measure cannot be used if earnings are negative.

Based on the 2015 annual accounts and a share price of $102, the figures for Apple are:

$$= \frac{\text{Share price}}{\text{Earnings per share}}$$
$$= \frac{\$102}{\$9.28}$$
$$= 10.99$$

Dividend Yield

A company's dividend yield measures the dividend earned as a percentage of the price.

$$\frac{\text{Dividend per share}}{\text{Share price}} \times 100 \qquad (3.12)$$

This is often seen as a popular measure as dividends are often seen as less volatile than earnings. Although it may be stating the obvious companies which do not pay dividends will not have a dividend yield.

Based on the 2015 annual accounts and a share price of $102, the figures for Apple are:

$$= \frac{\$1.98}{\$102} \times 100$$
$$= 1.94\%$$

P/E to Growth (PEG) Ratio

The PEG ratio takes a stock's P/E ratio and divides it by the percentage expected earnings growth rate. Suppose a company has a P/E of 10 and a projected earnings growth of 5 %, its PEG would be 2. All other things being equal a lower PEG is preferred to a higher PEG. The lower the number the less you are paying per unit of projected earnings growth. If the projected earnings growth is high, then mathematically this will reduce the PEG relative to a low projected growth. As a rule of thumb some practitioners have suggested that a PEG of 1 indicates that a company is fairly valued. From this it might be reasonable to construe that a PEG of less than 1 may represent good value. Extending the argument further a negative PEG indicates that earnings are expected to decline, but as with all ratio analysis further investigation may be warranted.

Dividend Per Share
Based on the dividend payout it is possible to calculate a dividend per share measure.

Price/Book Value
The numerator of this relationship is once again the company's share price. The denominator looks at the shareholders' equity component of the balance sheet and divides it by the number of shares in issue. It is referred to as a 'book' value as it represents a monetary value based on historical data rather than something that is driven by a market price. In a sense it is indicating whether the company has added any value (Vause 2005). A value greater than

1 indicates that value has been added while a value of less than 1 would indicate value has been taken away. The ratio is defined as:

$$\frac{\text{Share price}}{\text{Book value per share}} \qquad (3.13)$$

Based on the 2015 annual accounts and a share price of $102, the figures
for Apple are:

$$= \frac{\$102}{27,416,000,000 \Big/ 5,753,421,000}$$

$$= \frac{\$102}{4.7652}$$

$$= 21.41$$

Price/Free Cash Flow Yield

The P/E ratio has proved to be a popular metric by which to measure value
but some analysts argue that relating price to a company's cash flow is a more
appropriate measure that is less susceptible to different accounting choices. Set
against this is the fact that free cash flow can be very volatile due to changes
in capital expenditure and working capital. Price to free cash flow compares
a company's share price to its level of free cash flow. The appropriate measure
of cash flow should be free cash flow to equity. The inverse of this measure is
referred to a free cash flow yield.

Price to Sales
This measure divides the observed share price by the company's net sales.
Similar to price/cash flow yield measure, sales are perhaps less susceptible to
accounting differences between countries and companies.

3.4.4 Enterprise Value Multiples

EV multiples will relate the value of the firm to the profits it generates. Unlike
the equity price multiples, the convention for these measures is to use an earnings figure that is before taxation.

EV to EBIT or EBITDA

Two popular multiples relate EBIT and EBITDA to the enterprise value:

$$\frac{\text{Enterprise value}}{\text{Earnings before interest and taxation}} \qquad (3.14)$$

$$\frac{\text{Enterprise value}}{\text{Earnings before interest, taxation, depreciation \& amortisation}} \qquad (3.15)$$

The EV/EBITDA multiple is favoured as some analysts may use EBITDA as a measure of the company's gross cash flow. The measure is also popular as it is not affected by differences in capital structure (it is a pre-interest measure) and also less impacted by different accounting policies.

The earnings used in the P/E multiple is subject to different accounting policies (e.g. depreciation/amortization) and differences in the choices made by management as to how the business is financed (which will impact the amount of interest paid and the net income). At a simple level the metric tries to illustrate how much cash flow the company has relative to the amount of debt outstanding. It can be thought of as an approximation of how quickly the company could pay off its debt.

Similar to the interpretation of the P/E ratio a starting point to identify mispriced share would be a lower rather than higher measure. As ever this cannot be taken out of context and should be viewed in light of competitors or the sector or indeed the market as a whole.

Other measures at this level replace the denominator with sales revenues. This may be a useful measure if the company being analysed is not profitable at either the EBIT or EBITDA level. Other measures to which EV is expressed include FCFF.

Based on the 2015 annual accounts the figures for Apple are derived as follows:

Market capitalization
5,753,421 shares × $102 = $586,848,942,000
Net debt (in millions)
$64,462 (debt) minus $41,601 (cash) = $22,861
Enterprise value (full amount)
$609,709,942,000
EV/EBIT = $609,709,942,000/$71,230,000,000 = 8.56
EV/EBITDA = $609,709,942,000/$82,487,000,000 = 7.39

3.4.5 Identifying Mispriced Shares

There is no single approach to how one could use ratio analysis. There are perhaps some relatively simple techniques one could use to identify value within a cash equity framework.

Target Share Price

Having selected the appropriate ratio, the analyst could forecast a target share price based on some judgemental multiple. To illustrate the concept, consider the following hypothetical statement. *Based on ABC's ability to grow earnings in excess of its long-term forecast through improved revenue growth we view the upside share price scenario at $200 based on 14× our full year 2014 forecast of EPS of $14.29. This is in line with multinational industrial companies in the S&P 500. The downside scenario would be a share price of $142 based on 10× the full year 2014 EPS forecast. This is at the low end of the historical ranges but closer to industry peers.*

Current level versus historical levels—the analyst may decide that the metric is perhaps at some extreme relative to the historical performance of the measure. This view would perhaps suggest that the measure would be expected to revert to some long-term value.

Current level versus peer group—here the measure is considered to be relative to another equivalent company or perhaps a mean or median value for a group of companies. The analyst would then analyse the difference between the values and determine if it can be fundamentally justified. If the current level represents a substantial deviation from the comparison set then this may be an indicator of over or undervaluation.

3.5   Conclusion

The main message to reiterate is that price is determined by demand and supply, while equity value can be determined using a variety of analytical process such as discounted cash flow or comparable analysis. There is no single 'right' way to value an equity and different participants have developed to overcome perceived shortcomings in the traditional approaches. Interested readers who wish to gain an understanding of these models are referred to Viebig et al. (2008). Very often some of the techniques yield nonsensical results depending on the assumptions used. Hence an analyst may wish to apply a variety of techniques to come to an educated assessment of a company's value.

4

Valuation of Equity Derivatives

4.1 Chapter Overview

The chapter starts by discussing the valuation of single stock forwards and futures before extending the discussion to cover index futures. This provides a stepping stone to equity swap valuation before the final and longest section, that of equity options. Option valuation is a well-documented subject and so the coverage is designed to ensure the reader will be able to understand related topics presented elsewhere within the text.

4.2 Valuation of Single Stock Equity Forwards and Futures

In this section the focus is on single stock OTC forwards. However, the same principles can be applied to an equivalent futures contract. The valuation of single stock forwards and futures is based on principles that are sometimes referred to as 'no arbitrage' or 'cash and carry arbitrage'. This concept calculates the forward value of an asset based on the income and expense of a long position of a given maturity. Suppose a bank has received a request from a client for the purchase of Barclays Bank shares in 3 months' time. The quoted price will be such that at the point of delivery the bank will not incur any losses. The simplest way of ensuring this is to create a fully hedged position:

© The Author(s) 2017
N. Schofield, *Equity Derivatives*, DOI 10.1057/978-0-230-39107-9_4

- Buy the share for spot value.
- Borrow money for 3 months (say, at LIBOR) to finance the purchase of the share.
- Earn the dividend yield on the share.
- Lend out the shares for 3 months and earn a fee (i.e. the equity repo rate).
- Upon repayment of the stock loan, deliver the asset to the client in exchange for the pre-agreed price.

This suggests a simple relationship that ties together the income and expense incurred by the trader until the required maturity; the forward price will simply be the net cost of holding this position. As a result, the forward price of the asset can be derived as:

Forward price = Spot price + LIBOR borrowing cost − dividend income
− securities lending fee

From the client's perspective, by taking delivery in 3 months rather than for spot value they have 'saved' having to finance the position but have 'lost out' on receiving any dividend. As a result, the forward price they pay has to reflect these economics. This means that all expenses are added to the cost of buying the share, while all income components are subtracted.

The costs and income of holding this long hedge position are sometimes referred to as the 'carry' on the position. Some analysts may also refer to this concept as the 'net carry' or 'cost of carry'. There is often some degree of confusion and contradiction relating to the way in which carry is expressed. For clarification the text defines carry as follows:

- If income > expense, then a long position carries positively and the forward price will be below the spot price.
- If income < expense, then a long position carries negatively and the forward price will be above the spot price.
- If income = expense, then a long position incurs no carry and so the spot price and the forward price will be the same.

Returning to our forward calculation example, it will be assumed that the following rates apply in the market:

Spot price	235p
Prospective dividend yield	4.00 % p.a.
3-month GBP LIBOR	3.00 % p.a.
Securities lending fee	1.00 % p.a.

The cost of financing a long position in this share would be:

$$£2.35 \times 3.00\% \times 92 / 365 = £0.0178$$

Initially we will assume that the shares pay a constant dividend over the period:

$$£2.35 \times 4\% \times 92 / 365 = £0.0237$$

The fee earned from lending the security out for the period is:

$$£2.35 \times 1.00\% \times 92 / 365 = £0.0059$$

A quick glance at the results suggests that the income received from the long position exceeds the expense and so the position carries positively.

Recall the forward pricing formula

$$\text{Forward price} = \text{Spot price} + \text{LIBOR borrowing cost}$$
$$- \text{dividend income} - \text{securities lending fee}$$
$$\text{Forward price} = £2.35 + £0.0178 - £0.0237 - £0.0059$$
$$\text{Forward price} = £2.3382$$

From this example it is possible to make a number of conclusions:

- Since the position carries positively, the forward price is below the spot price.
- The price quoted to the customer is driven by the results of the hedging process.
- Today's forward price is neither a guess nor a forecast of where the spot price is expected to move.
- The forward price is simply today's breakeven price for delivery at some future time period.

Arguably in any asset class, where a forward market is quoted and traded, the forward should always act as a hurdle price. If the investor in the above example believes that in 3 months' time the actual price of a Barclays share will be greater than the forward price, then they should buy the share forward. This would also apply if they felt the price was going to fall by a penny to £2.34—it would still be cheaper to buy the asset on a forward basis. If they felt the price was going to be below the current forward price, then they would be better off doing nothing as their future purchase will be at a price less than the initially quoted forward. So an investor's trading decision should be based on where they think the share price will be in relation to the forward—the aim is always to beat the forward!

4.3   Valuation of Index Forwards and Futures

4.3.1 No Arbitrage Valuation Principles

Suppose the following data is observed in the market for settlement on the 17th February of a particular year.

Cash index FTSE 100	5899.87
June FTSE index future	5810.00
Futures expiry	15th June
Days from cash settlement to futures expiry	119
Index dividend yield	3.24 %
LIBOR rate to futures expiry	1.17 %
Securities lending fee (equity repo rate)	0.50 %

In this example a slightly different question is posed—is the June index future fairly valued?

The 'cash and carry arbitrage' principles introduced in Sect. 4.2 can be applied to answer the question but instead of using monetary values everything is expressed in index points:

The cost of financing a long position in the index for the period is:

$$5899.87 \times 1.17\% \times 119 / 365 = 22.5052 \tag{4.1}$$

Again assuming constant dividend payments, the income derived from holding a position is:

$$5899.87 \times 3.24\% \times 119 / 365 = 62.3220 \tag{4.2}$$

The income earned from lending the portfolio of equities is:

$$5899.87 \times 0.50\% \times 119 / 365 = 9.6176 \tag{4.3}$$

Therefore, the fair value of the future is:

$$5899.87 + 22.5052 - 62.3220 - 9.6176 = 5850.44$$

The main learning points are:

- The future is trading below the spot price as the position displays positive carry.
- The market price of the future (5,810.00) is below its theoretical value (5,850.44) and would be considered 'cheap' to fair value. The opposite situation (i.e. observed price greater than fair value) would be described as 'rich' rather than the more commonly recognized word 'expensive'.
- In calculating the fair value of the index the trader should arguably use the net rather than gross value of dividends to be received. This is based on the assumption that as a hedge the trader will be long the underlying shares and would be required to pay tax on the dividends.
- Over time the cash and futures prices will converge, such that at maturity they will be one and the same thing. To illustrate this, consider Eqs. (4.1, 4.2 and 4.3). If the forward price for the same fixed expiry date of 15th June is recalculated every day, then all other things being equal the individual carry components will decline to zero resulting in the convergence of the spot and forward prices. In reality, it is unlikely that this convergence will happen in a linear fashion, as the individual carry components (especially funding costs and equity repo rates) will be subject to short-term changes.

Although Chap. 9 considers how it is possible for an institution to make money from a future that is trading away from fair value, it is worth investigating why there is a relatively big difference of 40 index points between the observed market price and the theoretical value. This is most likely due to the dividend yield calculation. First of all, the calculation assumes there is a constant payment of dividends. However, the dividend element of the calculation can be more accurately restated as:

$$\text{Index value} \times \text{prospective annual dividend yield} \times P_{FUT} / P_{ANN}$$

Where:
P_{FUT} = dividend payments expected between now and the expiry of the futures
P_{ANN} = Total dividend payments expected in the full year ending on the expiry of the futures contract

Since the observed value of the future is below the fair value it could be argued that the market expects a greater dividend payment than that implied by the continuous payment calculation. Being able to accurately forecast dividends beyond 6–9 months in the future is very difficult and is one reason why these contracts are not quoted beyond these maturities.

Another popular technique favoured by some analysts used to calculate forward prices uses the following formula, which assumes continuous compounding:

$$\text{Forward price} = \text{Spot price} \times \text{EXP} \left((\text{Interest rates} - \text{Dividend yield}) \times \text{Time to expiry} \right) \quad (4.4)$$

Applying this formula to the previous values returns a different answer:

$$= 5899.87 \times 2.71828^{(1.17\% - 3.24\%) \times 0.326}$$

$$= 5860.19 \quad (4.5)$$

The time to expiry of 0.326 is calculated as 119 days divided by 365.

Some indices such as Germany's DAX are expressed in total return form. This means that the value of the index assumes that all dividends paid by the constituent stocks are reinvested. As a result, when calculating the value of an index future for this type of index, only the financing component need be taken into consideration.

4.3.2 Implied Equity Repo Rates

This chapter has shown that the forward valuation of an equity derivative is based on the following relationship:

$$\text{Forward price} = \text{spot price} + \text{LIBOR} - \text{dividend yield} - \text{equity repo rate} \quad (4.6)$$

Within the equity derivative market, it has been observed (Risk 2013) that the actual repo rate in the securities lending market often differs from the rate implied by the prices of index futures. Combescot (2013) notes that the implied equity repo rates for a variety of markets and maturities have been trading at negative values for a number of years. This negative value implies that if an investor wished to borrow some stocks they would receive a fee for doing so, which is counterintuitive.

Arguably negative implied repo rates embedded in futures prices came about due to technical and regulatory factors. One of the main buyers of equity futures are exotic option traders who tend to have a short forward position by virtue of the products that they structure and sell.[1] This demand to buy futures leads to upward pressure on price and, to avoid the possibility of arbitrage, needs to be accompanied by a change in one or more of the forward pricing components outlined in Eq. (4.6).

Consider the following example based on the EURO STOXX 50 using data observed in the market:

Value date:	1st September
Spot index value:	3175.05
September futures:	3178.00
Days to expiry of future:	18
EURIBOR:	0.05 %
Dividend yield:	3.13 %

Using a continuous compounding approach to valuation (i.e. Eq. 4.4) and assuming an initial equity repo rate of zero, these parameters would suggest a fair value for the future of approximately 3,170.00. However, it would be possible to calculate what equity repo rate would be needed to calibrate the fair value of the future with its observed value; the answer in this case is approximately −3.00 %. This is not an unreasonable approach since the future is relatively short-dated and so there will be little uncertainty over the prospective dividend yield. Suppose that in the securities lending market the actual repo rate was positive at a level of, say, 1 %. Using this observed repo rate returns a fair value of approximately 3169.

As a result, theory suggests that arbitrageurs would recognize that the future is trading above the fair value and would execute the following trade:

- Sell the over-valued future whose price includes an implied negative repo rate suggesting the arbitrageur will *receive* this implied rate.[2]
- Buy and hold a basket of shares for 18 days and lend them out to earn the actual repo rate.

---

[1] These desks typically create products that leave the banks structurally short calls and long puts, which means they will suffer a mark to market loss if the underlying price rises. In order to hedge this exposure these desks will buy futures. Structured products are considered in more detail in Chap. 12.

[2] A short forward position can be replicated by borrowing and then shorting a basket of shares. The proceeds of the short sale are placed on deposit to earn LIBOR but the investor will have to pay back to the lender any dividends and a securities lending fee (i.e. a repo rate). If the repo rate is negative the borrower is paid to borrow the shares.

If held to maturity this trade would generate a profit and if sufficient market participants act in the same the market should be kept in balance.[3]

Following the financial crisis, the implied repo rates on index futures became negative which persisted for several years. This meant that futures would tend to trade 'rich' to fair value and so exotic option desks were faced with increased costs to hedge their exposures.

The main reason for negative implied repo rates resulted from securities lending desks being under pressure to reduce the level of securities held as inventory (Risk 2013). This meant they were less likely to engage in the 'buy shares / sell futures' arbitrage needed to bring the markets back in line. These desks started to move away from holding the physical stock and replacing the exposures with 'delta one' derivatives (i.e. futures and total return swaps [TRS]), the demand for which exacerbated the magnitude of the negative implied repo rate. This change in activity was driven by a number of regulatory changes:

- *Balance sheet taxes*—since banks tended to be lenders of equity and this process creates a liability as they were also borrowing cash as part of the transaction—a number of jurisdictions (e.g. UK, Germany and France) had imposed taxes largely on the liability side of a bank's balance sheet reducing the attractiveness of the business.
- *Basle III regulations*—this impacted the banks in two ways. The regulations introduced a liquidity coverage ratio to address the issue of potential liquidity crises. These rules require banks to hold sufficient liquid assets to cover expected outflows over a 30-day period. In the original version of the policy this included securities lending and so banks would be required to buy high-quality low-yielding assets to support this business which would incur an extra borrowing cost. The other main aspect of the Basle regulations aimed to limit a bank's leverage, that is, the size of their assets relative to the capital base. Since securities lending constituted a very large part of the asset side of the balance sheet and is a high-volume, relatively low-yielding business, it would perhaps not be economically viable given the cost of holding capital against the positions.

4.3.3 Withholding Tax

Withholding tax is tax on income taken at source. The author (a UK resident), by virtue of previous employment, is still a share holder at a large US

---

[3] A worked example similar to this is detailed in Chap. 9.

investment bank and every quarter receives a dividend from which withholding tax has been deducted.

Since a long forward position can be replicated by a long position in the underlying asset it is logical to take into account any withholding tax that would be payable while holding the share. Suppose a bank has been asked to structure a 1-year equity forward for a client who normally receives their dividend gross (i.e. they are not required to pay withholding tax). The following values are observed in the market assuming an actual/actual day basis.

Spot price of share:	$100
12-month interest rates	3 %
Prospective gross dividend yields	2 %

The forward price implied by these values is $101 ($100 + $3 − $2). However, suppose that the structuring bank pays withholding tax at 10 % on the dividend they receive reducing their income to $1.80. The cost of carrying the hedge for the client is therefore $101.20 and so this is the price the bank would need to charge in order to break even.

Suppose further that there is an instantaneous rise in withholding tax to 20 %. From the bank's perspective, on a mark to market basis, the forward would now take a value of $101.40 ($100 + $3 − $1.60). The bank is short the forward at $101.20 and to close out the position they would need to buy it back at the higher price of $101.40. It follows that the seller of the forward has a short exposure to withholding tax, that is, an increase in withholding tax would result in a loss for a short forward position.

4.4 Valuation of Equity Index Swaps

4.4.1 Intuitive Approach to Equity Swap Valuation

An old market adage states that the price of any transaction is based on the cost of hedging the exposure—"if you can hedge it, you can price it". To illustrate this principle, consider the following example. A bank enters into a single name, 1-year price return equity swap (i.e. no dividends are payable) where they pay the equity return leg. In order to simplify the analysis, it is assumed that there will be a single exchange of cash flows at maturity. To hedge the equity price return payable under the swap the bank decides to buy the underlying asset, the purchase of which is financed by a money market borrowing (Fig. 4.1).

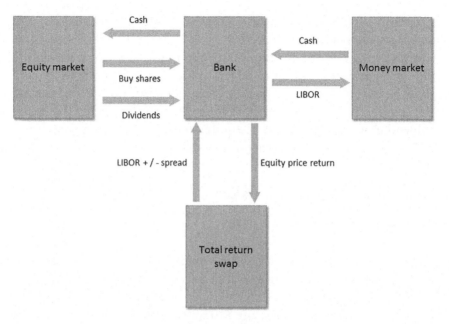

Fig. 4.1 Structuring and hedging a single name price return swap (*Source*: author)

The fair price of the equity swap can be calculated as the spread to LIBOR that ensures the transaction is an equitable exchange of cash flows. If the bank expected that the issuer was going to pay a 3 % dividend during the year, then the fair value of the spread to LIBOR is equal to this value, that is the floating leg is LIBOR—300 basis points. From the bank's perspective the 3 % dividends received on the underlying hedge is offset by a reduction in the LIBOR cash flow receivable under the swap.

It follows that if the swap was structured in total return form then the theoretical breakeven value of the spread to LIBOR would be zero. The floating leg would comprise just of a LIBOR cash flow as the bank forwards all dividends received on the hedge to the client. However, it is probable that a TRS may be priced with a positive spread to LIBOR for a variety of reasons:

- The cost of borrowing in the money market to finance the purchase of the hedge may not be possible at LIBOR 'flat'.
- The bank will want to build in a profit margin.
- The client may be happy to pay a positive spread to LIBOR if this is less than their normal borrowing cost.
- In order to protect themselves from the potential customer default the price of the swap would be adjusted to reflect the counterparty credit risk.

- If the bank is required to pay tax on the dividends received on the shares held as a hedge but must pay dividends gross under the terms of the swap, they may add a spread to LIBOR to ensure that overall they do not lose money.
- If the equity swap references an index, then the bank would probably use index futures to hedge the exposure. Since there are a limited number of maturities that trade, this hedge position would need to be 'rolled' on an ongoing basis which may incur a cost.[4] This cost would be factored into the swap by way of an increased margin to LIBOR.

4.4.2 Linking the Equity Repo and Equity Swaps Market

Section 4.4.1 considered the fundamental intuition of equity swap valuation. However, it did not consider equity repo rates.

The relationship between equity repo rates and TRS can be established using 'no arbitrage' valuation principles (Barclays Capital 2010). Suppose an investor has a long position in a portfolio of shares that exactly replicates a particular index. The investor observes that in the securities lending market the portfolio could be lent out to earn 20 basis points. If the investor decided to lend out the entire holding, they would:

- Deliver the shares to the borrower in return for cash,
- Invest the cash proceeds at, say, LIBOR,
- Pay a rebate to the borrower equal to LIBOR—20 basis points,
- Earn the equity repo rate (i.e. securities borrowing fee) of 20 basis points from the borrower.

Now consider a scenario where the investor sees that TRS on the same index are trading at LIBOR minus 30 basis points. It would be possible to make an arbitrage profit in the following way:

- Sell the portfolio of shares of cash,
- Invest the cash proceeds to earn, say, LIBOR,
- Enter into a TRS where they pay LIBOR—30 basis points and receive the equity total return.

In the first example the investor's net return was 20 basis points, while in the second it was 30 basis points (Fig. 4.2).

---

[4] See Chap. 9.

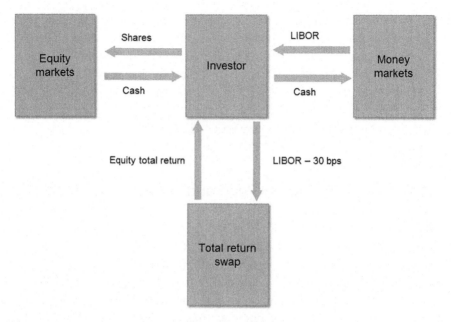

Fig. 4.2 Diagrammatic representation of possible arbitrage between the equity, money and equity swaps markets (*Source*: author)

Now consider the scenario where the TRS on the index is trading at LIBOR—15 basis points. To make an arbitrage profit the investor could:

- Borrow at LIBOR to buy the portfolio of shares.
- Lend out the shares to earn the equity repo rate of 20 basis points.
- Enter into a TRS where they pay the equity performance and receive LIBOR—15 basis points.

This structure is shown in Fig. 4.3 and results in a net profit to the investor of 5 basis points.

It is these two 'no arbitrage' mechanisms that ensure that equity repo rates and TRS prices are kept in line.[5] It follows that an increase in repo rates should result in an increase in the absolute value of the spread component of the LIBOR cash flow[6] and thus for the investor in Fig. 4.3 generate a mark to market profit. To illustrate this principle, consider just the equity swap in Fig. 4.3 from the investor's perspective. Suppose that repo rates increase to 25

---

[5] The example ignores taxation and assumes the investor funds at LIBOR.

[6] As a point of clarification, an 'increase in the absolute value of the spread component of the LIBOR cash flow' is defined as a situation where the floating cash flow moves from LIBOR—15 to LIBOR—25. This would mean of course that the magnitude of the LIBOR cash flow has decreased.

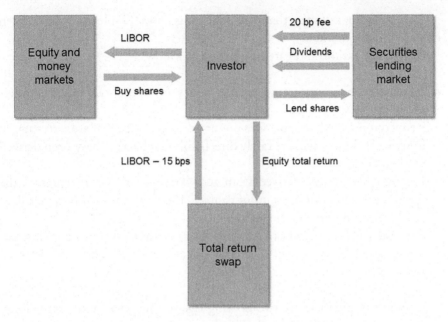

Fig. 4.3 Diagrammatic representation of possible arbitrage between the securities lending market and the equity swaps market (*Source*: author)

basis points and the 'price' of the swap moves in line to LIBOR—25 bps. If the investor were to enter into an offsetting swap position, then on a net basis they would receive LIBOR—15 bps but only have to pay LIBOR—25 bps to generate a profit of 10 basis points. This illustrates that an increase in equity repo rates would generate a mark to market profit for an entity paying the equity leg of a swap.

4.4.3 Discounted Cash Flow Approach to Swap Valuation

An alternative way of valuing swaps is to use a discounted cash flow technique. To illustrate these principles a new hypothetical transaction is introduced:

Effective date	Spot
Maturity	1 year
Payment frequency	Quarterly
Initial notional amount	£10,000,000
Equity notional reset	Applicable
Equity leg	Return on the FTSE 100 index without dividends (i.e. price return swap)
Initial starting value of index	5890
Interest rate leg	3-month GBP LIBOR
Spread to LIBOR	–3.39 % p.a.

The example assumes that the following rates (Table 4.1) have been observed in the market.[7]

Briefly, the various rates are interpreted as follows:

- The interest rate swap rates represent values for interest rate swaps of different maturities.
- Zero coupon yields are the rates on interest rate swaps that are zero coupon in style. As these values are rarely directly observable they have been derived mathematically.
- Discount factors are derived from zero coupon yields and represent the present value of a future sum of money. The discount factors were calculated from the zero coupon yields.
- Forward yields are interest rate swap rates for forward starting maturities. These can either be observed directly or calculated from other values such as the discount factors.

In this example there are two floating legs so the 'price' of the transaction will be a spread to LIBOR that is added or subtracted such that the initial net present value (NPV) of the transaction is zero. This ensures that on the trade date the transaction is considered to be an equitable exchange of cash flows.

All of the associated cash flows for this transaction are shown in Table 4.2. The different columns are interpreted as follows:

- *Forward index level*—this is derived using the same principles discussed in Sect. 4.3. The forward value is calculated as:
  Spot value + LIBOR expense − expected dividends
- For ease of illustration securities lending fees (i.e. equity repo rate) and withholding tax have been ignored.

Table 4.1 Market rates used for swap valuation example

Period	Interest rate swap rates (%)	Zero coupon yields (%)	Discount factor	Forward yields (%)	Projected dividend payments in index points
0.25	3.0000	3.0000	0.9926	3.0000	36
0.50	3.2500	3.2642	0.9839	3.5022	38
0.75	3.5000	3.5337	0.9742	4.0072	41
1.00	3.7500	3.8091	0.9633	4.5158	35

---

[7] A full derivation of the rates is beyond the scope of this book. Interested readers are referred to Schofield and Bowler (2011).

Table 4.2 Valuation of equity swap on trade date

Period	Forward index level	Notional value	Index cash flow	PV of index cash flow	LIBOR cash flow	PV of LIBOR cash flow
0.25	5898.18	10,013,879.46	13,879.46	13,776.14	−9832.78	−9759.58
0.50	5900.07	10,017,089.56	3210.11	3158.55	2,725.72	2,681.95
0.75	5901.03	10,018,732.80	1643.24	1,600.82	15,373.95	14,977.02
1.00	5911.09	10,035,805.54	17,072.73	16,446.27	28,114.00	27,082.39
			Totals	34,981.78		34,981.78
				Net present value	0.0000	

- *Notional value*—in this transaction the notional value will move in accordance with how the index evolves over the life of the transaction ('equity notional reset'). The logic behind the changing notional is that the transaction has been designed to mimic a long position in the underlying index. Its initial value is taken to be £10 m but from a pricing perspective the value in the three subsequent quarters is derived from the initial forward price for each future period.
- *Index cash flow*—this is calculated as the notional value at the start of each period multiplied by the percentage change in the index over the period.
- *PV of index cash flow*—this result is derived by taking the result of the index cash flow column and multiplying it by the discount factor applicable to that period.
- *LIBOR cash flow*—this cash flow is calculated as the notional value for a particular period multiplied by the applicable forward rate multiplied by the days in the period divided by the day basis. For ease of illustration we have assumed an exact quarter of a year. The LIBOR rate used in this calculation is adjusted by adding or subtracting a fixed number of basis points, which represents the price of the transaction.
- *PV of LIBOR cash flow*—the LIBOR cash flows are present valued using the appropriate discount factor.

In this example a fixed spread of 339 basis points has been subtracted from each LIBOR value. Since the initial NPV of the structure is zero the transaction would be considered an equitable exchange of cash flows and so the negative spread of 339 basis points would represent 'fair value'.

The notion of entering into a transaction with an initial profit of zero may seem strange but over time the NPV of the transaction will change as the underlying index, LIBOR rates and dividend yields evolve. Inevitably as market rates evolve the profitability of the swap will also change—that is the NPV of the cash flows will no longer be zero. The transaction will show a profit for the entity that expects to receive more in present value terms than they expect to pay.

Recall that a forward is used as a break even or hurdle rate. So at a simple level if an investor believed that the total return of the FTSE index was going to evolve faster than the forward LIBOR rates used to value the contract they should receive the equity leg. By the same token, they would also need to believe that LIBOR rates they are required to pay will be less than or equal to the initial forward rates used to value the interest rate leg.

Timing of Dividend Payments—Total Return Swaps
One aspect of the analysis that has been ignored is the timing of the dividend. The entity that is paying the equity leg on the swap would typically hedge themselves by buying the underlying. If the transaction is total return in nature, they will be required to pay across to their counterparty any dividends that are paid during each period at the same time they settle the equity return component. However, it is likely that the dividends on the underlying hedge will be received throughout the period and so therefore the bank will be able to reinvest these until the required swap payment date. As a result, this timing mismatch should be reflected in the spread to LIBOR.

4.4.4 Interest Rate Exposure of Equity Swaps

The swap structure does also have exposure to interest rates by virtue of the fact that interest rate swap rates are used in the valuation process. The most popular metric used to measure the interest rate exposure of a derivative is the 'dollar value of an 01' (DV01). In this case the DV01 measures the change in the mark to market of the equity swap transaction for a 1 basis point parallel movement of the interest rate swaps curve. In this case a one basis point movement of the curve changes the value of the swap by about $725. Although this may not be a significant amount the equity swaps trader may decide to hedge this exposure using some form of offsetting interest rate derivative such as a swap, forward rate agreement or interest rate future.

4.4.5 Overnight Index Swap (OIS) Discounting

Over the last few years there has been an increased focus on counterparty credit risk, which has resulted in banks now taking collateral for derivative provisions. The International Swaps and Derivatives Association (ISDA) Credit Support Annex (CSA) requires that any bank that receives (pays) collateral pays (receives) interest based on a specified overnight interest rate. Most money markets will publish a benchmark interest rate which is constructed based on overnight unsecured deposits traded in the market. Some of the more popular indices are:

- Sterling Overnight Index Average (SONIA)
- Euro Overnight Index Average (EONIA)
- Federal Funds Effective Rate

Prior to the financial crisis of 2007 the majority of swaps had been revalued using LIBOR rates while any collateral paid or received would have attracted an overnight interest rate. Dealers were exposed to the spread between the two rates but since the differential was small and stable few institutions were concerned. However, during the crisis the differential widened substantially and this led to a mismatch in values. To illustrate the concept, consider the following simplified example which is based on a classic 'fixed for floating' interest rate swap. Suppose a trader has a $10 m swap position with exactly 1 year to run. Rates instantaneously move by 1 % in his favour causing the swap to show a profit of $100,000. If the trader present values this profit at the current LIBOR rate of, say, 5 % then he would demand collateral of value $95,238. Typically, overnight rates will be lower than LIBOR rates as given their short-term nature they are perceived to have less credit risk. If it is assumed that overnight rates are at 4 % then the trader will put the collateral on deposit and will receive $99,048 at the end of the year. However, if the counterparty were to default prior to maturity the value of the swap will not have evolved in line with the accruing value of the collateral, leaving the trader with a loss.

As a result of the divergence of LIBOR and overnight rates the market has now moved to revaluing swaps using OIS rates rather than LIBOR rates.[8] The main impact of OIS revaluation is that the discount factors and forward LIBOR rates will be different from those derived when discounting using LIBOR values. Readers interested in knowing more about the process of OIS discounting are referred to either Schofield and Bowler (2011) or Nashikkar (2011).

---

[8] An OIS is a fixed-for-floating swap in which the floating payment is based on compounding at an overnight interest rate.

4.4.6 Hedging Equity Swaps

The hedging of equity swaps was alluded to in Fig. 1.3 but not analysed in any great depth. To hedge the equity cash flows the market maker would need to take an equal or opposite exposure in the underlying asset. So if they are paying the total return on a single stock then the easiest solution is to simply buy the stock. If the hedge is structured correctly, then any loss incurred on the swap would be offset by a profit on the underlying hedge.

If the swap references an index, then the trader would typically hedge the position using index futures. The same principles would apply; any loss on the swap should be offset by a profit on the future. This approach requires the trader to make a decision as to the appropriate hedge maturity. Table 4.2 illustrates a 1-year swap with four quarterly payments. The trader could hedge the entire swap exposure using a single maturity perhaps choosing the near-dated contract since it is likely to be the most liquid. However, this contract will mature after 3 months and so the trader would need to roll their hedge to the next contract; this is a so-called stack hedge. The other possibility is that they could hedge each individual cash flow with a future of a corresponding maturity; this approach is referred to as a 'strip' hedge.

4.5   Valuation of Equity Options

Much has been written on the subject of option valuation so to avoid reinventing the wheel the coverage here will be fairly high level. Reference is often made to option 'pricing models' but this is something of a misnomer. Like all traded assets an option's price will be determined by the interaction of demand and supply within the market. Arguably, option models serve two purposes: they help determine the 'fair value' of the option as well as guiding the user as to how to manage the associated market risk.

In this section we will consider only so-called closed-form solutions, that is, a Black Scholes Merton (BSM) framework. Two other popular techniques are used to value options, namely binomial and Monte Carlo. These techniques have been well documented in other texts and so interested readers are referred elsewhere, for example Schofield and Bowler (2011).

4.5.1 Intuitive Approach to Option Pricing

The UK National Lottery requires a player to select 6 numbers from 59. The odds of selecting the winning 6 numbers are about 1 in 45 million (1 in

45,057,474 to be a little more precise). According to Camelot's website their average jackpot is about £5 m. As a result, we can calculate the approximate expected value of the game (£5 m x 1/45 m), which is about £0.11. Since players have to pay £2 to play some people may view this as 'the idiot's income tax'. Although this example assumes that the lottery operator only offers a single prize, the logic gives an insight into the principles of option valuation.

UBS (1999) define a call option 'as a substitute for a long forward position with downside protection'. Equally they define a put option 'as a substitute for a short forward position with upside protection'. They argue that this way of defining an option gives an additional insight into how the option should be valued. Since the option is viewed as substitute for a forward then any advantage the option confers relative to the forward price must have additional value, which must be paid for by the buyer. So if the option is struck ITM with respect to the forward price this degree of "moneyness" will need to be paid for. An option struck OTM relative to the forward rate confers no advantage relative to the forward price but it does not mean that the option will be free. Irrespective of the degree of moneyness, options incorporate protection against adverse price movements as well as the possibility of making theoretically unlimited profits. These two additional features will also need to be paid for by the buyer.

The main factors that influence the value of an equity option are:

- The underlying price of the asset
- The strike price
- Time to maturity
- Dividend yield on the share
- Interest rates
- Implied volatility

Since European-style options cannot be exercised until maturity they are valued relative to an equivalent underlying instrument, which is a forward. This can be somewhat confusing as the instrument will often be exercisable into a spot position and will often have the spot price as a valuation input. Tompkins (1994) argues that 'all option pricing models estimate first what the expected forward price of the underlying asset will be at the expiration dates of the option and then from this knowledge, estimate the option price'.

The fundamental principle of option pricing is that the premium payable or receivable will be a function of the seller's payout at expiry. This payout will be dependent on the spot price of the asset at expiry but since this is not known with certainty until the option matures the pricing process requires

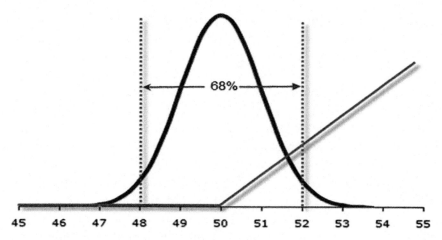

Fig. 4.4 ATM expiry pay off of a call option overlaid with a stylized normal distribution of underlying prices (*Source*: author)

the trader to estimate a range of possible outcomes and the probability of their occurrence. In order to estimate the range of possible payouts traditional approaches to option valuation attempt to overlay the option's expiry payoff with a (log) normal distribution.[9] The two key properties of a normal distribution are its mean and its standard deviation. The conventional approach is to centre the normal distribution over the current underlying price (i.e. the forward price). The standard deviation is a measure of spread from the mean, and it can be used to estimate the likelihood that a particular value or range of values will occur. The magnitude of a standard deviation will be a function of how volatile the asset is expected to be as well as the time to maturity. The width of the distribution (i.e. the dispersion of the returns) is referred to using the somewhat ambiguous term of 'volatility'.

Consider the following examples based on an ATM equity call option where the spot price is $50 and the net carry is zero. The exact maturity, volatility and premium are not specified in order to simplify the example.

The normal distribution in Fig. 4.4 shows that over the remaining life of the option the market expects the asset to trade within ± $2 of the underlying price with 68 % confidence. Note that to the left of the strike the seller's expected payout will be zero, that is, there is a 50 % chance that they will not have to make a payout. To the right of the strike there is no limit to how high the underlying price can move, but the normal distribution can be used to calculate the expected value of each outcome. The figure shows that as the

[9] The validity of this assumption will be considered in greater detail in Chap. 6.

payout increases the probability of it occurring diminishes and therefore the expected values at the extreme will be lower.

Figure 4.5 takes the same option and considers what the impact of an increase in the underlying price by $1 will be. Notice that the distribution is now recentred at the higher price of $51, which means the expected values to the right of the strike now increase making the option more expensive.

In Fig. 4.6, as a result of an increase in implied volatility the seller is now faced with the prospect of a wider range of prices trading at maturity, which will cause the value of the option to increase. Note that although implied

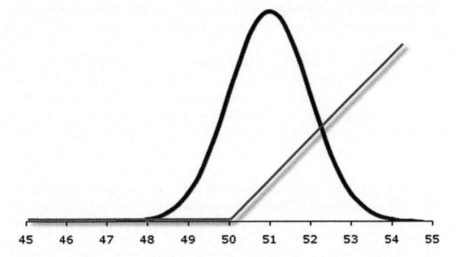

Fig. 4.5 ITM call option with a strike of $50 where the underlying price has increased to $51 (*Source*: author)

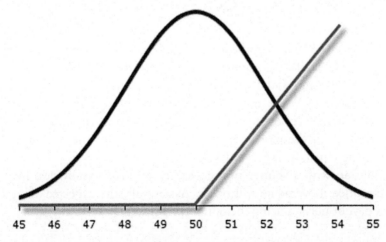

Fig. 4.6 Increase in implied volatility for ATM call option (*Source*: author)

volatility has increased the current underlying price is unchanged at $50. A common misunderstanding of options assumes that movements in the underlying price and movements in implied volatility are the same thing. This cannot be the case as the option pricing model has the two factors as independent variables. Vasan (1998) writing within an FX context argues that implied volatility measures "the market's expectation of how widely the exchange rate is likely to fluctuate…. (it) measures the expected movements around the forward price, as opposed to the spot price….likely means with about 2/3 probability (±1 standard deviation), with a 1/3 chance of being wrong….more formally the expected standard deviation in the FX rate, at an annualised per cent rate". Essentially, implied volatility quantifies the degree of uncertainty in the market.

There is, however, an indirect linkage between the movement of the spot price and implied volatility. Suppose that a trader had valued this option using an implied volatility of 30 %. Implied volatility is expressed in percentage per annum and so to convert this into a measure that applies to a shorter time period it is necessary to divide by the square root of the number of trading periods in the year. Since options are not traded at weekends the convention used to convert into a daily figure is to divide by the square root of 252. The different techniques used to convert between time periods are considered in greater detail in Chap. 6. Dividing the annualized implied volatility figure by the square root of 252 we derive an estimate of the expected daily volatility.

$$= 30\% \div \sqrt{252}$$
$$= 30\% \div 15.8745$$
$$= 1.89\%$$

So as a rule of thumb if the asset is trading at a price of $50 an implied volatility quote of 30 % per annum suggests that the price is expected to move between $49.05 and $50.95 on a daily basis (i.e. ± 1.89 % of the underlying price). If a trader saw the underlying price was trading consistently outside of this range, he may choose to alter his implied volatility quote appropriately.

The impact of the passage of time on the value of the option, all other things being equal, is shown in Fig. 4.7.

An option with a shorter time to expiry means it is now less likely that extreme price movements will occur. As a result, the expected value of the seller's payout falls reducing the option premium.

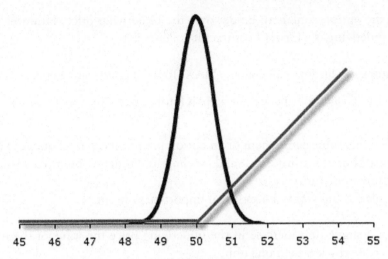

Fig. 4.7 The impact of time on the value of an ATM call option

4.6 Changes in an Option's Fair Value

This section illustrates how the fair value of an option changes within a BSM framework. Let us assume the following market parameters are observed in the market:

Spot price:	$15
Strike price	$15.15 (ATM forward)
Maturity	1 year
Implied volatility	30 %
Dividend yield	2 %
Interest rates	3 %

The BSM model returns an initial fair value of $1.75 for both the call and the put.

Consider now how the value of the two options changes as the individual underlying market parameters change but all of the other factors are held constant.

4.6.1 Change in the Spot Price

Option theory decomposes the premium into two components: intrinsic and time value. Intrinsic value is the amount that the holder of the option would realize if he could exercise his option straight away. If the option is European in style this would not be possible so we could redefine this as the advantage that the option confers to holder over the underlying price. However, since the underlying is a forward contract it is defined as:

Intrinsic value for a call option = MAX (forward price − strike price, 0)

Intrinsic value for a put option = MAX (strike price − forward price, 0)

The time value component of an option premium can be thought of as the potential future intrinsic value and is primarily a function of implied volatility and time to maturity.

Table 4.3 highlights a number of important concepts:

- For a single unit increase in the underlying price the value of the option increases by less than one unit.
- The relationship between the underlying price and the value of the option prior to expiry is non-linear. This is shown in Fig. 4.8.
- When the option is OTM and ATM the premium comprises entirely of time value.
- Time value is greatest when the option is ATM.
- When the option is ITM the premium consists of increasing intrinsic value and decreasing time value.

4.6.2 Change in Time to Maturity

Table 4.4 shows that the passage of time has a negative effect on both the call and the put option and that this accelerates as the option approaches expiry.

An alternative approach to analysing Table 4.4 is to view each line as a series of identical options with different maturities. Intuitively one might expect a 12-month option to be worth twice as much as a 6-month option; however, this is not the case. A 6-month call option priced using the same parameters

Table 4.3 Impact on the value of a call and a put from a change in the spot price

Spot price ($)	Value of a call ($)	Change in value of call	Value of a put ($)	Change in value of put
13	0.84		2.80	
14	1.25	0.41	2.23	−0.57
15	1.75	0.50	1.75	−0.48
16	2.34	0.59	1.36	−0.39
17	3.01	0.67	1.05	−0.31
18	3.74	0.73	0.80	−0.25

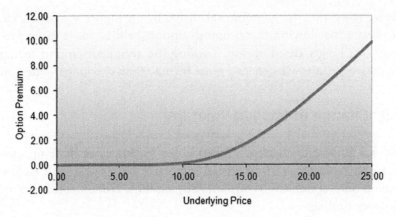

Fig. 4.8 Relationship between option premium and the underlying price for a call option prior to expiry

Table 4.4 Impact on the value of a call and put from the passage of time

Time to expiry	Value of a call ($)	Change in value of call	Value of a put ($)	Change in value of put
1.00	1.75		1.75	
0.80	1.56	−0.19	1.59	−0.16
0.60	1.34	−0.22	1.40	−0.19
0.40	1.08	−0.26	1.17	−0.23
0.20	0.74	−0.34	0.86	−0.31
0.00	0.00	−0.74	0.00	−0.86

costs $1.22 while a 12-month option is valued at $1.75. Vasan (1998) shows the mathematics behind the calculation as:

$$12 \text{ month variance} = 2 \times 6 \text{ month variance}$$
$$12 \text{ month standard deviation} = \sqrt{2 \times 6 \text{ month variance}}$$
$$= \sqrt{2} \times \sqrt{6 \text{ month variance}}$$
$$= \sqrt{2} \times 6 \text{ month standard deviation}$$

This suggests that the approximate premium on a 12-month option should be:

$$= \$1.22 \times \sqrt{2}$$
$$= \$1.22 \times 1.41$$
$$= \$1.73$$

As we saw earlier the premium calculated by the model was $1.75. He goes on to argue that buying two 6-month options will be more expensive than buying one longer-dated option. Turning the argument around selling two consecutive options will generate more income than one longer-dated option.

4.6.3 Change of Implied Volatility

Table 4.5 illustrates that as implied volatility increases both options will increase in value. Each 10 % rise in implied volatility will increase the premium on both options by a constant (ish) amount. Two other features are also worth mentioning:

- An option that has no intrinsic value and is priced using 0 % volatility is worthless. Zero volatility suggests that the underlying price is not expected to move over the remaining life of the option and so the options will expire worthless.
- The relationship between premium and volatility for an ATM option is proportional; doubling the volatility doubles the premium.

Table 4.6 looks at the impact of a change in implied volatility on an ITM and OTM call. Both options are valued using the original strike of $15.15 but

Table 4.5 Impact on the value of a call and a put from a change in implied volatility

Implied volatility (%)	Value of call ($)	Change in value of call	Value of put ($)	Change in value of put
0.00	0.00		0.00	
10.00	0.59	0.59	0.59	0.59
20.00	1.17	0.58	1.17	0.58
30.00	1.75	0.58	1.75	0.58
40.00	2.33	0.58	2.33	0.58
50.00	2.90	0.57	2.90	0.57

Table 4.6 Impact on the value of an ITM and OTM call from a change in implied volatility (premiums shown to just two decimal places)

Implied volatility (%)	Value of ITM call ($)	Change in value of call	Value of OTM call ($)	Change in value of call
0.00	4.90		0.00	
10.00	4.90	0.00	0.00	0.00
20.00	5.01	0.11	0.02	0.02
30.00	5.35	0.34	0.15	0.13
40.00	5.83	0.48	0.38	0.23
50.00	6.37	0.54	0.69	0.31

the spot price is assumed to be $20 and $10 for the ITM and OTM, positions respectively.

It is possible to make the following conclusions from Table 4.6:

- An increase in implied volatility causes the ITM and OTM premiums to increase at an increasing rate.
- At zero implied volatility the premium for the ITM option comprises entirely of intrinsic value. The implied forward price for a spot price of $20.00 (all other things being equal) is $20.20. The option premium returns the present value of the intrinsic value. This is $4.90 [($20.20 − $15.15) / 1.03].
- For the ITM option, intrinsic value is a constant, while for the OTM option it consists entirely of time value. As a result, Table 4.6 shows how an increase in implied volatility increases the time value component.
- At first glance the OTM option premia appear to be relatively insignificant but note what happens when implied volatility doubles from 20 to 40 %. The premium increases from $0.02 to $0.38—this is an increase of 1800 %. Looked at from this perspective, deeply out of the money options with low implied volatilities may be thought of as cheap lottery tickets. A sudden movement in implied volatility will increase the value of the option by a significant percentage resulting in a massive return on capital.

4.6.4 Change in Interest Rates

The main conclusions from Table 4.7 are that an increase in interest rates will increase the value of a call but will reduce the value of a put option. To illustrate why this is so, consider how a trader would hedge a short call position. If the option position were to be exercised they will be required to deliver the asset. As such the appropriate hedging strategy is to buy the underlying asset. Although the underlying asset is technically a forward many traders will

Table 4.7 Impact on the value of a call and a put from a change in the funding rate

Interest rates (%)	Value of call ($)	Change in value of call	Value of put ($)	Change in value of put
1.00	1.63		1.92	
2.00	1.69	0.06	1.84	−0.08
3.00	1.75	0.06	1.75	−0.09
4.00	1.82	0.07	1.67	−0.08
5.00	1.89	0.07	1.59	−0.08

actually prefer to use the spot market to hedge this potential exposure. The purchase of hedge will require an initial outlay of cash which will need to be financed. An increase in interest rates increases the cost of borrowing and so the option seller will pass this increased charge on to the buyer in the form of a higher premium. The opposite would be true for a put option. The hedge in this case is a short position in the underlying. The money received from the sale of the asset can be put on deposit to earn interest. An increase in interest rates will reduce the cost of carrying the position and hence the premium will be lower.

4.6.5 Change of Dividend Yield and Equity Repo Rates

Table 4.8 shows that an increase in dividend yields decreases the value of the call but increases the value of a put. Referring back to the hedging cost argument introduced in Sect. 4.6.4, the seller of a call will be long the underlying asset as a hedge and will therefore receive the dividend yield. An increase in the dividend yield reduces the cost of carrying the hedge and so the benefit is passed onto the buyer in the form of a lower premium.

If options can be thought of as a substitute for a forward, then intuitively the same carry components used to value a forward position need to be taken into account when valuing options. This means that equity option models need to take into account securities lending fees, that is equity repo rates. Recall from Sect. 4.2 the general relationship used to derive a forward price:

$$\text{Forward price} = \text{Spot price} + \text{LIBOR borrowing cost} \\ - \text{dividend income} - \text{securities lending fee}$$

Within the context of option valuation, a change in equity repo rates (i.e. the securities lending fee) will have the same impact as a change in the dividend yield.

Table 4.8 Impact on the value of a call and a put from a change in dividend yields

Dividend yield (%)	Value of call ($)	Change	Value of put ($)	Change
1.00	1.84		1.69	
2.00	1.75	−0.09	1.75	0.06
3.00	1.67	−0.08	1.82	0.07
4.00	1.59	−0.08	1.88	0.06
5.00	1.52	−0.07	1.95	0.07

4.7   Early Exercise of American -Style Options

One topic that is often raised by newcomers to the option market is whether an American-style option should always cost more than a European equivalent. This is based on the observation that an American-style option would appear to offer an investor more flexibility in terms of when it can be exercised. The answer is not immediately obvious and once again it can be explained in terms of the underlying hedge. Consider the seller of a call option who buys the underlying asset as a hedge against potential future delivery. If the cost of funding the purchase of the underlying asset is greater than the dividend earned on the asset the position will incur a carry cost which will be passed on to the buyer in the form of a higher premium. If the option buyer were to exercise the option, they would forfeit any time value and realize only the intrinsic value. In addition, they would now be holding a long position which carries negatively. This negative carry increases as the option becomes more ITM. As a result, where there is a cost associated with carrying the underlying asset the additional flexibility offered by American options is of little practical value as no rational investor would exercise early. Therefore, under these conditions the prices of an American and European option should be the same. The holder of an American option wishing to unwind the exposure would be better off taking an equal and opposite position in the option's market for which they will receive both intrinsic and time value.

Looked at from another perspective it may pay the holder of an American call option to exercise early in order to receive any income on the underlying security, which they would not be able to earn as an option holder. This may occur if the option holder believed the net value of the income receivable by holding the physical asset would be greater than any time value remaining on the option. Naturally, the market will see the possibility of early exercise and would price the option with additional time value over and above that on a comparable European option and to that extent it would probably tilt the balance in favour of not exercising early. The relationship between the different types and styles of options and the net carry is summarized in Table 4.9.

Table 4.9 Cost of American option vs. cost of European option in different cost of carry scenarios

	Interest rate > dividend yield	Interest rate < dividend yield
Call option	Cost of American option = Cost of European option	Cost of American option > Cost of European option
Put option	Cost of American option > Cost of European option	Cost of American option = Cost of European option

4.8   Put-Call Parity

The author started studying options in the late 1980s and was introduced quite quickly to the concept of put-call parity. I confess to have found it rather dull and boring until some 13 years later when I spent a useful afternoon with an FX options structurer (thanks James!) who showed me how the principles could be used to create and analyse a variety of structured products. We will return to the applications of the principle throughout the text but at this stage we merely outline the key principles. Notice that at the start of Sect. 4.6 we priced an ATM forward option on a theoretical equity which returned a premium for both the call and the put of $1.75. This is an example of put-call parity. In its simplest form it can be stated as:

$$+C - P = +F - E$$

Where:
C = premium on a call option
P = premium on a put option
F = Forward price
E = Strike rate on an option

The principles of put-call parity will hold when the strike, maturity and notional of the two options are the same. So the equation states that the premium on an option struck ATM forward will be the same for both a call and a put.

So how does this relationship help structure products? Tompkins (1994) argues that by restating the equation such that $+F - E$ is interpreted as a long forward position the equation can be interpreted to say that the purchase of a call and the sale of a put are equal to a long forward position in the underlying asset. From a structuring perspective it is therefore possible to create products that have a forward-style payoff but are actually created by combining calls and puts. This can create a very wide range of structures particularly if barrier options are included.

Tompkins (1994) points out that the nature of put-call parity will vary according to the underlying asset. For equity options the relationship is more formally stated as[10]:

---

[10] The equation presented by Tompkins does not include a value for equity repo rates but this can be accommodated for by making an adjustment to the dividend yield parameter.

$$+C - P = S \times \exp^{(DY \times t)} - E \times \exp^{(-\text{LIBOR} \times t)}$$

Where the additional terms are defined as follows:
S = spot price.
DY = dividend yield.
t = time to expiry.

4.9   Summary

There are two major themes that are important to understand when looking at derivative valuation.

- The price of the product is driven by the cost of hedging the exposure. The mantra was "if you can hedge it, you can price it!"
- Derivatives consist of a series of cash flows to be paid and received at different points in the future. A derivative's value is therefore linked to how much these cash flows are worth in present value terms.

The chapter looked at the principles of 'cash and carry' arbitrage as a way of valuing single stock and index forwards and futures. The discussion then widened to consider equity swaps. Here three different valuation approaches were considered but it was argued that they were all consistent with each other. The final section looked at the principles of option valuation. The major topics covered were the intuitive principles of closed-form valuation, early exercise of American options and put-call parity.

5

Risk Management of Vanilla Equity Options

5.1 Introduction

The main measures of vanilla option market risk are sometimes referred to collectively as 'the Greeks'. Numerous texts are available that provide closed form solutions for these metrics, for example, Haug (2007). Consequently, the focus of this chapter is the interpretation of these measures rather than their calculation. The Greeks for exotic options such as barriers and binaries are discussed in Chap. 7.

For consistency this chapter will use the long call option introduced in Chap. 4. The factors used to value the option were:

Spot price	$15.00
Strike	$15.15(ATM forward)
Expiry	1 year
Funding rate	3.00 %
Dividend yield	2.00 %
Volatility	30.00 %
Premium	$1.7534 per share

5.2 Delta

Figure 4.5 illustrated the relationship between the premium of an option and the underlying price[1]. This relationship was analysed in Chap. 4 but for ease of reference it is reproduced as Fig. 5.1.

---

[1] Strictly speaking the underlying price for a European-style option is a forward price with the same time to maturity as the option. However, anecdotally the author has seen many equity option practitioners

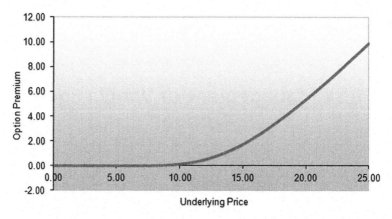

Fig. 5.1 Relationship between an option's premium and the underlying asset price for a long call option prior to expiry (*Source*: author)

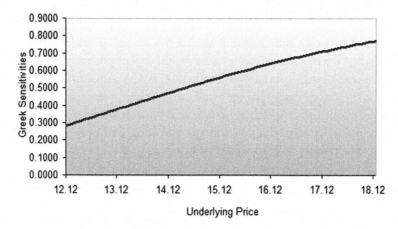

Fig. 5.2 Delta for a range of underlying prices far from expiry for a long-dated, long call option position (*Source*: author)

Delta measures the slope of this price line for a 'small' change in the underlying price. Figure 5.2 shows the initial values of delta for a similar range of underlying share prices.

The slope of the price line in Fig. 5.1 and the associated delta value will be positive or negative depending on the type of option. The logic behind this can be derived from Fig. 1.4 which illustrated the main at expiry option profiles. From this diagram it is possible to infer that the slope (and therefore the deltas) for either a long call option or a short put will be positive while for

refer casually to the spot price as the underlying price. Arguably it would be more accurate to refer to the 'moneyness' of the option in relation to the forward (ATMF) or relative to the spot price (ATMS).

a short call and long put option position the deltas will be negative. Based on this approach we can make the following statements:

- Delta is not a constant number as the slope of the price line will change as the underlying price changes.
- Since the slope of the pre-expiry price is non-linear, a one-unit change in the underlying price will not be associated with a one-unit change in the option's premium.
- As the option becomes more ITM the delta will approach +1 or −1 (depending on the type of option and whether the trader is long or short).
- As the option becomes more OTM, delta will tend towards zero.
- The delta value can be expressed as a percentage (e.g. 49 %) or as a decimal (e.g. 0.49).

For example, consider Fig. 5.3, which shows the delta of our example call option very shortly before maturity (all other market factors assumed to be constant). The line has become more "S" shaped in nature with delta tending towards one or zero. This is because the option is losing the curvature it displayed in Fig. 5.1 and is now starting to resemble the at expiry "hockey stick" profile of Fig. 1.4.

For the ATM forward call option the initial value of delta is 0.5486 or 54.86 %[2]. This means that if the spot price were to increase by a 'small' amount, the option premium would increase by 54.86 % of this change.

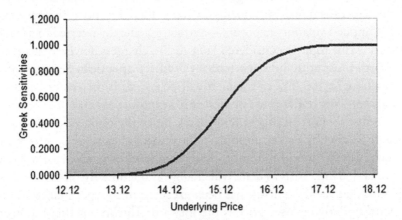

Fig. 5.3 Delta for a range of underlying prices close to expiry for a long call option position (*Source*: author)

---

[2] It is an urban myth to say that all ATM options always have a delta of exactly 50 %.

Suppose that the spot price were to increase by $0.01 to $15.01, we would expect the premium to change by $0.01 × 0.5486 or $0.005486. Given the initial premium value of $1.7534 delta would predict a premium price of $1.7534 + $0.005486 = $1.7589.

Delta can also be expressed as a 'delta equivalent value'. This value is calculated by multiplying the number of options traded by the value of delta. So if a trader had bought 100,000 call options on the underlying equity with a delta of 54.86%, the delta equivalent value is 54,860 shares[3]. This means that a long call option position with a notional amount of 100,000 will have the same exposure to small changes in the underlying price as a long position of 54,860 shares. A one-cent move in the underlying price will cause the option position to gain $548.60 (100,000 × $0.01 × 0.5486). The change in value of an equivalent long position of 54,860 shares for a $0.01 increase in price would generate a profit of the same amount.

Delta will therefore tell the trader the nature of their exposure to movements in the underlying price. If the trader's option position is delta positive (i.e. he is long a call or short a put), he knows that the profit or loss on his option position as a result of a small change in the underlying price will be the same as if he were long an equivalent amount of the underlying asset. If the trader's position were delta negative (i.e. short a call, long a put) he will benefit from a fall in prices but suffer from rising prices; the option position is bearish relative to the underlying market.

The option's delta value can also be used to hedge the position's directional exposure. One common strategy used by traders is to immunize the option's exposure to directional movements in the underlying price in order to isolate the implied volatility exposure—a strategy generally referred to as 'trading volatility'. This topic is considered later in the chapter; however, at this stage it is worth illustrating how the trader would set up a delta-hedged position. Having bought 100,000 calls which will behave as if the trader had bought 54,860 shares the trader could neutralize his exposure to small directional price movements by short selling 54,860 shares. Since the option's long directional exposure is offset by a short position in the underlying asset the trader is said to be 'delta neutral'. It is important to stress that this hedge will need to be managed on a dynamic basis as delta will change as the underlying price changes.

Notice that the delta hedge has been executed in the spot market although the 'true' underlying asset price is the forward. This means that the hedge is not 100 % perfect as the trader is exposed to a change in the net carry of the asset. In other words, a change in interest rates and dividend yields would have

---

[3] This calculation does assume that one option references one underlying asset so if each option references, say, 100 shares, the delta equivalent would be 100,000 options × 100 shares × 54.86 % = 5,486,000 shares.

a direct impact on the value of the option but not necessarily on the price of the shares. As was argued in Chap. 3 there is no single overarching method for valuing shares and so the impact of a change in the carry variables is arguably more ambiguous than it is for the valuation of the option.

Not only does delta vary with respect to movements in the spot price but it will also change with respect to the passage of time. Over time the option's price line loses its curvature such that it resembles a hockey stick at expiry (Fig. 1.4). So from this it is possible to say that at the moment of expiry the option will have a delta of either 0 (option not exercised) or 1 (option exercised). Figures 5.2 and 5.3 showed how delta evolves in relation to the passage of time. This effect is sometimes referred to as 'delta bleed' and again indicates that any delta hedge will need to be actively managed in order to remain delta neutral.

The value of delta is also sensitive to the level of implied volatility. Figure 5.4 shows the price line of the option under different implied volatility assumptions, all other things being equal.

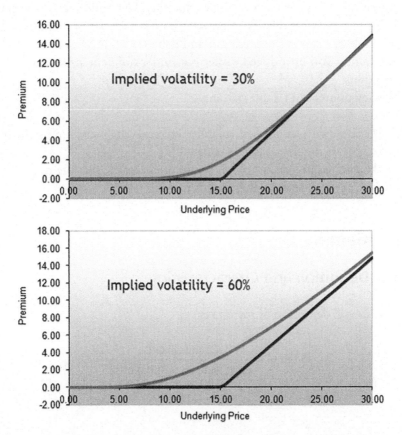

Fig. 5.4 Equity call option priced under different implied volatility assumptions (*Source:* author)

Table 5.1 Premiums and deltas for an ITM call and OTM option put under different implied volatility conditions. Underlying price assumed to be $15.00. All other market factors are held constant

	Long ITM call Strike rate $13.00	Long OTM put Strike rate $13.00
20 % volatility	Premium = $2.43 Delta = 0.7906	Premium = $0.35 Delta = −0.1896
30 % volatility	Premium = $2.88 Delta = 0.7307	Premium = $0.79 Delta = −0.2495

As implied volatility increases (right hand panel of Fig. 5.4) the price line is pushed outwards to the left and so for OTM and ITM options the pre-expiry payoff profile will tend to gain an element of curvature. As a result, the deltas of both ITM and OTM options tend towards +/− 50 %. Intuitively this suggests that there is a greater probability that the ITM option may possibly end up being OTM, while the OTM option now has a greater probability of being ITM. Table 5.1 shows the premium and delta for an ITM call and put based on the transaction introduced earlier but under different strike and volatility assumptions.

The key points from Table 5.1 are:

• *ITM call option*—as implied volatility increases the premium on the option increases but the delta falls towards +0.50.
• *OTM put option*—as implied volatility increases the premium on the option increases and the delta tends towards −0.50.

5.3   Gamma

5.3.1 Definition and Characteristics

The 'textbook' definition of gamma is:

$$\text{Gamma} = \frac{\text{Change in delta}}{\text{Change in underlying price}} \qquad (5.1)$$

However, for many people this relationship is not really intuitive and so here are some alternative definitions which with a supplemental explanation may help the reader's understanding. Gamma describes:

• How rapidly a delta-hedged position becomes unhedged due to a change in the option's delta.
• How quickly the profit and loss on an option position will change with respect to the underlying price.
• The option's exposure to actual volatility (as opposed to implied volatility).
• The option's sensitivity to significant price changes.

Consider the following example using our ATM forward call option with an initial delta of 0.5486. At this spot price the associated gamma value is 0.0859. However, this gamma figure is meaningless unless it is associated with a range of spot price movements. The typical way of expressing gamma is with respect to a 1-unit change in the underlying spot price. So rearranging the textbook formula (5.1) for gamma to solve for the change in delta, a $1 move in the underlying asset price from $15 to $16 should result in a change in delta from 0.5486 to 0.6345. It should be noted that gamma itself is an approximation and is sensitive to changes in the other inputs to the option price formula[4].

Gamma can also be expressed relative to a percentage movement in the underlying price (Eq. 5.2).

$$\text{Change in delta} = \text{Gamma} \times \frac{\text{Underlying price}}{100}$$

$$0.012885 = 0.0859 \times \frac{\$15.00}{100}$$

(5.2)

Based on the results of eq. 5.2, if the spot price were to move by 1 % to $15.15 (with the forward price moving to $15.30) then delta is predicted to move from 0.5486 to 0.5615. At this higher spot level, a BSM pricing model returns a delta value of 0.5614.

Like all Greeks, gamma will have a positive or negative value and (thankfully) compared to delta these are easier to remember. Option buyers are said to be gamma positive while option sellers are gamma negative. As an example,

---

[4] Indeed, it is possible to derive Greek measures that consider how gamma changes with respect to changes in implied volatility ('zomma'), the spot price ('speed') and the passage of time ('colour').

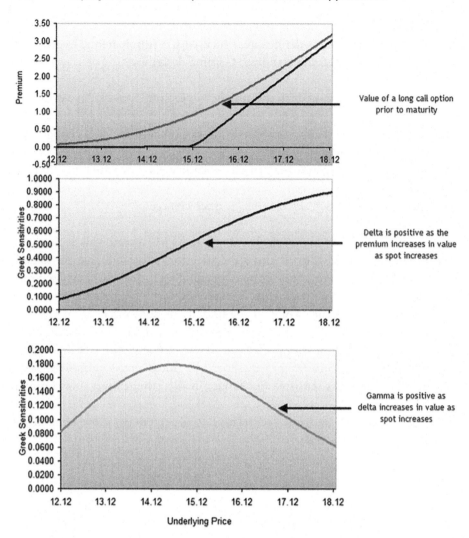

Value of a long call option prior to maturity

Delta is positive as the premium increases in value as spot increases

Gamma is positive as delta increases in value as spot increases

Underlying Price

Fig. 5.5 Positive gamma exposure for a long call position (*Source*: author)

Fig. 5.5 illustrates why a long call option will exhibit positive gamma. The top part of the diagram shows the pre-expiry and expiry payoffs of the long call option. The middle section shows the delta relationship for this option, which is derived from the slope of the pre-expiry payoff. The lower part of the diagram shows the gamma relationship, which is the measuring of the slope of the delta profile. Since delta is increasing with respect to the underlying price, its slope (and therefore gamma) is positive. The slope of delta at low and high underlying prices is relatively shallow and so the value of gamma will be correspondingly low. The peak of the gamma profile occurs when the slope of the delta profile is steepest, which is when the option is ATM.

The gamma exposures for the remaining three option building blocks are not illustrated but the logic behind their derivation is identical. For any type of vanilla option, gamma will be highest for short-dated ATM options and lower for long-dated ITM and OTM options.

5.3.2 The Delta–Gamma Relationship

When looking at gamma for the first time it is reasonable to wonder why anyone would be interested in the change in delta. As with many things a worked example often helps the understanding.

Suppose a trader observes that 1-month options on our share are trading with implied volatilities of 30 %, which he feels will fall back over the coming few days. He decides to express this view on implied volatility but does not want to have an exposure to movements in the underlying price. To express the view, he constructs a 'delta-neutral short volatility position'.

It is worthwhile digressing momentarily to point out that traders will often quote options in terms of their implied volatility. This is based on the idea that within the BSM framework, the market factor that is unknown is the implied volatility input. Essentially it can be thought of as a trader's best estimate as to the likely distribution of spot prices at maturity. Alternatively, it is a trader's estimate of future realized volatility. So a market maker may quote as follows (Table 5.2).

Table 5.2 Stylized quotation for option position

	Bid	Offer
Quote	30 %	31 %
Action	Buy options	Sell options
	(either calls or puts)	(either calls or puts)

The trader is in theory indifferent as to whether they trade calls or puts as Sect. 4.6.3 illustrated that there is a positive relationship between implied volatility and the value of options. The trader decides to sell 100,000 call options struck ATM spot[5]. The premium is \$0.52 per share or \$52,000 for the entire position. The option is initially delta negative with a value of −0.5203, meaning the position behaves as if the trader is short 52,030 shares. To offset this

---

[5] The option in this trading example is struck ATM spot rather than ATM forward which is used elsewhere in the chapter.

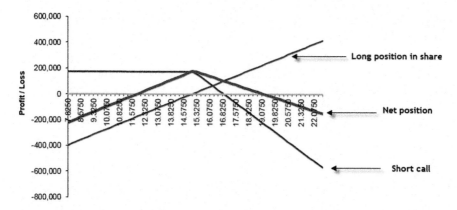

Fig. 5.6   Expiry profile of delta-neutral short volatility position (*Source*: author)

directional exposure, the trader buys this number of shares in the spot market to establish delta neutrality, that is, 52,030 shares purchased at $15.00. The different components of the transaction are shown in Fig. 5.6.

However, to better understand the nature of this trade consider Fig. 5.7 which shows only the net position at both the inception and expiry of the trade.

At first glance it would seem that as long as the underlying price does not move too much, the trade will be profitable. Although this is correct, it was not the motivation for the trade. The trader created a position that was delta neutral but would profit from a change in the level of implied volatility rather than a change in the spot price. A fall in implied volatility (say by 5 %) will generate a profit for the trader as the option will fall in value. This will result in an increase in the pre-expiry profit or loss of the position (Fig. 5.8).

Notice that the change in implied volatility is done under conditions where all other market factors are held equal; in particular, the spot price has not changed. Many people feel that changes in 'volatility' must go hand in hand with changes in spot prices; however, it depends what type of volatility one is referring to. Movements of implied volatility are not inextricably linked to spot price movements as they are independent variables within the BSM framework. So the spot price could remain unchanged but the trader would enjoy a profit as long as the implied volatility of the option falls.

However, let us return to the option trade to see what happens if the underlying price were to move. Suppose that shortly after putting on this position the share price rises sharply by $1.00 and as a result the option price increases

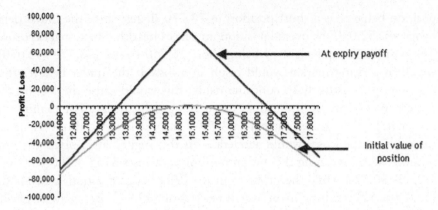

Fig. 5.7   Initial and expiry payoffs for delta-neutral short position (*Source*: author)

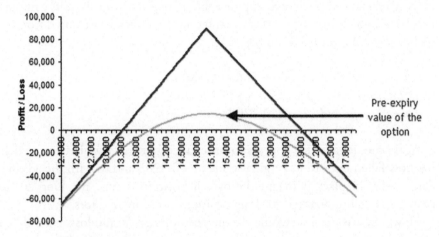

Fig. 5.8   Impact on profit or loss for a 5 % fall in implied volatility on the delta-neutral short volatility position (*Source*: author)

by $0.66 to $1.18 (all other things being equal). On a mark-to-market basis the position's profit and loss at this higher spot price will be:

- *Options*: 100,000 × $0.66 = $66,000 loss
- *Delta hedge*: 52,030 × $1.00 = $52,030 profit
- *Overall profit and loss* = $13,970 loss

It may seem strange that the position has experienced a loss as the purpose of the delta hedge was to protect the trader from movements in the underlying price and as such it has clearly failed to do so. This is because delta itself has changed and at the higher spot price is now −0.7877. That is, the option position behaves as a short position in 78,770 shares; since the initial delta hedge was 52,030 the overall position now has a bearish directional exposure. The position is equivalent to being short 26,740 shares (78,770–52,030), which in a rising market would result in a loss. If the trader believes that the share price is likely to continue rising, this would cause the loss on the option to increase by more than the existing delta hedge. For example, if the share price increased further to $17.00 and the trader did not rebalance the position the losses would accelerate. At this higher share price, the premium is $2.05 meaning the option position now loses $153,000 (100,000 × ($2.05–$0.52)) while the profit from the delta hedge position is $104,060 (52,030 × $2) resulting in an overall net loss of $49,940. Being aware of this risk we will assume that the trader decides to rebalance the position at the new spot price of $16.00 and so buys 26,740 more shares at this higher spot price. Having rebalanced the hedge, suppose the share price loses all of its gains and falls back to $15.00. The mark-to-market on the position measured from the higher price of $16.00 would be:

- *Options*: 100,000 x $0.66 = $66,000 profit
- *Delta hedge*: 78,770 x $1.00 = $78,770 loss
- *Overall profit and loss* = $12,770 loss

Again the delta hedge appears to have failed but this is only because delta has now fallen back to its original value of −0.5203 and so with the adjusted delta hedge in place it means the overall position is now net long 26,740 shares. In a falling market this long position would incur a loss.

However, it is possible to analyse the position's profit and loss in a different way. The example was constructed to assume that all other factors are equal and that the only parameter that changed was the spot price. Since the example illustrates an intra-day exposure the value of the option is unchanged. Equally, the initial delta hedge of 52,030 shares also shows zero profit and loss as they were bought at $15 at the start of the day and also finished the day at this level. As a result, the only component of the trade that has generated any profit or loss was the extra 26,740 shares purchased at $16.00 and subsequently revalued at the closing price of $15.00. This generates a loss of $26,740 which is equal to the sum of the two mark-to-market losses (i.e. $13,970 + $12,770). From this it possible to make the following conclusions:

- The hedge had to be rebalanced as the movement in the spot price caused delta to move (i.e. actual volatility).

- The source of profit and loss from the trade was from the trader's delta hedging activities.
- The magnitude of the movement in delta for a given movement in the spot price is gamma.

This example used a short-dated ATM option position where the gamma value was relatively high. So any movement in spot would cause delta to move by a relatively large amount incurring hedging losses irrespective of whether the price moved up or down. Longer-dated options that are not ATM would not experience such a significant gamma effect. That is, the same change in the spot price would not cause delta to move by much and so the profit and loss impact from the trader's hedging activities would be less pronounced.

So returning to a point made earlier, what type of volatility did the trader experience? Although his intention was to express a view on implied volatility, the source of profit and loss on this transaction was 'actual' or 'realized' volatility. Delta hedging will ensure that the trader is protected against small movements in the underlying price but a $1 move up and down in the share price—equivalent to a 6.67% change—would be considered significant. Recall that implied volatility focuses on the distribution of share prices at the option's maturity rather than what is happening right now, which is realized volatility. Arguably it is this time dimension that is perhaps the most misunderstood component of this transaction. So rather than describing this trade in relatively general terms as a 'volatility' trade it would be more accurate to describe it as either a gamma or a vega trade, depending on the motivation of the trader. Referring back to Fig. 5.8 the source of profitability from a vega[6] trade will cause the profit and loss payout to move along a vertical plane, whereas the profitability from a gamma trade is based on spot price movements which are movements along a horizontal plane (Fig. 5.9).[7]

At this point it is worth revisiting the relationship between implied volatility and spot. Although the concept of vega will be covered in Sect. 5.6, one way of understanding the linkage is to consider a simple rule of thumb used by some traders. The implied volatility figure used in the transaction was 30 % and like most volatility measures is typically quoted on an annualized basis. To derive the equivalent value for a single day the trader divides by the square root of the number of business days (rather than calendar days) in the year, which is often taken to be 252. This calculation (30 %/15.87) returns a daily volatility value of 1.89 % (rounded), which when applied to the initial

---

[6] Vega is an option's exposure to a change in implied volatility. See Sect. 5.6.
[7] Sometimes the process of trading options and delta hedging frequently is referred to as 'gamma scalping'.

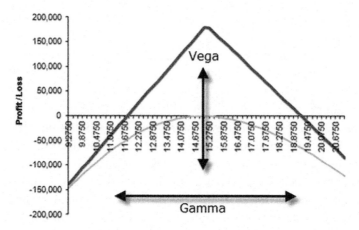

Fig. 5.9 Sources of profitability for a delta-neutral short volatility trade (*Source*: author)

spot price suggests a daily trading range of $14.72–$15.28. In our example the asset traded outside of this value suggesting that actual or realized volatility was greater than the implied volatility used to price the option. If the trader thought that this type of movement was perhaps just temporary, then they may decide not to change the implied volatility value they quote to the market. However, if they felt the spot price movement was perhaps a sign of a significant market move then they may decide to increase the implied volatility quote which would increase the value of the option.

Sometimes this type of trading activity can lead to a stock being 'pinned'. This concept relates to the observed range-bound movement of a stock price around a particular strike level. So an example would be where the price of share is rising but when it moves above the strike, option traders who are long volatility would sell the asset as part of hedging strategy but would need to buy it back if it then drifted below the strike.

5.3.3   The Delta–Gamma–Theta Relationship

Returning to our trade, had the trader executed a long vega trade (i.e. bought options and sold shares as a delta hedge) the position would have shown a profit in the scenario presented. So when considering both outcomes it may be tempting to think that if a trader sells options and delta hedges they will always end up with losses and when they buy options and delta hedge they will make profits, hence it is always better to be a buyer of volatility. This notion would be incorrect. There is an extra dimension that has not been considered and that is the passage of time. Although this will be considered in detail in Sect. 5.4 it is possible to say at this stage that option sellers will benefit from the passage of time, while buyers of options will suffer. So for a delta-neutral short volatility trade the challenge for the trader is to make sure that they make more money from the passage of time than they will lose from their delta hedging activities. The trading example used earlier indicated that the trader received $52,000 upfront in terms of premium. However, on an immediate mark-to-market basis the position would show a zero profit, that is, if the trader had to close out the position straight away, it would cost them $52,000. However, the next day, all other things being equal, the option will decay in value to $0.51 per share and so the entire position is cheaper to buy back resulting in a gain of $1000. The opposite is true for a long vega position. The trader will lose money from the decaying value of the option but will make money if the spot price moves significantly such that their delta hedging activities will generate a greater profit.

This is why traders sometimes refer to theta (the impact of the passage of time) as 'gamma rent'. If a trader has bought volatility, which will generate delta hedging profits, they will have an associated cost which is theta. However, the cost for a seller of volatility is his delta hedging activities and so the passage of time is his compensation for taking on this risk.

5.4   Delta and Gamma 'Cash' Limits[8]

Traders will be subject to gamma and delta trading limits, which are often expressed in cash equivalent terms. By expressing them in a cash equivalent it allows the risk management of a portfolio of options of different shares to be expressed in a uniform manner. So rather than having limits for each individual share there is one single cash limit for the entire portfolio.

By convention, traders like to think in percentage movements rather than absolute movements. A gamma trading limit would be expressed as 'gamma cash'. This is defined as the amount by which 'delta cash' changes for a 1 % move in the share price. Delta cash is defined as delta multiplied by the share price multiplied by the number of options. 'Gamma cash' can now be derived

---

[8] I am very grateful to Frans de Weert author of "An introduction to options trading (2006)" and "Exotic options trading (2008)" for his input into this section.

by calculating 'delta cash' for a 1 % share price movement and then deducting this value from the original 'delta cash' calculation.

Delta cash on a per share basis is:

$$\text{Delta} \times \text{share price} \qquad (5.3)$$

Delta cash after a 1 % change in the share price is:

$$\left(\text{Delta} \times \text{share price}\right) + \left(\text{gamma} \times \text{share price} \times \frac{\text{share price}}{100}\right) \qquad (5.4)$$

If delta cash (eq. 5.3) is subtracted from eq. 5.4 you are left with gamma cash, which on a per share basis is:

$$\text{Gamma} \times \text{share price} \times \frac{\text{share price}}{100} \qquad (5.5)$$

To illustrate the concept, consider the example used earlier. At the initial share price of $15.00 the delta cash exposure is:

$$\$15.00 \times 0.5203 \times 100{,}000 = \$780{,}450$$

Although not stated explicitly in the previous trading example gamma for a one-unit change in the underlying price was 0.3062, so the value of gamma cash for a 1 % move in the share price for the position is:

$$0.3062 \times \$15 \times \$15 \,/\, 100 \times 100{,}000 = \$68{,}895$$

When the delta-neutral short volatility trade is initially set up, the position has a delta cash position of zero as the delta cash exposure of the option ($780,450) is matched with a purchase of shares of the same monetary value. If the share price were to increase by 1 %, the trader would now be required to buy $68,895 worth of shares at the now higher price to be fully delta hedged.

So why have a gamma cash limit? One high-risk strategy for a trader would be to sell short-dated ATM options hoping that they would rapidly increase in value due to the passage of time but at the same time hoping that the market will remain stable. However, as the previous example has shown this could incur substantial losses if the market proves to be volatile. As a result, a gamma cash limit would help limit this exposure.

5.5   Theta

Theta measures an option's exposure to the passage of time. Recall from Sect. 4.6.1 that an option's premium can be decomposed into intrinsic value and time value. The time value component of an option is primarily influenced by the passage of time and changes in implied volatility. Theta describes how the time value of an option amortizes as the option approaches maturity and is typically measured in terms of one day. Theta is typically positive for sellers (time works in their favour) but negative for buyers (time is their enemy). The same section illustrated that option prices do not decay in a linear fashion with respect to time.

Figure 5.10 shows the initial values for theta for our example option.

At the initial spot price of \$15.00, the theta for the option is −\$0.0025. This value represents the amount by which the premium will change on a per share basis over a 24-h period. However, the theta profile will evolve over time (Fig. 5.10).

Figure 5.11 shows the same option as the previous diagram except there is now only 30 days to expiry. If the share price has not moved the option will now change in value by \$0.0088 over the next 24 h. So combining the results of the two diagrams indicates that shorter-dated options lose more value due to the passage of time than longer-dated options. Note also that irrespective of the maturity theta is at its greatest when the option is ATM.

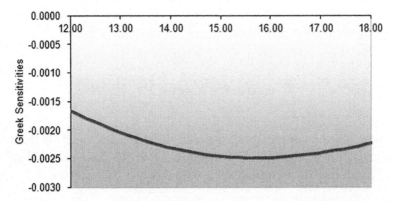

Fig. 5.10 Theta for a 1-year option over a range of spot prices (*Source*: author)

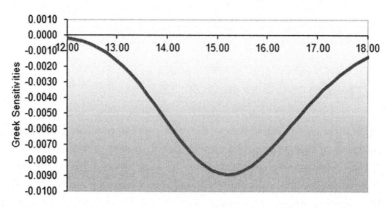

Fig. 5.11 The theta profile of a 1-month option for a range of spot prices (*Source:* author)

One aspect of theta that is worth mentioning is how a long option position may in fact increase in value as the position approaches maturity. This suggests that in some circumstances theta for a long option position could indeed be positive.

Consider the following call option:

Table 5.3 Valuation of a deeply ITM call option on a dividend-paying stock

Spot price	$125.00
Strike price	$100.00
Expiry	1 year
Funding rate	1.00 %
Dividend yield	5.00 %
Implied volatility	20 %
Premium	$22.01

Diagrammatically the pre- and expiry values of the option are shown in Fig. 5.12.

Using arguments based on Hull (2012), no-arbitrage principles show that the lower bound (i.e. minimum possible value) for a European call option maturing at date T on a stock that pays no dividends is:

$$\max\left(0,\, S_0 - K \times \exp^{(-rT)}\right) \tag{5.6}$$

Where S_0 is the current spot price, K is the strike price and r is the funding rate. Suppose that the option detailed in Table 5.3 paid no dividend. This would mean that its minimum value would be:

$$\max\left(0,\, \$125 - \$100 \times \exp^{(-0.01)}\right) = \$24.75 \tag{5.7}$$

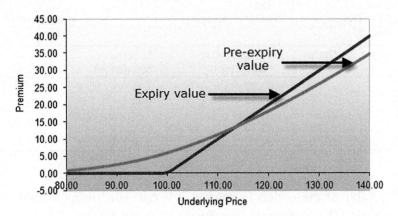

Fig. 5.12 Pre- and expiry payoff values for an option, which displays positive theta for ITM values of the underlying price (*Source*: author)

If the option was observed to be trading at $24.00, the trader could unlock an arbitrage profit by:

- Buying the call option at $24.00
- Short selling the stock for $125.00 (borrowing costs are ignored for ease of illustration)
- Investing the net proceeds ($101.00) for 1 year at prevailing rates of 1% to return $102.01

If the option expires ITM with the final spot price being, say, $103.00, the option will be exercised with the trader buying the stock at $100 to realize a profit of $2.01 ($102.01 − $100). If the option expires OTM the position lapses and the short stock position is repurchased in the market. If the spot price has moved to, say, $95 the position will show a profit of $7.01 ($102.01−$95.00).

Hull shows that the lower bound (i.e. its intrinsic value) for a European call option maturing at date T on a stock that pays a continuous dividend yield at rate q is:

$$\max\left(0,\ S_0 \times \exp^{(-qT)} - K \times \exp^{(-rT)}\right) \tag{5.8}$$

Table 5.4 shows the value of the long call position at different points in time, all other things being equal.

Table 5.4 The value of an ITM long call option on a dividend-paying stock with respect to time

Maturity (years)	Option value	Intrinsic value component	Time value component	Forward price
1.00	22.01	19.90	2.11	120.01
0.75	22.40	21.50	0.90	121.36
0.50	22.94	22.40	0.54	122.52
0.25	23.76	23.70	0.06	123.76
0.00	25.00	25.00	0.00	125.00

The value of the option in column 2 is calculated using a BSM option spreadsheet. The intrinsic value component of the option at a given maturity is calculated using formula 5.8. Time value is calculated as the difference between the option value and the intrinsic value component. The final column shows the forward price with the same residual time to maturity as the value in column 1. The table highlights the following concepts with respect to the passage of time:

- The value of the option increases.
- The intrinsic value component of the option increases.
- The time value component declines.

Since the option must trade at its intrinsic value at expiry, it is quite possible for European call options on dividend-paying stocks to have positive theta, that is, for the option to increase in value with respect to the passage of time, other things remaining equal. The conditions in which this occurs are relatively low implied volatilities, high spot prices, high dividend yields and low interest rates.

The effect of relatively high dividend payments and low interest rates, other things remaining equal, is to reduce the forward price of the asset. Since the forward price is lower than it would be if the stock did not pay dividends, the value of the option is worth less. When the option is deep in the money this can be sufficient to push the value of the option below its 'at maturity' intrinsic value.

Similar arguments apply in the case of European puts. Consider the following extreme example:

Spot price:	$0.00
Strike price:	$100.00
Dividend yield:	1.00 %
Interest rates:	5.00 %
Implied volatility:	20.00 %
Maturity:	1 year

Table 5.5 The value of an ITM long put option with respect to time

Maturity (years)	Option value	Intrinsic value component	Time value component	Forward price
1.00	17.61	15.92	1.69	83.26
0.75	17.92	16.92	1.00	82.44
0.50	18.35	17.93	0.42	81.62
0.25	19.01	18.92	0.05	80.80
0.00	20.00	20.00	0.00	80.00

Option value: $95.12

Since the option must trade at its intrinsic value at maturity then all other things being equal the option must increase in value with respect to the passage of time. This example of positive theta for a put option occurs when implied volatilities are low, spot prices are low, dividend yields are low and interest rates relatively high. Table 5.5 shows how this same put option would increase in value with respect to the passage of time, if the spot price was $80.00.

The intrinsic value of the put option is based on the lower boundary value of a put option on dividend-paying shares (Hull, 2012) which is:

$$\max\left(0, K \times \exp^{(-rT)} - S_0 \times \exp^{(-qT)}\right) \tag{5.9}$$

Similar to Table 5.4 the option increases in value with respect to time as does the intrinsic value of the option. The time value component decreases with respect to the passage of time.

5.6   Interest Rates and Dividend Yield

The option Greeks for the 'carry' components are sometimes referred to as 'rho' for interest rates and 'psi' for dividend yield. Table 5.6 shows the value of rho in tabular form for our original long call option:

- Different maturities for a given spot price (read vertically)
- Different spot prices for a given maturity (read horizontally)

From this it is possible to conclude:

Table 5.6 Rho for long call

Maturity (years)	$13.15	$14.15	$15.15	$16.15	$17.15
1.00	0.0409	0.0537	0.0667	0.0792	0.0907
0.75	0.0288	0.0398	0.0511	0.0620	0.0718
0.50	0.0169	0.0256	0.0349	0.0438	0.0517
0.25	0.0059	0.0114	0.0179	0.0242	0.0293
0.01	0.0000	0.0000	0.0008	0.0015	0.0015

Table 5.7 Psi for long call

Maturity (years)	$13.15	$14.15	$15.15	$16.15	$17.15
1.00	−0.0487	−0.0657	−0.0837	−0.1021	−0.1202
0.75	−0.0334	−0.0471	−0.0622	−0.0775	−0.0925
0.50	−0.0189	−0.0292	−0.0409	−0.0528	−0.0642
0.25	−0.0063	−0.0125	−0.0200	−0.0279	−0.0348
0.01	0.0000	0.0000	−0.0007	−0.0016	−0.0017

- Rho is positive for long calls and short put positions; it is negative for long puts and short calls.
- The impact on an option's premium of a change in interest rates decreases with respect to time.
- Rho is greatest for ITM options.

The two conclusions will also hold for put options, although rho will be negative for a long put position.

Table 5.7 shows the value of psi in tabular form for:

- Different maturities for a given spot price (read vertically)
- Different spot prices for a given maturity (read horizontally)

Psi is negative for long call and short put positions; it is positive for long puts and short calls. From this it is possible to conclude that the impact on an option's premium of a change in dividend yields is most pronounced for longer-dated ITM call options. A similar argument will also hold for put options.

5.7   Vega

Vega measures the change in an option's premium for a 1 % change in implied volatility. The initial value for vega for our stylized call option is +$0.058. So with an initial option premium of $1.7534, a 1 % increase in implied volatility should cause the premium to increase to \$1.8114 (i.e. \$1.7534 + \$0.058). Indeed, this is the value of the option returned by a BSM model at an implied volatility level of 31 %.

Section 4.6.3 illustrated that there was a positive relationship between the value of an option and implied volatility, suggesting that option buyers (calls or puts) are long implied volatility, while option sellers (again either calls or puts) will be short implied volatility. So it is possible to rephrase this statement to, say, option buyers are vega positive, while option sellers are vega negative. An option buyer pays the premium and so acquires the option's intrinsic and time value. An increase in implied volatility increases the time value component and so increases the value of the option, all other things being equal.

Vega for our example call option is illustrated in Fig. 5.13.

Figure 5.13 illustrates the main properties of vega in that it is greatest for longer-dated options that are ATM. Vega will be lower for OTM and ITM options that are shorter-dated.

Section 5.3 illustrated a short hand way of converting an annual implied volatility value into an approximate range of expected daily price movements. This is done by dividing the annualized volatility by the square root of the number of 'trading periods' in a year. So in a 12-month period there are approximately 252 trading days (i.e. periods) so the analyst divides the annual volatility figure by the square root of 252. The other common adjustments are:

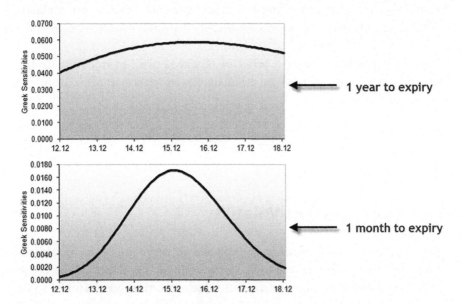

Fig. 5.13 Vega for a range of spot prices and at two different maturities (*Source*: author)

- Annual to weekly—divide by the square root of 52
- Annual to quarterly—divide by the square root of 4
- Annual to semi-annual—divide by the square root of 2

To derive the approximate range of daily price movements associated with a given annual level of implied volatility the following formula could be used:

$$\text{Range} = \frac{(\text{Annual volatility} \times \text{ spot})}{\sqrt{\text{Number of working days in a year}}} \qquad (6.10)$$

So for a spot price of $15.00, 252 working days and an annual volatility of 30 % formula 6.10 would return a range of daily price movements of 28 cents.

$$\text{Range} = \frac{(30\% \times \$15.00)}{\sqrt{252}}$$

$$\$0.28 = \frac{\$4.5}{15.87} \qquad (6.11)$$

Volatility is the financial market's term for an asset's standard deviation. Since a standard deviation is a measure of spread from a central value, it could be argued that for an annual implied volatility of 30% then in approximately 68 % of all outcomes the approximate daily expected price movements from the spot price are +/− $0.28.

It is also possible to take a series of observed price movements during a day and reverse the process to calculate the volatility implied from these observations.

$$\text{Annual volatility} = \frac{\text{Range of daily price movements}}{\text{Spot}} \times \sqrt{252} \qquad (6.12)$$

5.8 Non-constant Volatility

The characteristics of volatility are covered in detail in Chap. 6, although it is impossible to ignore the topic completely at this stage. In the original BSM framework the volatility used to value a position was assumed to be a constant. In other words, the same volatility would be used irrespective of whether the option was long- or short-dated or whether it was ITM, ATM or OTM. This relatively short section explains why this is not the case and provides some empirical evidence to support the claims.

Empirically volatility will vary with respect to an option's strike and this is termed as either 'the smile' or 'skew'. As is common in finance, the terms are often used interchangeably even though one could argue they are actually different concepts. Chapter 4 illustrated a simplified pricing example where a normal distribution was overlaid on a range of expiry payoffs. In reality analytical models such as BSM assume that prices are log normally distributed. The concept of smiles and skews occurs when the actual probability distribution implied by observed option prices is seen to have 'fatter tails'. Where the distribution is fatter on both sides this is termed a volatility smile. This means that OTM and ITM options will trade with higher implied volatilities than ATM options. Typically, the smile is relatively symmetrical and does resemble a physical smile. Figure 5.14 shows the smile for an FX option written on EURUSD at two different points in time.

Equity markets, however, tend to display a volatility skew, which means that low strike options trade at higher implied volatilities than higher strikes. This means that the implied distribution has a fatter left tail and a thinner right tail than the log normal distribution assumed by the model. An example of volatility skew is given for the S&P 500 (Fig. 5.15). The Y axis shows the levels of implied volatility for option strikes represented as a percentage of the current spot price. So if the underlying index was trading at 2000 points a 90 % strike option would have been executed at 1800 (i.e. an OTM put or ITM call).

Empirically, volatility also varies with respect to maturity and therefore displays a term structure. In 'normal' markets the term structure is upwards sloping, perhaps suggesting that there is greater uncertainty over future events and as such longer-dated options will trade with higher implied volatilities than shorter-dated options with the same parameters. It is possible for the term structure to invert in response to expected short-term uncertainty such as an election. An example term structure for the S&P 500 is shown in Fig. 5.16.

When both of these variations are graphed together the result is often referred to as a volatility surface (Fig. 5.17). When documented in tabular format it is sometimes referred to as a volatility matrix (Table 5.8).

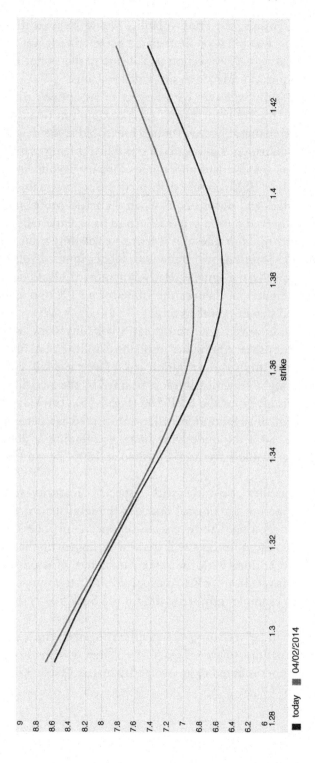

Fig. 5.14 FX smile for 1-month options on EURUSD at two different points in time (*Source:* Barclays Live)

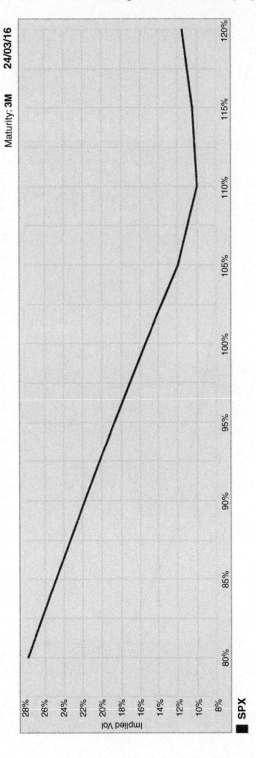

Fig. 5.15   Volatility against strike for 3-month options. S&P 500 equity index (*Source:* Barclays Live)

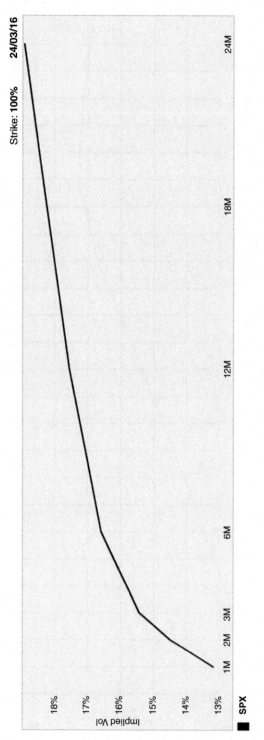

Fig. 5.16 Implied volatility against maturity for a 100 % strike option (i.e. ATM spot) S&P 500 equity index (*Source:* Barclays Live)

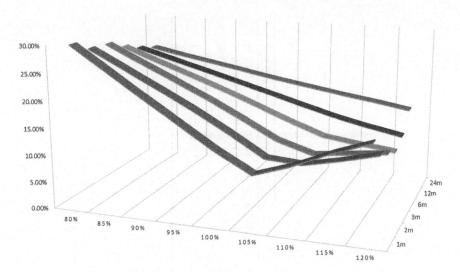

Fig. 5.17   Volatility surface for S&P 500 as of 25th March 2016 (*Source*: Barclays Live)

5.9   Second Order Greeks

Section 5.3 illustrated the concept of gamma, which is arguably the most common second order Greek measure. Although there are a number of second order Greeks there are perhaps two others which are worth mentioning in relation to vega.

5.9.1   Volgamma

Volgamma (sometimes referred to as 'convexity' or 'volga' or 'vomma') measures the sensitivity of vega to changes in implied volatility.

$$\text{Volgamma} = \frac{\text{Change in vega}}{1\% \text{ Change in implied volatility}} \qquad (5.13)$$

Volgamma is positive for buyers and negative for sellers and is greatest for long-dated ITM and OTM options (Fig. 5.18).

Consider the ATM call option used in this chapter. At an initial spot price of $15.00 this ATM option will have a vega value of $0.0580. Volgamma is zero meaning that if implied volatility increases by 1 % then the option's vega will remain unchanged. Now consider a situation where

Table 5.8 Volatility matrix for S&P 500 as of 25th March 2016

	80 %	85 %	90 %	95 %	100 %	105 %	110 %	115 %	120 %
1 m	30.00 %	25.80 %	21.60 %	17.40 %	13.20 %	9.60 %	11.80 %	14.70 %	17.10 %
2 m	28.10 %	24.90 %	21.60 %	18.20 %	14.50 %	10.60 %	10.10 %	11.50 %	13.20 %
3 m	27.80 %	24.80 %	21.80 %	18.70 %	15.40 %	12.00 %	10.00 %	10.75 %	11.50 %
6 m	26.20 %	23.80 %	21.50 %	19.10 %	16.60 %	14.00 %	11.60 %	10.70 %	9.90 %
12 m	24.80 %	23.00 %	21.20 %	19.40 %	17.60 %	15.70 %	13.90 %	12.40 %	11.10 %
24 m	23.80 %	22.50 %	21.30 %	20.10 %	18.90 %	17.80 %	16.70 %	15.70 %	14.60 %

Source: Barclays Live

all of the input parameters remain unchanged but the spot price has fallen to $10.00. At this price level, the premium is $0.1457, vega has a value of $0.0190 while volgamma is now $0.0011. So a 1 % increase in the options implied volatility will cause the premium to increase to $0.1647 ($0.1457 + $0.0190). At this higher level of implied volatility, however, vega will now take a value of $0.0201 ($0.019 + $0.0011). So for ITM/OTM options the premium will increase at an increasing rate for a given rise in implied volatility.

So if you are long options (i.e. long vega) you want to have as high a positive volgamma as possible. If you are short options (and short vega) you want to have a negative volgamma. Positive volgamma tells you that you earn more for every percentage point increase in volatility and if implied volatility is falling you will lose less and less. Put another way if you are long volgamma you get longer volatility when volatility moves up and shorter volatility when volatility moves down. It is a form of convexity and so the more the better! However, this benefit should not be free and so the price of the option will usually be adjusted by the trader to take account of this.

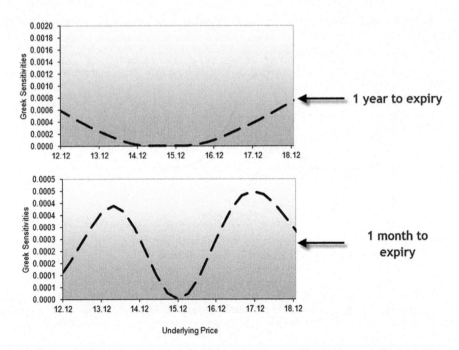

Fig. 5.18 Volgamma profile of a long call option for different maturities for a range of spot prices. Strike price = $15.15 (*Source*: author)

5.9.2 Vanna

Vanna measures how much vega will change by for a change in the spot price.

$$\text{Vanna} = \frac{\text{Change in vega}}{\text{Change in spot price}} \qquad (5.14)$$

Consider Fig. 5.19, which shows both the vega and the vanna exposure for a 3-month call option over a range of spot prices.

If one were to draw a tangent on the vega profile the gradient would be vanna. So to the right of the vega peak in Fig. 5.19 an increase in spot will result in a fall in vega (negative vanna), while to the left of the peak a decrease spot results in a decrease in vega which is a positive relationship.

Vanna profiles for a range of maturities are shown in Fig. 5.20.

Whether or not vanna is desirable depends on whether volatility is skewed across strikes. Suppose that there is a belief that a particular cash market will fall and this will be associated with an increase in implied volatility[9]. To profit from this, participants could buy OTM puts and finance the position by selling OTM calls, a strategy that is termed a risk reversal[10]. As a result of this trading activity, lower strike option volatilities will increase in value while

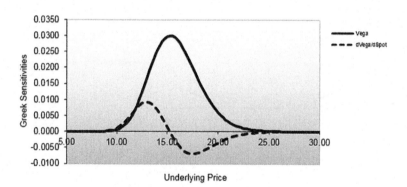

Fig. 5.19 Vega and vanna exposures for 3-month call option for a range of spot prices. Option is struck ATM forward (*Source*: author)

---

[9] The relationship between the level of the cash market and implied volatility will be considered in Chap. 6. In general terms the relationship tends to be inverse but like all things in finance there are always exceptions.

[10] The trader may also delta hedge such a position as both of these options as described would be delta negative.

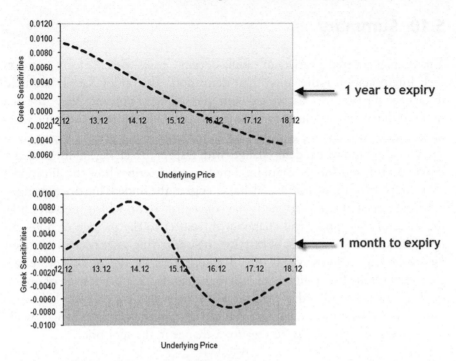

Fig. 5.20 Vanna profile of a long call and put option for different maturities and different degrees of 'moneyness' (*Source*: author)

higher strike option volatilities will fall. Suppose further that the option displays positive vanna to the downside (see Fig. 5.20). This means that a fall in spot will lead to an increase in vega. If the fall in the spot market is associated with an increase in volatility the trader will become longer volatility in a rising volatility environment.

Table 5.9 shows the vanna exposures for different options by strike and position. Figure 5.18 shows the vanna profiles for a long call option. A long put option will have a similar profile. The exposures for the equivalent short positions are simply the opposite of the longs.

Table 5.9 Vanna exposures by strike and position

	Call options			Put options		
	ITM	ATM	OTM	ITM	ATM	OTM
Buy	–	0	+	+	0	–
Sell	+	0	–	–	0	+

5.10 Summary

This chapter covered a variety of vanilla option Greeks with the focus more on their interpretation rather than their derivation. The option Greeks are used to manage the price risk associated with the trading of options. They arise as a result of the parameters used to value an option. *Delta* measures how the value of an option will change with respect to the underlying price. *Gamma* measures the extent to which delta changes with respect to a change in the underlying price. This measure is useful for a trader as it describes how the directional characteristics of the option (i.e. delta) change as the underlying price changes. Closely associated with gamma is the concept of *theta*, which measures how the value of the option will change with respect to the passage of time. An option's exposure to the cost of carrying the underlying asset relates to interest rates (*rho*) and dividend yields (*psi*). *Vega* measures the option's exposure to a change in implied volatility. Since 'trading volatility' is a key feature of option markets, two second order vega measures were also considered. *Volgamma* measured the extent to which vega changed as implied volatility changed while *vanna* measured the change in vega for a change in the spot price.

6

Volatility and Correlation

6.1   Introduction

Implied volatility is central to both the valuation and trading of options as it is the only uncertain variable in the BSM model. Over the last decade there has also been growing interest in equity market correlation, and this chapter covers some of the key characteristics relating to both of these concepts.

The first part of the chapter consists of a short statistics refresher covering variance, volatility, covariance and correlation. The main part of the chapter concentrates on the characteristics of both volatility and correlation highlighting some important empirical relationships. The final part considers some techniques that could be used to determine if volatility or correlation is trading at fair value.

6.2   Definitions

6.2.1 Variance and Volatility

Definitions

For a sample of data, it is often important to know how representative the mean is of all of the observations. This can be assessed by measuring the dispersion of data around the mean.

Variance is a statistical measure of how a sample of data is distributed around its mean. The variance of a sample of numbers is derived by the following ways:

© The Author(s) 2017
N. Schofield, *Equity Derivatives*, DOI 10.1057/978-0-230-39107-9_6

(a) Calculating the mean of the series
(b) Subtracting the mean from each value within the series and then squaring the result
(c) Calculating the sum of all of the squared results
(d) Dividing the result of (c) by $n-1$, where 'n' is the sample size

However, the result of the variance calculation is expressed as 'squared units' of the underlying. For example, the variance of a sample of ages would be 'squared years' while for investment returns it would be 'squared returns'. It is perhaps as a result of this unintuitive unit of measurement that it is more common to convert the variance into a *standard deviation*. This is calculated as the square root of the variance and the result is expressed in the same units of measurement as the underlying data. So in our previous examples this would be just 'years' or 'returns'. Within finance, standard deviations are often used to describe the spread of asset prices or returns around a mean value which inevitably means the analysis will involve some discussion of 'normal distributions' such as that shown in Fig. 6.1.

Statistical theory tells us that a normal distribution is symmetrical with 68.3 % of the observations lying within +/−1 standard deviation of the mean. Of the data 95.4 % lies within +/−2 standard deviations of the mean while +/−3 standard deviations from the mean captures 99.7 % of the observations.

Although it is tempting to think that prices can be described by a normal distribution, this would not be technically correct. Galitz (2013) argues: 'It turns out that, while prices are not normally distributed, returns mostly are'. For example, a normally distributed variable needs to be able to take a value

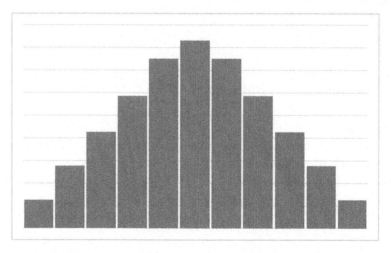

Fig. 6.1 A stylized normal distribution (*Source*: author)

from positive infinity to negative infinity, which would immediately create a problem for share prices as they cannot take negative values. To avoid this issue option valuation principles hypothesize that future spot rates are lognormally distributed around the forward rate[1]. A lognormal distribution is characterized by a left tail that is bounded by zero but with a right tail that extends to infinity. Although the spread of these future spot prices around the forward can be described in standard deviation terms, financial markets use the term *volatility*[2] instead. It is important to note that the degree of uncertainty about future spot price movements does not necessarily depend on where the spot price is trading today.

Interpreting Volatility—An Intuitive Approach
To convey the intuition behind these concepts, suppose there is an index option whose current underlying forward price is 1000 points and is trading with an implied volatility of 30 %. By convention this volatility quote represents one standard deviation and so it would be possible to say that in 68.3 % of all possible outcomes the index is expected to trade within a range of +/−300 index points of the forward price over the next 12 months. It is worth noting that informally many participants will often describe this range of expected price movements relative to the current spot rate rather than the forward.

Volatilities are quoted as a percentage per annum but often traders like to know the equivalent value for another period. Market practice is to take the annualized figure and divide it by the number of applicable trading periods in a year.

- *Annual to daily volatility:* Divide by the square root of 252,[3] that is, 15.87 (or 16 as an approximation). For an implied volatility quote of 30%, this would suggest a daily range of price movements of +/−1.89 %.
- *Annual to weekly volatility:* Divide by the square root of 52, that is, 7.2. So for an annualized volatility of 30 % this would equate to a weekly range of expected price movements of +/−4.16 %.
- *Annual to monthly volatility:* Divide by the square root of 12, that is, 3.46, which would return a monthly range of expected price movements of +/−8.67 % for an annual level of 30 %.

---

[1] Galitz (2013) provides an excellent overview of these concepts and calculations.
[2] The term 'risk' is also used interchangeably.
[3] This convention assumes that option markets are closed at weekends and on public holidays and so represents the approximate number of business days in a year.

Another aspect of interpreting realized volatility quotes relates to the sampling period and the interval between observations. Suppose an investor sees a research piece which states that '3-month annualized daily realized volatility was 16 %'. This means that the sample used in the calculation comprises of daily closing prices taken from the last 3 months of trading. The result was then annualized by multiplying by the square root of 252.

6.2.1.1 Different Types of Volatility

Natenberg (1994) and Tompkins (1994) make reference to a number of different types of volatility:

* *Historical volatility*: the volatility over some period in the past. Sometimes referred to as 'realized' volatility.
* *Future realized volatility*: the volatility that best describes the actual future distribution of prices for an underlying contract. This parameter is unknowable in advance.
* *Forecast volatility*: A model-based estimate of the future volatility of a contract.
* *Forward volatility*: A measure of volatility whose value is known today but applies to a future time period. Analogous to a forward interest rate, that is, the 6-month rate in 6 months' time. This is not a forecast but is a 'no arbitrage' value. An example calculation of forward volatility is given in the appendix to this chapter.
* *Seasonal volatility*: Volatility that relates to seasonal factors such as those experienced by commodities.
* *Implied volatility*: This is often defined as the volatility implied by an observed option price. But defining implied volatility in this manner introduces an element of circularity into the definition—from where did the other market participants obtain their volatility input? Kani et al. (1996) define implied volatility 'as the market's estimate of the average future volatility during the life of the option'. Natenberg (1994) defines it as 'a consensus volatility among all market participants with respect to the expected amount of the underlying price fluctuations over the remaining life of the option'. Tompkins (1994) defines it as 'the risk perceived by the market today for the period up until the expiration of a particular option series'. These definitions bring out the idea that volatility is a perception and is therefore subjective—or to put it crudely, a guess.

A further useful distinction to make is the difference between risk and uncertainty, which is usually attributed to the American Economist, Frank Knight. Risk relates to situations where a future outcome is uncertain but where the odds or probabilities can be objectively measured. Examples would include things like the odds of rolling a six from the throw of a die or the probability of winning a lottery. Uncertainty occurs where it is impossible to assign values to uncertain future outcomes; examples of this include where a share price or equity index will be in the future. In this sense, implied volatility could perhaps be viewed as the degree of *uncertainty* involving the magnitude of future price movements.

6.2.2 Covariance and Correlation

Definitions

Covariance measures how two random variables behave relative to each other, measuring the degree of linear association between the two variables. If the price of asset A generally rises (falls) at the same time that the price of asset B rises (falls), the covariance will be positive. If generally the price of asset A is associated with a fall in the price of asset B, the covariance will be negative. One of the problems relating to the interpretation of covariance is that the magnitude of the result is a function of the value of the assets under analysis—it is an unbounded number. So a higher value for covariance could be explained either by the fact that the two variables may deviate significantly from their mean values or that they display a high degree of association.

The degree of association between two variables can also be measured by converting the covariance into a *correlation coefficient*. This is a 'standardized covariance' measure whose values range from 0 to +1 or 0 to −1 and indicates the strength and direction of a linear relationship between two variables. One possible interpretation of the correlation coefficient is:

0.0 to 0.2	Negligible
0.2 to 0.4	Low
0.4 to 0.7	Moderate
0.7 to 0.9	High
0.9 to 1.0	Very high

These interpretations would apply irrespective of whether the coefficient is positive or negative.

It is worth noting:

- Correlation can also be expressed as a percentage number, for example, 40 %.
- If two assets are deemed to be correlated it does not imply any form of causality.
- A correlation measure does not give any indication of the magnitude of movement experienced by the two variables. So if asset A and asset B display a correlation of, say, +0.4 (or 40 %) it does not mean that a 1 unit move in the price of A will be associated with a 0.4 unit move in the price of asset B.

By way of illustration, the correlation between two equity markets (Hang Seng and the S&P 500) is shown in Fig. 6.2.

Similar to volatility the equity market distinguishes between realized and implied correlation. Realized correlation is the actual correlation experienced over some historic period. Implied correlation represents the market's current expectation of future realized correlation.

Correlation and Portfolio Theory

Modern portfolio theory argues that the variability of a portfolio's returns (i.e. the risk or volatility) is calculated as the weighted sum of the individual volatilities adjusted by the degree to which they are correlated. Provided that the assets in the portfolio are not perfectly positively correlated the volatility of the portfolio will be less than the weighted sum of the volatilities of the constituent assets that form that portfolio.

Equation 6.1 shows the composite volatility for a two-asset portfolio.

$$\sigma_{\text{basket}} = \sqrt{\left(w_{x_1}^2 \sigma_{x_1}^2\right) + \left(w_{x_2}^2 \sigma_{x_2}^2\right) + 2 \times \left(w_{x_1} w_{x_2} \rho_{x_1 x_2} \sigma_{x_1} \sigma_{x_2}\right)} \qquad (6.1)$$

where:
$\sigma_{x_1}^2$ = Variance of asset 1
$\sigma_{x_2}^2$ = Variance of asset 2
$\rho_{x_1 x_2}$ = Correlation between asset 1 and asset 2
σ_{x_1} = Volatility of asset 1
σ_{x_2} = Volatility of asset 2
w_{x_1} = Proportion of asset 1
w_{x_2} = Proportion of asset 1

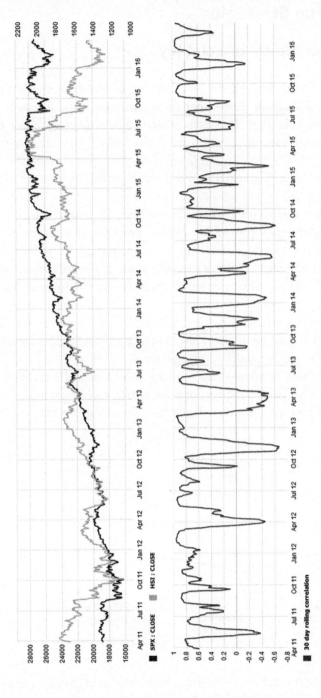

Fig. 6.2 *Upper panel*: Movement of Hang Seng (left hand side) and S&P 500 index (right hand side) from March 2013 to March 2016. *Lower panel*: 30-day rolling correlation coefficient over same period (*Source*: Barclays Live)

6.3   Overview of Volatility and Correlation Trading Strategies

6.3.1 Market 'Flows' of Volatility

Figure 6.3 illustrates the 'market flows' of the demand for and the supply of volatility. The diagram shows that term structures exist for both single-stock and index volatility. The term structure of single-stock volatility is a weighted average measure derived from the individual shares within the overall index.

In Fig. 6.3 the main participants and their respective motives are:

- *Fund managers and insurance companies*—they will tend to use options as a way of protecting their portfolios against downside price movements. This implies they are buyers of OTM index puts, perhaps struck 10 % away from the current price (1). From a single-stock perspective, they may also decide to sell OTM calls in order to enhance the yield on an individual position (2).
- *Corporates*—one source of single-stock volatility will involve some form of equity-linked financing such as the issuance of convertible bonds. This leaves the issuer with a short equity call position (3).
- *Structured product vendors*—these entities would typically include investment banks who issue products that are either capital protected or yield enhanced. For a capital protected structure the investor is long a call on an

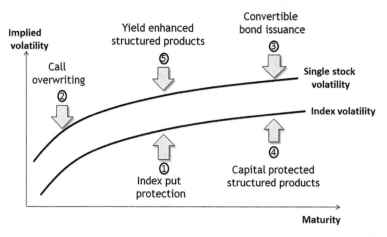

Fig. 6.3 The term structure of single-stock and index volatility indicating the different sources of participant demand and supply (*Source*: author)

index while a yield-enhanced product typically results in the investor being short a put on an individual share. These are shown as positions (4) and (5) respectively, in Fig. 6.3. The options embedded within these structures may present the structuring banks with exposures that they will then seek to hedge[4].

- *Hedge funds and investment banks*—these entities will be looking to trade volatility as an individual asset class. They may be buyers or sellers of index and/or single-stock volatility and may simply be looking to exploit opportunities as they arise. In some cases, they may take opposing positions in index and single-stock volatility which results in a correlation exposure.

Figure 6.3 illustrates that in general terms index volatility is in demand while single-stock volatility is in supply. At first glance these statements would appear to be inconsistent with the diagram which illustrates that average single-stock volatility will tend to trade above index volatility. At some point it would seem to be logical that the selling pressure from single-stock activity combined with the buying pressure of index volatility would force the two curves to switch position. However, this would violate the basic principle of portfolio theory shown in Eq. 6.1; that is the volatility of a portfolio (i.e. the index) is lower than the volatility of its individual components. This also gives an insight into the trading of correlation which, in essence, is based on taking views on the convergence or divergence of average single-stock volatility relative to index volatility.

6.3.2 Trading Volatility—An Overview

Within the context of option valuation, the only uncertain variable is implied volatility, which consequently offers market participants a number of trading opportunities.

At a wholesale level a market maker seeking to trade volatility may structure a quote as follows:

Bid	Offer
25.00 %	25.10 %
Motivation	
Buy volatility	Sell volatility
Example trades	
Buy options and delta hedge	Sell options and delta hedge
OR	OR

---

[4] These risks relate primarily to dividends and correlation and are considered in greater detail in Chap. 12.

Buy straddles   Sell straddles

A buyer of volatility will profit if implied volatility rises, while a seller of volatility will profit if implied volatility falls. The strategy highlighted in Sect. 5.3 illustrates that there are two ways of profiting from trading volatility:

- *Changes in the mark to market of the position*—the trader profits from entering the trade at a given level of implied volatility and closes out the position at another level sometime in the future ('vega trading').
- *Delta hedging*—here the initial implied volatility used to value the option initially differs from the volatility actually realized over the life of the option ('gamma trading').

6.3.3 Trading Correlation—An Overview

Equation 6.1 demonstrated that correlation provided the link between the volatility of an index and that of the constituent stocks. A popular shorthand way of expressing this relationship is the 'correlation proxy' (Granger and Allen 2005):

$$\text{Index volatility} \approx \sqrt{\text{correlation}} \times \text{average single stock volatility} \qquad (6.2)$$

The correlation measure in Eq. 6.2 represents the average of the correlations between all possible pairs of constituent shares within an index. Granger and Allen (2005) argue that there are two ways of measuring this value. The first approach calculates the value as the equally weighted average pairwise correlations of the constituent stocks. This is given by Eq. 6.3:

$$\rho_{\text{average}} = \frac{2}{N(N-1)} \sum_{i<j} \rho_{ij} \qquad (6.3)$$

Where:
N = number of stocks
ρ_{ij} = pairwise correlation of the ith and j^{th} stocks

The second technique is to calculate the correlation implied by the observed implied volatilities of the index and the constituent stocks. Recall Eq. 6.1, which calculated the volatility of a portfolio based on the volatilities of the two constituent assets and their correlation. For a portfolio consisting of multiple stocks the fundamental principles of the equation would still apply except that the calculation would need to include a greater number of correlations. If the implied volatilities of the index and the constituent assets are traded in the market it should be possible to rearrange the formula to derive a single implied correlation measure that is consistent with these observations. This is illustrated in Eq. 6.4 (Granger and Allen 2005).

$$\rho_H = \frac{\sigma_I^2 - \sum_i w_i^2 \sigma_i^2}{\left(\sum_i w_i \sigma_i\right)^2 - \sum_i w_i^2 \sigma_i^2} \qquad (6.4)$$

Where:
ρ_H = implied index correlation
σ_i = volatility of constituent stock
σ_I = volatility of index
w_i = weight of constituent stock within the index

Generally speaking, banks tend to be short correlation by virtue of their structured product portfolios. Equation 6.2 gives an insight into how this correlation exposure could be mitigated. Implied correlation can be isolated by taking opposing positions in instruments that reference index volatility and single-stock volatility. For example, a long position in index volatility combined with a short position in single-stock volatility results in a long correlation exposure. This is referred to as dispersion trading and will be considered in greater detail in Chap. 15.

6.4 Characteristics of Volatility and Correlation

In order to profit from anticipated movements of volatility and correlation it is important to understand how these market factors evolve over time. A common technique is to chart the evolution of the variable relative to another market factor.

6.4.1 Characteristics of Volatility

6.4.1.1 Implied Volatility Versus the Level of the Market

Figure 6.4 indicates that there is an inverse relationship between implied volatility and the absolute level of the cash equity market. So as equity prices fall then implied volatility rises. Note also that implied volatility has a tendency to 'spike' upwards and then gradually 'grind down'[5].

6.4.1.2 Implied versus Realized Volatility

Figure 6.5 illustrates the relationship between index implied volatility and index historical ('realized') volatility.

Figure 6.6 shows the relationship between average single-stock implied volatility and average single-stock realized volatility.

Taken together, Figs. 6.5 and 6.6 show that implied volatility has a tendency to trade at higher levels than realized volatility. That is, market participants value their option positions using a level of implied volatility that on average will be in excess of the volatility actually realized by the market. One concept used to explain why implied volatility trades higher than realized is the so-called risk premium argument. This is based on the idea that since option sellers are faced with potentially open-ended losses it is not unreasonable that they should earn some form of supplemental return.

The figures also illustrate that when implied volatility increases significantly, then realized volatility tends to increase by a greater amount.

6.4.1.3 Index Volatility Versus Single Stock Volatility

Recall that Eq. 6.1 illustrated the relationship between the volatility of a portfolio and the volatility of the constituent stocks. The equation highlighted that the volatility of a portfolio is less than the volatility of the constituents and this principle is confirmed by the data in Fig. 6.7.

Figure 6.8 illustrates the relationship between realized volatility for the index against the average realized volatility of the constituent stocks. This shows that the realized volatility of the index is lower than that of the constituent assets by virtue of realized correlation.

---

[5] One trader described this to the author as 'going up in an elevator and coming down on an escalator'.

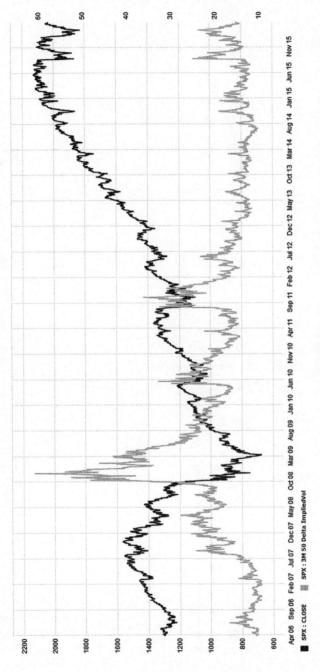

Fig. 6.4 Level of the S&P 500 and 3-month implied volatility for a 50 delta option. March 2006–March 2016 (*Source:* Barclays Live)

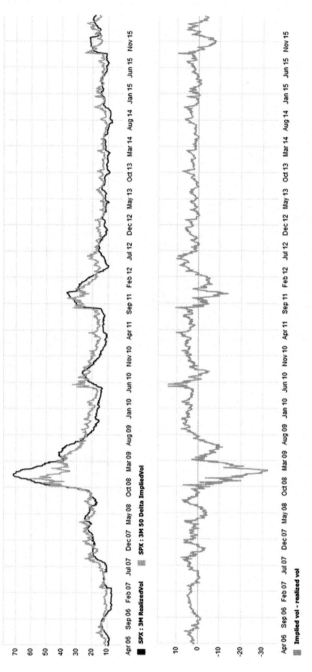

Fig. 6.5 Implied volatility for 3-month 50 delta index option versus 3-month historical index volatility (*upper panel*). Implied volatility minus realized volatility (*lower panel*). March 2006–March 2016 (*Source:* Barclays Live)

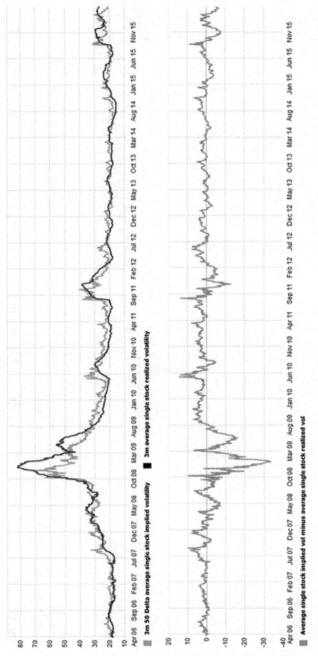

Fig. 6.6 Average single-stock implied volatility versus average single-stock realized volatility (*upper panel*). Implied volatility minus realized volatility (*lower panel*). March 2006–March 2016 (*Source:* Barclays Live)

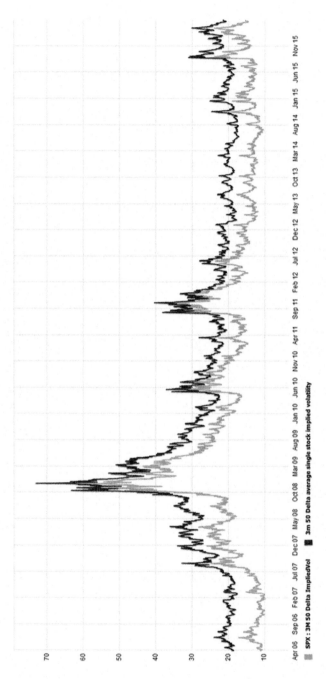

Fig. 6.7 Implied volatility of 3-month 50 delta S&P index option versus average implied volatility of 50 largest constituent stocks. March 2006–March 2016 (*Source*: Barclays Live)

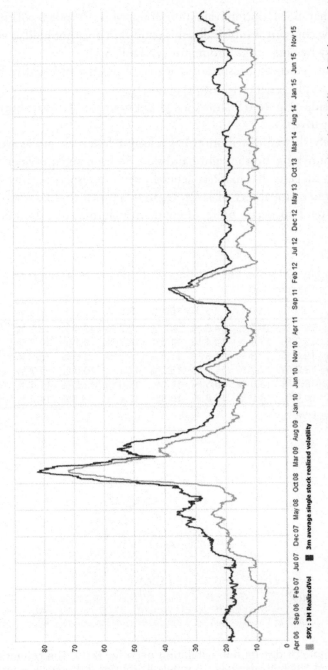

Fig. 6.8 Realized volatility of 3-month 50 delta S&P 500 index option versus average realized volatility of 50 largest constituent stocks. March 2006–March 2016 (*Source:* Barclays Live)

6.4.1.4   Volatility Skew

In the original BSM option valuation framework, implied volatility was assumed to be constant. Empirically, this condition does not hold as volatility is seen to vary by both strike and maturity (Table 6.1).

Statistically, skewness measures the degree of positive or negative bias displayed by a sample of data with equity markets being characterized as 'skewed to the downside'. Figure 6.9 shows a stylized example of a distribution that displays a negative skew.

A negatively skewed distribution has a longer fatter left tail as well as an element of 'bunching' on the right hand side. So from an equity perspective, although this suggests that markets generally tend to display positive returns, there is a greater probability of large negative returns, that is, stock market crashes will tend to occur more often than a normal distribution would predict.

Table 6.1 Volatility surface for S&P 500. Data as of 26th July 2014. Strikes are shown as a percentage of the spot price

	80 %	85 %	90 %	95 %	100 %	105 %	110 %	115 %	120 %
1 m	28.9 %	24.4 %	19.6 %	14.6 %	9.7 %	7.8 %	10.4 %	12.9 %	15.1 %
2 m	23.7 %	20.7 %	17.6 %	14.4 %	11.0%	8.3 %	9.1 %	10.8 %	12.4 %
3 m	22.2 %	19.8 %	17.3 %	14.6 %	11.8%	9.3 %	9.0 %	10.1 %	11.3 %
6 m	21.0 %	19.2 %	17.2 %	15.2 %	13.2%	11.3 %	10.0 %	9.7 %	9.9 %
12 m	21.0 %	19.5 %	18.0 %	16.5 %	15.0%	13.6 %	12.3 %	11.4 %	10.8 %
24 m	21.1 %	20.0 %	18.9 %	17.8 %	16.8%	15.8 %	14.8%	14.0 %	13.3 %

Source: Barclays Live

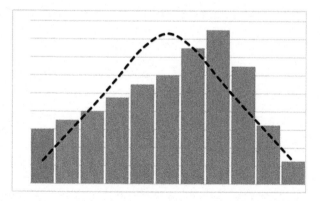

Fig. 6.9 Example of distribution exhibiting negative skew. The columns represent the skewed distribution while a normal distribution is shown by a *dotted line* (*Source*: author)

This negative skew translates into a situation where low strike options will tend to trade with higher implied volatilities than options with higher strikes (Fig. 6.10). An option whose strike is 90 % of the current market[6] would have to be either an ITM call or OTM put. Conversely, an option struck at 110 % would be an OTM call or ITM put option. However, the mathematics of option valuation mean that even if the market is negatively skewed, ATM options will still trade with a higher premium than OTM options.

Although the type of 'downside skew' illustrated in Fig. 6.10 is very common in equity markets there are exceptions. For example, consider Fig. 6.11 which charts the relationship between implied volatility and a variety of different call option deltas for Blackberry. Notice that this relationship is roughly symmetrical in nature; this is referred to as a volatility smile.

Figure 6.11 indicates that the implied volatility for high strike, low delta OTM call options (right hand side of the diagram) is virtually the same as it is for low, high delta ITM calls (left hand side of the diagram).

In order to link this diagram to the implied volatilities for put options recall the principles of put-call parity; the combination of a call and a put with the same strike and maturity will be equal to a long forward position in the underlying asset. So, if prior to maturity an investor was short an ITM call strike with a delta of −75 then an OTM put option struck at the same price must have a delta of approximately −25, that is, the combination of the two options is equivalent to a short forward position. This means that the implied volatility of the −75 delta ITM call and the −25 delta OTM put must be equivalent as a forward position has no exposure to implied volatility. Therefore, on the left hand side of Fig. 6.11 OTM puts will trade with the same level of implied volatility as the equivalent ITM call option.

At the time Blackberry was in the process of a major restructuring having lost market share to other smartphone producers such as Apple and Samsung. Although the company had avoided bankruptcy, the smile perhaps reflects the fact that the market was still split as to their future prospects. The higher volatilities for lower strikes would be driven by those participants who had bought downside put protection, while the higher volatilities for the higher strikes was probably a result of participants buying cheap OTM call options in case the stock experienced a significant recovery.

It is also possible for an asset to display a positive skew, such as that for the Indian company Reliance Industries (Fig. 6.12). Here the volatility for OTM calls is greater than that for OTM puts.

---

[6] Note that for equities the 'current market' is commonly interpreted to mean spot rather than the forward.

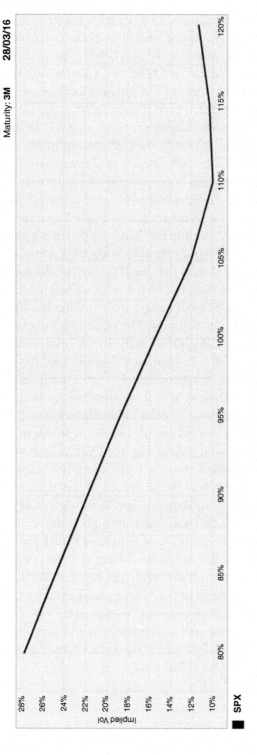

Fig. 6.10 Volatility skew for 3-month ATM options written on the S&P 500 equity index. The *X* axis is the strike of the option as a percentage of the current spot price (*Source*: Barclays Live)

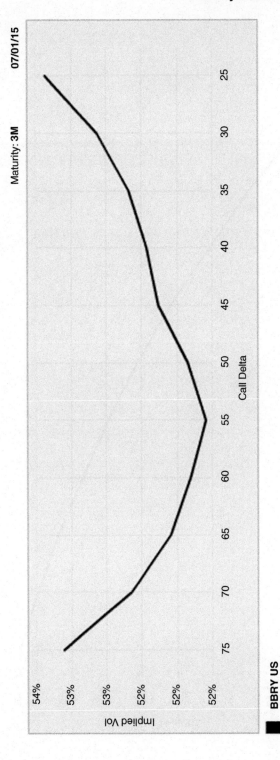

Fig. 6.11 Volatility smile for Blackberry. Implied volatility (*Y* axis) measured relative to the delta of a 3-month call option (*Source:* Barclays Live)

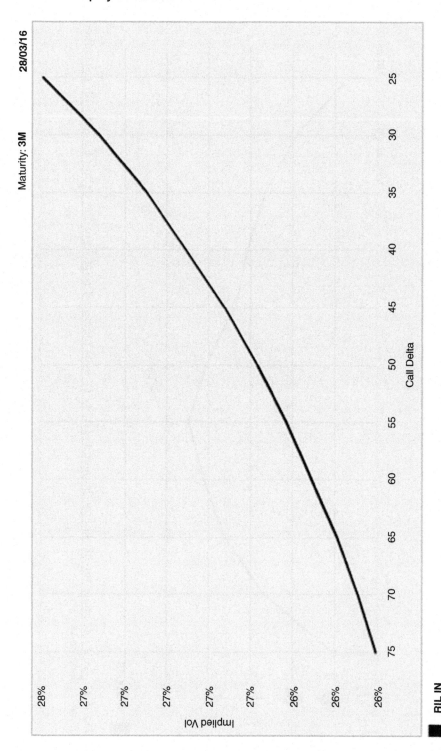

Fig. 6.12 Volatility skew for Reliance industries (*Source: Barclays Live*)

Why Does the Volatility Skew Exist?

A number of reasons have been suggested to explain the existence of volatility skew. They include:

- *Fat tails*—this is the belief that the incidence of extreme market movements is greater than the lognormal distribution assumed by the BSM valuation framework. Since a trader knows they will occur with greater frequency than the statistics suggest, OTM puts which offer equity investors downside protection will be priced with higher implied volatilities.
- *Pre-emptive pricing*—De Weert (2006) argues that traders who sell OTM puts will delta hedge their directional exposures by shorting the underlying stock. As the market falls, the gamma exposure on the position will increase as the option now tends towards the ATM level. As was shown in Sect. 5.3 this rebalancing could result in losses if the underlying price movements are significant. So where a trader is delta hedging a short put position a falling spot price would require them to sell more of the asset, which would result in losses. In anticipation of these possible hedging losses the trader will charge relatively more by increasing their implied volatility quote.
- *Simple demand and supply*—the vast majority of participants in the cash equity market hold long positions. As a result, participants are more likely to buy downside protection in the form of an OTM put pushing up the cost in volatility terms relative to the ATM volatility. This OTM put could be financed by the sale of an OTM call with the strike set in a region that is not expected to trade. This selling pressure pushes down the volatility of higher strike options. It is also possible for implied volatility to increase for higher strike options (see Fig. 6.12). This would suggest that there is some demand for OTM call options perhaps as a result of some expectation of a sharp increase in price.
- *Behavioural finance*—writers such as Daniel Kahnemann have suggested that the pain suffered by investors from losing money is twice as great as the pleasure they derive from making money. This is perhaps reflected in Fig. 6.4 which illustrates the relationship between implied volatility and the underlying market. The diagram suggests that as markets fall sharply, investors will tend to panic and overreact.

How Is the Volatility Skew Measured?

There are a number of ways in which volatility skew can be measured (Deb and Brask 2009):

The cost of a collar struck at 90 % and 110 % of the market—a collar is an option combination, which from an equity investor's perspective consists of a long OTM put option and a short ITM call option. Briefly, an investor is able to obtain downside protection on an equity position by virtue of the purchased put option, the cost of which is subsidized by the sale of an OTM call option. Although the cost of protection is reduced, the impact of the short call prevents the investor from enjoying any upside beyond the 110 % strike call.

Suppose the underlying market is trading at 2000 index points. Using the values in Table 6.1, a 3-month long OTM put struck at 90 % of this value (i.e. 1800 index points) would return a premium of approximately 10 index points. A short OTM call option struck at 110 % of spot (i.e. 2200 index points) with the same maturity would generate a premium of about 0.5 of an index point. So in this instance the cost of the structure would be approximately 9.5 index points.

Using this method of calculating the skew it would suggest that the greater the net premium the more pronounced is the skew to the downside.

Volatility spread between 90 % and 110 % options—whereas the cost of the 90–110 % collar measured the skew in terms of premium, this particular metric measures the differences in volatility terms. To illustrate how this would be calculated consider again the 3-month collar position used in the previous example:

- 90 % volatility = 17.3 %
- 110 % volatility = 9.0 %
- Volatility spread = 8.3 %

This suggests that a greater volatility spread is associated with a greater degree of skew to the downside—sometimes referred to as a 'steep' skew. A lower spread would be therefore indicative of a 'flatter' skew.

Percentage skew—empirically it has been observed that in a high volatility environment skew has a tendency to flatten. This can be illustrated by expressing the skew as a percentage. This is calculated by taking the 90–110 % volatility spread and dividing it by the ATM volatility.

Figure 6.13 shows that as implied volatility rises the degree of skewness declines and vice versa. This could be explained by mean reversion (Deb and Brask 2009): 'when volatility is already elevated, there is less risk of a large increase in volatility should the underlying market move lower still. This calls for a flatter skew.... Equally, when volatility is low (typically when markets are rising) the primary risk to volatility is a sharp increase should markets fall. This translates into a steep skew....'

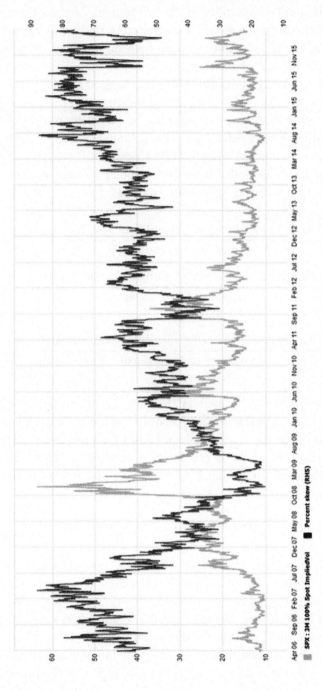

Fig. 6.13 S&P 500 index volatility (left hand side) plotted against the skew measured in per cent (right hand side). March 2006–March 2016 (*Source*: Barclays Live)

Delta skew—suppose an analyst is looking at a 3-month OTM 110 % S&P 500 call. With implied volatility at 20 % the delta of the option is about 17 %. However, the same option with the same strike will have a delta of about 27 % if implied volatility were to increase to 30 %, all other things being equal. So instead of holding the degree of moneyness constant (and allowing delta to change as implied volatility changes) this measure holds the delta constant and allows the degree of moneyness to vary. Delta skew can be measured either as a ratio (i.e. volatility of a 25 delta put divided by the implied volatility of a 25 delta call) or as a difference (i.e. volatility of a 25 delta put minus the implied volatility of a 25 delta call).

Normalized delta skew—this is another popular measure that is used and can be calculated in different ways (Eqs. 6.5 and 6.6):

$$\frac{\left(\text{Volatility of 25 delta put} - \text{volatility of 25 delta call}\right)}{\text{Volatility of a 50 delta option}} \tag{6.5}$$

$$\frac{\left(\text{Volatility of 25 delta put} - \text{volatility of 50 delta put}\right)}{\text{Volatility of 50 delta put}}$$
$$\text{minus} \tag{6.6}$$
$$\frac{\left(\text{Volatility of 25 delta call} - \text{volatility of 50 delta call}\right)}{\text{Volatility of 50 delta call}}$$

Variance skew—this is defined as the ratio of the variance swap strike expressed in volatility terms to the ATM forward volatility. Variance swaps are considered in greater detail in Chap. 12 but Deb and Brask (2009) argue 'since a variance swap strike is essentially a weighted average of volatilities across option strikes, comparing it to ATM volatility is a measure of skew'. This is shown in Fig. 6.14.

Characteristics of the Volatility Skew

The volatility skew itself will not remain stable but will evolve over time. Figure 6.15 is a time series that illustrates the degree of skewness exhibited by a 3-month S&P 500 option over time. The degree of skewness is measured as the difference between the implied volatility of an option struck at 90 % of spot minus the implied volatility of an option struck at 110 %.

The movement of skew over time does not in itself reveal much information unless it is put into a wider context. Figure 6.16 shows how the

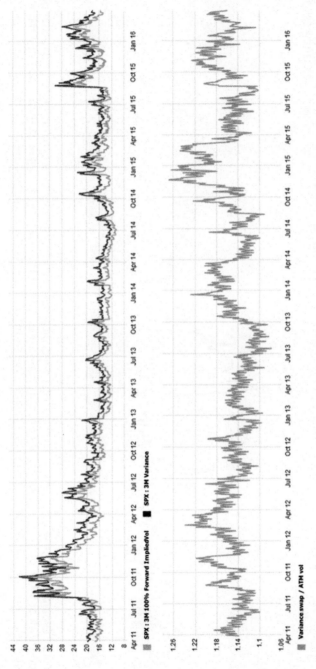

Fig. 6.14 Variance swap strike and ATM forward implied forward volatility for S&P 500 (*upper panel*). Variance swap divided by ATM forward volatility for S&P 500 (*lower panel*). March 2011–March 2016 (*Source:* Barclays Live)

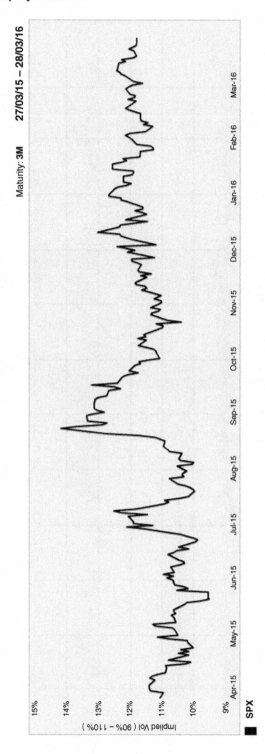

Fig. 6.15 Evolution of the volatility skew over time. Skewness measured as the difference between the implied volatilities of an option struck at 90 % of the market less that of an option struck at 110 %. The higher the value of the number the more the market is skewed to the downside (i.e. skewed towards lower strike options) (*Source:* Barclays Live)

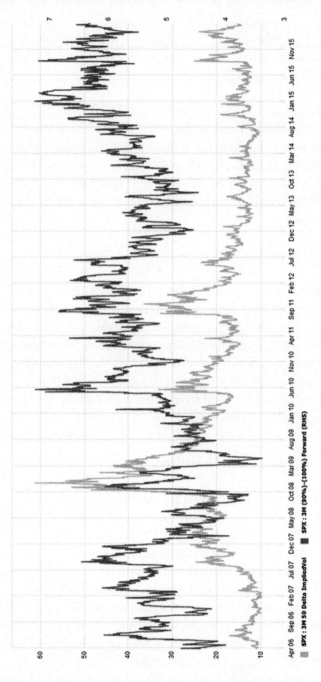

Fig. 6.16 Implied volatility of 3-month ATM S&P 500 option plotted against the 3-month volatility skew (*Source:* Barclays Live)

Table 6.2 Premium on a 90–110 % collar under different volatility assumptions

	Original net premium	1 % parallel increase in volatility	1 % increase in the 90/110 volatility spread
90 % put @ 17.3 % 110 % call @ 9.0%	9.64 index points	11.21 index points	10.78 index points

skew moves in relation to the level of implied volatility. The figure shows that as implied volatility rises (and so the cash market is likely falling) the degree of skewness towards lower strike options increases. This is perhaps intuitive—a falling cash market should lead to an increase in the demand for OTM puts. This increased demand will translate into an increase in implied volatility which in turn will lead to an increase in cost, all other things being equal.

Does Volatility Skew Matter?

How significant is the skew? Consider Table 6.2 which revisits the net premium on a 3-month 90–110 % collar using the values in Table 6.1, the net cost of the structure being 9.64 index points. Table 6.2 shows what would happen if the absolute level of volatility increases by 1 % (column 3) against the impact of a 1 % increase in the 90–110 % volatility spread (column 4). Although perhaps somewhat simplistic the table indicates that movements in the absolute level of volatility will have a greater impact on the premium than the same change in the shape of the skew.

6.4.1.5   Term Structure of Volatility

Figures 6.17, 6.18 and 6.19 illustrate the existence of a term structure of volatility. The different diagrams illustrate the term structure for options struck at different levels: 80 % of spot, Fig. 6.17; ATM strike options, 100 % of spot, Fig. 6.18 and high strike options, 120 % of spot, Fig. 6.19.

The most common representation of the term structure is that of the ATM option shown in Fig. 6.18. This shows that 'normally' volatility is upward sloping with respect to maturity. In these cases, it would suggest that uncertainty increases with respect to maturity. For low and high strike options the charts show that shorter-dated options trade with higher volatilities which then dip down before rising. This would suggest the opposite—there is greater uncertainty with shorter-dated options struck at these levels. However, it is

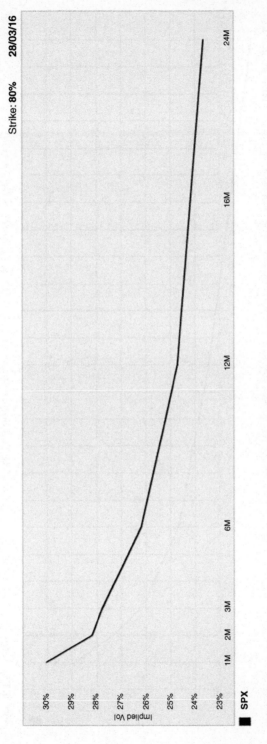

Fig. 6.17 Term structure of volatility for an S&P 500 option struck at 80 % of spot (*Source:* Barclays Live)

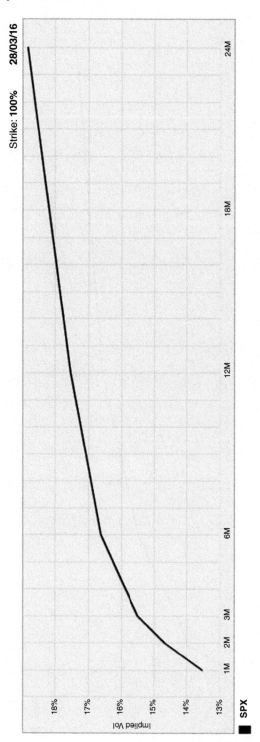

Fig. 6.18 Term structure of volatility for an S&P 500 option struck at 100 % of spot (*Source:* Barclays Live)

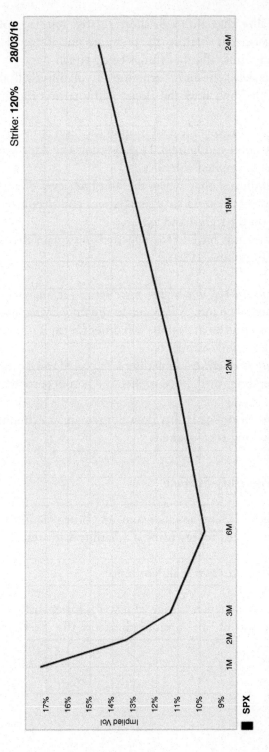

Fig. 6.19   Term structure of volatility for an S&P 500 option struck at 120 % of spot (*Source*: Barclays Live)

important to realize that although shorter-dated implied volatility may be higher than longer-dated volatility the premium on a longer-dated option will be greater in cash terms, all other things being equal.

Similar to the skew, the term structure of volatility will also evolve over time. Figure 6.20 shows how the slope of the term structure evolves with respect to time.

However, similar to skew the evolution of the term structure slope needs to be put into some context. Figure 6.21 shows how the slope evolves relative to the absolute level of implied volatility.

Figure 6.21 indicates that when the absolute level of implied volatility increases the slope of the term structure flattens and may invert (as shown by a negative value on the right hand axis).

A number of reasons have been suggested to explain the existence of the term structure (Tompkins, 1994):

* *Non-stationarity in the underlying price series*—if analysts anticipate that some fundamental change will occur to the underlying asset in the future then implied volatilities of options will differ for expiration periods prior to and after the economic event.
* *Non-uniformity of volatility*—volatility is expected to be different on different days depending on the occurrence (or non-occurrence) of 'economic events'.
* *Reversion to the mean*—volatility does not remain at extreme levels but will tend towards a long-term average.

6.4.1.6   The Volatility Surface

Table 6.1 and Fig. 6.22 illustrate the concept of the volatility surface. A volatility surface is a way of representing a volatility with respect to both strike and maturity.

Figure 6.22 illustrates two main concepts:

* The equity options market is skewed towards lower strike options.
* As the maturity of an option shortens the skew becomes more pronounced.

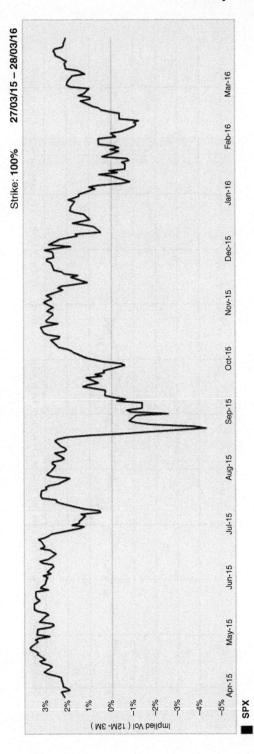

Fig. 6.20 Slope of term structure of S&P 500 implied volatility. Term structure is measured as 12-month implied volatility minus 3-month volatility. An increase in the value of the *Y* axis indicates a steepening of the slope (*Source*: Barclays Live)

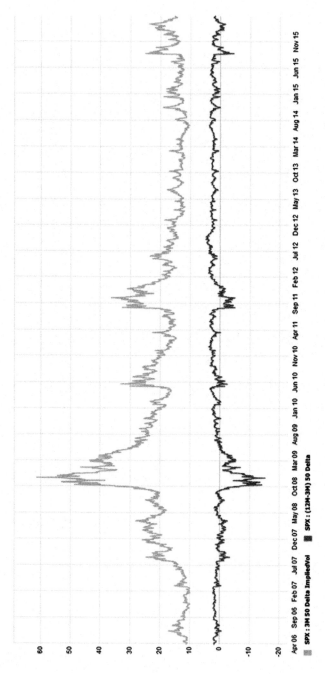

Fig. 6.21 Implied volatility of 3-month 50 delta S&P 500 index option (Left hand axis) versus the slope of the index term structure (right hand axis). March 2006–March 2016

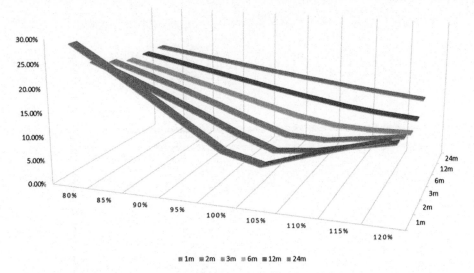

Fig. 6.22 Volatility skew for S&P options with different maturities. Data based on values shown in Table 6.1 (*Source*: Barclays Live)

6.4.1.7   How Volatile Is Volatility?

Figure 6.23 illustrates that shorter-dated implied volatility is more volatile than longer-dated volatility, which has important risk management implications.

To reflect these different degrees of volatility, some traders make a distinction between headline and weighted vega. Headline vega is defined as the model-determined vega exposure for any given maturity. Since the term structure of volatility does not move in a parallel fashion (see Fig. 6.20) many traders do not add together their volatility exposures across maturities but rather use the concept of weighted vega. This is defined as the maturity-weighted vega exposure, expressed relative to a chosen maturity. Suppose a trader's S&P 500 option portfolio has a $100,000 model-determined vega exposure in both the 3-month and 36-month maturities. This implies that a 1 % change in implied volatility will result in the option portfolio gaining or losing $100,000 in each maturity. However, from a risk management perspective the two would not be considered equivalent due to the non-parallel movement of the term structure. The trader decides to calculate the weighted vega for the 36-month exposure relative to the

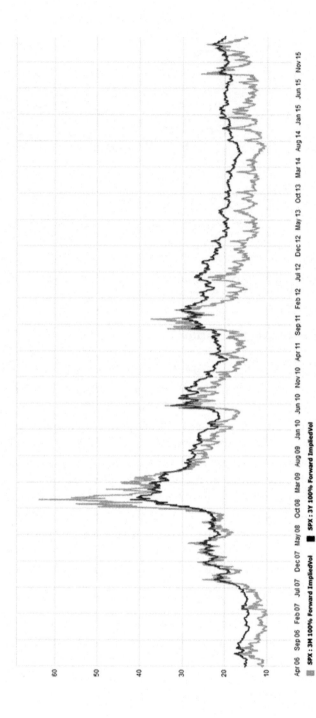

Fig. 6.23 Time series of 3-month index implied volatility plotted against 36-month index implied volatility. March 2006–March 2016 (*Source*: Barclays Live)

3-month maturity. One of the ways to calculate the weight is to use the following formula:

$$\sqrt{\frac{\text{Base maturity}}{\text{Comparative maturity}}} \qquad (6.7)$$

The 36-month maturity (1080 days) is taken to be the comparative maturity while the 3-month maturity (90 days) is the base maturity. The weight is

$$\sqrt{\frac{90}{1080}} = 0.2887 \qquad (6.8)$$

So if 3-month volatility moves by 1 % there would be a gain or loss of $100,000 (headline vega) in that maturity and this would likely be associated with a smaller move in the 36-month volatility that would result in a gain or loss of $28,700 (the weighted vega).

An alternative approach would be to use regression analysis, which is a popular technique used in similar circumstances in the fixed income market[7]. This technique describes the relationship between a 'dependent' and 'independent' variable. In this instance the dependent variable would be 36-month vega whose value is predicted based on movements in the independent variable which is 3-month vega. Figure 6.24 shows a time series of the daily changes in implied volatilities for both maturities and a casual 'eyeballing' of the data does confirm the assertion that shorter-dated volatility changes by more than longer-dated volatility.

The next step is to plot a scattergraph of the data and to determine a 'line of best fit' (Fig. 6.25) whose mathematical form would be:

$$\Delta y_{36m} = \alpha + \beta \Delta x_{3m} + \varepsilon_t \qquad (6.9)$$

Where:
Δy_{36m} = the change in 36-month vega (the dependent variable)
α = a constant; the value of Y even if X has zero value
β = the regression coefficient. This represents the slope of the line of best fit.
Δx_{3m} = the change in 3-month vega (the independent variable)

---

[7] See Schofield and Bowler (2011) for applications within a fixed income environment. Watsham and Parramore (1997) is an excellent reference for the underlying mathematics.

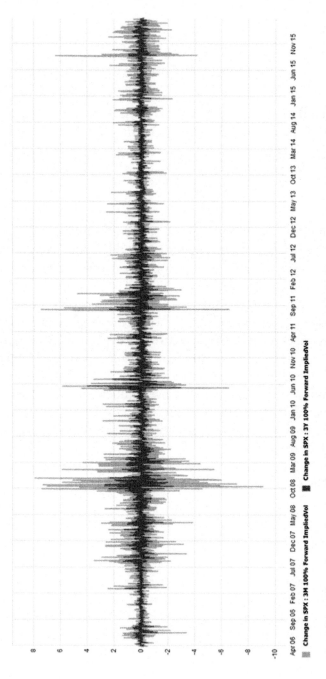

Fig. 6.24 Chart shows the change in 3-month ATM spot implied volatility vs. change in 36-month ATM spot volatility for the S&P 500 index. March 2006–March 2016 (*Source*: Barclays Live)

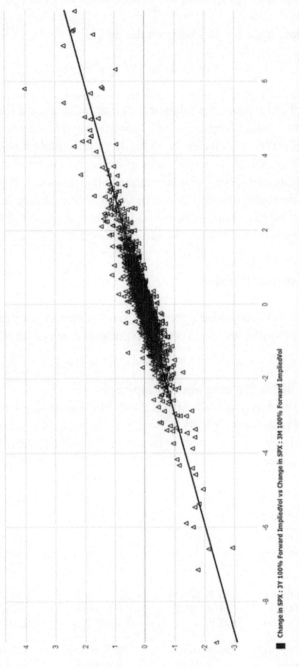

■ Change in SPX : 3Y 100% Forward ImpliedVol vs Change in SPX : 3M 100% Forward ImpliedVol

Fig. 6.25 A 'line of best fit' for a scattergraph of changes in 36-month implied volatility (Y axis) against changes in 3-month implied volatility (x axis). S&P 500 index, March 2006–March 2016 (Source: Barclays Live)

ε = the error term. This reflects the fact that other factors may influence the value of Y and are not captured by the specification of the equation.

The regression equation derived from the data is:

$$Y = 0.001244 + 0.338310x \qquad (6.10)$$

If, for ease of illustration, the value of the constant is ignored then Eq. 6.10 shows that a one-unit change in X (i.e. 3-month implied volatility) is associated with a 0.338310-unit change in Y (i.e. 36-month implied volatility). The regression equation also returns an R^2 value of 0.84. This means that 84 % of the variance of the 36-month vega can be explained by the model. Equation 6.10 confirms that short-dated volatility is more volatile than longer-dated volatility and is also close to the short cut method outlined in Eq. 6.8. However, the value of the regression coefficient will also be a function of the sample period.

6.4.1.8   Volatility Regimes

This section covers how volatility trading has an impact on observed spot prices. All the examples are based on the hypothetical values for the S&P 500 (Table 6.3).

Sticky Strike, Strike Pinning and Whippy Spot
Consider first the different levels of volatility indicated on day 1 in Table 6.3. If the underlying market were to subsequently stay unchanged but implied volatility were to rise or fall for all strikes, then this would indicate a shift in the volatility surface.

Table 6.3   Implied volatilities for different market levels and strikes over a 3-day period

Day 1	Underlying market 2000	95 % strikes (i.e. 1900) 25.0 %	100 % strikes (i.e. 2000) 22.0%	105 % strikes (i.e. 2100) 19.0 %
Day 2	Underlying market 1900	95 % strikes (i.e. 1805) 28.0 %	100% strikes (i.e. 1900) 25.0 %	105 % strikes (i.e. 1995) 22.1 %
Day 3	Underlying market 1805	95 % strikes (i.e. 1715) 28.0 %	100% strikes (i.e. 1805) 25.0 %	105 % strikes (i.e. 1895) 22.1 %

Now consider the movement in the market from day 1 to day 2. On day 1 the volatility associated with an ATM spot strike of 2000 index points was 22.0 %. The following day the market moves down by 5 % to reach a new level of 1900. The volatility associated with a specific strike price of 1900 (now the ATM strike) is the same as it was on day 1—25.0 %. This is the concept of 'sticky strike'—a situation where the volatility associated with a particular strike price remains constant, although its relative 'moneyness' may have changed. Note also that the 22.1% volatility for the higher strike options on day 2 (the 105 % strike which corresponds to a level of 1995 index points) is consistent with the day 1 volatility for options struck at 2000. Citigroup (2008) argue 'we tend to observe sticky strike moves over the short term as the market tends to anchor a certain underlying level with a certain implied vol. We would move away from this sticky strike regime once there has been a genuine rally or sell-off (or change of risk perception)'.

Another manifestation of 'sticky strike' is termed 'strike pinning'. This relates to a market activity, most often observed in the single-stock markets, where the share price will trade around a popular strike price. Section 5.3 analysed a transaction where the intention was to exploit an anticipated change in the level of implied volatility. However, movements in the underlying price led to an element of directional exposure and so to neutralize this the trader had to buy and sell the underlying asset. The trade as presented involved a delta-hedged short option position and is sometimes referred to as a 'short gamma' exposure. A long gamma trade would require a trader to buy options (either calls or puts) and hedge the directional exposure by trading the underlying share. Share price rises would require the trader to sell shares while share prices fall would require the trader to buy shares. This long gamma hedging activity could lead to the share price being 'pinned' to a particular strike.

The delta hedging activities of the different volatility strategies are summarized in Table 6.4.

Bennett and Gil (2012) make the following observations in relation to strike pinning:

- There must be a significant amount of option trading relative to the normal traded volumes of the asset.
- It is more likely to happen in shares that are relatively illiquid where there is no strong trend to drive the price away from the strike.
- It is difficult to pin an index given the relatively high trading volumes.

Table 6.4 Associated delta hedging activities when trading volatility using the four option basic 'building blocks'

Initial position	Initial delta hedge	Asset price moves up?	Asset price moves down?
Buy call	Sell asset	Sell more of the asset	Buy asset
Buy put	Buy asset	Sell asset	Buy more of the asset
Sell call	Buy asset	Buy more of the asset	Sell asset
Sell put	Sell asset	Buy asset	Sell more of the asset

'Whippy' spot relates to short gamma positions (i.e. either a short call or a short put) and would be characterized by significant spot price volatility around a particular strike.

Sticky Moneyness and Sticky Delta

Returning to Table 6.3, if on day 3 the market falls by another 5 % then the ATM strike is now 1805. In this example, the implied volatility for an option struck at 100 % of the market is unchanged from day 2 at 25.0 %, although the level of the underlying market has changed. This is an example of 'sticky moneyness'[8] and represents a situation where the implied volatility for a particular percentage of the strike (i.e. the moneyness or the delta of the option) remains the same. Citigroup (2008) argue 'we tend to see sticky moneyness in a longer time horizon, where the perception of implied vols per given moneyness will not change even if the underlying does.'

6.4.2 Characteristics of Correlation

6.4.2.1 Correlation Versus Market Level Versus Implied Volatility

Figure 6.26 illustrates the relationship between index volatility and implied correlation, while Fig. 6.27 looks at the absolute level of the cash market and implied correlation. Taken together these charts indicate that when volatility is elevated and the market is falling, stocks within the index tend to become increasingly correlated. Similar to volatility, correlation also exhibits a tendency to mean revert.

In times of crisis both volatility and correlation have a tendency to spike up. This would suggest that a short correlation position may offset a long volatility position. If the markets are calm, then both correlation and volatil-

---

[8] This can also be calculated relative to the option's delta and as such would be referred to as 'sticky delta'.

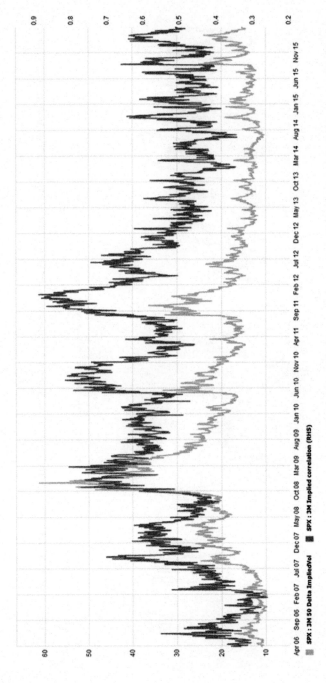

Fig. 6.26 Implied volatility of 3-month 50 delta S&P 500 index against 3-month implied correlation. March 2006–March 2016 (*Source*: Barclays Live)

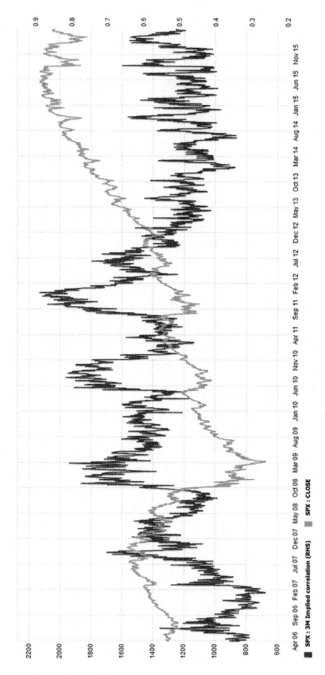

Fig. 6.27 Level of S&P 500 cash index against 3-month index implied correlation. March 2006–March 2016 (*Source:* Barclays Live)

ity grind down. Again a short correlation position may offset a long volatility position.

One interesting exception to the concept of portfolio theory and the impact of correlation is shown in Fig. 6.28 which charts the evolution of index correlation for the Hong Kong Hang Seng Index. Notice that on several occasions short-dated index correlation exceeded the theoretical value of 1.

6.4.2.2   Implied Versus Realized Correlation

Figure 6.29 shows that similar to implied volatility, implied correlation will tend to trade above realized volatility apart from periods of high volatility.

6.4.2.3   Correlation Skew

The concept of volatility skew was considered in Sect. 6.4.1.4. Since single stocks will also display a volatility skew then it follows from Eq. 6.2 that correlation will also display a skew.

6.4.2.4   Term Structure of Correlation

Figure 6.30 shows that similar to implied volatility, implied correlation will tend to display an upward sloping term structure.

However, the slope is not always positive. Figure 6.31 shows that again similar to implied volatility the slope of the term structure of correlation will flatten and possibly invert when the absolute level of implied volatility is high.

6.5   Identifying Value in Volatility and Correlation

The author recalls a discussion with a senior bank sales person who became frustrated with the approach of some of his junior colleagues when constructing client hedging strategies. They would often market zero premium strategies such as collars (e.g. buy an OTM call and finance with the sale of an OTM put) on the basis that the lack of premium represented an attractive proposition. Although this may be true at a simple level, the senior sales person argued that they only represented good value if the implied volatility of

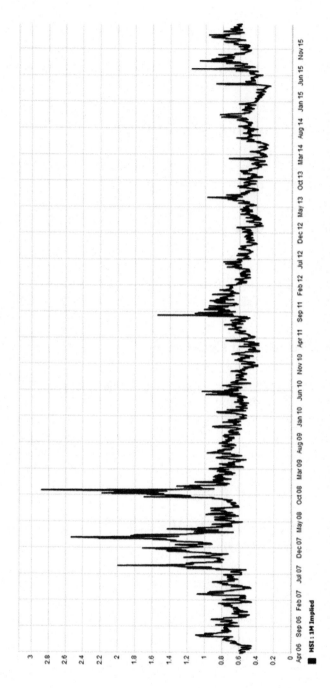

Fig. 6.28   One-month implied correlation of Hang Seng Index. March 2006–March 2016 (*Source:* Barclays Live)

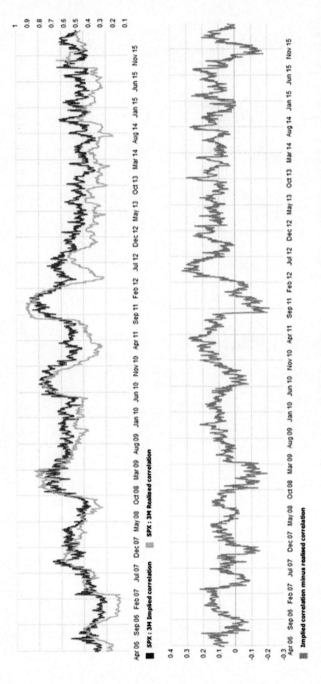

Fig. 6.29   Three-month Implied correlation minus realized correlation. S&P 500 equity index (*Source*: Barclays Live)

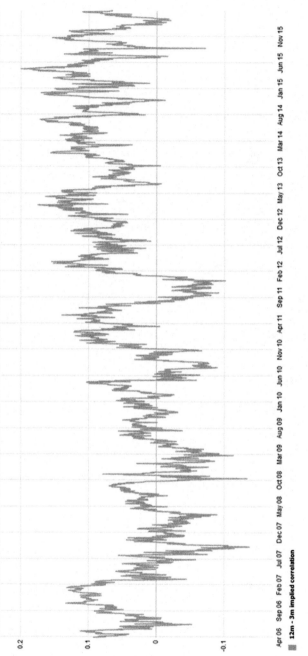

Fig. 6.30 Term structure of S&P 500 implied correlation. Twelve-month minus 3-month implied correlation. March 2006–March 2016 (*Source: Barclays Live*)

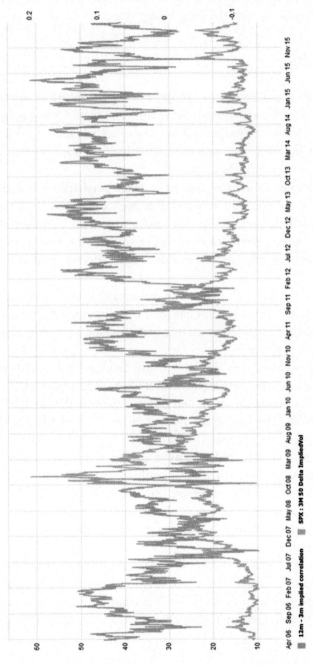

Fig. 6.31 Implied volatility of 3-month 50 delta S&P 500 index option (left hand axis) plotted against slope of correlation term structure (right hand axis). The correlation term structure is calculated as 12-month minus 3-month implied correlation. A negative value indicates an inverted term structure (*Source*: Barclays Live)

the purchased option was trading at a relatively low level and the implied volatility of the sold option was trading at a relatively high level. Moral of the story? Price and value are not the same thing!

6.5.1 Volatility

One of the trickiest tasks faced by an option trader is to formulate the most appropriate strategy for the prevailing volatility climate (Natenberg 1994). This usually involves some judgement as to whether implied volatility is currently trading at 'fair value' or some technique that forecasts how the volatility of the underlying asset is likely to evolve[9].

The concept of fair value may suggest to some participants that there is a single 'true' price for every asset, which has been calculated by a top secret supercomputer, which never reveals its results to market participants. Since this is not an accurate representation it is perhaps why looking at the appropriateness of a strategy relative to the current market environment is a better approach.

A casual review of research literature produced by the various investment banks suggests that each institution has their own 'house' technique for identifying value relating to different strategies. Generally speaking, there are a number of common themes:

Mean reversion—over a long period volatility (realized or implied) will tend to revert to some long-term average. Consider Figs. 6.32 and 6.33. These diagrams illustrate the evolution of implied and realized volatility of the S&P 500 from 1996 to 2016. The long-term average of implied volatility is 19.13 % while the same measure for realized volatility is 17.45 %.

Knowing these long-term values would allow the analyst to determine if the current level of implied volatility is trading significantly away from the mean and whether it is likely to revert. However, there is no single agreed timeframe over which the mean is calculated and it is impossible to say with certainty the speed with which it will revert. This would make it difficult to rely on from a trading perspective.

Implied volatility is trading away from recent levels—if a stock has been trading at an implied volatility level of 25 % over some period but is now trading at 20 %, the investor may believe that it warrants further investigation to determine if it is trading cheap to fair value.

---

[9] See for example Tompkins (1994) or Natenberg (1994), for details of volatility forecasting techniques.

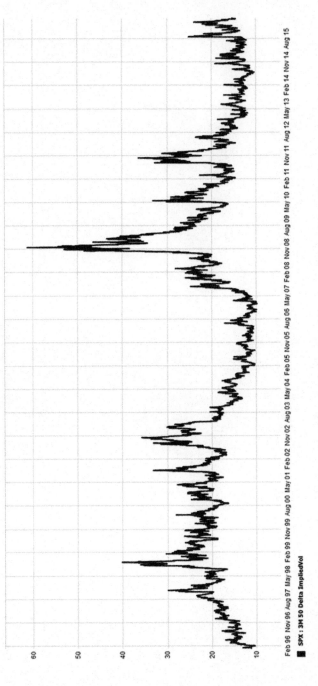

Fig. 6.32 Implied volatility of S&P 500 index options from 1996 to 2016 (*Source*: Barclays Live)

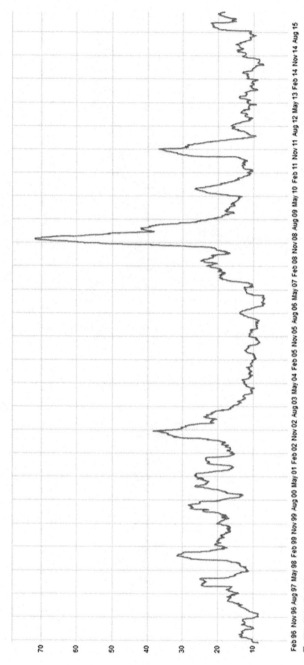

Fig. 6.33   Realized volatility of S&P 500 from 1996 to 2016 (*Source*: Barclays Live)

Predictive ability of implied volatility—this is based on the notion that observed option implied volatilities reflect market views on how the actual volatility of the underlying asset will evolve over the remaining life of the option. As a result, the different techniques analyse current implied volatility relative to realized volatility. As a simple example consider Fig. 6.34. Both implied and realized for the S&P 500 are trading away their long-term averages for the market (19.13 % and 17.45 %, respectively) but does this mean that they are both likely to mean revert in the short term? Perhaps there are a number of trade possibilities; for example:

• At the moment implied volatility has stabilized since falling from a mid-February peak. If the trader believed that implied volatility was going to increase they may decide to implement a long vega trade.
• If the trader believed that realized volatility would fall below implied, he may decide to implement a short gamma trade.

Realized volatility is expected to evolve at a different rate than implied volatility—Section 5.3 analysed a vega/gamma trade where a trader had sold options in anticipation of lower implied volatility. However, realized volatility was greater than the initial levels of implied and so the trader lost money through their delta hedge. From this it follows that:

• If the option trader sells options, the challenge is to ensure that the premium income is greater than the losses incurred from delta hedging.
• If the option trader buys options, the challenge is to ensure that the premium expense incurred is less than the profits generated from delta hedging.
• The trader will not profit if realized volatility evolves exactly in line with the initial levels of implied volatility, ignoring all transaction costs.

Volatility cones—another popular technique used to identify value is the concept of the volatility cone. There are a number of different ways in which these can be constructed and the following represents just one approach. Consider Fig. 6.35, which was constructed in the following manner:

• A number of maturities were selected for the *x* axis, for example 1-month, 2-month and so on.
• A sample period for the underlying asset was chosen, for example 2 years.
• The realized volatility for each maturity was measured on a rolling basis. So 1-month realized volatility is calculated using daily observations for pre-

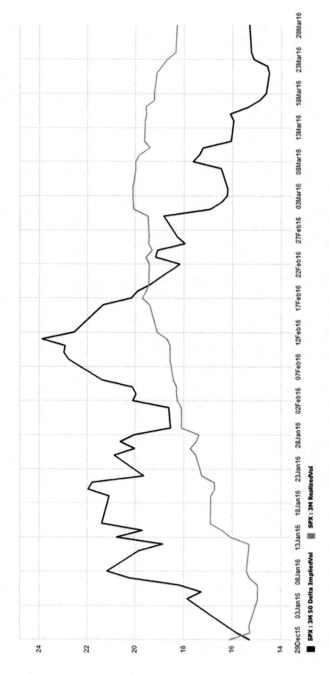

Fig. 6.34 Three-month implied and realized volatility for S&P 500 (*Source*: Barclays Live)

ceding 4 weeks of data, the result of which is then annualized. The calculation is then repeated for each day of the sample period each time moving the measurement period forward by one day.

- From the data produced the minimum, maximum and average values for each maturity were collected and plotted on the graph.
- The current term structure of implied volatilities was then superimposed on the chart.

What is the rationale for this approach? Tompkins (1994) argues:

....when evaluating the volatility input into an options pricing model, it would be fairly safe to say that this input would probably not exceed the highest actual volatility that had occurred over a comparable time period in the past or be below the lowest actual volatility that had ever occurred.

Figure 6.35 shows that as the maturity of the option increases the difference between the highest and lowest realized volatilities narrows. This would confirm the idea suggested earlier that shorter-dated volatility is more volatile higher than longer-dated volatility. The average realized volatility for each maturity over this sample period is about 11 % and perhaps the fact that this average is quite flat across all maturities is further confirmation of mean reversion.

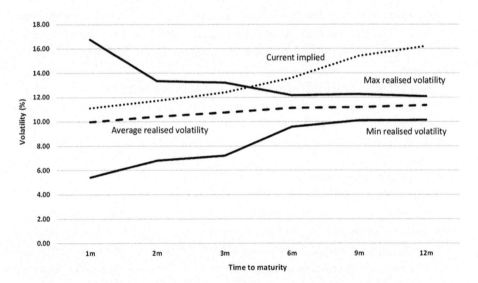

Fig. 6.35 Volatility cone for S&P 500 index options. Data as of 28th July 2014 (*Source*: Barclays Live)

Notice that the current term structure of implied volatility sits outside the maximum boundary for realized volatility. This could perhaps be an indication that longer-dated implied volatility may be trading above some notion of fair value and that it may revert to a lower level, even though it is still below the long-term value of 19.46 %.

6.5.2 Correlation

Figures 6.36 and 6.37 show the path of implied and realized correlation since 1996, respectively. The long-term average values are 0.47 (implied) and 0.37 (realized), indicating that similar to volatility, implied correlation trades higher than realized.

Figure 6.38 adapts the concept of the volatility cone and applies it to correlation. The figure charts realized correlation for a variety of maturities charting the maximum, minimum and average values. Overlaid on the diagram is the current term structure of implied correlation, which similar to implied volatility suggests that perhaps longer-dated implied correlation may revert to lower levels.

6.6   Conclusion

Two popular market factors traded in the equity derivatives market are implied volatility and correlation. An understanding of how these variables move provides a solid foundation for the construction of hedging and trading strategies.

The chapter started off with a short statistics refresher which focused on how these measures are defined and interpreted. The two measures were then linked by means of modern portfolio theory as well as the demand and supply characteristics of single-stock and index implied volatility. This illustrated that due to the effects of correlation, index volatility should trade lower than average single-stock volatility.

Section 6.4 considered some of the characteristics of volatility and correlation. Although the original option valuation framework assumed that volatility was constant it was highlighted that there is no empirical support for this assumption. For example, implied volatility displays not only a term structure but will also vary according to strike. These two characteristics taken together give rise to the concept of the volatility surface. A similar analysis was performed with respect to correlation looking at how this the metric moved in

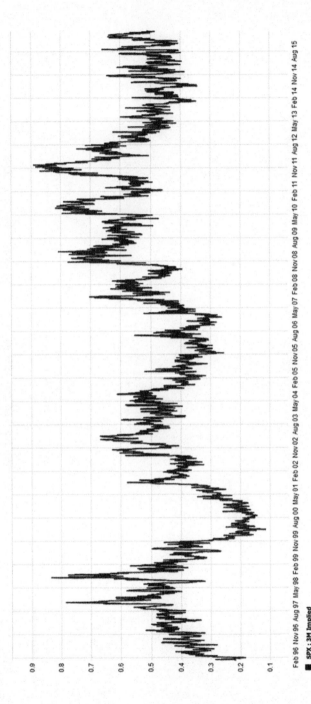

Fig. 6.36   S&P 500 index implied correlation. March 1996–March 2016 (*Source*: Barclays Live)

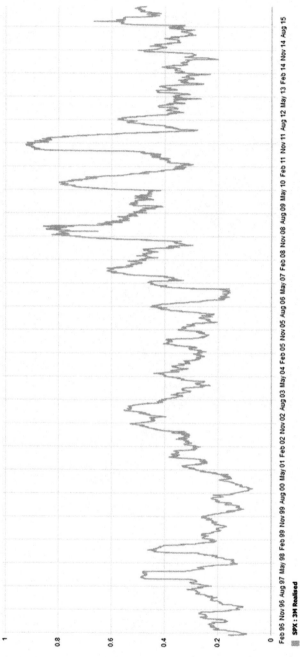

Fig. 6.37 S&P 500 index realized correlation. March 1996–March 2016 (*Source:* Barclays Live)

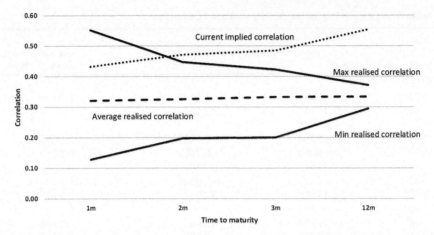

Fig. 6.38 Correlation cone for S&P 500. Data as of 28 July 2014 (*Source*: Barclays Live)

relation to such factors as the absolute level of the cash market and implied volatility.

The final section of the chapter considered a number of general principles that are used by practitioners to identify if volatility is fairly valued.

6.7   Appendix 1

6.7.1   Calculating Variance, Standard Deviations ('Volatility'), Covariance and Correlation

This appendix provides a short review of how measures of dispersion and association are calculated.

6.7.1.1   Calculating Variance and Standard Deviation ('Volatility')

Variance is often used in finance to describe risk and uncertainty and within the context of this book its most obvious use is variance swaps. Standard deviation/volatility is commonly used within an option valuation framework. Table 6.5 shows how variance and the standard deviation are calculated.

Table 6.5 Calculating variance and standard deviation

FTSE 100 levels	Continuously compounded returns (%)	Returns minus mean (%)	(Returns minus mean)² (%)
5966			
5903	−1.0616	−1.0182	0.0104
6130	3.7734	3.8168	0.1457
6003	−2.0935	−2.0501	0.0420
5953	−0.8364	−0.7930	0.0063
5905	−0.8096	−0.7662	0.0059
5945	0.6751	0.7185	0.0052
5823	−2.0735	−2.0301	0.0412
6007	3.1110	3.1544	0.0995
5809	−3.3517	−3.3083	0.1094
6058	4.1971	4.2405	0.1798
5824	−3.9392	−3.8958	0.1518
5864	0.6845	0.7279	0.0053
6019	2.6089	2.6523	0.0703
5925	−1.5740	−1.5306	0.0234
6093	2.7960	2.8394	0.0806
5848	−4.1041	−4.0607	0.1649
6108	4.3500	4.3934	0.1930
6055	−0.8715	−0.8281	0.0069
5917	−2.3055	−2.2621	0.0512
Sum	−0.8246	0.0000	1.3928
Mean	−0.0434		Variance 0.0774
		Standard deviation	2.7821

The first column shows 20 hypothetical closing prices for the FTSE 100 index. The second column calculates 19 daily returns. Rather than using the 'traditional' method of calculating returns $((P_{t+1}/P_t)-1)$ the calculation is performed using logarithms. The returns are therefore calculated as $\ln(P_{t+1}/P_t)$. In the same column these returns are summed and the mean is calculated.

Column 3 considers how clustered these returns are around the mean. If they are widely dispersed around the mean the difference between any individual return and the mean would be large. If they are tightly clustered around the mean the difference between the individual return and the mean would be small. Since the sum of the deviations will always be zero, the individual values in column 3 are squared and shown in column 4. These values are then summed and then divided by $n-1$, which in this case is 18, to return the variance which is expressed as squared units of the underlying making this result a 'squared percentage', which is not immediately intuitive.

Taking the square root of the variance returns the standard deviation, which is shown at the bottom of the fourth column. By convention in financial markets, volatility is measured as one standard deviation. This figure could then be converted into an annualized equivalent using the principles outlined in Sect. 6.2.1.

6.7.1.2 Calculating Covariance and Correlation

Covariance indicates how two random variables behave in relation to each other. This is often converted into a correlation coefficient which is a unit-free measure of the strength and direction of a linear relationship between two variables.

An example of how these metrics could be calculated is shown in Table 6.6, which uses hypothetical values from the FTSE 100 and S&P 500. Columns 1 and 2 are identical to those shown in Table 6.5. The third and fourth columns show the index values for the S&P 500 and their returns, respectively. The

Table 6.6 Calculating covariance and correlation

FTSE 100 returns	FTSE continuously compounded returns (%)	S&P 500 levels	S&P 500 continuously compounded returns (%)	FTSE returns minus mean (%)	S&P returns minus means (%)	FTSE*S&P (%)
5966		1987				
5903	−1.0616	1951	−1.8284	−1.0182	−1.9177	0.0195
6130	3.7734	2074	6.1137	3.8168	6.0244	0.2299
6003	−2.0935	2026	−2.3416	−2.0501	−2.4309	0.0498
5953	−0.8364	2038	0.5906	−0.7930	0.5013	−0.0040
5905	−0.8096	1989	−2.4337	−0.7662	−2.5230	0.0193
5945	0.6751	1927	−3.1668	0.7185	−3.2561	−0.0234
5823	−2.0735	1904	−1.2007	−2.0301	−1.2900	0.0262
6007	3.1110	1950	2.3872	3.1544	2.2979	0.0725
5809	−3.3517	1971	1.0712	−3.3083	0.9819	−0.0325
6058	4.1971	2009	1.9096	4.2405	1.8203	0.0772
5824	−3.9392	1973	−1.8082	−3.8958	−1.8975	0.0739
5864	0.6845	2099	6.1906	0.7279	6.1013	0.0444
6019	2.6089	1912	−9.3311	2.6523	−9.4204	−0.2499
5925	−1.5740	1982	3.5957	−1.5306	3.5064	−0.0537
6093	2.7960	1931	−2.6068	2.8394	−2.6961	−0.0766
5848	−4.1041	2044	5.6871	−4.0607	5.5978	−0.2273
6108	4.3500	1986	−2.8786	4.3934	−2.9679	−0.1304
6055	−0.8715	2097	5.4385	−0.8281	5.3492	−0.0443
5917	−2.3055	2021	−3.6915	−2.2621	−3.7808	0.0855
Sum	−0.8246		1.6968	Sum		−0.1439
				Covariance		−0.0080
Mean	−0.0434		0.0893	Correlation		−6.97

fifth and sixth columns measure the extent to which these values are clustered around the mean. Column 7 is the product of columns 5 and 6. Column 7 is then summed and divided by $n-1$ to give a covariance of -0.0080 %.

The correlation coefficient, ρ, is calculated by dividing the covariance by the product of the standard deviations of the two underlying assets. The standard deviation for the FTSE 100 was 2.7821 % and was 4.1267 % for the S&P 500[10]. This returns a value of -0.0697 or -6.97 %.

6.8   Appendix 2

6.8.1 Calculating Forward Volatility

Forward volatility is an implied volatility quote, whose value is known today but applies to a future time period. The formula is:

$$\text{Forward vol} = \sqrt{\frac{\text{vol}_2^2 \times T_2 - \text{vol}_1^2 \times T_1}{(T_2 - T_1)}}$$

T_1 (in years) = Shorter option maturity
T_2 (in years) = Longer option maturity
Vol_1 = Implied volatility for an option that matures at T_1
Vol_2 = Implied volatility for an option that matures at T_2

What is the 1-year forward, 3-month forward implied volatility given the following parameters?

$T_1 = 1$ year
$T_2 = 1.25$ years
$\text{Vol}_1 = 13.50$ %
$\text{Vol}_2 = 13.70$ %

$$14.47\% = \sqrt{\frac{13.7\% \times 1.25 - 13.5\% \times 1}{(1.25 - 1.00)}}$$

---

[10] The calculation of the S&P 500 standard deviation is not shown.

7

Barrier and Binary Options

7.1 Introduction

Chapter 1 provided a brief explanation of two popular exotic options, barriers and binaries—but what is an exotic option? There is no accepted definition but broadly speaking, it can be thought of as an option whose payoff is different from a vanilla, non-exotic option, for example, a payoff that is different from those shown in Fig. 1.4.

Detailed pricing of these options is not covered as it has been extensively documented elsewhere (e.g. De Weert 2008 or Marroni and Perdomo 2014) but for the sake of completeness, valuation principles are covered in an intuitive manner. In addition, the chapter considers the various market risk exposures of each of these options, that is, their respective Greeks.

7.2 Barrier Options

7.2.1 Features of Barrier Options

Barrier options are European-style options where an extra element of conditionality influences the final payout. The extra condition relates to a barrier price, which, if breached, will result in the option either being activated or deactivated. This barrier is sometimes referred to as either the 'outstrike' or 'instrike'.

Figure 7.1 illustrates a full taxonomy of barrier options. The first level differentiates between regular and reverse barriers. This category relates to the placement of the barrier relative to the current spot price. Regular barrier

© The Author(s) 2017
N. Schofield, *Equity Derivatives*, DOI 10.1057/978-0-230-39107-9_7

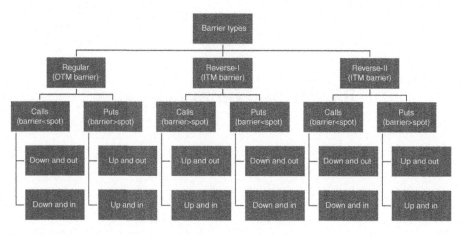

Fig. 7.1 Taxonomy of barrier options (*Source*: author)

options have an OTM barrier, that is, the barrier is placed in a region where a conventional option would not be exercised. For call options the barrier is below the spot price, but for put options, it will be above the spot price. The first category of reverse barriers (reverse—I in Fig. 7.1) have the barrier placed ITM region, that is, the barrier is set above the spot price for a call option and below spot for a put option meaning the option knocks in or out when the spot rate moves past the strike becoming more ITM.

The lower part of Fig. 7.1 indicates what will happen to the option if the barrier is breached. The option will either be activated ('knocked in') or will be deactivated ('knocked out'). From this, the market has adopted a series of shorthand phrases to describe the nature of the barrier option. So a regular knock in call option with the barrier set below the spot is termed a 'down and in', that is, the spot price has to fall past the barrier for the option to be activated.

There is one apparent inconsistency that arises from Fig. 7.1 and relates to the second category of reverse barrier options (reverse—II in Fig. 7.1). The placement of the barrier appears to be contradictory to what has just been described and so this type of option is best understood in terms of the position that results if the option is activated. Although the diagram seems to suggest that they have similar properties to regular barrier options, consider the following example of a down and in call option.

Regular	Reverse
Spot = 100	Spot = 100
Strike = 95	Barrier = 95
Barrier = 90	Strike = 90

The holder of the regular down and in call has the right to buy at 95 if the spot price falls to 90. If this price movement did occur, the holder would now own a European-style call option which would be 5 units OTM. In the case of the reverse down and in call option the holder will be granted the right to buy at 90 if the asset trades at a price of 95, which means they would be in possession of a European-style call option which is 5 units ITM. Looked at in this way the regular knock in call yields an OTM option, while the reverse knock in call returns an ITM position.

Bennett and Gil (2012) point out that put barriers are three to four times more popular than call barriers. This is due to the fact that down and in puts are often embedded within structured products such as reverse convertibles, while down and out puts are an inexpensive way of obtaining cheap protection.

Barrier Monitoring

Typically, the movement of spot is monitored on an ongoing basis[1] by one of the parties. This is why the option is referred to as being 'path dependent'— whether the option will be knocked in or out will depend on how the spot price evolves over the life of the transaction.

There are a number of issues that relate to the monitoring of the barrier.

- Which party should be responsible for determining if spot has hit the barrier?
  - This will be outlined in the confirmation and will usually be the market maker.
- How does one know for sure that a barrier has traded?
  - There is no real solution to this but one possible solution is to use third party evidence such as confirmation from a broker.
- How do the participants know if the price was just quoted by the market against whether it was actually traded?
  - Again, third party confirmation may be useful.
- Even if spot has traded through the barrier, is there a minimum amount that is acceptable?
  - There are a number of different opinions in this respect:

    - The size of the trade should be pro rata—for example, $2 m cash trade knocks in/out a $2 m barrier trade.
    - Only 'commercially sized' transactions activate the barrier.

---

[1] Sometimes referred to casually as an American barrier.

- Any trade size will qualify.
- Parties agree to the trade size in the confirmation

- What is stopping banks from pushing the spot price through or away from the barrier?
  - This is in effect market manipulation which is illegal but is typically very difficult to prove.

7.2.2 Valuation of Barrier Options

This section illustrates the intuition that sits behind the pricing of barrier options. Those readers interested in a more rigorous formula-based approach are referred to other texts such as Haug (2007).

Compared to vanilla options, a barrier option with the same parameters (i.e. strike, maturity, notional) will have a lower premium. To understand this argument, it is useful to note that the valuation of any option could be looked at from two perspectives:

- From the buyer's perspective the option price is the expected payout of the option.
- From the seller's perspective the option price is the expected cost of hedging the exposure.

At a simple level, the holder of a knock out option could lose the position before expiration while for the knock in, the option may never be activated. From the buyer's perspective this suggests that they will own an option whose payout will either be equal to or less than a vanilla equivalent.

To illustrate the main principles of barrier valuation the following regular barrier call options will be used in the analysis that follows.[2] Table 7.1 shows the premium of the barrier options as well as that of a comparable European equivalent.

Position of the Barrier to Current Spot Level
The value of a 'down and in' call option for a variety of barrier levels is shown in the second column of Table 7.2. If the barrier is moved further away from the current spot price of 100, the probability of the option being activated ('knocked in') diminishes and so the value of the option falls. If the barrier was set equal to

---

[2] Although not explicitly covered, the principles will apply to regular barrier put options as well as reverse barriers.

Table 7.1 Parameters of regular knock in and out call options

Type of option	Knock in call	Knock out call
Spot	100	100
Strike	100	100
Barrier	90	90
Expiry	1 year	1 year
Carry[3]	0 %	0 %
Implied volatility	20 %	20 %
Premium	1.47	6.34
Vanilla European premium	7.81	7.81

Table 7.2 How the position of the option barrier relative to the spot price impacts the value of knock in and knock out call options. Spot price assumed to be 100

Barrier	Price of knock in call	Price of knock out call
100	7.81	0.00
95	3.79	4.02
90	1.47	6.34
85	0.43	7.38
80	0.09	7.72
75	0.01	7.80

the current spot price, then as soon as it is traded the option would immediately be activated and would become a conventional vanilla option. At this level of spot the price of the barrier would be equal to that of an equivalent vanilla option.

For the knock out call option the opposite is true. The more distant the barrier from the spot price the less likely the option will be deactivated ('knocked out'). Notice that at a barrier level of 75 with a spot level of 100, the chances of the option being knocked out are very slim; for all intents and purposes this is indistinguishable from a regular European option and so trades very close to this value.

The Impact of Remaining Time to Maturity

Table 7.3 shows how the value of the two barrier call options and a vanilla call option vary with respect to the passage of time.

To interpret Table 7.3 consider the scenario where the options have 0.2 of a year to run. Like vanilla options, barrier options will decay in value with respect to the passage of time. By this time the price of a knock out option has nearly converged with that of the vanilla equivalent indicating that under current market conditions there is only a small chance of the option being

[3] Carry is defined as the net of the income received from the share's dividend plus any fees earned from lending the security less the interest expense incurred from funding an assumed long position.

Table 7.3 How the passage of time impacts the value of a knock in and knock out call option

Option maturity (in years)	Price of knock in call	Price of knock out call	Price of vanilla call
1.0	1.47	6.34	7.81
0.8	1.03	5.98	7.01
0.6	0.61	5.49	6.10
0.4	0.25	4.75	5.00
0.2	0.03	3.53	3.56
0.0	0.00	0.00	0.00

knocked out. From this it could be concluded that the passage of time makes it less likely a knock out option will be terminated and less likely that a knock in option will be activated, all other things being equal.

The Impact of Implied Volatility

Table 7.4 shows the value of the two barrier options and the vanilla call at different levels of implied volatility.

At relatively low levels of implied volatility the probability of the knock in being activated and the knock out being deactivated are relatively low. This suggests that the knock in is virtually worthless but the knock out trades at virtually the same price as the vanilla call.

The price of the knock out call increases as implied volatility increases but at a slower rate. The increase in implied volatility increases the probability that the option will become more profitable but also increases the probability that the spot price will fall resulting in the deactivation of the position.

Barriers with Rebates

It is also possible to structure barrier options with rebates. Consider again the parameters of the two regular barrier call options in Table 7.1. Suppose that the knock in call option is sold with a 5-unit rebate that would only be paid if the option is never activated. This increases the premium from 1.47 to 3.28. Alternatively, the knock out call could include a 5-unit rebate, payable if the position is terminated. This also increases the premium (since the seller is faced with the possibility of paying the rebate) from 6.34 to 9.47.

Table 7.4 The impact of different levels of implied volatility on barrier and vanilla options

Implied volatility (%)	Price of knock in	Price of knock out	Price of a vanilla call
5	0.000013	1.95	1.95
10	0.06	3.85	3.91
15	0.53	5.33	5.86
20	1.47	6.34	7.81
25	2.72	7.03	9.75
30	4.16	7.53	11.69

7.2.3 Risk Management of Regular Barrier Call Options

The following examples are based on the options outlined in Table 7.1.

7.2.3.1 Regular Knock in Call Option

For the knock in call option the holder of the option is granted an option contract which will only be activated if the spot price falls to 90. At this point the holder would now own a European-style call option that is indistinguishable from an equivalent vanilla structure. However, at a price of 90 a call option with a strike of 100 is OTM and so spot would have to increase back towards the strike price for the option to be exercised.

Figure 7.2 shows the value of the regular knock out call (i.e. down and in) outlined in Table 7.1, prior to maturity.

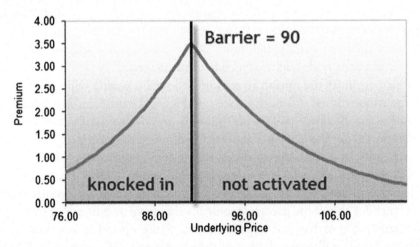

Fig. 7.2 Value of 'down and in' call option prior to maturity. Initial spot 100, strike 100, barrier 90 (*Source*: author)

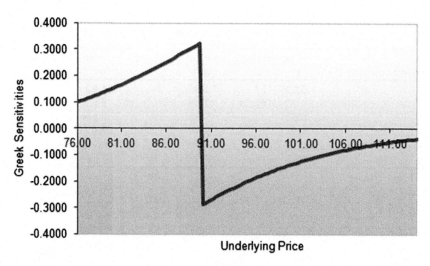

Fig. 7.3 Delta of the down and in call option. Initial spot 100, strike 100, barrier 90 (*Source*: author)

If the barrier is activated, then the holder takes possession of a European-style call option, whose value will resemble that of a vanilla equivalent with the same parameters. This is why the left hand side of Fig. 7.2 has the same shape as Fig. 4.5. Indeed, once the barrier is activated the value of the option will behave in the same manner as a vanilla call and the profile will resemble those shown in Figs. 1.4 and 4.5 depending on the residual maturity. The right hand side of Fig. 7.2 shows that as the spot price rises, the value of the option falls as it becomes increasingly unlikely that the barrier will be activated. Consider the delta of this option (Fig. 7.3). Again the diagram illustrates the delta of the option if the barrier trades (left hand side of the diagram) and the delta if the barrier does not trade (right hand side of the diagram).

Once again, if the option is activated the delta profile will resemble that of the conventional call option (see e.g. Figs. 5.2 and 5.3). But notice that the delta for the down and in call option is negative for spot prices above 90, when the barrier has not been activated. Following on from Fig. 7.2 when the barrier price has not traded, a rise in the underlying price is associated with a fall in the premium, which is a negative relationship. In this case at very high prices the option is OTM and so the option's delta will tend towards zero.

Figure 7.4 shows the gamma profile for the down and in call option, when the barrier has or has not been activated. If the option is knocked in, the gamma profile will resemble that of the regular call option (see Fig. 5.5) and

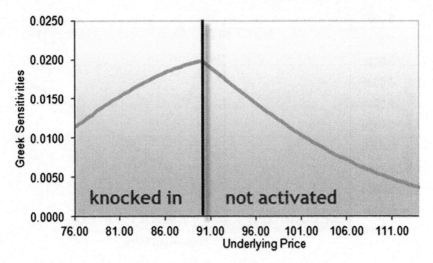

Fig. 7.4 The gamma for a down and in call option. Initial spot 100, strike 100, barrier 90 (*Source*: author)

this is the area to the left of the barrier in Fig. 7.4. If the barrier is not activated, then gamma will fall as the price rises. Although the option's delta is negative at this point, it is increasing (i.e. becoming less negative) with respect to price and so gamma is positive. However, the slope of delta is tending towards zero and as such gamma will also fall towards the same value.

Again similar to gamma, the theta profile when the option is knocked in will be that of a vanilla European call option (see Figs. 5.9 and 5.10). Figure 7.5 shows that the option position is less sensitive to the passage of time at high underlying prices where the barrier has not been activated.

The behaviour of vega (Fig. 7.6) follows the same principles as those discussed so far. If the option is knocked in, the profile will resemble that of the vanilla European call option (i.e. the area to the left of the barrier). To the right of the barrier the probability of the spot price hitting the barrier declines and so the option becomes less sensitive to changes in implied volatility.

7.2.3.2   Regular Knock Out Call Option

For the knock out option the holder starts with a European-style option but this contract will be terminated if the spot price falls beyond the barrier (Fig. 7.7).

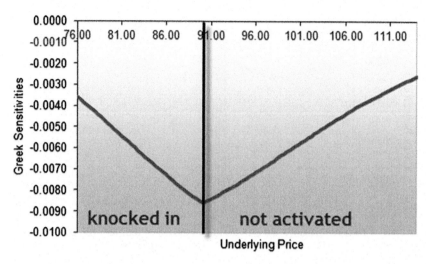

Fig. 7.5 Theta profile for down and in call. Initial spot 100, strike 100, barrier 90 (*Source*: author)

In this case though, one might consider this as an example of a 'benign' barrier. A conventional call option will offer protection against a movement in the underlying price above the strike rate. But a fall in the underlying price would reduce the need for the option. If the option has a barrier which deactivates the position if the price falls this may not be a bad thing as the holder can now buy the asset at a lower price in the market. However, if the

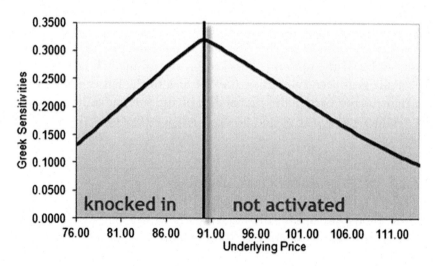

Fig. 7.6 Vega profile for down and in call option. Initial spot 100, strike 100, barrier 90 (*Source*: author)

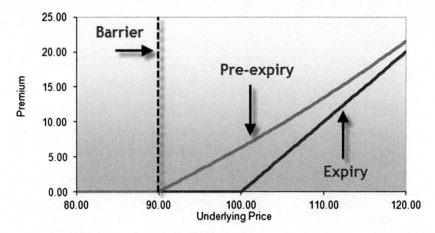

Fig. 7.7 Payoff profile of down and out call option. Initial spot 100, strike 100, barrier 90 (*Source*: author)

spot price were suddenly to spike upwards there is no longer any protection in place.

The Greeks associated with the down and out barrier options are relatively straightforward since as long as the option is active they will have the same characteristics as those of a non-barrier equivalent. However, if the barrier trades the option will terminate and so the option Greeks will take a value of zero. The main option Greeks are shown in Figs. 7.8 (delta), 7.9 (gamma), 7.10 (theta) and 7.11 (vega).

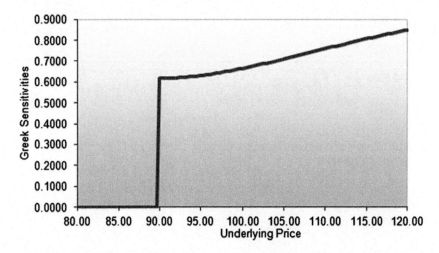

Fig. 7.8 Delta of a down and out call option with a barrier of 90 and a strike of 100 (*Source*: author)

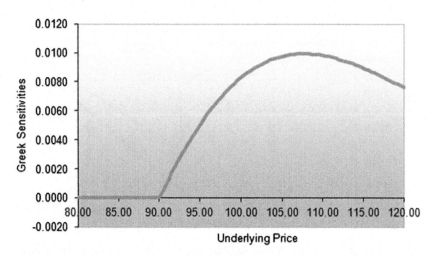

Fig. 7.9 Gamma of a down and out call option with a barrier of 90 and a strike of 100 (*Source*: author)

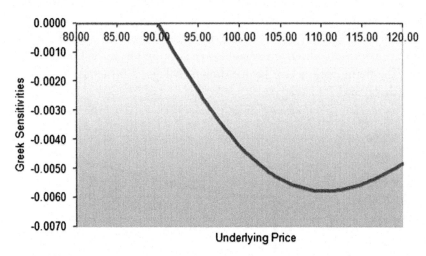

Fig. 7.10 Theta of a down and out call option with a barrier of 90 and a strike of 100 (*Source*: author)

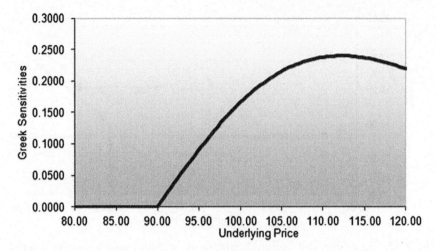

Fig. 7.11 Vega of a down and out call option with a barrier of 90 and a strike of 100 (*Source*: author)

7.2.4 Risk Management of Reverse Barrier Call Options—I

This section will focus on two stylized reverse barrier call options, the parameters of which are shown in Table 7.5. The general characteristic of this type of reverse structure is that the barrier is placed in the ITM region, which for a call option means the barrier would be placed above the spot price.

7.2.4.1 Reverse Knock in Call Option—I

In the case of a reverse knock in call, the holder of the option will be granted a 100 strike option if a price of 110 trades (Fig. 7.12). This means that the option position is 'born' with 10 units of intrinsic value plus some element of

Table 7.5 Parameters of reverse barrier call options

Type of option	Knock in call	Knock out call
Spot	100	100
Strike	100	100
Barrier	110	110
Expiry	1 year	1 year
Carry	0 %	0 %
Implied volatility	20.00 %	20.00 %
Premium	7.69	0.12
Vanilla European premium	7.81	7.81

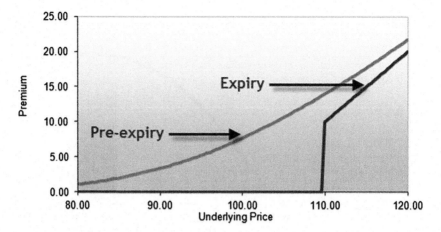

Fig. 7.12 Up and in call option. Premium vs. underlying price; strike price 100, barrier 110 (*Source*: author)

time value. So even if the spot price moves a little way beyond the 100 strike the option is still considered to OTM as it has not been activated.

The delta for the up and in call is shown in Fig. 7.13. The profile of delta is in one sense intuitive because the payoff profile shows that as the price of the underlying asset increases so does the premium on the option. This means that delta will be positive and will slope upwards in a similar fashion to the delta of a vanilla option. Observant readers may notice a small 'kink' on the delta profile around the level of the barrier. To the right of the barrier,

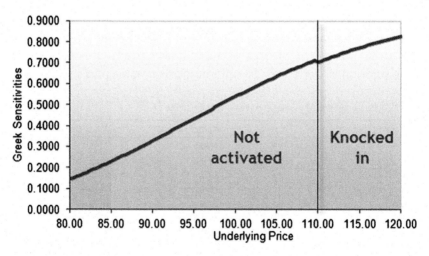

Fig. 7.13 Delta profile of an up and in call option. Strike price 100, barrier 110 (*Source*: author)

the delta profile will be that of an ITM option, while to the left of this value the profile will be that of a barrier option that has not been activated. For example, if the barrier has not been breached then the delta for an OTM barrier at a spot price of 109 (all other factors being equal) is 70.12 %. However, the barrier for a vanilla option with the same parameters would have a delta value of 68.83 %.

The comments made with respect to the delta profile apply to the option's other risk management profiles shown in Figs. 7.14 (gamma), 7.15 (theta) and 7.16 (vega). Once the option is activated, the profiles will resemble that of an ITM call option. However, at this level of spot the various risk management values will be relatively low with the exception of delta.

7.2.4.2   Reverse Knock Out Call Option—I

The next profile to consider is the up and out call option.[4] In this case the holder starts with a vanilla option with a barrier set above the spot rate, which means that the expiry payout will be limited to the difference between the strike price and the barrier. So in this example, the intrinsic value of the option at expiry cannot exceed 10 units (Figs. 7.17 and 7.18).

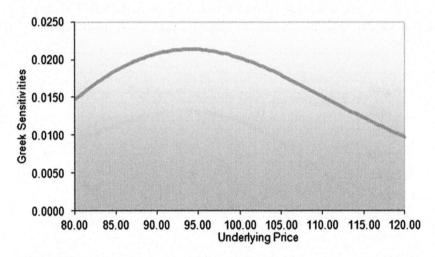

Fig. 7.14 Gamma profile of an up and in call option Strike price 100, barrier 110 (*Source*: author)

---

[4] In the up and out call option examples the profiles shown in Figs. 7.17, 7.18, 7.19, 7.20, 7.21 and 7.21 were drawn for the option with only 3 months to expiry. This was done for purely aesthetic purposes and does not substantially alter the key learning points.

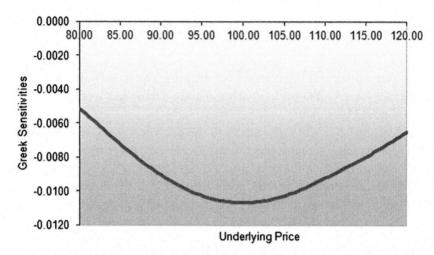

Fig. 7.15 The theta value of an up and in call option. Strike price 100, barrier 110 (*Source*: author)

In this case the profile shows that the delta for this long call position can be either positive or negative depending on the level of the spot price. When the spot price is relatively low the option is OTM and delta will behave as per a regular non-barrier option. However, as the spot price rises, the chances that the barrier will trade increases and as a result the value of the option will gradually fall. As a result, a rising spot price will be associated with a

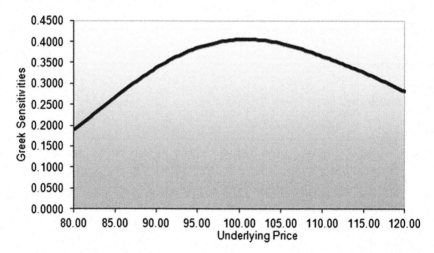

Fig. 7.16 The vega value of an up and in call option. Strike price 100, barrier 110 (*Source*: author)

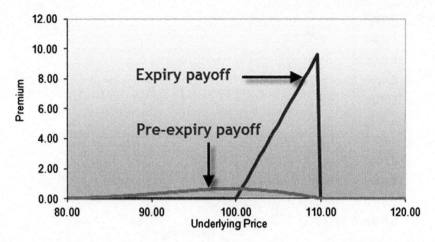

Fig. 7.17 Payoff diagram of spot price vs. premium for up and out call option (*Source*: author)

falling premium and so the delta will turn negative. Once the barrier trades the option is knocked out and so delta will take a value of zero.

The gamma profile of the option is shown in Fig. 7.19. At low spot prices delta increases as the spot price increases and so gamma is positive. As spot moves towards the barrier delta eventually starts to fall towards zero and so gamma will turn negative and then also tend towards zero as the probability of being knocked out increases.

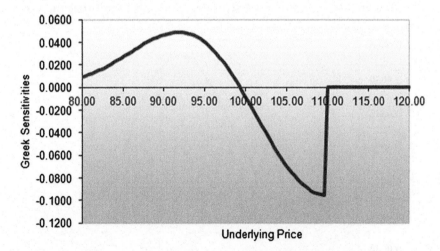

Fig. 7.18 The delta profile for an up and out call option. Strike price 100, barrier 110 (*Source*: author)

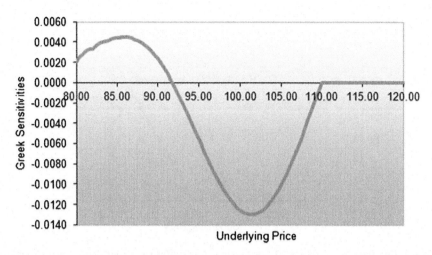

Fig. 7.19 Gamma exposure of the up and out call option. Strike price 100, barrier 110 (*Source*: author)

The theta profile for the long up and out call option does not conform to the vanilla European profile shown in Figs. 5.9 and 5.10. In order to interpret Fig. 7.20, the concept of theta in this context, consider the following two examples. Suppose that the underlying spot price is at 90 (i.e. the call option is OTM) and that the barrier has not traded. At this level of spot with 3 months to go until maturity the option is worth 0.16 and since it is OTM then it will fall in value with respect to the passage of time (all other things being equal). Now consider the situation where the spot price is at 105. Since spot is now moving towards the barrier Fig. 7.17 illustrates that the value of

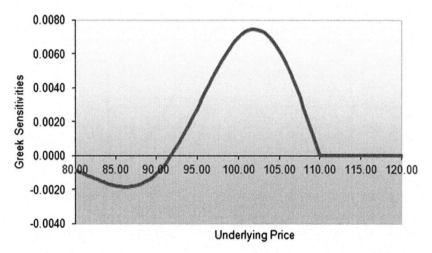

Fig. 7.20 Theta profile for long up and out call option. Strike price 100, barrier 110 (*Source*: author)

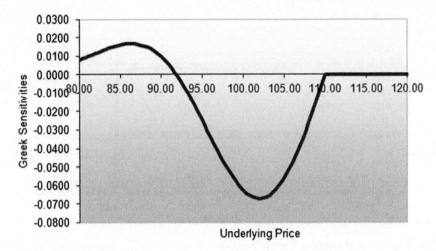

Fig. 7.21 Vega profile of up and out call option. Strike price 100, barrier 110 (*Source*: author)

the option is being pulled downwards as it is more likely the option will be knocked out. Indeed, with 1 year to go to expiry, the option at this level of spot will be valued at 0.06. However, if the price remains at 105 then eventually (again all other things being equal) the option will expire with 5 units of intrinsic value. This means that the passage of time will have a beneficial effect on the value of the option and so theta is positive.

Figure 7.21 illustrates the vega profile of the up and out call option. At very low prices an increase in implied volatility will increase the value of the option. However, as the spot price rises, increases in implied volatility will have a negative impact on the barrier option as it increases the probability that the option will be terminated. So, whereas a long vanilla call option will be vega positive the up and out call option will be vega positive at low prices but vega negative as the spot price approaches the barrier.

7.2.4.3 Barrier/Exit Risk

One of the interesting features of the up and out call option is the behaviour of delta as it approaches expiry and where the spot price is close to the barrier. Figure 7.22 shows the option's payoff profiles and Fig. 7.23 the associated delta profile under these conditions.

Note the value of delta as spot moves closer to the barrier. With a few days to go before expiry the delta value takes a maximum value of −267 %. This is due to the fact that the pre-expiry payoff steepens considerably as spot approaches the barrier (Fig. 7.22). So the concept that delta could not exceed

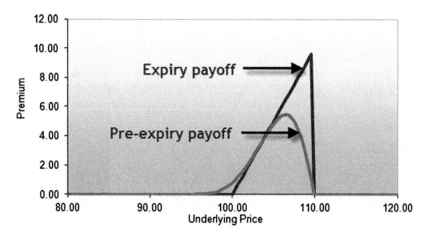

Fig. 7.22 Payoff profiles for up and out call option close to and at expiry. Strike 100, barrier 110 (*Source*: author)

+/−100 % clearly no longer applies. This has important considerations for a trader who is attempting to delta hedge the position. Under these market conditions the long up and out call behaves as if the trader is short 267 % of the underlying asset and so the appropriate delta hedge would be a purchase of the same amount. However, if the barrier is suddenly breached the trader is left with a long hedge position but no underlying option. In this case this is not a bad thing as he is long the underlying asset in a rising market. A simi-

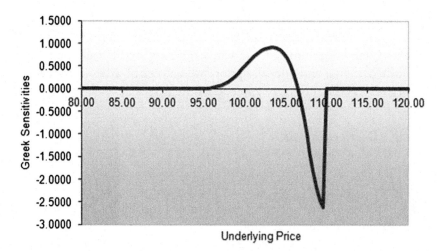

Fig. 7.23 The delta of an up and out call option close to expiry. Strike 100, barrier 110 (*Source*: author)

lar situation will occur where the trader is short a down and out put option. Consider the following scenario:

Spot price	91.00
Strike price	100.00
Barrier	90.00
Expiry	2 days
Carry	0 %
Implied volatility	20 %

In this example, the trader's option position will be delta negative (-348 %) and so the appropriate delta hedge will be a long position which will be almost 3.5 times the option's notional amount. If the option is then knocked out the trader will be forced to sell the hedge into a falling market, meaning they could incur a significant loss. De Weert (2008) uses the concept of the 'barrier shift', which is a technique used to manage this type of 'exit risk'. Consider the issue of hedging a long down and in barrier put option[5] with the following parameters:

Spot price:	90.50
Strike price:	100.00
Barrier:	90.00
Expiry:	1 week
Carry:	0 %
Implied volatility:	20 %

The position is shown in Fig. 7.24.

The option's delta is -308 % meaning that the trader must be long 308 % of the transaction's notional in order to remain delta neutral. If the spot price goes through the barrier the trader is now long a short-dated ITM option, whose delta is close to -100 %. They would need to sell a large amount of their existing delta hedge, which in a falling market would result in a loss. The trader knows in advance there is a possibility that they could be faced with this situation and so the terms of the trade quoted to the client may well be different from what he chooses to risk manage on the bank's systems. For example, the trader could agree a contractual barrier of 90 with the client but choose to price and risk manage a barrier placed at, say, 88.00. At a spot price of 90.50 the delta of the 1 week long put position with a barrier at 88 is -230 % and if the 90.00 barrier confirmed to the client is hit, the delta of the risk-managed position moves to -277 %. At this point the trader is still risk managing a live option position although the contractual commitment with

---

[5] This position would be representative of an institution that has structured a reverse convertible bond (see Chap. 12).

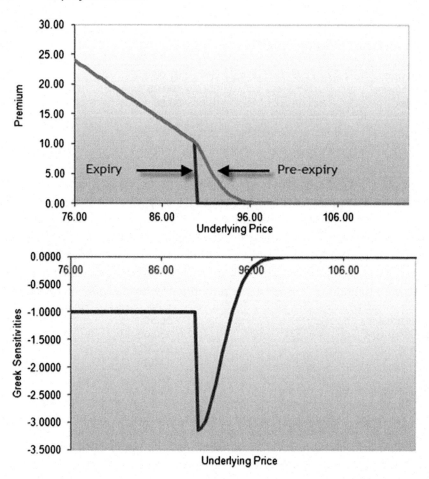

Fig. 7.24 The pre- and post-expiry values of a down and in put option (upper diagram) with associated delta profile (lower diagram) (*Source*: author)

the client has now ended. If the market is trending lower, it is unlikely to stop at a level of 90.00. So it is more likely that the trader would have to close out his delta hedge at a lower level, hence the lower risk-managed barrier. This technique should allow the trader to unwind the hedge with less pain than a position with a higher barrier as the position requires a smaller delta hedge.

How would this option have been priced at inception? Suppose the following market parameters existed at the start of the trade:

Spot price	110
Strike price	100
Barrier	90
Maturity	1 year
Carry	0 %
Implied volatility	20 %
Delta	−27.78 %

The cost of the option with these characteristics is 3.97 but the same option with a barrier at 88.00 would cost 3.80 and have a delta of −27.51 %. The transaction would be confirmed with the client as having a contractual barrier of 90.00 and the trader would charge a premium based on this level (i.e. 3.97). However, the position would be revalued and hedged with a knock in barrier of 88.00. De Weert (2008) points out that there are four barrier options that have significant barrier risk, all of which are reverse structures:

- Down and in put
- Down and out put
- Up and in call
- Up and out call

It has been shown that a long down and in put option will have a large 'adverse' exist risk so it follows that it is possible to have 'favourable' exit risk; that is a movement in spot which will have a beneficial impact on the trader's delta-hedged position. It could be argued that 'favourable' exit risk occurs when the trader is long knock out options and short knock ins. 'Adverse' exit risk occurs when the trader is short knock outs and long knock ins and this is shown in Table 7.6 where it is assumed that the option position is close to expiry and that spot is trading close to the barrier.

Table 7.6 Examples of 'adverse' exit risk for four barrier options where the position is close to expiry and spot is trading near the barrier

Option type	Trader's option position	Underlying delta hedge	What happens if barrier is hit?	Impact on delta hedge
Down and in put	Long	Long more than 100 % of the underlying	Trader becomes long ITM put option whose delta is close to −100 %	Trader must sell part of delta hedge in falling market
Down and out put	Short	Long more than 100 % of the underlying	Trader's option position disappears	Trader closes out entire delta but is selling into a falling market
Up and in call	Long	Short more than 100 % of the underlying	Trader is long an ITM call option whose delta is close to +100 %	Trader must buy back part of short delta-hedged position in a rising market
Up and out call	Short	Short more than 100 % of the underlying	Trader's option position disappears	Trader must buy back entire delta hedge in a rising market

The reader should hopefully be able to develop their understanding of 'favourable' exit risk by using the same options but changing the original option position and the associated delta hedge.

De Weert (2008) argues that there are five factors that may influence the magnitude of the barrier shift:

- *The size of the transaction*—the larger the transaction the greater the potential loss on the delta hedge if the barrier is breached.
- *The difference between strike price and the barrier*—De Weert uses the example of a down and in put and points out that if the difference is large, the position could rapidly be transformed from having no option exposure to suddenly being a deeply ITM option. So the greater the distance between the strike and the barrier the greater the barrier shift.
- *The volatility of the underlying price*—if the asset displays considerable volatility there is a greater probability that the barrier will be breached resulting in a delta hedging loss. In this case the trader may decide that with greater volatility they will apply a larger barrier shift.
- *The absolute level of the barrier*—in Chap. 6 it was shown that there is an inverse relationship between the level of implied volatility and the absolute level of the market. If the trader has chosen a relatively low barrier, then as the spot price falls the asset will tend to become more volatile further increasing the likelihood that the barrier will be breached. So all other things being equal a lower absolute barrier level may require a greater barrier shift.
- *Remaining time to expiry*—in Figs. 7.22 and 7.23 it was shown that for an option where there is significant barrier risk, the delta of the option will increase if the spot price is trading close to the barrier. Since the value of delta will therefore now be quite large the risk of losing money on the delta hedge becomes more significant. Therefore, shorter-dated barrier options should be priced with a greater barrier shift than longer-dated options.

7.2.5 Risk Management of Reverse Barrier Call Options—II

The parameters of the second type of reverse barrier call options are shown in Table 7.7. In this second category the barrier is placed below the spot price but above the strike price.

Table 7.7 Parameters of two reverse barrier call options

Type of option	Knock in	Knock out
Spot	100	100
Strike	90	90
Barrier	95	95
Expiry	1 year	1 year
Carry	0 %	0 %
Implied volatility	20.00 %	20.00 %
Premium	7.52	5.80
Vanilla European premium	13.32	13.32

7.2.5.1   Reverse Knock in Call Options—II

Figure 7.25 shows the expiry and pre-expiry payoff profiles for the knock in call option.

Prior to expiry the option will remain deactivated as long as the spot price is above the barrier. In these conditions, if the spot price continues to increase the value of the call option will decline as the likelihood of exercise diminishes. However, if the spot price falls and hits the barrier the option holder is granted an ITM option whose payoff profiles will resemble that of the vanilla call option. Figure 7.25 only shows the payoff profile for the activated option below the barrier; as mentioned above, the barrier will resemble that of a vanilla European.

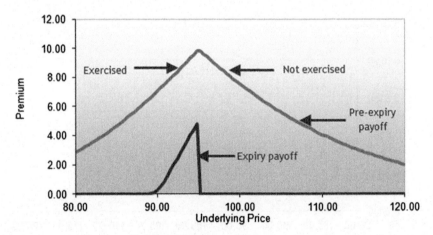

Fig. 7.25 Expiry and pre-expiry payoffs for a knock in call ('down and in'). Strike price 90, barrier 95 (*Source*: author)

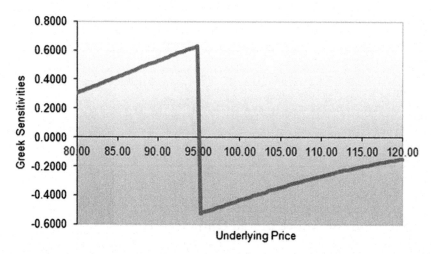

Fig. 7.26 Delta of down and in reverse barrier call option. Strike price 90, barrier 95 (*Source*: author)

The option's delta is shown in Fig. 7.26.

The figure illustrates that to the right of the barrier when the option has not been activated, the delta will be negative. This is because an increase in the spot price is associated with a decrease in the value of the position. To the left of the barrier the option is now activated and so the delta is positive and will possess the same properties as a vanilla European option with the same characteristics.

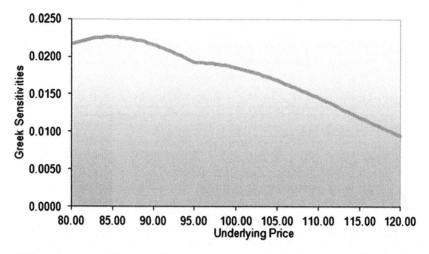

Fig. 7.27 Gamma of down and in reverse barrier call option. Strike price 90, barrier 95 (*Source*: author)

The option's gamma is shown in Fig. 7.27.

Note that above the barrier, there appears to be a kink in the gamma profile. Similar to the option's delta, values to the right of this point represent the gamma profile under the assumption that the barrier has not been hit. In these circumstances gamma is positive but decreasing. This can be traced back to the delta profile in Fig. 7.26; in these circumstances delta is increasing (becoming less negative) with respect to the underlying price. Once again, when the barrier is hit the gamma profile will take on the properties of a vanilla European call.

The theta profile is shown in Fig. 7.28.

Again the profile has a kink at the barrier indicating that to the right of this point the option has not been activated while to the left the option is now live. Referring back to the pre-expiry payoff diagram for this option in Fig. 7.25 it can be seen that if the spot price does not breach the barrier the option will fall in value. The magnitude of this fall will be greatest slightly beyond the barrier of 95. To the left of the barrier the fall in the value of the option will be less pronounced and its theta characteristics will resemble that of the vanilla European call.

The option's vega profile is shown in Fig. 7.29.

Again the profile's kink occurs at the level of the barrier. To the right of the option the holder of the down and in call option is vega positive. An increase in volatility increases the value of the option; however, the further away the spot price is from the barrier, the lower the impact. To the left of the barrier

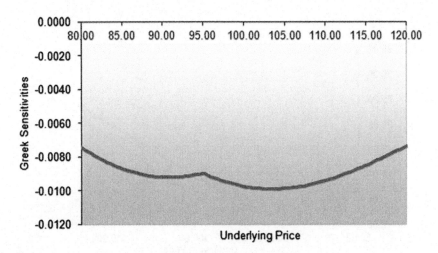

Fig. 7.28 Theta of down and in reverse barrier call option. Strike price 90, barrier 95 (*Source*: author)

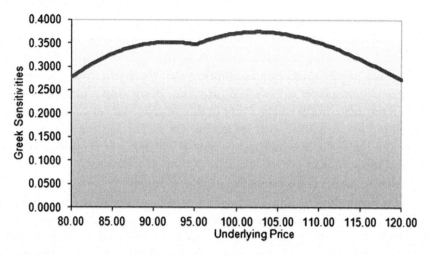

Fig. 7.29 Vega of down and in reverse barrier call option. Strike price 90, barrier 95 (*Source*: author)

where the barrier is activated, the vega profile is that of a regular European call option.

7.2.5.2 Reverse Knock Out Call Options—II

The final profile to consider is that of the 'down and out' call reverse barrier option. Figures 7.30 and 7.31 illustrate the pre-expiry and expiry payoffs of the option.

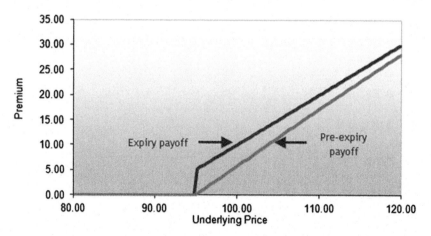

Fig. 7.30 Down and out call option. Strike price 90, barrier 95 (*Source*: author)

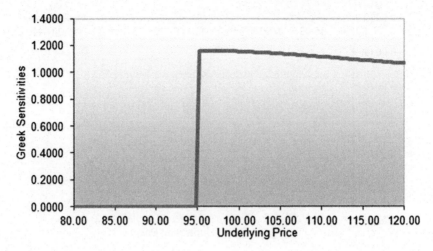

Fig. 7.31 The delta of a down and out call option. Strike price 90, barrier 95 (*Source*: author)

With the spot price at 100 the option holder is in possession of an ITM option. However, in this case notice that the pre-expiry value is lower than the expiry payout, all other things being equal. At a spot price of 100, the expiry value of the option would be 10 units assuming the option has not been knocked out but with 1 year remaining, the premium is only 5.8 units reflecting the probability that it could be deactivated.

To the left of the barrier, delta is zero as the option is no longer in existence. To the right of the barrier delta is positive and around the barrier is greater than 100 % but as spot increases delta declines towards 100 %. To understand why this is the case, consider the pre-expiry value of the option in Fig. 7.30. At the expiry of the option, assuming that the option is still live, the payoff is linear with a slope of 45 degrees—a so-called delta-one profile. The diagram shows that as a result of the passage of time the value of the option rises and the two payoff lines will converge, meaning that the slope of the pre-expiry payoff will initially have a steeper slope and therefore a higher delta than the expiry payoff line.

To the left of the barrier in Fig. 7.32 the option is knocked out and so the position's gamma value will be zero. To the right of the barrier a long position in this option will have a negative gamma value. This is because of the behaviour of delta shown in the previous diagram. When the option is still live, delta will fall as the underlying price increases.

The theta profile in Fig. 7.33 (in 3-D for ease of interpretation) should be viewed with respect to the pre- and expiry values of the options in Fig. 7.30.

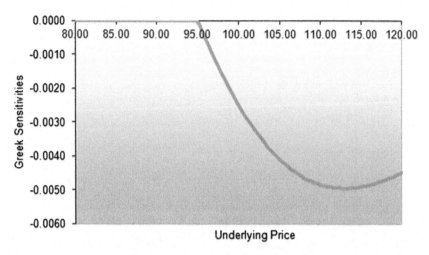

Fig. 7.32 The gamma of a down and out call option. Strike price 90, barrier 95 (*Source*: author)

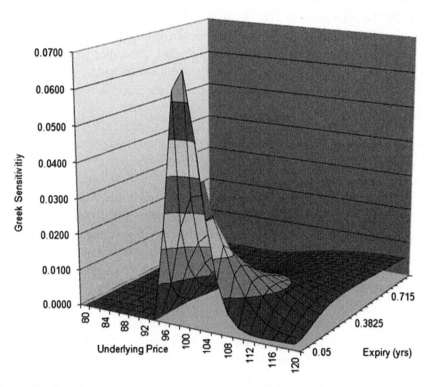

Fig. 7.33 The theta of a long down and out call option. Strike price 90, barrier 95 (*Source*: author)

Since the value of the long barrier option position increases with respect to the passage of time, theta will have a positive value. It will be greatest for options that are close to expiry and where the spot price is closest to the barrier. This is where the convergence between the payoff lines will be at their greatest.

A long position in this 'down and out' call option will be vega negative. The intuition behind Fig. 7.34 is not immediately obvious but once again reference to the pre- and expiry payoffs can help clarify. Suppose that the spot price has fallen to 95.01 (all other things being equal). The value of the option to four decimal places is 0.0116. An increase in implied volatility will push the pre-expiry payoff line down to the right as there is a significant chance that the option will be deactivated. But since the option's value is already very low and cannot fall below zero an increase in implied volatility will have a relatively small absolute impact on the position. Vega at this level of spot is therefore −0.0001. However, at a relatively high price of say 115 the option has a value of 22.6793 and so the zero premium boundary is quite distant. At this price level vega is now −0.1296. At extremely high spot prices the pre- and expiry values of the option are very close as the position now resembles the underlying asset. Since the underlying asset does not by definition have any exposure to implied volatility, vega will be relatively low.

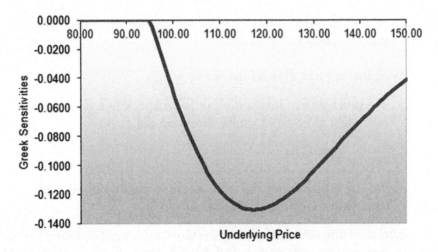

Fig. 7.34 The vega of a down and out call option. Strike price 90, barrier 95 (*Source*: author)

7.2.6 Barrier Parity

Barrier parity ensures that the value of barrier options and their non-barrier equivalent do not violate 'no arbitrage' principles. The principles hold as long as the notional, maturity, strike and barrier are the same.

From Table 7.5, the premiums for the various options were:

- Reverse knock in call = 7.69
- Reverse knock out call = 0.12
- Vanilla European option = 7.81

Note that the premiums on the barrier options sum to the price of the vanilla option. The logic for barrier parity is relatively straightforward. If an investor owned both barrier options, then at any time during the life of the transactions the position will be equivalent to being long a European call option. Suppose that the barrier never trades; in this case the reverse knock in is not activated while the reverse knock out will remain live. If barrier did trade, the reverse knock out ceases to exist but the investor is granted a European call option by virtue of the activation of the reverse knock in position. So:

> Price of reverse knock in + Price of the reverse knock out =
> Price of vanilla European option

and

> Price of regular knock in + Price of regular knock out =
> Price of vanilla European option

This could also be phrased in an alternative way:

> The purchase of a knock out call and a knock in call is
> equivalent to buying a vanilla European call.

So it follows that:

> Buying a knock out call and selling a vanilla call is
> equivalent to selling a knock in call.

This relationship will also hold for the Greeks. Using the pricing parameters for the reverse barrier options in Table 7.5, the respective option Greeks are shown in Table 7.8, confirming that the parity conditions do hold.

Table 7.8 Barrier parity for option Greeks

	Reverse knock in call	Reverse knock out call	European call
Delta	0.5380	−0.0089	0.5291
Gamma	0.0202	−0.0007	0.0195
Theta	−0.0106	0.0004	−0.0102
Vega	0.4050	−0.0159	0.3891

7.2.7   Other Barrier Options

Double Barrier Options

A double barrier option is a European option with two trigger levels. One barrier is placed above the spot price and one is placed below. Generally speaking, the most common structures are 'ins' and 'outs'. A double barrier 'in' option means that the investor is only granted an option position if either barrier is activated. A double barrier 'out' option means that the investor starts with an active option position, which will be terminated in the event of either barrier being activated.

Window Barrier Options

This is a single barrier option where the barrier is active only for a certain period of time during the life of the position. So a 12-month up and out call option with a barrier between 6 and 9 months means that the option can only be knocked out during the 3-month window.

European Barriers

The barrier options considered so far all had a so-called American-style barrier in that the activation or deactivation of the position could happen at any time during the life of the option. This subset of barrier option has a trigger level which will only be observed at the expiry of the option.

7.3   Binary Options

7.3.1   Overview

Binary options are often described using a variety of different terms such as 'digitals' or 'bet' options. A binary option is an option that pays a single fixed sum if exercised but this sum only becomes payable if the option ends up

ITM. If the option expires OTM then, like other options, it will be worthless to the holder. Binary option payoffs are shown in Fig. 1.6.

A European-style binary option expresses the view that the underlying asset will be higher (binary call) or lower (binary put) than a certain level at expiry. They differ from American-style binary options in that the latter pay the fixed amount upon the underlying reaching the pre-agreed level at anytime between inception and expiration.

Somewhat confusingly practitioners will apply terminology to binary options that is perhaps more often associated with barriers. For example, the strike rate on the binary option is sometimes referred to as the barrier or trigger. Equally when the binary option is ITM or OTM it may be described as having being 'knocked in' or 'knocked out' respectively. It may also be that the words call and put are replaced with the terms 'up' and 'down'.

American-Style Binary Options

For American-style binary options it is common to distinguish between one touch and no touch structures as well as double one touch and no touch structures. For a one touch structure the holder of the position pays a premium but will receive a pre-agreed fixed amount if the spot rate ever touches the barrier. If this condition is not met they will receive nothing. A no touch means the holder will pay a premium but will only receive the fixed payout if spot never reaches the barrier. A taxonomy of American-style binary options is provided in Table 7.9.

Table 7.9 Taxonomy of American-style binary options

	One touch	No touch	Double touch	Double no touch
Up	Fixed payout if spot rises and goes through a barrier anytime prior to expiry	Fixed payout as long as spot is less than a barrier at all times prior to expiry	Fixed payout if spot rises and goes through an upper barrier or spot falls and goes through a lower barrier at anytime prior to expiry	Fixed payout as long as spot is less than an upper barrier or spot is greater than a lower barrier at all times prior to expiry
Down	Fixed payout if spot falls and goes through a barrier anytime prior to expiry	Fixed payout as long as spot is greater than a barrier at all times prior to expiry		

European-Style Binary Options

A European-style binary option is where the barrier condition will only be observed and applied on the option's expiry date. A digital call will make a fixed payout if the spot price is greater than the 'barrier' (i.e. the strike price) at expiry. A digital put option will make a fixed payment if the spot price is less than the barrier at expiry.

7.3.2 Pricing of Binary Options

There may be a number of ways in which the premium of a binary option could be quoted:

- As a cash amount
- As a percentage of the lump sum payout (i.e. 10 %, 25 %)
- In the form of odds (i.e. the payout in relation to the premium i.e. '10 to 1', '4 to 1')

The price of a European-style binary option is calculated as the discounted value of the lump sum payout multiplied by the probability that the spot price will be equal to or greater than the strike price at expiration. The price of an American-style binary is calculated in a similar fashion, but it must take into account the probability that the strike price will be hit at any time during the life of the trade.

Section 12.7.2 outlines the principles of hedging and pricing of binary options but readers interested in a more detailed practitioner's perspective on the issues are referred to Marroni and Perdomo (2014).

Similar to barrier options there is also the concept of 'binary parity'. This will apply as long as the characteristics of the option (e.g. maturity, strike, lump sum payout) are the same:

> Price of a one touch + Price of a no touch =
> Present value of lump sum payout

Or

> 80%probability that strike will *be* touched paying out $100 +
> 20%probability that strike will *not be* touched paying out $100 =
> 100%probability of $100 payout

7.3.3 Risk Management of American-Style Binary Options

The use of barrier-style terminology provides an insight into how these options could be analysed. Consider the one touch 'up' binary option outlined in Table 7.9. Suppose the investor is offered the following barrier option termsheet:

Spot price:	100
Strike price:	110
Barrier:	110
Maturity:	1 year
Fixed rebate:	10 units, payable if the barrier is hit
Premium:	4.96

This is a binary call option which has been modelled as an 'up and out' barrier call option with a 10-unit rebate. The barrier and the strike price are set equal to each other. So as a result, the option is active but OTM until the spot price hits the strike. If this event occurs the option is then knocked out with the investor receiving the 10-unit rebate.

The pre-expiry and expiry values of this option are shown in Fig. 7.35.

The delta of this option is shown in Fig. 7.36.

The shape of the delta profile follows from the option's pre-expiry payoff shown in the previous diagram. To the left of the 110 barrier (i.e. strike price) the value of the option increases with respect to the underlying price. As a result the delta exposure is positive. However, as soon as the barrier is hit the option is knocked out so the premium is zero; as a result delta will also be zero.

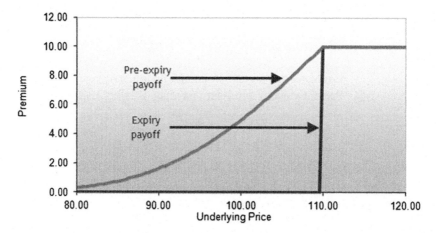

Fig. 7.35 Pre-expiry and expiry payoff values of a 'one touch' option (*Source*: author)

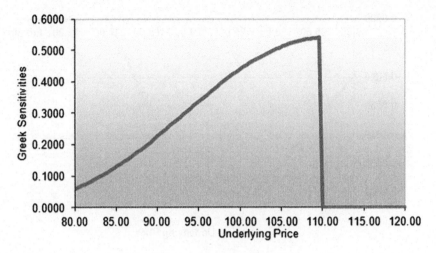

Fig. 7.36 Delta of one touch binary option (*Source*: author)

Figure 7.37 shows the option's gamma profile. Delta is increasing with respect to the underlying price and so gamma will take a positive value. However as the spot price approaches the barrier, delta tends to increase at a slower rate and so gamma will decline. As with delta, gamma will have a zero value beyond the barrier.

The theta profile of the one touch option is illustrated in Fig. 7.38. Prior to the option being knocked out theta will take a negative value. This can be seen from Fig. 7.34 as the pre-expiry value of the option will fall towards the expiry

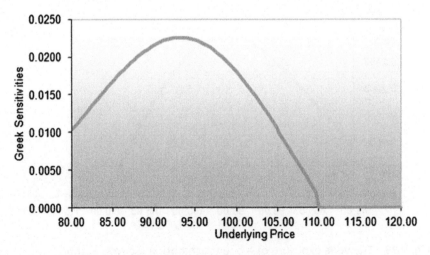

Fig. 7.37 Gamma value of a one touch option (*Source*: author)

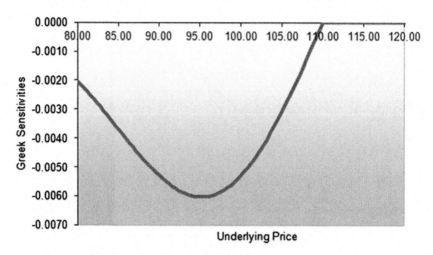

Fig. 7.38 Theta profile of a one touch option (*Source*: author)

value in the region that the option is OTM. Once again the termination of the option at a price of 110 will result in a zero value for theta.

The vega profile of the one touch option is shown in Fig. 7.39. When the option is live but trading in the OTM region the position will exhibit positive vega. An increase in implied volatility will increase the value of the option. Once the option is terminated and the rebate paid the vega value falls to zero.

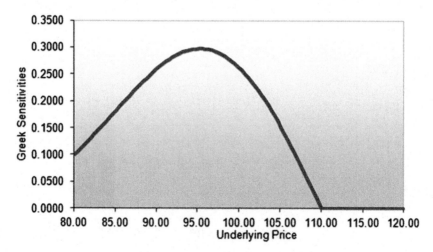

Fig. 7.39 The vega exposure of a one touch option (*Source*: author)

7.3.4 Features of European-Style Binary Options

Consider the following European-style binary call option.

Spot price:	100
Strike price:	110
Payout:	10
Expiry:	1 year
Premium:	2.34

The expiry and pre-expiry values of the option are shown in Fig. 7.40.

This option will pay the holder a fixed amount of 10 units if the spot price is greater than the 110 strike at maturity. Unlike the American-style version of this option it is possible for the spot price to breach the strike several times during its life without triggering a payout. The key factor is whether the spot price is higher than the strike on the day the option expires. Notice that reducing the number of times the 'barrier' is monitored to one single point in time results in considerable reduction in price. A typical rule of thumb used by market practitioners is that American-style binary options are twice as expensive as their European equivalent. In our examples, the American binary cost 4.96 units while the equivalent European option cost only 2.34 units.

One point to highlight at this stage is that the payoff profile of the binary call option resembles the delta exposure of a vanilla call option.

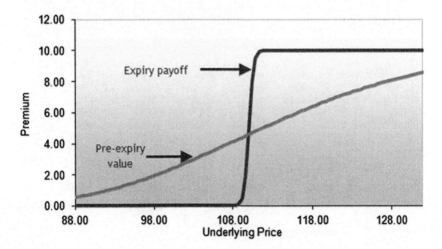

Fig. 7.40 Pre- and expiry payoffs for a European-style binary option (*Source*: author)

7.3.5   Risk management of European-Style Binary Options

The main risk management profiles of this type of option are significantly different from the American binary. In the following figures, the option risk management profiles are shown in 3D to illustrate how the measures move in relation to both the underlying price and expiry.

The delta profile for this type of option is shown in Figs. 7.41 and 7.42. Note that the delta profile of this European binary option resembles the gamma profile of a vanilla European option. Recall that the expiry and pre-expiry values of the European binary option in Fig. 7.40 resemble the delta of a vanilla European option (see Figs. 5.2 and 5.3). The delta values of the European binary increase with respect to the passage of time and are at their greatest when the option is ATM, which is also a feature of the plain vanilla gamma.

Notice as well the value of the delta. No longer does the number have a range between 0 and +/− 100 %. For a European-style binary option the pre-

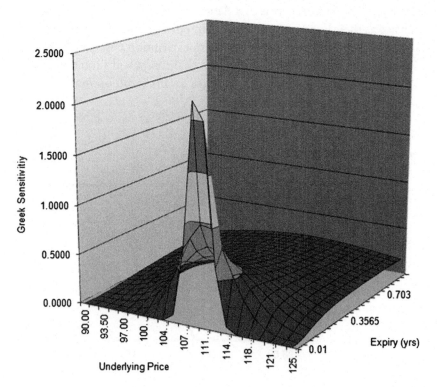

Fig. 7.41   The delta profile of a European binary call option against the underlying price and maturity (*Source*: author)

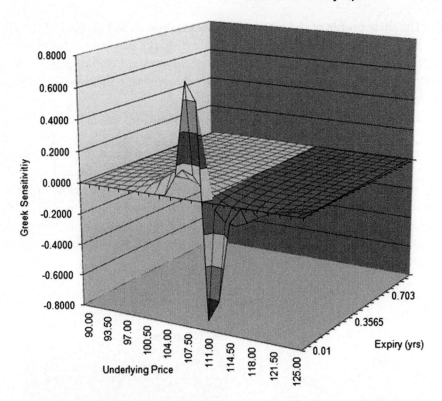

Fig. 7.42 The gamma profile of a European binary call option against the under-lying price and maturity (*Source*: author)

mium is most sensitive when the position is close to expiry and when the spot price is near the strike. Small movements up or down of the spot price could lead to either the fixed payout or nothing. In theory the delta figure could get infinitely large as the underlying approaches the strike, which would make hedging decisions extremely difficult.

The option's gamma is positive below the strike price and then negative thereafter. At extreme spot prices irrespective of maturity the gamma value is very low. Otherwise, gamma increases generally with the passage of time. In this instance gamma is at its highest numerically when the underlying price is at 108 and 112, which lie on either side of the strike. This can be seen by look-ing at the sides of the 'peak' of the option's delta in Fig. 7.41. Below the strike an increase in spot increases the delta (positive gamma) but further increases result in a decline in delta (negative gamma). Because the delta of the binary resembles the gamma of the vanilla option then it would be fair to say that the gamma of the binary resembles the third derivative of the plain vanilla option (the rate of change of gamma with respect to the spot price).

The theta profile of the binary call option is shown in Fig. 7.43.

Theta can be best interpreted by considering the pre-expiry payoff on the option in Fig. 7.40. Note that to the left of the strike price the option will fall in value with respect to time (theta negative), whereas to the right of the strike price they will increase in value (theta positive).

The vega profile of the binary option is shown in Figs. 7.44 (in 3D) and 7.45. Below the strike price the option displays positive vega. As implied volatility increases the probability of the option being exercised improves increasing its value. However, beyond the strike an increase in implied volatility increases the chances that the underlying price could end up below the strike price meaning the option will not be exercised. This will lead to a fall in the value of the option. Therefore if the spot price is below the strike the option displays positive vega, whereas at, or above, the strike it will display negative vega.

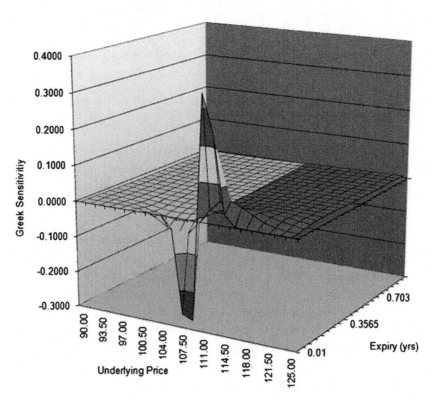

Fig. 7.43 The theta profile of a European binary call option against the underlying price and maturity (*Source*: author)

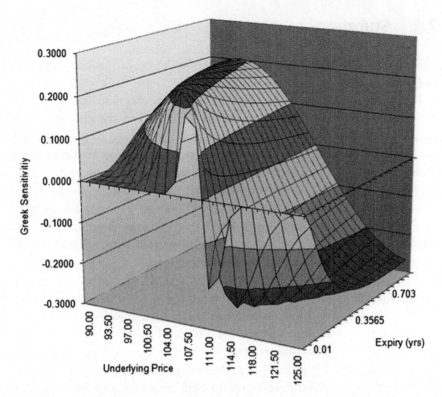

Fig. 7.44 The vega profile of a European binary call option against the underlying price and maturity (*Source*: author)

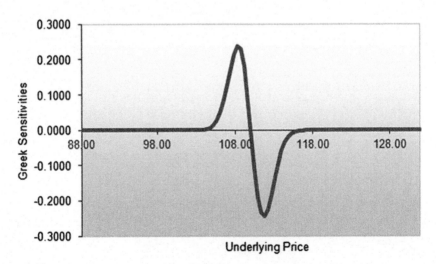

Fig. 7.45 The vega profile of a European binary option shortly before expiry (*Source*: author)

7.4   Summary

This chapter considered two of the most popular exotic options, namely barriers and binaries.

In the section on barrier options a distinction was made between regular and reverse barrier options which primarily related to the placement of the barrier relative to the prevailing spot price. The pricing of the options was considered in an intuitive manner followed by an analysis of their respective 'Greek' exposures. The key point was that these risk management measures are very different from those of a vanilla equivalent. The topic of barrier 'exit risk' was considered as well as how a trader could manage a substantial hedge position in adverse market conditions. Barrier parity highlighted that the possession of a regular and reverse barrier position with the same parameters would always result in an equivalent European equivalent.

Binary options are typically traded in two forms, either American or European. The payout could be structured based on whether the spot price of the asset did or did not go through a particular strike price. The section noted that there was often very ambiguous use of terminology with respect to binary options as practitioners often use barrier terminology—for example, the strike price is often referred to as the barrier. The chapter concluded with a review of the major Greek exposures for both American and European binary options.

8

Correlation-Dependent Exotic Options

8.1   Introduction

Although financial markets have toyed with the concept of correlation for almost three decades, it is perhaps only in the last 10–15 years that it has become more 'mainstream'.

This chapter describes a number of popular correlation-dependent exotic options, while the trading of correlation is covered in greater depth in Chap. 15.

The style of the chapter follows the book in general in that the coverage will be more intuitive than mathematical. For readers interested in the pricing formulas used to value the various options, Haug (2007) is an excellent reference.

8.2   Basket Options

8.2.1   Introduction

A basket option allows an investor to hedge multiple underlying exposures with a single structure. They would be of interest to asset managers who wish to protect the value of a portfolio of equities without having to buy an option on each individual asset. Basket options tend to be cash-settled as delivery of the underlying assets can be time consuming and operationally difficult.

The simplest form of basket option is an option on an index such as the FTSE 100. The investor is buying an option on the constituent stocks, which

© The Author(s) 2017
N. Schofield, *Equity Derivatives*, DOI 10.1057/978-0-230-39107-9_8

are weighted according to their market capitalization. Inevitably some of the share prices will rise and fall and as a result, their weight within the index will also change. It is also possible for the constituent members of the index to change over the life of an index option. A basket option differs from an index option in that the constituent members and their respective weights do not change.

The payoff of a basket option is based on the premise that within a portfolio, asset prices will never all rise and fall in tandem. That is, the correlations between the underlying shares in the basket work as a form of natural hedge. This is based on the notion that the risk of a diversified portfolio of assets is less than the sum of the individual risks.

8.2.2 Example of a Basket Option

Let us take an example of two shares within the US energy sector: Chevron and ExxonMobil. Figure 8.1 shows the share price of both assets and the 30-day rolling correlation over a 5-year period.

Suppose the following prices were observed in the market for options with a maturity of 3 months (Table 8.1):

Table 8.1 Initial market parameters for Chevron and ExxonMobil

Share	Share price	Dividend yield (%)	Financing costs (%)	3-month option volatility (%)	ATM spot vanilla option premium
Chevron	$110	3.6	0.25	16	$3.05
ExxonMobil	$90	2.8	0.25	15	$2.40
Totals					$5.45

Suppose an investor has a position in both shares and is looking to hedge the exposure using a basket call option. The example that follows assumes that the basket is denominated in the same currency as the underlying shares and that each asset has an equal weight of 50 %. To construct a single basket option on both of the shares requires the calculation of the initial market value of the basket:

$$\text{Strike} = \left[(50\% \times \$110) + (50\% \times \$90) \right]$$
$$= \$55 + \$45$$
$$= \$100$$

Since the option is ATM, this value will also be the strike of the option.

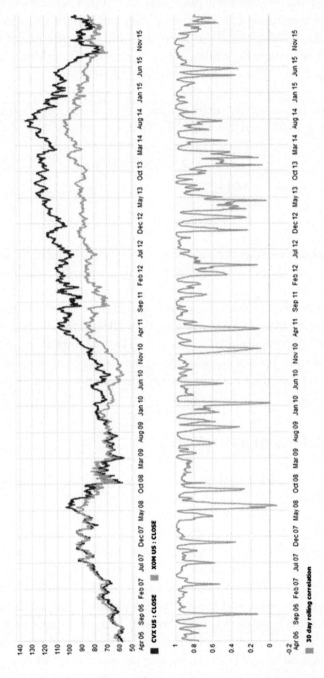

Fig. 8.1   Thirty-day rolling correlation (right hand axis) between Chevron and ExxonMobil (*Source:* Barclays Live)

At maturity let us assume that the underlying share price for Chevron rises to $120 and the ExxonMobil price rises to $100. Consider first what the payoff to the investor would have been if they had bought a vanilla option on each asset. An ATM spot call on Chevron would have paid out $10 ($120 − $110) on a per share basis, while a similar option on ExxonMobil would have also paid out $10 ($100 − $90) also on a per share basis.

In order to compare these payoffs to those of a basket option it is necessary to determine the 'at expiry' market value of the basket, which similar to its initial value is a weighted average of the final spot prices:

$$
\begin{aligned}
&= && \left[\left(50\% \times \$120\right) + \left(50\% \times \$100\right)\right] \\
&= && \$60 + \$50 \\
&= && \$110
\end{aligned}
$$

The payoff of the basket option will be the difference between the initial strike price ($100) and the price of the basket ($110) at maturity, which will be $10. Notice that two vanilla call options would have paid out a total of $20 while an equally weighted basket would have paid out half this amount. The premium of the basket option ($2.33), however, is less than 50 % of the combined premium of the two vanilla options ($2.73); this is the effect of correlation.

In this example, both of the underlying share prices had increased. If, however, one had fallen the final spot price of the basket would have been pulled down resulting in a lower basket payoff.

8.2.3 Volatility of a Portfolio

The valuation of basket options needs to take into account the correlation that exists between the underlying assets using principles of modern portfolio theory. This approach is not required for index options as the underlying is regarded as a single asset with a single price.

Chapter 6 introduced the concept of correlation and highlighted its application within a portfolio of assets. The concepts are briefly reconsidered here for ease of reference. From portfolio theory the risk associated with a portfolio consisting of two assets is calculated as the weighted sum of the individual risks adjusted for their correlation. Provided that the assets in the portfolio are not perfectly positively correlated the volatility of the portfolio will be less than the weighted sum of the volatilities of the assets that form that portfolio.

Equation 8.1 shows the composite volatility for a two-asset portfolio.

$$\sigma_{\text{basket}} = \sqrt{\left(w_{x_1}^2 \sigma_{x_1}^2\right) + \left(w_{x_2}^2 \sigma_{x_2}^2\right) + 2 \times \left(w_{x_1} w_{x_2} \rho_{x_1 x_2} \sigma_{x_1} \sigma_{x_2}\right)}$$ (8.1)

where:
$\sigma_{x_1}^2$ = Variance of asset 1
$\sigma_{x_2}^2$ = Variance of asset 2
$\rho_{x_1 x_2}$ = Correlation between asset 1 and asset 2
σ_{x_1} = Volatility of asset 1
σ_{x_2} = Volatility of asset 2
w_{x_1} = Proportion of asset 1
w_{x_2} = Proportion of asset 1

The same formula can be used for multiple assets except there would then be multiple correlations that need to be taken into account.

Table 8.2 shows how a change in correlation leads to a change in the composite volatility, all other things held equal.

Table 8.2 shows that an increase in correlation will increase the volatility of the two-asset portfolio. Using this composite volatility, an estimate of the premium for a basket option could then be derived using a BSM framework using the basket strike and basket spot price. So when correlation is +0.50 and the associated composite volatility is 13.43 % a BSM model returns an option premium of $2.33.[1]

Table 8.2 Calculation of composite volatility for a given level of implied volatilities

Correlation	Volatility (%)
−1	0.50
−0.5	7.76
0	10.97
+0.5	13.43
+1	15.50

[1] This calculation used a funding rate of 0.25 % and a composite dividend yield of 3.20 %, which was a weighted average of the two underlying shares.

Note one other point. The weighted sum of the individual volatilities was

$$
\begin{aligned}
&= && \left(50\% \times 16\%\right) + \left(50\% \times 15\%\right) \\
&= && 15.50\%
\end{aligned}
$$

Which is equal to the composite volatility of the basket when correlation is +1. Here once again there is no diversification benefit and so the volatility of the basket is equal to the weighted-average volatility of the underlying shares.

From this it is possible to conclude that an increase in either of the constituent volatilities will increase the composite volatility, which in turn will increase the value of the basket option.

8.2.4 Correlation and the Basket Option Premium

The effect of a change in the basket correlation input assuming the volatility is constant can be shown as follows (Table 8.3):

Table 8.3 Relationship between correlation and premium for a basket option

Correlation input	Option premium (USD)
+1.00	2.74
+0.75	2.54
+0.50	2.33
+0.25	2.10
0.00	1.85
−0.25	1.57
−0.50	1.25
−0.75	0.83
−1.00	0.20

Table 8.3 shows that there is a positive relationship between the price correlation of the two assets and the premium on the option. This relationship is sometimes referred to as the 'correlation vega'—the change in the premium for a change in the correlation. The use of the term vega in this context illustrates the fact that the impact of a change in correlation is via the composite volatility input to the model (see Eq. 8.1). Looking at the expiry payoff on the option, the payment is maximized when both of the assets increase in value, that is, when they display positive price correlation.

Although somewhat unrealistic, consider what would happen if the correlation between the assets were +1; here the premium increases to $2.74. This is relevant, as if we were to buy 50 % of the two individual vanilla call options the total premium would also be $2.73 (small rounding difference). With the correlation set at +1, a move in one direction by one of the assets is associated with a similar directional movement in the other asset. In this instance the 'self-hedging' properties of the basket are lost and the basket starts to behave like a single asset.

8.3   Best of and Worst of Structures

8.3.1 Introduction

'Best of' and 'worst of' options allow investors to express a view on the under- or outperformance of two or more assets in a particular direction. Bouzoubaa and Osseiran (2010) argue that such structures are examples of dispersion trades. That is, the payoff of these trades is a function of the distance between the returns on the underlying assets: 'uncorrelated returns result in a high dispersion. If a trader is long dispersion, this also means that he is short correlation since a low correlation implies a high dispersion'.

8.3.2 Expiry Payoffs

The different terms and payoffs used to describe these types of option can be bewildering. For example, many transaction termsheets do not make clear if these types of option are either calls or puts.

The expiry payouts on the different options are listed below[2]:

- Best of call: The investor is long a call on the best performing stock.
    - MAX (MAX $(r_1, r_2....r_n)$, 0)
- Best of put: Investor is long a put on the best performing stock.
    - MAX ($-$MAX $(r_1, r_2....r_n)$, 0)
- Worst of call: The investor is long a call on the worst performing stock.
    - MAX (MIN $(r_1, r_2....r_n)$, 0)
- Worst of put: Investor is long a put on the worst performing stock.
    - MAX ($-$MIN $(r_1, r_2....r_n)$, 0)

---

[2] Based on notation in Bennett and Gil (2012).

Like many correlation-dependent structures the payoff is expressed in terms of percentage returns, so 'r' in the above expressions represents the return on the asset. To avoid confusion, it is worth clarifying how to interpret the 'best of' and 'worst of' put payoffs. Suppose there are two assets, A and B, whose returns over a given period are −1.11 and +4.55 %, respectively. For the 'worst of' put the minimum payoff is from asset A and is equal to −1.11 %. The sign is then changed making the final payoff equal to the maximum of either +1.11 % or 0, which would be 1.11 %. The investor would then receive 1.11 % of the agreed notional amount. This is consistent with the definition of the option, which says the investor is long a vanilla put on the worst performing stock which was asset A. For the 'best of' put using the same values, the maximum return is that of asset B, +4.55 %. The sign on this return is then changed so the final payoff is the maximum of either −4.55 % or 0, which will be 0. The reader may quite reasonably wonder why the payoff is not based on the −1.11 % fall in the price of asset A. This is because the investor is essentially long a vanilla put on the best performing stock. Since the best performing stock (asset B) displayed positive returns, a long vanilla put option written on this asset would expire OTM.

To illustrate the concept, consider the two shares introduced in Sect. 8.2, Chevron and ExxonMobil whose spot share prices were $110 and $90, respectively. Table 8.4 shows four possible share price scenarios and calculates the associated percentage returns. Table 8.5 shows the associated payoffs for 'best of' and 'worst of' options assuming they were struck ATM spot.

Table 8.4 Four price scenarios for the two underlying shares. Scenarios are both prices rising (#1); both prices falling (#2); price of ExxonMobil rises while price of Chevron falls (#3) and the price of ExxonMobil falls while price of Chevron rises (#4)

Scenario	Initial share price	Final share price	Percentage return
#1	ExxonMobil $90	ExxonMobil $91	ExxonMobil 1.11 %
	Chevron $110	Chevron $115	Chevron 4.55 %
#2	ExxonMobil $90	ExxonMobil $89	ExxonMobil −1.11 %
	Chevron $110	Chevron $105	Chevron −4.55 %
#3	ExxonMobil $90	ExxonMobil $91	ExxonMobil 1.11 %
	Chevron $110	Chevron $105	Chevron −4.55 %
#4	ExxonMobil $90	ExxonMobil $89	ExxonMobil −1.11 %
	Chevron $110	Chevron $115	Chevron 4.55 %

Table 8.5 Option payoffs from 'best of' and 'worst of' option structures. The four scenarios in the first column reference Table 8.4

Scenario	Best of call payoff MAX (MAX (r_1, r_2),0)	Best of put payoff MAX (-MAX (r_1, r_2),0)	Worst of call payoff MAX (MIN (r_1, r_2),0)	Worst of put payoff MAX (-MIN (r_1, r_2),0)
#1	MAX (MAX (1.11 %, 4.55 %), 0) = 4.55 %; Chevron	MAX (-MAX (1.11 %, 4.55 %),0) = 0; no payout	MAX (MIN (1.11 %,4.55 %),0) = 1.11 %; ExxonMobil	MAX (-MIN(1.11 %, 4.55 %),0) =0; no payout
#2	MAX (MAX (-1.11 %, -4.55 %), 0) = 0; no payout	MAX (-MAX (-1.11 %, -4.55 %),0) = 1.11 %; ExxonMobil	MAX (MIN (-1.11 %,-4.55 %),0) = 0; no payout	MAX (-MIN (-1.11 %,-4.55 %),0) = 4.55 %; Chevron
#3	MAX (MAX (1.11 %, -4.55 %), 0) = 1.11 %; ExxonMobil	MAX (-MAX (1.11 %,-4.55 %),0) = 0; no payout	MAX (MIN (1.11 %, -4.55 %),0) = 0; no payout	MAX (-MIN (1.11 %,-4.55 %),0) = 4.55 %; Chevron
#4	MAX (MAX (-1.11 %, 4.55 %), 0) = 4.55 %; Chevron	MAX (-MAX (-1.11 %,4.55 %), 0) = 0; no payout	MAX (MIN (-1.11 %, 4.55 %), 0) = 0; no payout	MAX (-MIN (-1.11 %, 4.55 %),0) =1.11 %; ExxonMobil

8.3.3 Valuation and Risk Management of 'Best of' and 'Worst of' Options

This section considers aspects of the valuation and risk management of 'best of' and 'worst of' call options on Chevron and ExxonMobil.[3] The parameters of the two trades are:

Expiry:	3 months
Funding rate:	0.25 %
Spot price of Chevron	$110
Strike price of Chevron	$110
3-month implied volatility	16.00 %
Spot price of ExxonMobil	$90
Strike price of ExxonMobil	$90
3-month implied volatility	15.00 %
Premium of a best of call	$4.75 (correlation assumed to be +0.50)
Premium of a worst of call	$1.55 (correlation assumed to be +0.50)

The price of a 3-month ATM spot European call option on each stock individually would be $3.05 for Chevron and $2.40 for ExxonMobil.

8.3.4 'Best of' Call Option

For the 'best of call' option the premium is greater than that charged for either of the vanilla call options. Suppose the seller of the 'best of' call option decided to charge the more expensive premium of the two individual options (That of Chevron, $3.05). The seller knows that their final payout could be that of Chevron but there is also the possibility that it could be ExxonMobil. Intuitively, the seller will charge more than this amount given this element of uncertainty. Since the 'best of' premium is higher than the individual vanilla call option premiums this type of structure is a popular choice to sell for yield enhancement purposes.

From a risk management perspective, the option's sensitivities to a change in market factors are:

- If the price of either share were to increase (all other things being equal) the value of the option will increase so in this sense the position is delta positive with respect to individual share price movements.

---

[3] For a more detailed analysis of the Greeks, readers are referred to Marroni and Perdomo (2014).

Table 8.6 The relationship between correlation and the value of a 'best of' call option

Correlation	Premium
+1.0	3.29
+0.5	4.75
0.0	5.45
−0.5	5.92
−1.0	6.32

- An increase in the implied volatilities of either of the shares would also increase the premium of the option, so it is possible to say that the position is vega positive.
- The passage of time will cause the option to decrease in value and so the position will be theta negative.
- For the 'best of' call option an increase in interest rates will cause the premium to increase, while an increase in dividend yields will cause the value of the option to fall. In this respect the option's sensitivity to carry is similar to that of a vanilla call option.

The option's sensitivity to changes in correlation is shown in Table 8.6.

Table 8.6 shows that the 'best of' call position is short correlation. That is, an increase in the correlation between the assets will cause the value of the position to decline. To understand the rationale behind this result, consider the different payoffs for the 'best of' call option in Table 8.5. In the two cases where the assets are negatively correlated there is always some payout. But in the case where the assets are positively correlated there is only one scenario where the option pays out.

8.3.5 'Worst of' Call Option

The 'worst of' call option is cheaper than either of the single vanilla call options on the individual stocks. As a result, this is often seen as a relatively inexpensive way for a buyer to express a view on the underperformance of one of the assets within the basket. Bennett and Gil (2012) argue that 'worst of' of structures are generally the more popular than 'best of' options.

From a risk management perspective:

- An increase in the price in either asset (all other things being equal) will lead to an increase in the value of the option so the position is delta positive.
- An increase in the implied volatility of one asset (all other things being equal) will lead to an increase in the value of the option so the position is vega positive.

Table 8.7 The relationship between correlation and the value of a 'worst of' call option

Correlation	Premium
+1.0	2.93
+0.5	1.56
0.0	0.87
−0.5	0.36
−1.0	0.00

- The option position loses money with respect to the passage of time and so is theta negative.
- An increase in interest rates will result in an increase in the value of the option. An increase in dividend yields will therefore cause the value of the option to fall. In this respect the option's sensitivity to carry is similar to that of a vanilla call option.

The 'worst of' call option's sensitivity to changes in correlation is shown in Table 8.7, which shows that a long position in a 'worst of' call option is long correlation.

Again the impact of correlation can be illustrated by referring back to Table 8.5. In the two scenarios where the assets are negatively correlated (#3 and #4) there is no payout on the option. Since the option will never pay out under these conditions the premium is smaller. This is reinforced by the results of Table 8.7 which shows that at the extreme correlation of −1.0 % the option will never pay out and so the premium is zero.

The other popular option within this category is a 'worst of' put, which tends to be relatively expensive and as such investors will typically sell such structures. A long position in this option is short correlation and so the investor community tends to be buyers of correlation (i.e. banks will be sellers of correlation).

8.4   Outperformance Options

8.4.1 Introduction

An outperformance option can be used by investors to express a view on the relative performance of two assets, while not necessarily requiring any directional view. Within an equities context there are a number of different ways of structuring a trade, which could include:

- Single stock versus single stock
- Single stock versus index

- Index versus Index
- Equity versus alternative asset class (e.g. commodities)

Bennett and Gil (2012) point out that by convention they tend to be quoted as call options, that is, the return of asset 'A' over asset 'B'.

8.4.2 Expiry Payoffs

Suppose an investor believes asset A will outperform asset B over some given time period. Equation 8.2 shows the expiry payoff at a future time period, t, of an outperformance asset written on two assets, A and B.

$$\text{Notional amount} \times \text{MAX}\left(\frac{\text{Asset}_{A,t}}{\text{Asset}_{A,0}} - \frac{\text{Asset}_{B,t}}{\text{Asset}_{B,0}}, 0\right) \tag{8.2}$$

Consider the two assets introduced in this chapter, Chevron and ExxonMobil, the initial prices of which were $110 and $90, respectively. Suppose an investor has no view on the direction of either asset but simply believes that ExxonMobil will outperform Chevron. The payoff under a number of different scenarios is shown in Table 8.8.

Table 8.8 also illustrates the dispersional aspects of the option. In the second scenario where both share prices fall, ExxonMobil falls by less than Chevron, which is defined as an outperformance. Notice also that the payout on the option is greatest when the price of ExxonMobil increases and the price

Table 8.8 Payout of outperformance option of ExxonMobil vs. Chevron

Final share price	Outperformance option payoff
ExxonMobil:$91 (up) Chevron:$115 (up)	MAX[(91/90) – (115/110),0] MAX(1.01 – 1.05,0) = 0 Chevron outperforms ExxonMobil
ExxonMobil:$89 (down) Chevron:$105 (down)	MAX[(89/90) – (105/110),0] MAX(0.99 – 0.95,0) = 0.04 ExxonMobil outperforms Chevron
ExxonMobil:$91 (up) Chevron:$105 (down)	MAX[(91/90) – (105/110),0] MAX(1.01 – 0.95,0) = 0.06 ExxonMobil outperforms Chevron
ExxonMobil:$89 (down) Chevron:$115 (up)	MAX[(89/90) – (115/110),0] MAX(0.99 – 1.05,0) = 0 Chevron outperforms ExxonMobil

of Chevron falls; this gives a hint as to the nature of the option's negative correlation exposure.

8.4.3 Valuation Principles

One useful way of understanding the principles of valuing an outperformance option is to treat it as a variation of a spread option. A spread option allows the holder to express a view on the spread between two prices relative to a pre-agreed strike price. The payoff on a spread call option, written on two assets A and B is:

$$\text{MAX}\left(\text{Expiry price A} - \text{Expiry price B} - \text{strike}, 0\right) \qquad (8.3)$$

An outperformance option is regarded as a special case of a spread option where the strike is set equal to zero. Therefore, Eq. 8.3 can be rewritten as follows:

$$\text{MAX}\left(\text{Expiry price A} - \text{Expiry price B}, 0\right) \qquad (8.4)$$

Another popular way of valuing the outperformance option is to treat it as an exchange option, which was an approach pioneered by Magrabe (1978). The model does not rely on a strike price as the exchange at maturity is cashless. So the holder of the option at expiry has the right to exchange asset B for asset A without any payment. The expiry payoff on an exchange option is: (Haug (2007)):

$$\text{MAX}\left(Q_A S_A - Q_B S_B, 0\right) \qquad (8.5)$$

Where:
Q_A is the quantity of asset A
Q_B is the quantity of asset B
S_A is the value of asset A at expiry
S_B is the value of asset B at expiry

If the exchange option references one unit of each asset, then Eq. 8.5 is equal to Eq. 8.4.

So how do these two approaches relate to the valuation of a performance option? If the at expiry values of the asset (i.e. S_A and S_B in Eq. 8.5) are redefined as price ratios (i.e. final value of the asset/initial value of the asset) then Eqs. 8.2, 8.4 and 8.5 are all consistent. The full formula for a Magrabe exchange option is:

$$S_A e^{-q_A T} \times N(d_1) - S_B e^{-qT} \times N(d_2)$$

$$d_1 = \ln\left(\frac{S_A}{S_B}\right) + \left(q_A - q_B + \frac{\hat{\sigma}}{2}\right)T$$

$$d_2 = d_1 - \hat{\sigma}\sqrt{T}$$

$$\hat{\sigma} = \sqrt{\sigma_A^2 + \sigma_B^2 - 2\sigma_a \sigma_B \rho}$$

(8.6)

Where:

S_A, S_B = spot price of asset A and B, respectively
q_A, q_B = yield on asset A and B, respectively
T = Option's time to maturity
σ_A, σ_B = volatility of asset A and B, respectively

When trying to value an outperformance option using this approach, it is not obvious what initial values should be used for the terms S_A and S_B in Eq. 8.6. Equation 8.2 illustrates that the outperformance option's expiry payout is based on price relatives rather than spot prices. In order to be consistent, the initial asset values used in the exchange option formula would also need to be based on some ratio. Derman (1992) shows that for both assets their initial value is just 1. Since the expiry payout of an outperformance option is based on the ratio of the final share price to the initial share price, then the initial ratio for an ATM option would have to be the initial spot price divided by... the initial spot price, that is, 1!

8.4.4 Impact of Correlation

The Magrabe framework uses a composite volatility, which is shown on the lower part of Eq. 8.6. The value of the composite volatility for the two assets for different measures of correlation is shown in Table 8.9.

Some of the key points of Table 8.9 are:

- If correlation is −1 the volatility is equal to the sum of the two underlying volatilities. Since both of the markets are moving in the opposite direction it is possible to simply add the volatilities together.
- At the other theoretical extreme, that is, a correlation of +1, the volatility of the portfolio is the difference between the volatilities of each asset.
- A correlation of 0 % returns a composite volatility that is greater than either of the individual assets.

The option's value as function of a change in correlation is shown in Table 8.10.[4]

Table 8.10 shows that the option is correlation negative; that is a decrease in correlation increases the value of the option. This is reasonably intuitive—the payoff to the holder of an outperformance option will be greatest when the prices of the two assets diverge.

If the premia in Table 8.10 appear to be low recall the payoffs from Table 8.8 which are of a similar magnitude. Suppose that an investor buys our outperformance option when correlation is trading at +0.75 and the associated premium is 0.042. The cost to the buyer for a $1 mm position would be $42,000 ($1 m × 0.042). Suppose further that the returns on the assets then diverge and display negative correlation as per the third scenario in Table 8.8. ExxonMobil outperforms Chevron resulting in an expiry payoff of 0.06,

Table 8.9 Impact of correlation on composite volatility of an outperformance option

Correlation	Composite volatility (%)
+1.0	1.00
+0.5	15.52
0.0	21.93
−0.5	26.85
−1.0	31.00

Table 8.10 Sensitivity of an outperformance option premium to a change in correlation

Correlation	Premium
+1.0	0.0009
+0.5	0.0630
0.0	0.0952
−0.5	0.1219
−1.0	0.1458

[4]All other option input parameters are the same as the previous types of option except the following examples all have a maturity of 1 year.

which on a notional amount of $1 m would result in a payoff of $60,000 and a net profit of $18,000. This would represent a return of about 43 % on the investor's initial investment.

8.4.5 Impact of Volatility

The absolute and relative levels of volatility will also impact the price of the option (Brask et al. 2007). With correlation set at 0, a doubling of the constituent volatilities increases the value of the option to 0.2263, which is more than double the original premium. These higher levels of volatility suggest that any possible divergence between the assets will be of a significant amount and so could result in a higher possible payoff.

Table 8.11 shows two scenarios where the average volatility is the same but the difference between the two volatilities varies. Where the assets display positive correlation an increase in the volatility differential has the greatest impact on the value of the option. The increase in the relative volatilities has a lower impact when the correlation is negative.

Why is this the case? When correlation is negative the assets will always tend to move in the opposite direction, resulting in a payoff. When the assets are positively correlated and the volatilities are similar it would seem reasonable to suggest that any payoff would be relatively small. However, if under the same conditions the volatility differential were large then again it could suggest the possibility of a greater price divergence and hence a larger payout.

From a risk management perspective, the outperformance option has the following exposure to changes in the remaining model inputs:

• The option is theta negative in that it will lose value with respect to the passage of time.
• The option will increase in value for an increase in interest rates but will decrease in value for an increase in dividend yields.

Table 8.11 Impact of relative volatilities on the premium of an outperformance option

Implied volatilities (%)	Volatility differential (%)	Average volatility (%)	Premium (correlation = +1)	Premium (correlation = 0)	Premium (correlation = −1)
15 & 16	1	15.5	0.0009	0.0952	0.1458
10 & 21	11	15.5	0.0346	0.0934	0.1362

8.5   Quanto and Composite Options

8.5.1 Plain Vanilla Call with No Currency Protection

Consider the scenario where a US investor decides to buy 10,000 1-year ATM spot call options on Barclays Bank.[5] The initial market data is:

Spot price	£2.50
Dividend yield	2.7 %
LIBOR	0.5 %
Implied volatility	20 %
GBPUSD exchange rate	£1 = $1.60
Vanilla call premium	£0.1701 (i.e. 17 pence per share)

Suppose the option ends up ITM at a spot price of £2.60. The USD investor's payoff in GBP will be £1000 (£0.10 × 10,000) but the USD value will be dependent on the spot exchange rate at the time the option expires. Table 8.12 shows the USD value of this payoff under three different FX scenarios.

Table 8.12 shows that as the USD appreciates/GBP depreciates, a USD investor suffers a fall in USD income; a USD depreciation would result in a rise in the GBP income.

Table 8.12 The payoff to a USD investor in USD of a 1-year GBP call option

Spot FX rate at expiry	Type of exchange rate movement	USD investor receives
£1 = $1.50	GBP depreciation/USD appreciation[6]	$1500 (£1000 × $1.50)
£1 = $1.60	No change	$1600 (£1000 × $1.60)
£1 = $1.70	GBP appreciation/USD depreciation	$1700 (£1000 × $1.70)

8.5.2 Quanto Call Option

A quanto option allows the holder to benefit from a favourable movement in the price of a foreign currency denominated asset while having no exposure to movements in the exchange rate. In our example, a quanto call option would offer the USD investor protection against an adverse movement in the GBPUSD exchange rate by fixing the exchange rate of any payout. The payoff on the quanto call option is:

---

[5] It is assumed that 1 option = 1 share.

[6] GBP depreciation means that 1 unit of sterling will buy a smaller amount of USD; USD appreciation can be thought of as having to give up fewer USD to obtain a fixed amount of GBP. GBP appreciation means one unit of sterling will buy a greater amount of USD; USD depreciation means giving up a greater amount of USD to obtain a fixed amount of GBP.

$$\text{MAX}\left(0,\left[\text{Spot}_{fc}-\text{Strike}_{fc}\right]\times FX_{0}\right) \qquad (8.7)$$

Where
Spot_{fc} = Expiry price of share denominated in the foreign currency
Strike_{fc} = Strike price of share denominated in the foreign currency
FX_{0} = A fixed foreign exchange rate agreed at the start of the transaction

In this example the exchange rate is quoted as the number of USD per unit of GBP.

Using the same figures as the previous example the USD investor agrees with the option seller that the fixed exchange rate that will be applied to the transaction will be the original spot rate of £1 = $1.60. Table 8.13 shows the payoffs to the USD investor in different exchange rate scenarios, assuming the share ends up £0.10 ITM.

Table 8.13 shows that the USD investor's profits on the underlying asset are immune from any adverse exchange rate movement, although he will not be able to benefit from an appreciation of sterling.

For a quanto option the correlation exposure measures the relationship between the FX price and the underlying asset. The position is correlation negative—that is, a decrease in correlation increases the value of the option (Table 8.14).

The easiest way to see why the quanto call is correlation negative is to consider Table 8.15, which shows a number of 'at expiry' payoffs. Recall that the

Table 8.13 The payoff to a USD investor in USD of a 1-year quanto call option referencing a GBP denominated share

Spot FX rate at expiry	Type of exchange rate movement	USD investor receives
£1 = $1.50	GBP depreciation / USD appreciation	$1600 (£1000 × $1.60)
£1 = $1.60	No change	$1600 (£1000 × $1.60)
£1 = $1.70	GBP appreciation / USD depreciation	$1600 (£1000 × $1.60)

Table 8.14 The impact of correlation on the USD price of a quanto option

Correlation	Premium (USD)
+1.00	0.2431
+0.50	0.2577
0.00	0.2729
−0.50	0.2887
−1.00	0.3051

Table 8.15 Intuition behind negative correlation exposure of quanto option. Scenario #1 is a rising share price and a rising exchange rate (GBP appreciation); scenario #2 is a falling share price and falling exchange rate; scenario #3 is a falling share price and rising exchange rate while scenario #4 is a rising share price and falling exchange rate

Scenario	Expiry values	Correlation	Vanilla option payoff	Quanto call option payoff
#1	£1 = $1.70; Share = £2.60	Positive	£1000 $1700	$1600
#2	£1 = $1.50; Share = £2.40	Positive	£0.00 $0.00	$0.00
#3	£1 = $1.70; Share = £2.40	Negative	£0.00 $0.00	$0.00
#4	£1 = $1.50; Share = £2.60	Negative	£1000 $1500	$1600

initial value for the share was £2.50 and the exchange rate was £1 = $1.60. The payoffs are expressed in terms of the original option position that referenced 10,000 shares and illustrate a number of different scenarios of rising or falling share prices in tandem with rising or falling exchange rates.

In scenario #1 an increase in the share price is associated with an increase in the exchange rate (i.e. a GBP appreciation). In this instance the vanilla call has a payoff of £0.10 per share which at the expiry exchange rate of £1 = $1.70 translates into $0.17 or $1700 on the vanilla option position. However, the payoff on the quanto call option is $1600 (£0.10 × $1.60 × 10,000). The only other scenario where there is a payoff is #4. Here an increase in the share price is associated with a fall in the exchange rate (GBP depreciation). In this instance the vanilla call option again pays out £1000 which translated into USD at the expiry exchange rate is $1500. Again the quanto payoff is $1600 per share as by definition it is immune to changes in the exchange rate. This analysis suggests that when the share price and the exchange rate exhibit positive correlation (scenario #1) the vanilla call is more valuable than the quanto. However, under conditions of negative correlation (scenario #4) the quanto is more valuable than the vanilla. Hence a quanto option will increase in value as correlation declines.

From a risk management perspective, the quanto option's sensitivities to a change in the remaining model inputs are:

- The quanto option requires two interest rate inputs, the domestic (i.e. USD) and foreign currency (GBP) rates. An increase in the domestic interest rate decreases the value of the option while an increase in the foreign interest rate increases the value of the option.
- An increase in dividend yields decreases the value of the option.

- The quanto option requires two volatility inputs—that of the FX rate as well as the underlying asset. An increase in one or both of these volatilities increases the value of the option.
- The option will decay in value with respect to the passage of time.

8.5.3 Composite Call Option

With a composite option the initial strike rate is denominated in the investor's domestic currency (USD in our example) using the exchange rate that prevailed at the inception of the deal. This fixes the initial value of the share in the investor's own currency, that is, USD. The expiry payout is also made in the investor's home currency but its magnitude is dependent on the spot FX rate that prevails at the option's maturity.

The payoff on the composite call option is:

$$\text{MAX}\left(0, \left[\text{Spot}_{fc} \times \text{FX}_E\right] - \left[\text{Strike}_{fc} \times \text{FX}_0\right]\right) \qquad (8.8)$$

Where

Spot_{fc} = Expiry price of share denominated in the foreign currency

Strike_{fc} = Strike price of share denominated in the foreign currency

FX_E = The foreign exchange rate at the expiration of the option. In this example the exchange rate is quoted as the number of USD per unit of GBP

FX_0 = A fixed foreign exchange rate agreed at the start of the transaction. In this example, the exchange rate is quoted as the number of USD per unit of GBP

In Table 8.16 it is assumed that the spot FX rate at the inception of the trade was £1 = $1.60 which is used to determine the USD value of the GBP ATM spot strike price. The example assumes the investor has bought 10,000 calls, ATM spot and that at expiry the share ends up £0.10 per share ITM.

Table 8.16 The payoff to a USD investor in USD of a 1-year composite call option referencing a GBP denominated share

Spot FX rate at expiry	Type of exchange rate movement	Option payout	USD investor receives
£1 = $1.50	GBP depreciation / USD appreciation	MAX(0, [£2.60 × $1.50] − [£2.50 × $1.60])	$0
£1 = $1.60	No change	MAX(0, [£2.60 × $1.60] − [£2.50 × $1.60])	$1600
£1 = $1.70	GBP appreciation / USD depreciation	MAX(0, [£2.60 × $1.70] − [£2.50 × $1.60])	$4200

Table 8.17 The impact of correlation on the USD price of a composite option

Correlation	Premium (USD)
+1.00	1.5035
+0.50	1.4956
0.00	1.4899
−0.50	1.4869
−1.00	1.4863

Table 8.18 Intuition behind negative correlation exposure of composite option

Scenario	Expiry values	Correlation	Vanilla option payoff	Composite call option payoff
#1	£1 = $1.70; Share = £2.60	Positive	$1700	$4200
#2	£1 = $1.50; Share = £2.40	Positive	$0.00	$0.00
#3	£1 = $1.70; Share = £2.40	Negative	$0.00	$800
#4	£1 = $1.50; Share = £2.60	Negative	$1500	$0.00

The correlation exposure of the composite option measures movements between the FX price and the underlying asset. The position is correlation positive—that is, an increase in correlation increases the value of the option. This can be seen from Table 8.17, which shows a positive relationship between the FX rate—share price correlation and the option's premium.

Again the intuition behind the correlation relationship is shown by way of an example (Table 8.18) which is similar in style to that of Table 8.15. Again the initial exchange rate is assumed to be £1 = $1.60 and the payoffs are shown on the original option position of 10,000 shares.

To understand how the payoffs for the composite option were derived consider scenario #1. The expiry payoff of the composite option is:

$$\text{MAX}\left(0, [£2.60 \times \$1.70] - [£2.50 \times \$1.60]\right) = \$0.42 \times 10,000 \text{ shares} = \$4,200$$

In the positive correlation scenario #1, the composite option has a greater value than the vanilla equivalent. In the negative correlation scenario #4 the vanilla call option has a greater value than the composite.[7]

---

[7]Admittedly in the other negative correlation scenario (#3) the composite option does outperform the vanilla but hopefully the reader will be happy to accept the intuition behind the argument shown by scenarios #1 and #4.

Table 8.19 Expiry payoffs from vanilla, composite and quanto options. Quanto and composite options are priced with zero correlation and FX volatility assumed to be 8 %

Spot FX rate at expiry	Vanilla option	Quanto	Composite
£1 = $1.50	$1500	$1600	$0
£1 = $1.60	$1600	$1600	$1600
£1 = $1.70	$1700	$1600	$4200
Initial premium (on a per share basis)	$0.2722[8]	$0.2729	$1.4899

From a risk management perspective, the composite option's sensitivities to a change in the remaining model inputs are:

- An increase in interest rates increases the value of the option.
- An increase in dividend yields decreases the value of the option.
- The option requires two volatility inputs—that of the FX rate as well as the underlying asset. An increase in one or both of these volatilities increases the value of the option.
- The option will decay in value with respect to the passage of time.

A summary of the USD payoffs is shown in Table 8.18.
Table 8.19 illustrates that:

- The quanto option costs more than the vanilla option as it offers currency protection.
- The composite option costs more than the quanto as the USD payout at expiry is potentially higher.

8.6   Summary

The aim of the chapter was to introduce a number of correlation-dependent options namely:

- Basket options
- 'Best of' and 'worst of' structures
- Outperformance options
- Quanto options and composite options

---

[8] This is the GBP per share premium of £0.1701 converted at the original exchange rate of £1 = $1.60.

Table 8.20 Summary of correlation-dependent options covered in the chapter and their respective correlation exposures

Option	Correlation position of long position	Investor demand	Investors' correlation position	Hedging banks' correlation position
Basket call option	Long	Buyer	Long	Short
'Best of' call	Short	Sellers	Long	Short
'Worst of' call	Long	Buyers	Long	Short
Outperformance call option	Short	Buyers	Short	Long
Quanto option	Short	Buyers	Short	Long
Composite option	Long	Buyers	Long	Short

The coverage was designed to give readers an understanding of the features of the products as well as how the values of the options are affected by changes in correlation.

Table 8.20 summarizes the correlation exposures of each of the options, whether an investor would typically buy or sell the instrument and the resultant correlation exposure of each participant.

9

Equity Forwards and Futures

9.1   Introduction

This chapter covers single-stock and index futures as well as their forward equivalent; dividend futures are analysed in Chap. 13. Chapter 1 introduced the basic features of forwards and futures (Sect. 1.3.1) and also outlined the contract specification for the FTSE 100 index future. Sections 4.2 and 4.3 illustrated the valuation principles associated with these products. This chapter assumes that the reader is comfortable with this content.

This chapter starts off by considering the risk embedded within an equity forward or future, which relates to changes in the spot price and the net carry—short-term interest rates, dividend yields and withholding tax and equity repo rates. The discussion then moves on to consider the concept of index arbitrage—the idea that an index future and its constituent stocks may not move in tandem.

In the section on hedging the focus will be on how futures could be used to hedge a portfolio of equities. Since it is likely that the target portfolio will differ from the benchmark index, the concept of beta weighting is introduced. Other popular applications that are illustrated include the use of index futures for tactical asset allocation purposes as well as other 'view–driven' strategies.

9.2   Forward and Futures Risk

This section considers the inherent risk of a forward position. In order to identify the various risk components, Fig. 9.1 illustrates the relationship between the spot and forward price of an equity. The basic logic of the diagram is that

© The Author(s) 2017   **271**
N. Schofield, *Equity Derivatives*, DOI 10.1057/978-0-230-39107-9_9

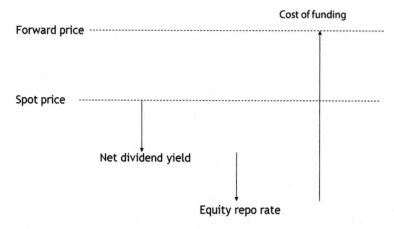

Fig. 9.1   Relationship between spot and forward prices (*Source*: author)

a forward position can be replicated by buying and holding the underlying asset for a time period equal to the forward's maturity. This approach is sometimes referred to as 'cash and carry'. In this example, the income elements of the long position's carry (i.e. dividend yield and equity repo rates) reduce the forward price, while the expense component (i.e. the cost of funding) will push the forward price higher. If the investor is subject to withholding tax, this would reduce the value of the dividend increasing the forward price. The impact of withholding tax is reflected by the net dividend yield component of Fig. 9.1.

So the current market value of a forward position (as opposed to a futures position) can be calculated using the principles outlined in Chap. 4. Suppose an investor has a long forward position in an equity with exactly 12 months remaining, which was executed at a given price, which will be referred to here as 'the strike', the present value (PV) of that long forward position is:

$$PV \text{ of Forward position} = PV \text{ of current 12 } - \text{month forward price less } PV \text{ of}$$
$$\text{strike} = \text{Spot} - PV(\text{dividends} - \text{equity repo} - \text{withholding tax}) - PV \text{ of strike}$$

Table 9.1 considers how a change in each of these market factors influences the forward price (under the assumption that all other things remain unchanged) and the impact on a participant who holds a long or short forward position.

The other element not considered in Table 9.1 is the passage of time. This is, in effect, similar to the concept of an option's theta (see Sect. 5.4). If the forward price for a given settlement date is higher than the spot price (i.e.

Table 9.1 The impact of a change in the market factors that influence forward prices, all other things assumed unchanged

Change in market factor	Impact on forward price	Long forward position	Short forward position
Increase in spot price	Increase	Profit	Loss
Decrease in spot price	Decrease	Loss	Profit
Increase in dividend yields	Decrease	Loss	Profit
Decrease in dividend yields	Increase	Profit	Loss
Increase in withholding tax	Increase	Profit	Loss
Decrease in withholding tax	Decrease	Loss	Profit
Increase in equity repo rates	Decrease	Loss	Profit
Decrease in equity repo rates	Increase	Profit	Loss
Increase in funding costs	Increase	Profit	Loss
Decrease in funding costs	Decrease	Loss	Profit

the position displays negative carry) then the impact of time will reduce this differential[1] causing the forward price to fall and converge towards the spot price. This is because the carry component of the spot–forward relationship will fall in value all other things being equal. If the forward price is lower than the spot price (i.e. the position carries positively), then the passage of time will result in the forward price rising towards the spot price. The convergence is unlikely to occur in a linear fashion as the carry component will evolve in a dynamic way as views on the market evolve.

9.3 Rolling a Futures Exposure

Index futures are often used as an efficient way of taking an exposure to the underlying market. However, by their nature, they will have a finite maturity. As a result, it will be necessary for market participants who wish to maintain their exposures to 'roll' their positions shortly before expiry. In order to roll a contract, the participant must first 'close out' their existing futures exposure by taking an equal and opposite exposure and then re-establish their position in the new contract. Suppose an asset manager is long a future for June delivery and wishes to roll his exposure into the September contract. Shortly before expiry of the June contract he would terminate his exposure by selling the June future and would then simultaneously buy a September future.

Many market makers will quote the roll as a single price capturing both the close out and the re-establishment of the price. It is quoted as the price

---

[1] This differential is sometimes referred to as 'the basis'.

of the front month contract minus the price of the back month contract. For example, from a market maker's perspective it could be quoted as[2]:

Bid price	Offer price
Pay 71 index points	Receive 72 index points
Buy the roll	Sell the roll
Buy the near-dated contract	Sell the near-dated contract
Sell the far-dated contract	Buy the far-dated contract

At the bid price the market maker will incur a 'cost' of 71 index points, which suggests that the longer-dated contract is trading at a lower value than the shorter-dated contract.

The decision as to when the roll will be executed will be at the discretion of the participant and will be done at a time when the differential between the maturities is considered to be favourable. One of the considerations is dividend risk on the longer-dated contract. A long-dated future may well have been priced based on anticipated dividends, but with the passage of time, these estimates may need to be revised leading to a change in price.

9.4   Index Arbitrage

Section 4.3 considered the principles of index future valuation. The position that was analysed was for value on 17 February of a particular year and for convenience the data is restated here:

Cash index FTSE 100	5899.87
June 2012 FTSE index future	5810.00
Futures expiry	15th June
Days from cash to futures expiry	119
Index dividend yield	3.24 %
LIBOR rate to futures expiry	1.17 %
Securities lending fee (equity repo rate)	0.50 %

The fair value for this particular settlement date was calculated as 5850.44 although it was acknowledged that this value was based on a number of assumptions. Assumptions aside, the calculation indicated that the future was trading 'cheap' to fair value. If the trader knew he could execute trades at the prices and values shown in the example (and ignoring bid–offer spreads) then

---

[2] Quoting conventions may differ between markets.

it would be possible to make a risk-free profit. Using the values calculated in Sect. 4.3 and expressing the results in index points, the trader could

- buy the index future at the quoted price of 5810 index points;
- borrow the stock for 119 days paying a fee equivalent to 9.6176 index points;
- sell the stock for spot value to earn the equivalent of 5899.87 index points;
- place the proceeds of the spot sale on deposit for 119 days to earn the equivalent of 22.5052 index points;
- pay to the lender of the stock the dividends due over the period which were assumed to be the equivalent of 62.3220 index points.

Suppose that at the future's maturity the FTSE closes at a price of 6000 index points, which is also the Exchange Delivery Settlement Price (EDSP)[3]. Assuming the cash position can be closed out at this level, the trader's gross profit and loss will be:

- *Profit on the long index future* = 6000 − 5810 = 190 index points
- *Loss on the short cash position* = 5899.87 − 6000 = 100.13 index points
- *Gross profit* = 190 − 100.13 = 89.87

The net profit and loss will be a function of the income or expense from the carry components. The trader pays the stock lending fee (9.6176) and the dividends (62.322) but earns interest on the proceeds of the spot sale (22.5052). So on this transaction the position carries negatively to the tune of 49.4344 index points. When this net expense is subtracted from the gross profit of 89.87 it results in a net profit of 40.44 (rounded), which was the difference between the observed market price of the future (5810) and the calculated fair value (5850.44). It is also important to note that the final EDSP is irrelevant to the net profit and loss calculation. Although not shown here the final result would have been exactly the same irrespective of whether the index had risen or fallen.

A related type of transaction is where an investor will construct a smaller basket of physical shares and trade this against the index future. This is not strictly an arbitrage trade but is perhaps a transaction that expresses a particular view on the correlation between the components.

The arbitrage examples illustrated above do not take into account the fact that dividends on a physical shareholding will be subject to taxation. That is,

---

[3] See Sect. 1.3.1

the holder of a cash equity may be required to pay withholding tax and/or income tax on the dividend, which would reduce the value of the position. In addition, if an investor short sells the asset they must pay the gross dividend to the lender. This gives rise to the concept of the 'arbitrage channel', that is, a range of values within which the future can trade without being subject to arbitrage trades.

9.5 Hedging Applications

9.5.1 Using Futures to Hedge a Portfolio of Shares

One of the simplest ways in which an index future can be used is to hedge a portfolio of equities. Suppose that a fund manager has a USD 10 m equity portfolio that comprises of four assets which are also constituents of the S&P 500. The assets are shown in Table 9.2.

The fund manager is fundamentally bullish on the portfolio but is concerned that their value may dip as a result of some forthcoming economic data. He decides to implement a futures hedge to manage this risk. The observed prices are:

S&P 500 cash index	1923.00
Near-dated e-mini S&P 500 index future[4]	1924.00
Index multiplier	$250.00

The formula to be used to hedge the exposure is:

$$\text{Number of futures contracts} = \frac{\text{Value of portfolio} \times \text{Portfolio beta}}{\text{Cash index level} \times \text{Index futures multiplier}} \quad (9.1)$$

Two issues arise from using formula 9.1. The first is the concept of portfolio beta. This was first introduced in Sect. 3.3.4, within the context of the Capital

Table 9.2 Composition of equity portfolio to be hedged

Stock name	Beta	Market value	% of portfolio
Apple	0.93	2,000,000	20
ExxonMobil	0.82	1,000,000	10
Goldman Sachs	1.62	4,000,000	40
Time Warner	1.18	3,000,000	30
	TOTAL	10,000,000	100

---

[4] The e-mini S&P 500 contract has a contract multiplier of $50

Asset Pricing Model (CAPM). For convenience the relationship is reproduced as Eq. 9.2:

$$R = R_f + \beta \times \left(R_m - R_f \right) \qquad (9.2)$$

Where:

R = Expected return on a security.

R_F = The return on a risk-free security.

R_M = The estimated return on a market portfolio of stocks.

β = The stock's beta (the percentage change in the return on a stock for a 1 % change in the market return). This measures the riskiness of the asset's returns relative to the risk on a market portfolio.

A value of 0 suggests that the security adds no risk to the market portfolio and therefore its return should be the same as that of a risk-free investment.

A value of less than 1 means that the security is relatively less risky than investing in the market portfolio and therefore its return should be lower than the market's.

If beta is equal to 1 the security has the same risk as the market portfolio and therefore its return should be the same as the market's.

Finally, a value of greater than 1 suggests that the security is riskier than an investment in the market portfolio and so therefore its expected return should be higher.

It is important to note that stock betas can vary and are not a static number. For example, they are sensitive to the period of measurement that is used in their calculation. Typically, they are calculated using historical data and so there is no guarantee that the observed relationship will extend into the future. This type of beta measure is often referred to in a variety of different ways:

- Raw beta
- Fundamental beta
- Historical beta

One alternative measure of beta that is sometimes used is the concept of 'adjusted beta' which is essentially an estimate of the expected future beta, assuming that over time each measure will tend towards a value of 1. The formula to calculate the adjusted beta is:

$$(0.67 \times \text{raw } \beta) + (0.33 \times 1) \qquad (9.3)$$

The second issue relates to which index level should be used in the denominator of Eq. 9.1. Although there is no definitive 'rule' on this, there are two arguments used to support the inclusion of the cash index rather than the futures price. One school of thought suggests the cash index is appropriate as this is the measure the investor is trying to hedge. The second view suggests that since beta is measured from cash market data, then for consistency the denominator should also be the cash market.

The first step is to calculate beta of the portfolio, which will be a weighted average of the betas of the constituent stocks:

$$
\begin{aligned}
&= (0.93 \times 0.20) + (0.82 \times 0.1) + (1.62 \times 0.4) + (1.18 \times 0.3) = \\
&= 0.19 + 0.82 + 0.65 + 0.35 \\
&= 2.01
\end{aligned}
$$

A beta value of more than 1 means a position would likely outperform the index in a bull market but underperform in a bear market. Since this position is likely to be twice as volatile as the index the appropriate hedge ratio is:

$$
\text{Number of futures contracts} = \frac{\$10,000,000 \times 2.01}{1,923 \times \$50}
$$
$$
= 209 \text{ futures (rounded)}
$$

This type of hedge will only protect against what is sometimes referred to as 'systematic market risk'. That is, the hedge will give protection against movements in the market which will affect all stocks. However, there are arguably two other sources of risk which could influence the effectiveness of the hedge:

- *Non-systematic or specific risk*—this relates to factors which will affect the performance of a given stock relative to the index.
- *Basis risk*—this relates to the fact that a change in the value of the portfolio to be hedged does not move in tandem with the index future. If the beta weighting of the portfolio to be hedged resulted in a one-for-one change relative to the cash index there is no assurance that the future would move by the same amount. The index future could change in value as a result of

a change in the net carry components (e.g. financing costs, equity repo rates and dividend yields) that may not have an impact on the cash index.

9.5.2 Using Forwards to Hedge the Delta Risk of an Exotic Option Portfolio

Chapters seven and eight highlighted that exotic option positions will have some element of directional exposure. One of the ways in which this delta risk can be hedged is by the use of forwards rather than futures. The trader may prefer a forward position if the exposure is longer-dated thereby removing the need to trade futures which may only have limited liquidity.

9.5.3 Use of Futures to Short the Market

One of the restraints that a fund manager may face is the inability to take a short or bearish position in an equity or an index. However, it may be possible that the fund's mandate may allow for some exposure to index futures. If this is the case, the fund could use the future as a way of taking a bearish view on the market or a single stock by shorting the future. This position would be profitable if the share price or single-stock price were to fall.

9.5.4 Tactical Asset Allocation

Suppose you are an international fund manager responsible for a 'Global Opportunities' fund. The fund is well established with a variety of investments in a wide range of countries. Despite ongoing concern that the long-running bear market in the US market is set to continue, you firmly believe there will be a rally in US equities and wish to take advantage. You decide to implement this view by increasing your US weightings at the expense of your UK holdings. The chosen exposure is set at £15,000,000.

Index futures provide a method whereby an exposure to the USA can be taken quickly, without immediate unwinding of the underlying position in UK equities.

The following market prices are observed.

The spot foreign exchange rate between the two currencies is £1 = $1.60.

To implement his view, the fund manager should buy E-mini S&P 500 index futures while selling FTSE 100 futures. One of the first issues faced by the investor is which maturity of futures contract should be traded. In an ideal

Table 9.3 Initial values for FTSE 100 and
S&P 500 spot indices and index futures

	FTSE 100	S&P 500
Cash index	6863	1923
SEP futures	6850	1924

Table 9.4 Values for indices and
futures after 1 month

	FTSE 100	S&P 500
Cash index	6,883	1,953
SEP futures	6,870	1,954

world the asset manager would look to buy futures that are trading 'cheap' to fair value, while selling futures that are 'rich' to fair value. For ease of illustration, we have ignored an in-depth analysis of the pricing of the futures in Table 9.3 and will assume that they are fairly valued.

The first step is to convert the chosen GBP exposure into USD at the prevailing exchange rates; £15 m at a rate of exchange of £1 = $1.60 equates to a USD exposure of $24 m. From this it will be possible to calculate the number of E-mini S&P futures required using Eq. 9.1. The required number is 250 contracts[5] (rounded) purchased at a futures price of 1924 index points. The same method could be used to calculate the number of FTSE 100 index futures to cover the £15 m exposure. The required number is 219[6] (rounded) and is based on an index multiplier of £10 per point. The FTSE 100 future would be sold at a price of 6850 index points.

Once the trade has been implemented by the asset manager there are a number of possible options. If the market evolves according to his initial view he could simply enter the cash market to buy US equities, sell UK equities and then unwind the futures position. But this need not be done in one single action. The asset manager may choose to do this over a period of time in an attempt to identify 'good value' within each of the markets.

Suppose that after 1 month prices have evolved as given in Table 9.4.

If the spot FX rate has also moved to £1 = $1.61 then the profit and loss in GBP are:

Short FTSE 100 index futures
(6850 − 6870) × 219 × £10 = £43,800 loss
Long S&P 500 index futures
(1954 − 1924) × 250 × $50 = $375,000/$1.61 = £232,919 profit
Net profit = £189,119

---

[5]$24,000,000/(1923 × $50).
[6]£15,000,000/(6863 × £10).

9.6 Trading Strategies

9.6.1 Futures Spread Trades

This section will focus primarily on spread trades which are characterized by the simultaneous purchase and sale of contracts. What would be the motivation for such trades? Essentially the key theme that sits behind all of these transactions is a belief that the underlying contracts are mispriced. In very simple terms the trader must believe that the contracts to be purchased are undervalued ('cheap') while the contracts to be sold are overvalued ('rich').

In order to consider some of the possible trading strategies used in the equity derivatives market, suppose that the following values for three popular index futures have been observed (Table 9.5).

For any asset that displays a term structure of prices there are a number of 'view driven' strategies that are popular:

- *An outright or directional trade*—this would involve the purchase or sale of the asset at a single maturity. This is done in anticipation of the asset rising or falling in price.
- *A slope trade*—sometimes referred to as a time or calendar spread. Here the investor takes two offsetting positions in the asset in separate maturities, for example, buy June, sell September. The motivation is that the difference between the two prices (i.e. the slope) will either increase or decrease. Consider the following example using the figures in Table 9.5. A trader decides to express a view between the prevailing price of the June and September E-mini S&P 500 index future. By convention the spread is defined as:

Price of a near month contract – price of a far month contract.

'Buying the spread' means that the trader would buy the near month and sell the far month. 'Selling the spread' means selling the near month and buying the far month. The trader expects that the initial spread (7.4 index points)

Table 9.5 Term structure of index futures prices

	S&P 500	FTSE 100	EURO STOXX 50
June	1925.70	6807.0	3,236
September	1918.30	6759.0	3,233
December	1910.60	6732.5	3,223

between the June and September contracts will fall—that is, the September contract will rise in relation to the June contract with the possibility the spread as defined will turn negative. On the basis of this belief the trader sells the spread. Suppose that over the following week the market evolves as per the trader's expectation and the prices move as follows:

- June 1930.80
- September 1925.40

The spread is now 5.4 index points and so the trader will show a profit of 2 index points per contract. If the position had been initiated with, say, 100 contracts on both legs of the deal then the profit would be $10,000 (100 contracts × 2 index points × $50).

- *Curvature trades*—whereas a slope trade consists of two transactions, a curvature trade consists of three transactions:
- Buy June—Sell September—Buy December or,
- Sell June—Buy September—Sell December

Here the motivation is that the curvature of the term structure will alter in some way. So in the two examples indicated above, there is a sense that the September contract ('the belly') is misvalued relative to the June and December contracts ('the wings').

- *Intermarket spreads*—here the trader would execute the transaction between markets. In one sense the tactical asset allocation example shown in Sect. 9.4.3 between the US and UK markets would be an illustration of this concept.
- *Intra-market spreads*—In this example the two contracts would reference different indices within the same geographical market. For example, in the USA, exchange-traded contracts are available for the S&P 500 as well as other indices such as the Dow Jones Industrial Average.
- *Single stock or bespoke basket versus an index*—a popular transaction may be to trade a single stock future against the index. Some exchanges do quote single-stock futures and it would also be possible to extend this idea and trade a basket of equity futures against an index.

9.6.2   Forward Trades

A popular strategy used by hedge funds is to use forwards to create trades that are neutral to overall movements in the market but are based on the anticipated convergence or divergence of stock prices. The investor may prefer to use forwards as it will be possible to create bespoke transactions rather than be limited by the availability of futures. Typical strategies may include:

- Stock versus sector (e.g. ExxonMobil vs. energy sector)
- Sector versus sector (e.g. Energy sector vs. Mining sector)
- Stock versus market (e.g. ExxonMobil vs. S&P 500)
- Market versus sector (S&P 500 vs. energy sector)
- Stock versus stock (ExxonMobil vs. Chevron)

9.7   Exchange for Physical

9.7.1   Product Fundamentals

An exchange for physical (EFP) is a transaction that straddles the OTC and exchange-based markets. EFPs are privately negotiated between two entities and involve the simultaneous exchange of a futures position for an 'equivalent' OTC position for an agreed price.

Equivalence is typically defined according to the rules of the exchange under whose auspices the transaction is executed. For example, an index EFP may allow the offsetting position to be:

- A basket of stocks which comprises a significant proportion of the underlying index
- An exchange-traded fund that is highly correlated with the reference index
- An equity index swap[7]

Since the transaction involves a purchase and a sale, the price of the EFP is effectively the differential between the forward and spot price, which is sometimes referred to as 'the basis':

---

[7] If the transaction involves a swap it may sometimes be referred to as an 'exchange for swap' (EFS).

Basis = Futures price – cash price

Basis = LIBOR – (Expected dividends – withholding tax) – equity repo

Buying the EFP is a combined position where the investor is short the stock and long the forward; a short or selling position would be long the stock and short the forward.

The prices for these markets are quoted on an OTC rather than an exchange basis but once the transaction has been agreed both sides of the deal submit the futures component of the transaction to the central clearing counterparty associated with the exchange under whose rules they have chosen to trade. The future is subject to the standard settlement procedures of the relevant exchange and the offsetting position will settle according to the existing cash market conventions.

9.7.2 Using EFPs to Trade the Implied Equity Repo Rate

A trader may decide to express a view on the evolution of the various components of the basis. For example, the trader may believe that interest rates or expected dividends may change over the life of the transaction such that the basis will change in his favour. In reality many equity derivative traders may not wish to have any exposure to changes in interest rates as they may feel uncomfortable with managing a risk from a market in which they do not frequently trade. Since many EFPs are short term in nature they may choose to hedge this with short-term interest rate derivatives such as interest rate futures or Forward Rate Agreements.

EFPs can also be used to profit from a change in the implied repo rate. To illustrate this concept, suppose the following hypothetical values were observed in the market[8]:

Cash price of share	$100
12 m future share price	$101
Observed basis	$1
12 m LIBOR	4 %
Prospective net dividend yield	2 %
Implied equity repo rate	1 %

A trader sees that the equity repo rate implied within the observed futures price is currently 1 %, which he notes is less than the actual repo rate of 1.5 %

---

[8] All calculations assume an actual/actual day basis.

being quoted in the securities lending market to borrow the same basket of stocks. He decides to buy the basis (i.e. buy the stock, sell the future) in anticipation that the equity repo rate implied in the futures price will converge towards the actual repo rate. Once taking delivery of the shares they are then lent out to earn the actual repo rate of 1.5 %. Since the investor is short the future, economically he is 'paying' the implied equity repo rate.

To avoid the impact of the passage of time, suppose that the implied equity repo rate does converge to the actual repo rate shortly after the trade is put on. All other things being equal the forward price should move to $100.50 ($100 + $4 − $2 − $1.50) causing the observed basis to fall to $0.50. The trader could then reverse the position (i.e. buy the future, sell the stock) and unlock a profit of $0.50. At first glance it would seem that the trader could profit from a fall in the implied repo rate by simply shorting the future. This strategy would show a profit if the market moved as expected but carries the risk that the implied repo rate would increase. The benefit of expressing the trade using a basis trade is that the profit is based on the convergence of the repo rates; so if both the actual repo rate and the implied repo rate were to increase the trade could still be profitable if the rates were to converge, that is, the actual repo rate increases by more than the implied repo rate.

9.8   Summary

In some ways forwards and futures are the most straightforward equity derivatives product. The chapter started by looking at the risk associated with holding a position in a futures contract, which is would be relevant to a trader who decides to use futures or forwards to hedge some form of optionality. The discussion then moved on to the concept of index arbitrage where a trader identifies a mispriced future or forward and so buys and sells the assets to unlock some degree of profitability. The main part of the chapter focused on the applications of futures illustrating how they could be used to hedge a portfolio of equities as well as considering a number of 'view driven' strategies.

10

Equity Swaps

10.1 Introduction

The fundamental principles of equity swaps were introduced in Chap. 1; Sect. 1.3.2 outlined some of the basic features of the instrument while Fig. 1.3 illustrated the principles with a simple cash flow diagram. The valuation of equity swaps was considered in Sect. 4.4.

The main objectives of this chapter are as follows:

- Review the fundamental concepts of equity swaps
- Outline the different equity swap variations
- Describe the different motivations for executing an equity swap
- Outline the main product applications
- Describe the main features of contracts for difference

10.2 Fundamentals of Equity Swaps

An equity swap is a derivative instrument that allows an investor to take a long or short exposure to an underlying equity, index or basket of shares. It is an exchange of cash flows where one party will pay an equity-linked return in exchange for LIBOR +/− a spread. The entity paying the LIBOR leg will also be obliged to pay any decrease in the price of the underlying.

Equity swaps can be structured to reference only the change in the price of the underlying ('price return swap') or can reference both the change in

© The Author(s) 2017
N. Schofield, *Equity Derivatives*, DOI 10.1057/978-0-230-39107-9_10

the price and any dividends paid ('total return swap'—TRS). Note that it is possible that the underlying could experience a fall in price but still pay a dividend. This would mean that an investor who has opted to pay the LIBOR leg would also pay this decrease in the price but would receive a cash flow determined by the dividend payment. This is not unreasonable as the swap aims to replicate an actual holding in the underlying without the need to buy the asset itself.

The main features of an equity swap are as follows:

- *The underlying*—this could be an index, a single stock, a basket of shares, a basket of indices or perhaps a specific investment fund.
- *Style of swap*—price or total return. If the swap is traded in total return format, the two parties would also need to agree what percentage of dividends would be paid.
- *Notional amount*—there are a number of ways in which the notional could be expressed, namely:

  - A monetary amount ('$20,000,000')
  - A number of shares ('100,000 shares of Apple')
  - Index 'units'. ('5000 FTSE 100 units'). The use of index units is a convenient way of converting an index value into a monetary amount and allows for the notional amount to be increased in line with changes in the value of the index. Suppose that the FTSE 100 is trading at a level of 7000 index points and two parties have agreed a transaction based on 5000 units. To determine the current monetary value of the swap the two figures are multiplied together; so in this case the transaction would have a monetary equivalent of £35,000,000.

- *Paying or receiving*—it is common for participants to use the phrases 'buy', 'sell', 'long', 'short', 'receiver' and 'payer' when describing swap transactions but these terms are rarely defined formally and could easily be misinterpreted. Generally speaking, the entity that is 'long' the swap ('the receiver') is the entity that is the receiver of the equity-linked cash flow and therefore the payer of the LIBOR leg. The 'short' ('the payer') would have the opposite exposure. Suffice to say it is always advisable to be explicit about which cash flow is being paid or received.
- *Choice of floating benchmark*—arguably, the most common floating rate benchmark to which swaps are referenced is LIBOR, although like most things in finance there are always exceptions. For example, a USD equity swap executed in the USA is likely to reference the money market bench-

mark at which the trader normally borrows; typically, this will be the overnight Federal Funds rate.

- *Price of the swap*—since the swap is an exchange of two variable cash flows the concept of a price becomes somewhat ambiguous. Typically, the price is taken to be the fixed component of the transaction which for equity swaps is the spread applied to the LIBOR leg. If an investor considers that a swap is 'cheap' they are describing a situation where the spread to LIBOR they are receiving is greater than what is considered to be fair value. A swap that is 'rich' is where the spread to LIBOR is lower than fair value.

- *Effective date*—many banks may decide to hedge their swap exposure by buying or selling the underlying shares. Typically, these may settle two or three business days after they have been traded depending on the market convention. As a result, the effective dates for swaps will vary between jurisdictions. At the time of writing, GBP and EUR equity swaps are effective 2 days after the trade date ('T+2') while USD equity swaps are effective T+3.

- *Maturity*—equity swaps tend to be relatively short-dated compared to, say, interest rate swaps. Some equity investors' performance is measured over a relatively short period (i.e. every quarter) and they are sometimes reluctant to be tied to long-dated structures. Another reason is that from the investment bank's perspective it may be difficult to find a suitable long-dated hedge.

- *Frequency of cash flow exchange*—although any permutation is possible, one of the popular conventions is to exchange cash flows on a quarterly basis.

- *Fixed or variable notional amount*—the notional amount on the equity swap could be fixed for the duration of the transaction or it could be reset on a periodic basis. If the notional amount is reset, then at every settlement date the monetary equivalent amount of the notional would change in accordance with the change in the underlying. So if the underlying index or share price rises by 1 % during a settlement period, then in the subsequent period the notional amount will increase by 1 %. Again this follows the principle that the swap should mimic the exposure of an investor who actually owns the underlying asset. Some equity swaps will also have a provision for 'dividend reinvestment'. This means that every time the underlying asset pays a dividend rather than make a payment under the terms of the swap, the notional amount is increased by this amount in the next period.

In order to illustrate some of the key principles consider the following transaction:

Maturity:	1 year
Underlying:	S&P 500 index
Notional amount:	$100m
Type:	Total return
Floating leg:	12-month LIBOR + 10 bps
Value of 12-month LIBOR:	1 %
Day basis for floating leg:	Actual/360
Initial level of index:	2000
Cash flow settlement:	Single payment at maturity

Suppose that at maturity the S&P has risen by 5 % to 2100. The cash flows are as follows:

- Equity payment: $100m × (2100 / 2000 − 1) = $5,000,000
- Floating payment: $100m × 1.1 % × 365 / 360 = $1,115,278 (rounded)
- Net payment by payer of equity leg = $5,000,000 − $1,115,278 = $3,884,722

10.3 Equity Swaps Variants

The structures described so far are somewhat 'vanilla' in nature but banks have offered different variations:

- *Index versus index*—in this example the investor swaps the return on one index for that of another, for example, FTSE 100 versus S&P 500. This type of structure is often structured to be zero coupon in style; that is, all of the cash flows will take place at maturity.
- *Index versus individual share*—here the investor is taking a view on how a share performs relative to an index, of which it may—or may not—be a constituent.

Beyond such variations it is also possible for the equity swaps to be structured with some form of embedded optionality. Some possible examples include the following:

- *Equity index caps/floors*—in this structure the LIBOR leg is subject to a maximum cap or a minimum floor level, while a collared structure would combine both components.
- *'Best of' and 'worst of' returns*—these exotic options were analysed in Chap. 8. When embedded into a total return swap it would transform the equity

leg by paying, say, the 'best of' the return on two indices such as the Nikkei 225 or S&P 500.

- *Quanto options*—equity swaps can be structured to have a quanto-style payoff, that is, an investor receives the positive performance of the FTSE 100 in USD.
- *Outperformance options*—an embedded outperformance option would mean the investor would receive a return based on the relative outperformance of two or more indices or shares.

10.4 Motivations for Using Equity Swaps

There are a number of motivations for the use of equity swaps:

- *Simplicity*—there is no need for an investor to buy the underlying assets.
- *Mandate restrictions*—some investors have internal restrictions that may prevent them from directly investing in certain stocks or markets.
- *Rebalancing*—if the composition of the underlying index changes there is no need for the investor to buy and sell any shares as the cash flows on the swap will automatically adjust to reflect the change.
- *No requirement to 'roll' the position*—an investor who has chosen to use futures as a means of maintaining an ongoing exposure to an equity market would need to 'roll' the exposure as the maturity of the contract approaches (see Sect. 9.3). Depending on when the position is rolled the 'price' of the roll could move against the investor.
- *Tracking error*—futures will not necessarily always trade at fair value and so will not replicate the movement in the underlying index on a one-for-one basis. This is sometimes referred to as 'tracking error'.
- *Longer maturities*—a further disadvantage of using futures to express a view on the market is that the liquidity for many contracts is concentrated in the near-dated maturities and many contracts will not trade out beyond 9 months. Equity swaps could be traded with maturities of several years.
- *Exposure to 'difficult to access' markets*—some emerging markets have restrictions on foreign investor activity, for example, China and India. Many investment banks will often have obtained the necessary trading permissions and as such would be able to hedge and structure equity swaps accordingly.
- *Currency exposure*—the swap could be structured to reference a foreign currency index but with the cash flows payable in the domestic currency. This would be a 'quanto' equity swap.

- *Liquidity*—it may also be the case that an investor has concerns over the liquidity of a particular share or market that would make them reluctant to invest.
- *Initial outlay*—in a vanilla equity swap the investor will not be required to pay for the underlying assets as they are not taking ownership of the underlying. This can be an advantage for investors who perhaps face some constraint in terms of the availability of cash. However, many banks will insist on their clients posting some form of initial margin as well as requiring subsequent exchanges of collateral as the mark-to-market value of the contract evolves.
- *More cost effective than buying the underlying assets*—Fig. 1.3 illustrated the cash flows on a vanilla equity swap. One of the ways in which the transaction could be hedged is for the structuring bank to buy the asset and hold it on their own balance sheet. Any price appreciation experienced by the underlying asset will be passed on to the investor under the terms of the swap. One of the sources of the profitability for the bank is the difference between the LIBOR-related cash flow received from the investor in the swap and that which has to be paid to finance the physical purchase of the underlying. So if the bank finances, say, at LIBOR 'flat' (i.e. no spread) then they may charge their client LIBOR + 10 basis points. The client would still be amenable to executing this transaction as long as the LIBOR cost they would pay under the swap is cheaper than the cost they would incur if they bought the physical asset outright. In one sense the client has effectively paid 10 basis points to 'rent' the balance sheet of the structuring bank.

  Since the investor does not actually own the shares they will not have to pay any custody fees. However, if the structuring bank hedges the deal by purchasing the asset there is a possibility that they would pass on this charge to the investor in the form of a higher spread to the floating leg.
- *Express both a long and short view on the performance of an asset*—typically many large equity investors are characterized as being 'long only' in that they are not allowed to take short positions in an equity or an index. Additionally, some clients may not be able to lend out shares to short sellers who wish to express a bearish view on the market thus losing out on potential lending fees. Equity swaps would allow an investor to express a bearish view on the market and would generate a LIBOR cash flow.

10.5 Institutional Applications

10.5.1 Dividend Taxation Arbitrage

The subject of 'taxation optimisation' (!) is always a sensitive issue and regulators around the world continually seek to find ways to prohibit the use of derivatives that seek to avoid such payments. Since any text relating to taxation would soon become dated, this section aims to convey a sense as to how equity swaps have been used in this context.

Suppose an investor is a non-resident of a country that withholds 15 % of any income paid to foreign investors. The investor has a position of 1 million shares in a company which is based in the same jurisdiction and is therefore required to pay this tax. He discusses with a financial institution the possibility of structuring an equity swap to increase his yield from dividends paid by the issuer.

The following represents a possible way of structuring the transaction:

Step #1—initial sale of shares to the financial institution

The investor sells all of his shares to the bank at the prevailing share price, which is assumed to be €10. The bank becomes the registered owner of the share and delivers €10m to the client.

Step #2—structuring of an equity swap

Simultaneously the two parties enter into a total return equity swap that references the underlying share. For ease of illustration it is assumed that the transaction has a maturity of 1 month (31 days) and will have a single exchange of cash flows at maturity. The floating leg is referenced to 1-month EURIBOR flat, which fixes at, say, 0.75 % per annum and will be payable by the investor.

Under the terms of the swap the bank will pay to the investor any increase in the share price, while the investor will pay any decrease in the price. Since the bank is the registered owner they will receive the gross dividend,[1] of which they agree to pay 95 % of the value to the investor under the terms of the equity swap. In this example it is assumed that during the life of the transaction there is a dividend of €1 per share.

---

[1] The structure only works if the financial institution pays withholding tax at a lower rate than the investor.

Step #3—sale of shares back to investor and settlement of swap cash flows

Suppose that at the maturity of the transaction the share price has fallen to €9 a share.

- The bank sells back to the investor the original 1m shares at this price and receives €9m.
- However, under the terms of the equity swap the investor must pay any price depreciation and so the bank will receive a further €1m.
- Having received a gross dividend of €1m from the issuer, the bank must also forward 95 % of this sum to the investor i.e. €950,000. This is €100,000 greater than the amount the investor would have received had they not entered into the swap.
- The investor pays to the financial institution a cash flow of €6458 (€10m × 0.75 % × 31 / 360, rounded), which is their obligation under the floating leg of the swap.

A summary of the cash flows is shown in Table 10.1.

From the investor's perspective they have received an enhanced dividend (95 % instead of 85 %) which amounts to an additional €100,000 of income. The investor has paid a LIBOR cost for having use of the initial sale proceeds for the duration of the transaction so from this perspective the client can view it as a form of secured borrowing. From the financial institution's perspective, they retained 5 % of the dividend (€50,000) and earned a LIBOR return on the monies lent to the client for the duration of the transaction.

Table 10.1 Cash flows to investor and bank from sale of shares combined with equity swap

	Investor	Financial institution
Initial sale of shares to bank @ €10	+€10,000,000	−€10,000,000
Repurchase of shares from the bank @ €9	−€9,000,000	+€9,000,000
Equity cash flow due under swap	−€1,000,000	+€1,000,000
Dividends received from issuer		+€1,000,000
Dividends payable under swap	+€950,000	−€950,000
Interest payable under floating leg of swap	−€6458	+€6458
Net cash flows	+€943,542	+€56,458

10.5.2 'Covered Swap' Transaction

This trade idea is based on Combescot (2013). Suppose an investor owns an Exchange Traded Fund (ETF) that references a major index, for example, SPDR S&P 500. It may be possible to execute a transaction involving this asset and a total return swap to earn a return based on LIBOR but which is immune to equity price movements.

The investor places the requisite number of shares into a segregated account and cannot dispose of the shares during the life of the swap. The investor would then enter into a total return swap where they would pay the increase in the shares' performance in return for receiving a LIBOR cash flow. Consider the investor's position under the following two 'at maturity' scenarios:

- *Index falls in value*: the investor's physical position will show a mark-to-market loss, but under the terms of the swap, they will receive a cash flow from the bank to compensate for this, as well as earning the pre-agreed LIBOR return.
- *Index increases in value*: the investor's physical position will show a mark-to-market profit, but they will be required to make a cash flow payment to the bank. Since the profit on the underlying shares is 'unrealized', that is, it does not involve the receipt of a cash flow, the investor would have to sell part of their shareholding to settle any liability under the swap. However, as the remaining shares have increased in value, the investor should be neutral to market movements.

10.5.3 Trading the Implied Equity Repo Rate

10.5.3.1 Term Structure of Equity Repo Rates

The concept of the equity repo rate was first introduced in Sect. 1.2.6 and its applicability within the concept of derivative valuation was considered in both Chaps. 4 and 9. For example, Table 9.1 showed that an increase in equity repo rates would lead to a decrease in the forward price, that is, a long futures position with a mark-to-market loss as a result of an increase in repo rates ('short repo exposure'). From this it is possible to argue that an investor receiving the equity amount on a total return swap also has a short repo exposure as the swap is economically equivalent to a long futures position, that is, both positions will make money from a rise in the underlying market.

Since options are forward instruments with upside or downside protection, a long call or short put will also possess a short repo exposure. This logic would also hold true for any exotic option that is long the market, that is, an exotic option where the delta exposure is positive. The exposure to equity repo rates of a variety of instruments is shown in Table 10.2.

Since all of these instruments will have different maturities it would also be possible to construct a term structure of equity repo rates.

Combescot (2013) gives some examples of market activity that will influence the term structure of equity repo rates:

- The purchase of long-term index puts by insurance companies
- Structured products that embed a long-dated, long call option (for capital protection) or a short-dated short put option (for yield enhancement)
- The hedging of autocallable structured products (see Chap. 12)

10.5.3.2   Trading the Equity Repo Rate

One of the ways to trade the term structure of equity repo rates is the use of offsetting total return equity swaps with different maturities. One possible way of structuring a trade for an investor would be as follows:

- Receive the equity leg on a 1-year total return swap and pay 12M LIBOR + 0.05 %.
- Pay the equity leg on a 6-year total return swap and receive 12M LIBOR + 0.15 %.

For ease of illustration assume that both the equity and the floating leg settle annually. Figure 10.1 shows that the position will carry positively for the investor in the first year of the transaction.

As a result of this position the investor is effectively locking in the 5-year spread to LIBOR, 1 year forward.

Table 10.2 summary of equity repo exposures for a variety of derivative positions

Positions that benefit from an increase in equity repo rates ('long repo exposure')	Positions that benefit from a decrease in equity repo rates ('short repo exposure')
Short a forward or future	Long a forward or future
Paying the equity leg in a swap	Receiving the equity leg in a swap
Short a call or long a put	Long a call or short a put
Any exotic that is delta negative	Any exotic option that is delta positive

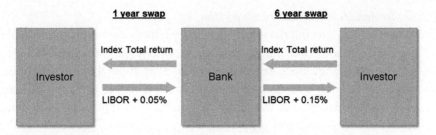

Fig. 10.1   Using total return equity swaps to exploit expected movements in the term structure of equity repo rates (*Source*: author)

The calculation of a forward interest rate or spread can be determined using 'no arbitrage' principles.

$$\left(1+{}_0R_6\right)^6 = \left(1+{}_0R_1\right)\times\left(1+{}_1R_6\right)^5$$

$$_1R_6 = \sqrt[5]{\frac{\left(1+{}_0R_6\right)^6}{\left(1+{}_0E_1\right)}} - 1$$

$$_1R_6 = \sqrt[5]{\frac{\left(1.0015\right)^6}{\left(1.0005\right)}} - 1$$

$$_1R_6 = 0.170\%$$

(10.1)

Where:
R = spread to LIBOR

Equation 10.1 calculates the 6-year spread (${}_0R_6$) as being the product of the 1-year spread (${}_0R_1$) and the compounded value of the 5-year spread in 1 year's time (${}_1R_6$). By rearranging the formula, it is possible to solve for the unknown forward spread which returns a value of 0.170 %. Such a forward is not a forecast or 'the market's best guess as to where the spot rate will be in the future', it is mostly accurately defined as a breakeven value.[2]

At the end of the first 12 months the 1-year swap will mature and the investor would then be faced with a decision as to whether he replaces the maturing position or unwinds the remaining swap.

---

[2] See Schofield and Bowler (2011) for more details on this concept.

- *Trader decides to unwind entire position*
  If, they were to unwind the remaining swap position, the transaction would be marked to market and the participant for whom the transaction was ITM would receive a cash flow. Another way of thinking about the concept of mark-to-market is that it is economically equivalent to taking an equal and offsetting position. In this case that would require the investor to pay the equity return on a new 5-year swap and receive LIBOR plus a spread. This means that the transaction will be ITM for the investor if, after 1 year, the spread to LIBOR on a 5-year total return swap was less than 17 basis points—the initial forward breakeven spread. Notice that the investor can suffer a rise in the spread by 2 basis points per annum before losses are incurred (see Fig. 10.2). This is a reflection that the investor earns 10 basis points of positive carry in the first year which provides him with a cushion of profitability. Consequently, the position can experience a small adverse change in the spread before losses are incurred.
- *Trader decides to rollover short-dated swap transaction*
  If when the short-dated swap matures, the prevailing price to replace this transaction is still attractive, the investor could execute another 1-year trade and continue to benefit from the positive carry.

But how would the evolution of other market factors impact the investor's profitability?

- The investor is neutral to absolute movements in the equity market as long as the notional amounts on the transaction are equal—whatever they are required to pay will be exactly offset by what they will pay.
- Since the transaction is a total return swap they are also neutral with respect to any dividends paid on the index.

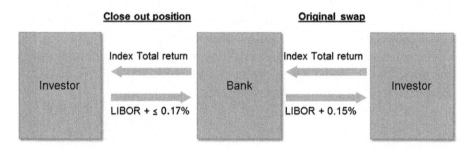

Fig. 10.2 Closing out a 6-year total return swap, 1 year after inception with a 5-year total return swap (*Source*: author)

- The same will apply to the floating leg; if they have referenced the cash flows to the same interest rate index (say 12-month LIBOR) then this component will net out.

So the only remaining component to which the investor has exposure is the term structure of equity repo rates. The original position took its value from 6-year rates but now will be revalued using 5-year rates. If equity repo rates decrease, then the absolute value of the spread to LIBOR on the equity swap should also fall resulting in a profit.[3]

10.5.4 Cross-Currency Equity Swaps

The motivation for entering into an equity swap with a currency component is to access finance at an attractive rate.

Consider the situation of a US bank that is naturally long USD. It is not unreasonable to suppose that this institution would also have to make EUR payments, which would normally be financed by borrowing from another market participant. If the bank holds surplus USD this position would incur an opportunity loss as it could be invested to earn a higher rate of return. Although some US banks may finance themselves at the Fed Fund rate, this example assumes a borrowing rate of USD LIBOR. Their EUR exposures would probably be financed on an overnight basis, which would incur a cost of EURIBOR plus a spread.

Figure 10.3 shows how a possible transaction could be structured, using Google as the reference asset and assuming a 1-month (31-day) maturity.

The bank first borrows $10.5m from the money markets (1). This sum represents the current price of the reference share ($500) plus cash collateral set at 105 % of this value (i.e. $10m × 105 %). The bank uses these proceeds (2) to borrow 20,000 Google shares from the securities lending market (3). These shares are then sold to a swap counterparty (4) in exchange for the current EUR equivalent. These proceeds could then be used to help finance some of the firm's EUR-denominated commitments (not shown). This EUR sum will be determined by reference to the current spot rate, which is assumed to be €1 = $1.25 and so would result in proceeds of €8m.

Figure 10.4 illustrates the flows that will occur 1 month later upon the maturity of the swap. Under the terms of the swap the bank repurchases the 20,000 shares (6) at the prevailing price of $510 (7). However, since there is

---

[3] See Sect. 4.4.2 for an explanation.

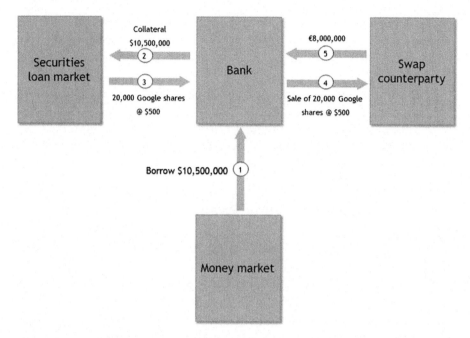

Fig. 10.3 Setting up an equity swap with a currency component (*Source*: author)

a total return swap component the swap counterparty will be required to pay to the bank any share price appreciation (8). The shares are then redelivered under the terms of the original loan of the asset (9). Under the terms of the swap the bank will pay 1-month EURIBOR 'flat' to the swap counterparty (10). The bank receives back the cash collateral that supported the loan of the share (11) having earned interest at an assumed rate of 3 % and incurring borrowing costs of 0.20 %.[4] These proceeds are then used to repay the USD loan (12).

The key points of the transaction are as follows:

- The bank has no exposure to the movement in the underlying share price.
- The cost of borrowing the USD in the money markets is financed by the lender of the shares.
- The net costs to the bank are the securities lending fee and the EURIBOR cash flow of the swap.

---

[4]$10,500,000 × (3.00% − 0.20%) × 31 / 360 = $25,317.

Recall that the normal cost of borrowing EUR for the bank was EURIBOR + a spread but the swap has achieved a EURIBOR 'flat' funding rate. This would suggest that the transaction would only be worthwhile if this reduction in spread is greater than the cost of borrowing the securities.[5]

There are a number of permutations that could be structured from this basic idea. For example:

- If the swap counterparty has experienced difficulty in sourcing the underlying stocks, then it could be that the structuring bank could pass on the securities borrowing fee via the EURIBOR leg. In this case the bank would pay EURIBOR minus a spread.
- If the lender of securities does not finance itself at LIBOR, the repayment of the cash collateral (step 11 in Fig. 10.4) could be at a positive spread to this benchmark.

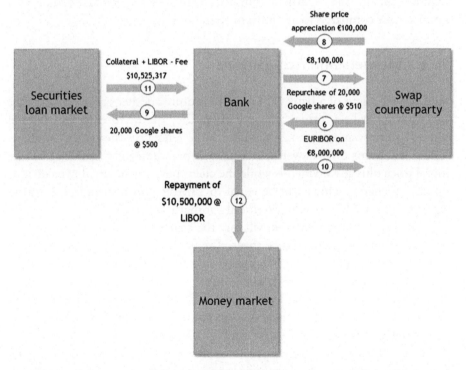

Fig. 10.4 Cash and asset flows at the maturity of the swap (*Source*: author)

---

[5] This ignores bid-offer spreads and all other transaction costs.

10.6 Corporate Applications

Although the text has mainly focused on institutional applications, total return swaps are also used within a corporate context. Equity swaps have been used in a number of high-profile takeovers:

- Hermes and LVMH
- Children's Investment Fund management and CSX
- Schaeffler Group and Continental Tyres

One of the reasons why these cases received a substantial amount of press attention was whether the acquirer's attempt to bypass each jurisdiction's rules on disclosure of shareholdings was ethical. The use of total return swaps as a tactic is still popular as depending on the target's jurisdiction, the disclosure requirements for such synthetic transactions may be less well defined or even non-existent compared to an outright shareholding.

10.6.1 Mergers and Acquisitions

Suppose the client of a bank is looking to acquire another company but does not want to make a formal takeover offer. They decide to enter into a total return equity swap with a bank, whose value references the target company. Under the terms of the swap the bank will pay the equity upside from the initial price plus any dividends while the client pays any equity downside plus a funding charge, which will be equal to LIBOR plus a spread. The voting rights will be available to the client only at maturity.

To hedge the swap the bank will buy the shares in the market, retain title and hold them on their balance sheet. The bank will need to borrow money to fund this purchase which is assumed to be done at LIBOR. The client is effectively 'renting' the bank's balance sheet for the transaction and so will be charged for doing so in the form of the LIBOR plus a credit spread. From the bank's perspective this spread is also a source of profitability. The different components of the trade are shown in Fig. 10.5.

Another feature of these corporate equity swaps is that the client will be required to make an upfront margin payment of, say, 30 % of the notional, resulting in a 'loan to value' (LTV) of 70 %. As part of this agreement the swaps will also include a collateral trigger which will be activated when the share price reaches some pre-agreed level. So if the price of the share falls additional cash will be called from the client. Depending on the nature of

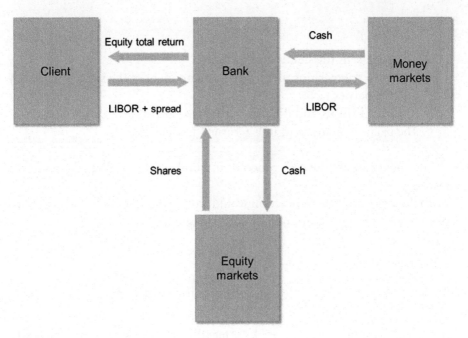

Fig. 10.5 Total return equity swap used for acquiring a target company (*Source*: author)

the agreement a rise in the share price could result in a return of collateral to the client. Although it is likely that the bank will have to pay interest on this margin, it may also be able to lend out the cash at a profit.

Typically, these swaps will require quarterly exchanges of cash flows. So the bank will pay across 100 % of any dividends received while the client will pay LIBOR plus a spread.

At the maturity of the swap the client can then choose to either physically or cash-settle the transaction:

Physical settlement

- The shares are delivered to the client against a payment equal to the bank's initial cost.
- The final LIBOR and dividend cash flows are settled.
- The balance of any margin is returned to the client.

The client now owns a proportion of the target company's outstanding shares.

Cash settlement

- The bank sells the shares in the market.
- The price appreciation/depreciation component of the swap is settled by the two parties.
- The final LIBOR and dividend cash flows are settled.
- The balance of any margin is returned to the client.

The client can use the cash proceeds to purchase the required shares in the market.

To illustrate how the transaction would work, consider the following example. For ease of illustration, margin calls are ignored.

Acquisition:	Target company
Initial share price:	€50
Number of shares:	1,000,000
Dividend:	€1 per share per quarter
3-month LIBOR:	2 % p.a.
Client credit spread:	1 % p.a.
Transaction maturity:	3 months (example assumes this is an exact quarter of a year)
Final share price:	€55

Physical settlement

- The bank delivers 1,000,000 shares at a price of €50/share against a payment of €50,000,000.
- The client pays the bank €375,000 on the funding leg (€50m × 3 % × 3/12).
- The bank pays €1m of dividends to the client.

The net economics is that the client now owns 1m shares at a net cost of €49,375,000 (€50m + €375,000 − €1m) or €49.375/share.

Cash settlement

- The bank sells its hedge of 1 million shares into the market at the prevailing price of €55/share.
- The bank pays €5m to the client to settle the price appreciation leg of the swap.

- The client pays the bank €375,000 on the funding leg (€50m × 3 % × 3/12).
- The bank pays €1m of dividends to the client.

The client could now use these swap proceeds of €5,625,000 to acquire 1m shares at the prevailing share price of €55 resulting in a net cost of €49,375,000.

So irrespective of how the client settles the deal the effect of the swap is that it fixes the price of the shares for future delivery. This single period swap is actually a forward as the cash flows comprise of a spot component plus the carry elements of funding and dividends.

10.6.2 Financing Shareholdings

Another way to finance the building of a stake is by means of a prepaid forward plus a price return swap (rather than the total return variation). As the name suggests this transaction is made up of two contracts, which are executed simultaneously: the client enters into a forward share sale and a total return equity swap. The main components of the trade are as follows:

- Client enters into a cash-settled forward transaction with the bank. A 'vanilla' forward would resemble a single period swap, that is, the client would deliver the market value of the shares at maturity in return for receiving a pre-agreed fixed cash flow. This fixed cash flow would be determined using 'no arbitrage' principles outlined in Sect. 9.2. However, a prepaid forward means that the cash flows will be slightly different. At the start of the transaction the client will receive a cash flow equal to the net present value of the shares, which is simply the initial spot value. At maturity they will pay to the bank a cash flow equal to the prevailing value of the shares. The fact that the transaction is cash-settled means that the client is able to retain ownership of the shares.
- Client enters into a total return equity swap where they will receive any equity upside and pay any downside as well as receiving any dividends. In addition, they will pay interest on the initial proceeds.
- The shares are pledged to the bank rather than being sold. The shares would be placed in a segregated account with restrictions placed on their sale. However, the client would still be able to enjoy any economic benefit.
- Since this is a collateralized structure it would be cheaper than alternative sources of finance.

The transaction is depicted in Fig. 10.6.

To illustrate how this transaction would work, consider the following example based on a position in a single share.

Initial share price:	£100
Dividend yield:	3 %
Interest rates:	5 %
Tenor:	1 year
Final share price:	£105

Using 'no arbitrage' principles the initial forward value of the share would be £102 (£100 + £5 − £3). However, the prepaid amount is the net present value of this sum, which is just the spot price of £100.

If at maturity the share has increased to £105 in value, the following cash flows are then settled:

Final market value of shares

- Client pays bank £105

Financing component:

- Client pays bank interest of £5 on the initial market value of the shares (£100 × 5 %).

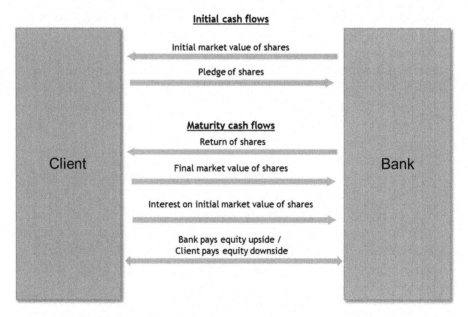

Fig. 10.6 Prepaid forward plus equity swap (*Source*: author)

Equity swap price return component

- Bank pays client £5

The net of all of the cash flows at maturity is £105.
So in summary the client has

- Borrowed £100 for 12 months.
- Pledged an equity position as collateral, but retained all of the economic benefits.

Repaid the £100 loan at the end of the transaction plus interest of £5.

10.6.3 Monetization of Cross Shareholdings

A TRS could be used to transform the returns of an existing shareholding, sometimes referred to as a 'monetization' strategy. The client is able to hedge a stake in a listed company giving away both the up and downside of the share price movement in return for a LIBOR-based fixed income return. Again this could be customized for the client. For example, a call spread could be added to the deal (see Sect. 11.3.2) to alter the risk-return profile. Since a call spread is a debit strategy the client would need to pay a premium but this could be achieved by increasing the spread to LIBOR on the funding leg. This would have the impact of reducing the size of the cash flow paid to the client.

Figure 10.7 assumes that a client has a shareholding in a particular company. They then enter into a total return swap where they give away the full economic exposure associated with the underlying shares. At maturity

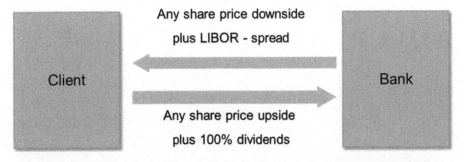

Fig. 10.7 Synthetic sale of shares using a total return swap (*Source*: author)

the equity swap could be settled in cash or by delivery of the underlying shares. Similar to the example in Sect. 10.6.1, the client has been able to lock in a forward sale price of the shares, while retaining all of the voting rights.

10.6.4 Diversification of Cross Shareholdings

A relative performance swap allows a client to fully hedge an existing cross shareholding, while gaining total exposure to an alternative equity asset, which could be a stock, a basket of stocks or an index. Economically, it is equivalent to selling the original stake and investing the proceeds into a new security. Similar to the previous example, the client is able to lock in a disposal price for both the original stake as well as the new security. One benefit though is that they will retain voting rights on the original position. The transaction is shown in Fig. 10.8.

Figure 10.8 shows that both counterparties will pay the total equity return meaning that they will pay any price upside as well as any dividends and receive any price downside.

This type of structure also allows for some degree of flexibility in terms of the customization. For example, the client could request that a zero premium collar be added to either or both of the legs.

10.7   Contracts of Difference

Sometimes the terms 'swaps' and 'contracts for difference' (CFD) are used interchangeably but within the equity market there are some subtle differences.

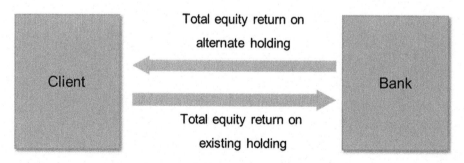

Fig. 10.8   Relative performance swap (*Source*: author)

10.7.1 Product Fundamentals

Definition
A CFD is an agreement between two entities to exchange a pre-agreed fixed cash flow for a variable cash flow established at the contract's maturity, the values of which reference the performance of a specific company's share price.[6]

Characteristics
The product has become popular for a number of reasons:

- The investor does not have to finance the entire purchase price of the underlying asset.
- CFDs can be traded for shares in countries that may be difficult for an investor to access such as those classified as being 'emerging'.
- The transaction retains all of the underlying economic benefits of owning the shares without the need for actual ownership, for example, share price change, receipt of all dividends paid by the issuer.
- Dividends are paid gross of any taxation.
- The investor can express both long and short views on the anticipated movement of the underlying.
- The transactions may be exempt from taxes that might be levied on a cash market purchase e.g. Stamp Duty in the UK.
- CFDs do not carry any voting rights that would be associated with a long position in the underlying stock.

Example
Suppose an investor wishes to express a bullish view on the UK media company BSkyB, whose share price is currently 900p. The terms of the agreed CFD are as follows:

Initial price	900p
Number of shares	500,000
Initial market value	£4,500,000
Initial margin	10 % (£450,000)
Investor receives	Share price appreciation plus dividends
Investor pays	Share price depreciation plus financing charges
Financing charges	Overnight LIBOR + 1 %
Initial LIBOR	2 %

[6] A CFD can also be structured to reference a sector or an equity index.

Dividend payment frequency	Dividends remitted on the date they are paid
Commission	2 basis points (£900)
Maturity	Open

This example supposes that the investor would typically finance themselves at LIBOR plus a spread. If the investor had decided to use the CFD as a way of expressing a view on a declining share price, then the financing charge they would have earned would have been LIBOR minus a spread. Typically, CFDs are traded without an agreed maturity and counterparties can give notice to terminate the contract on any trading day.

Suppose that the following day the share price has increased by 2p. The profit on the transaction would be:

Share price appreciation: $500,000 \times (902p - 900p) = £10,000$

Financing: $£4,050,000 \times 3\% \times 1/365 = £332.88$

Net profit: $£9,667.12$

Although the investor and the bank can negotiate any mutually acceptable transaction terms, these cash flows would typically be settled on a daily basis.

Note that the financing that the client pays is based on the market value of the shares less the initial margin that has been paid to the bank. This reflects the fact that the bank has probably purchased the underlying shares as a hedge on which it will need to pay a borrowing cost. The bank effectively passes this financing cost through to the client, net of the initial margin. Another way of thinking about this is to treat the difference between the market value of the shares and the initial margin as a loan to the client.

Leverage

This 1-day profit represents a 2.19 % return on their investment (i.e. the initial margin of £450,000). Although this may not seem like an enormous return the change in the share price over the 24-hour period represents a return of just 0.22 % and so the example illustrates the impact of being able to do this transaction while only being required to deposit a 10 % margin. This concept is sometimes referred to as 'leverage'[7] and is one of the reasons why entities such as hedge funds find this type of structure attractive.

---

[7] Defined here as the ability to use a small amount of money to control a larger exposure.

Break Evens

As a rule of thumb CFDs tend to be held for a maximum of a month or two. This can be seen by considering the breakeven position of the trade. Using the figures from the previous example, if the investor had bought the share they would have been required to pay Stamp Duty, which if assumed to be levied at 50 basis points would incur an additional cost of £22,500 (£4.5m × 0.50 %). The CFD incurs a daily financing cost of about £333, which would suggest that after approximately 68 days it becomes less economical to hold the CFD. A similar logic would hold for a short CFD position. In this case the investor would receive LIBOR minus a spread while holding the CFD but would have to pay lending fees to their counterparty.[8] So in this case it would be economical to trade the CFD only if the borrowing costs are less than the interest earned on a short CFD position.

Hedging a CFD Position

In order to hedge the CFD exposure the market maker will trade the underlying. So if a client has bought a CFD, the market maker will go long the physical stock. This means that if the price of the share rises, the hedge will show a profit that can be passed on to the client along with any dividends received. If a client sells a CFD, the market maker will need to borrow the stock the cost of which is passed on to the client. If the share price were to fall the short physical hedge position held by the market maker will show a profit that can be passed on to the end client. If a dividend is paid during the life of the transaction the market maker will remit a 'manufactured dividend' but this will again be financed by the end client.

Delta Hedging

This process of trading the underlying to hedge the CFD exposure is referred to as 'delta hedging' using the same terminology as the option market. If the trader were to trade the underlying in the same size as the CFD notional then the delta exposure would be zero ('delta neutral').

If the trader has chosen not to delta hedge the exposure, it would be possible to measure the 'gamma' of the position. This gamma value would represent the change in the delta equivalent value for a change in the underlying price. In the previous example assume that the trader decides to hedge the exposure by buying only 400,000 rather than the required 500,000 shares. His delta cash expo-

---

[8] These fees are payable as it is likely that the bank will short sell the shares as a hedge. The investor is therefore financing the bank's associated securities lending fees.

sure at this initial share price is −£900,000 (100,000 shares at 900p) indicating that he would lose money if the share price were to increase. His gamma for a 1 % increase in the share price would be −£9000 (100,000 shares × 9p). In other words, if the share price increases to 909p the delta equivalent exposure would increase to −£909,000. This confirms that the trader is losing money in a rising environment because if he chose to establish delta neutrality he would need to buy the residual 100,000 shares at the now higher price of 909p.

10.7.2 Applications

General
CFDs can be used for expressing short-term views on the evolution of the market. At the simplest level they could be used to express either a long or short view of market movements. This would be particularly attractive for jurisdictions such as the UK where the instrument is classified as a derivative and is therefore not subject to Stamp Duty, which is a tax levied on the purchase of shares. Extending this idea, CFDs could be used to hedge a physical share (or portfolio) against a possible adverse short-term move.

Corporate Actions
One popular CFD trade is referred to as *dividend stripping*. This transaction is based on the concept that the share price of a company should fall on the 'ex-dividend' date.[9] Theory would suggest that the share price should fall by the amount of the dividend although in practice this is unlikely to occur. An investor who takes a short CFD position would be able to realize a profit if the share did fall after the ex-dividend date.

Stock splits are usually implemented by companies that are seeking to reduce the absolute level of their share price.[10] One argument put forward to explain the rationale is that investors may perceive that a high share price may in some sense be 'expensive'.[11] As a result, the company may decide to split the stock to give the impression that it is more 'affordable'. However, anecdotally stock splits are often interpreted as a bullish sign by the market with the share price subsequently experiencing an increase in price.

---

[9] An investor buying a share on or after the ex-dividend date will not be eligible to receive the dividend.
[10] See Sect. 2.8 for an example.
[11] This is an over simplistic argument as it is possible for a share to be under- or overvalued irrespective of its price.

A *share buyback*[12] occurs when a company repurchases its own shares at a price that might be slightly higher than the prevailing price. Again this is often interpreted as a bullish move and is sometimes used as a legitimate tactic to drive up a company's share price. A CFD could be used to profit from this anticipated movement.

Pairs trading is a technique that is based on the potential for the price of two related shares to converge or diverge. The share that is expected to fall in value is sold, while the share that is expected to rise in value is purchased. This strategy is considered to be market neutral as it will only show a profit if the spread between the shares move in the way expected. Suppose that an investor believed that the spread between the two UK media companies BSkyB (900p) and ITV (200p) was too great. Consequently, the investor sells BSkyB and buys ITV. Suppose that shortly after opening the trade the price of BSkyB rises to 905p, while the price of ITV rises to 210p. The investor will lose 5p on the short position but will gain 10p on the long position. The overall direction of the market is irrelevant as the spread between the two prices has decreased resulting in an overall profit.

10.8 Summary

This chapter expanded the discussion about equity swaps that were first introduced in Chaps. 1 and 4. This chapter placed a greater emphasis on why investors may prefer swaps to other instruments such as futures. The chapter then discussed the way in which banks have developed variations on the basic structure to meet investor demand. Different applications were considered within an institutional and corporate context which included examples that focused on tax optimization as well as 'view driven' strategies such as trading the term structure of equity repo rates. The chapter concluded with an overview of the CFD market.

---

[12] See Sect. 2.12.

11

Investor Applications of Equity Options

11.1 Introduction

This chapter focuses on investor applications of equity options and covers five themes:

- Portfolio downside protection
- Expressing directional views
- Trades that benefit when the market is trading in either a volatile or range-bound manner
- Yield enhancement
- Outperformance strategies

The assumption in the majority of the examples is that the positions are held to maturity.

11.2 Portfolio Downside Protection

One of the most fundamental applications of equity options is to protect the value of a portfolio. In Sect. 6.3, it was argued that one of the key sources of the demand for equity market volatility was institutional investors who buy put index options to protect the value of their portfolios. There are a number of ways in which this strategy could be implemented.

© The Author(s) 2017
N. Schofield, *Equity Derivatives*, DOI 10.1057/978-0-230-39107-9_11

11.2.1 Buy a Put Option

Suppose an investor who holds a diversified portfolio of European equities is concerned that the markets in 'Euroland' may fall in the next 3 months as a result of ongoing economic problems. As such he is considering buying some form of protection against a dip in the EURO STOXX 50 index. Intuitively it seems appropriate to buy a put option since the market is expected to fall; however, this is not quite right. It would only make sense to buy the put option if the fund manager was fundamentally bullish but could not afford for his view to be wrong. If the fund manager was bearish, then they should simply sell the asset. Buying an option incurs premium which means that if he were to exercise the option, the effective sale price achieved for the underlying asset would be reduced by this amount.

The investor decides to 'overlay' his portfolio with the purchase of an ATM forward 3-month put on the EURO STOXX 50 index future. Market conditions at the time of the trade are assumed to be as follows:

Value of equity portfolio:	€3 m
Index futures price:	3000
Value of an index point:	€10
Index futures value:	€30,000
Number of options:	100
Option exposure:	€3 m
3-month ATM implied volatility:	17 %
Premium on 3-month ATMF option:	100 index points per contract (i.e. €1000 per contract)

For ease of illustration it is assumed that the spot market is trading at the same level as the futures market. Since the option is referencing an index future the investor will not be required to sell any underlying shares since settlement will take place in cash. Figure 11.1 shows all of the strategy's constituent components.

From Fig. 11.1 it is possible to make the following conclusions:

- The net position resembles a synthetic call on the underlying index.
- The maximum loss of €100,000 is equal to the premium paid (100 contracts × 100 index points × €10 an index point).
- The index future has to rise by 100 points to 3100 before the premium outlay is recouped and the strategy breaks even.

The reason the net payoff resembles a long call position can be traced back to the shorthand version of put call parity that was introduced in Sect. 4.7. For convenience it is reproduced here:

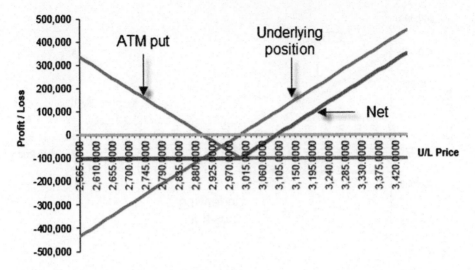

Fig. 11.1   Net position resulting from a long cash equity portfolio and a long ATM put option (*Source*: author)

$$+C - P = +F \qquad\qquad (11.1)$$

That is, the purchase of a call ($+C$) combined with the sale of a put ($-P$) is economically identical to being long the underlying asset ($+F$). So rearranging the formula to match the strategy, we have:

$$+C = +F + P \qquad\qquad (11.2)$$

That is, the combination of a long position in the underlying and a long put results in a synthetic long call.

Given many clients' reluctance to pay premium, it is probably more likely that they would buy OTM protection.[1] Suppose that they decided to buy an option that was 10 % OTM (i.e. a strike of 2700). Suppose that implied volatilities are skewed to the downside with the appropriate implied volatility input being 22 %. Despite this higher level of implied volatility, the cost of the option is now only 28 index points. Again, although this is less expensive in cash terms, it does not mean that it represents better value as it is possible that this implied volatility may be trading 'rich' to its 'normal' value. The profit and loss profile for this position is shown in Fig. 11.2.

The main points from Fig. 11.2 are:

---

[1] Even then the investor would only pay for this protection if they believed that implied volatility was trading cheap to some notion of fair value.

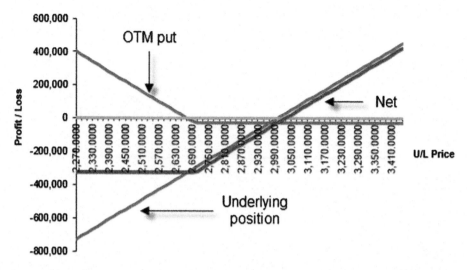

Fig. 11.2 Profit and loss profile for a long equity position overlaid with an OTM put (*Source*: author)

- The investor would lose the equivalent of 300 index points on the underlying equity portfolio before the put is exercised. This index movement is 10 % of the portfolio's value and so is equal to €300,000.
- The maximum loss on the entire position is equal to €328,000. This is made up of the €28,000 premium and the 300 index point loss incurred before the option is exercised.
- If the market rallies the option will break even earlier than the ATM strategy in Fig. 11.1 due to the lower premium. In this OTM example, the breakeven point is 3028 index points.

11.2.2 Put Spread

One of the popular arguments against the purchase of a single put is the premium cost. An alternative strategy for an investor is to sell some form of optionality in order to finance the desired long option position. The first strategy considered here is to sell an OTM put option to finance the long put position. The transaction is illustrated in Fig. 11.3 and comprises:

- Long position in the underlying established at 3000 index points.
- Long an ATM put option priced with an implied volatility of 17 % at a cost of 100 index points.

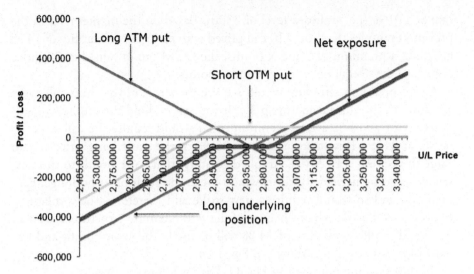

Fig. 11.3 Long position in an index future combined with the purchase of an ATM put and the sale of an OTM put (*Source*: author)

- Short an OTM put struck at 2850 (95 % of the initial spot price) priced with an implied volatility of 19 % to return an income of 51 index points.
- The net premium would be a cost of 49 index points.

Although the strategy is not zero premium the investor will still be able to enjoy any upside in the movement of the index although the position will underperform the market by the 49 index points of premium. This underperformance is less than the single put strategy illustrated in Fig. 11.1 as the premium is lower (49 index points vs. 100 index points). There is only a limited degree of downside protection between the two option strikes as this is part of the trade-off an investor must accept for the lower upfront premium. As a result, the investor is now faced with losses on the position below the strike of the short put. However, Fig. 11.3 shows that even if the position does lose money the losses are lower than if the investor had done nothing.

11.2.3 Collars

Collars are another popular technique that can be used to reduce the cost of portfolio protection. In this transaction the investor selects the desired strike for the long put option and then sells a call option to finance the purchase. One common way of structuring the deal is a 90—110 collar. Here the long put which provides the desired downside protection is struck at 90 % of the initial spot price (i.e. an index level of 2700) while the short call has a strike rate of 110 % (i.e. an index level of 3300). Based on the market data in the previous examples the short 110 call priced with an implied volatility of 14 % generates a premium of 9 index points, the OTM put is valued at 28 index points, so the overall net cost is 19 index points.

A zero premium structure would require the strike of the short call to be set closer to the current market price. If we were to hold the implied volatility constant at 14 % a zero premium collar would require the call strike to be set at 3159. This strike is about 105 % of the underlying price but to value this option correctly the implied volatility that corresponds to this new strike would be needed. But this would mean the position is no longer zero premium and so would require a new strike and therefore a new volatility! However, to illustrate the principles of the zero premium structure a strike of 3159 and implied volatility of 14 % will be used. The expiry profit and loss payoff for this position is shown in Fig. 11.4.

The key learning points from Fig. 11.4 are as follows:

• The position is zero premium. Many practitioners caution against describing this as a zero *cost* collar as arguably there is an opportunity cost associated with the strategy, that is, the investor cannot benefit from any upside beyond the strike of the short call option.
• The long OTM put establishes the lowest price at which the asset will be sold (2700 index points); losses cannot increase beyond this point.
• The short OTM call establishes the highest price at which the asset will be sold (3159 index points); profits cannot increase beyond this point.

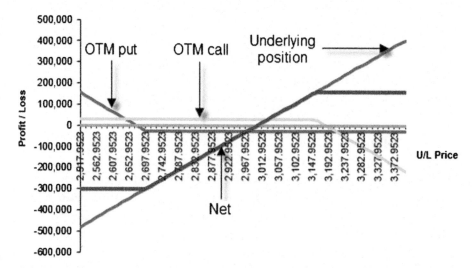

Fig. 11.4   Expiry pay off from a zero premium collar (*Source*: author)

- Between the two strikes, neither of the options are exercised and the investor has a long position in the underlying asset.

Over the years the banks have been faced with the challenge of varying the attractiveness of these strategies. Consider the following variation. The investor buys a put struck at 2850 index points (95 % of the market rather than 90 %) and finances this by selling a call struck at 3300 (110 % of the market rather than 105 %) all at zero premium. This structure increases the minimum and maximum sale price of the asset and is achieved by replacing the vanilla options with 'knock out' barrier options. In order to achieve zero premium at these two strikes the required options are as follows:

- Long a 'down and out' put option. Option strike is 2850 with the knock out barrier placed at 2650.
- Short a 'down and out' call option. Option strike is 3300 with the knock out barrier placed at 2650.

The impact of the two barriers on the profit and loss profile is shown in Fig. 11.5.
The key features of Fig. 11.5 are:

- The transaction is zero premium.
- Between the two strikes, neither of the options are exercised and so the investor is long the underlying market.

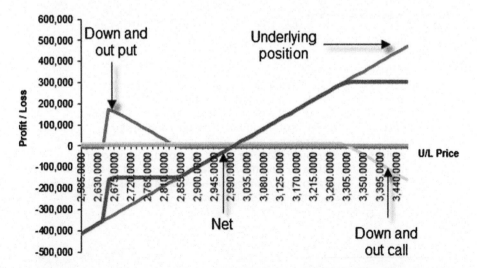

Fig. 11.5 Zero premium collar constructed using 'down and out' options (*Source:* author)

- The maximum and minimum prices achieved for the sale of the underlying asset are 3300 and 2850, respectively, both of which are more attractive than those achieved by the 'vanilla' zero premium call option.
- Below the barrier level of 2650 index points both options are knocked out removing all of the option protection. If the market continues to fall the investor's losses will move in line with the market. Equally, if the market were to recover the profit and loss would also move in line with the market.

11.2.4 Prepaid Variable Forward

Another strategy based on the collar idea is the 'prepaid variable forward' (PVF). This is sometimes described as a financing transaction as it allows the investor to borrow money against a future sale of shares. The structuring bank prepays a sum of money to the investor on the understanding that the investor will deliver shares to the bank at maturity. However, the number of shares that will be delivered at maturity will be a function of the final stock price. The PVF allows the investor to receive downside protection below a pre-agreed floor price while being allowed to participate in the appreciation of the underlying security to a pre-agreed ceiling price. Consider the following termsheet:

Seller:	Investor
Buyer:	Bank
Underlying security:	IBM
Initial share price:	$188.00
One-year interest rates:	5 %
Net dividend yield & repo rate:	2.5 %
ATMF implied volatility:	15 %[2]
Number of shares	50,000
Maturity:	1 year (actual/actual day count convention)
Floor price:	100 % of the initial share price ($188)
Ceiling price:	120 % of the initial share price ($226, rounded)
Purchase price:	91.84 % of the initial share price multiplied by the number of shares
Investor receives:	The purchase price at the start of the transaction
Bank receives:	Either (a) a number of shares determined by the settlement ratio multiplied by the number of shares or (b) the cash equivalent of such amount

---

[2] Example assumes constant volatility.

Divindends: Client retains any dividends paid by the issuer
Premium on 100 % $8.71
 put (i.e. floor)
Premium on 120 % $2.33
 call (i.e. ceiling)

The settlement ratio is determined according to the following conditions:

• If the final price is less than or equal to the floor price:

$$1$$

• If the final price is greater than the floor price but less than the ceiling price:

$$(\text{Floor price} / \text{Final price})$$

• If the final price is greater than or equal to the ceiling price:

$$1 - \left(\frac{\text{Ceiling price} - \text{Floor price}}{\text{Final price}} \right)$$

The PVF is a structure where the investor owns the asset and buys a 100 % put option, to give them downside protection under current market conditions; this would cost $8.71. The put is partly financed by the sale of a call struck at 120 % of spot to give an income of $2.33 although this will limit the investor's upside benefit. This results in a net cost to the client of $6.38 or $319,000 (50,000 shares × $6.38). The bank will then forward to the investor a sum of money equal to the present value of the shares based on the 'floor' strike of the put. This amount will be:

$$= \frac{50,000 \times \$188}{1.05} = \frac{\$9,400,000}{1.05} = \$8,952,381 \qquad (11.3)$$

However, from this amount the option premium of $319,000 will be subtracted to give a net amount of $8,633,381.[3]

---

[3] The option premium is already a present value.

Table 11.1 Cash flows at maturity for a prepaid variable forward transaction

Cash advanced to client	Maturity value of cash advance	Share price at maturity	Settlement ratio	Shares deliverable at maturity	Cash equivalent of deliverable shares	Market value of shares at maturity	Net value of cash delivered and shares retained	Net future value of package
(1)	(2)	(3)	(4)	$50,000 \times (4) =$ (5)	$(3) \times (5) = (6)$	$50,000 \times (3) =$ (7)	$(6) + (7) =$ (8)	$(2) + (8) = (9)$
$8,633,381	$9,065,050	$144	1	50,000	($7,200,000)	$7,200,000	0	$9,065,050
$8,633,381	$9,065,050	$157	1	50,000	($7,850,000)	$7,850,000	0	$9,065,050
$8,633,381	$9,065,050	$171	1	50,000	($8,550,000)	$8,550,000	0	$9,065,050
$8,633,381	$9,065,050	$188	1	50,000	($9,400,000)	$9,400,000	0	$9,065,050
$8,633,381	$9,065,050	$207	0.90821256	45,410.628	($9,400,000)	$10,350,000	$950,000	$10,015,050
$8,633,381	$9,065,050	$226	0.83185840	41,592.92	($9,400,000)	$11,300,000	$1,900,000	$10,965,050
$8,633,381	$9,065,050	$244	0.84426229	42,213.1145	($10,300,000)	$12,200,000	$1,900,000	$10,965,050

The amount to be repaid at maturity is shown in Table 11.1 and the following description gives an insight into how the structure works. In the following analysis it is assumed that the investor opts for cash rather than physical settlement.

- Column (1) is the present value of the sum of money forwarded to the client. This comprises the present value of the shares based on the strike of the floor ($8,952,381) less the net premium ($319,000).
- Column (2) indicates the amount the cash advance will be worth at maturity. The upfront proceeds in column (1) are future valued using the prevailing interest rate of 5 %.
- Column (3) indicates a range of possible share prices at maturity ranging from approximately 70 % to 130 % of the initial share price.
- Column (4) shows the calculation of the settlement ratio using the formulas outlined in the termsheet.
- Column (5) shows how many shares would need to be delivered if the investor opted for physical settlement. This is calculated as the settlement ratio multiplied by the transaction size of 50,000 shares.
- Column (6) calculates how much the investor will have to pay since they opted for cash settlement. This is based on the number of shares to be delivered (column (5)) multiplied by the expiry share price (column (3)). The brackets are used to denote an outgoing cash flow from the investor's perspective.
- Column 7 calculates how much the 50,000 shares will be worth at the expiry of the transaction and is calculated as the initial 50,000 holding multiplied by the expiry share price shown in column (3). These shares will be retained by the investor.
- Column (8) shows the net of the cash paid to settle the PVF (column [6]) and the value of the retained shares (column [7]).
- Column (9) indicates the overall value of the transaction to the investor and includes the fact that even though the investor has settled in cash, they retain the future value of the initial proceeds.

Another way in which the transaction could be viewed is that the net economic value to the investor is calculated as:

The maturity value of the initial proceeds – Cash paid to settle the *PVF* + Value of retained shares

By 'eyeballing' the figures in the final column the reader can hopefully recognize the characteristics of the long put/short call collar. Below the strike of the put option ($188) the package has a fixed minimum value; above the strike of the call option ($226) the package will have a fixed maximum value. Between the strikes the package moves in line with the market price. From the values in the final column it is possible to infer the price per share realized by this strategy.

- $9,065,050/50,000 = $181.30
- $10,015,050/50,000 = $200.30
- $10,965,050/50,000 = $219.30

Note that the minimum and maximum values achieved by the strategy are not exactly equal to the floor price (i.e. the $188 strike of the put) or the ceiling (the $226 strike of the call). The differences in both cases is $6.70 and this is equal to the future value of the net premium that was charged at the inception of the transaction. The client was charged $6.38 upfront and when this sum is future valued at a 5 % rate of interest it returns a value of $6.70 ($6.38 × 1.05). The same argument also holds for the value of the package at a price of $207.

11.2.5 Cash Extraction

A cash extraction strategy allows an investor to retain some upside exposure with limited down side risk, as long as they initially own the underlying stock. Typically, this is constructed by selling the inventory of a stock they own and using part of the proceeds to buy an ATM or perhaps slightly OTM call option. By selling the stock the trade unlocks the cash value of the asset while the call option retains the long upside exposure to the stock. This would be perhaps appropriate if the investor believed that the asset was going to fall in value but was prepared to pay a premium to maintain upside potential in case their view was wrong.

11.3 Expressing Directional Views

The examples in this section are based on Blackberry (BBRY) and the following market parameters have been used to value the associated options.

- Share price = $10.00
- 3-month forward price = $10.03

- Dividend yield = 0 %
- Interest rates = 1 %
- Maturity = 3 months
- ATM implied volatility = 52 % (volatility is assumed to be a constant unless otherwise specified).
- ATM option premium = $1.04

An investor believes that all of the bad news has been priced into BBRY's share price and is fundamentally bullish on the firm's prospects. The investor looks at the share's annual implied volatility of 52 %, which over a 3-month time period implies a range of movements of ± 26 %,[4] that is, a range of prices from $7.40 to $12.60.

11.3.1 Buying the Underlying Versus Buying a Call Option

A very popular notion is that buying a call is a 'better' strategy than buying the underlying asset. So, although a long call option will be delta positive and will therefore benefit from a rise in prices, it is also long vega and so will have some exposure to movements in implied volatility. If the investor did not have a view on volatility, then arguably a more appropriate directional strategy would be to simply buy the underlying option.

Suppose that an investor bought one BBRY share at $10.00 and 3 months later it is trading at $12.50. The investor's return is therefore 25 % [($12.50/$10) − 1]. If the trader bought an OTM call struck at $10.50, the cost would have been $0.83 and the investor's return in the same scenario would be 141 % [($2.00/$0.83) − 1]. In this case the option is effectively giving the investor more 'bang for their buck'. But consider the consequences of a smaller rise in the share price to $10.20. Now the return on the purchase of the share is 2 % but the return on the long call is −100 % as the option will not be exercised and the investor will lose their entire premium.

One of the key questions is to try and establish the optimum strike for the option position. One approach is to use a simple return on investment (ROI) calculation (Table 11.2).

The ROI is calculated as:

---

[4] This was calculated as 52 % divided by the square root of the number of 3-month trading periods in a year, that is, the square root of 4, which is 2.

Table 11.2 Return on investment for a variety of option strikes and final share prices

		Final share price				
		$10.50	**$11.00**	**$11.50**	**$12.00**	**$12.50**
Strike price and	**$10.50**	−100 %	−39.75 %	20.48 %	80.72 %	140.96 %
associated	$0.83					
premium	**$11.00**	−100 %	−100 %	−24.24 %	51.52 %	127.27 %
	$0.66					
	$11.50	−100 %	−100 %	−100 %	−3.85 %	92.31 %
	$0.52					
	$12.00	−100 %	−100 %	−100 %	−100 %	21.95 %
	$0.41					
	$12.50	−100 %	−100 %	−100 %	−100 %	−100 %
	$0.32					

$$MAX\left[\frac{(\text{Final share price} - \text{Strike price}) - \text{Premium}}{\text{Premium}}, -100\ \%\right] \quad (11.4)$$

The formula 'floors' the ROI at a maximum of −100 % which reflects that the buyer of an option cannot lose more than their initial premium. Table 11.2 does assume that the trader holds the option until maturity rather than trying to earn a profit by closing out the exposure prior to maturity as a result of a favourable mark-to-market valuation.

The author recalls a casual conversation many years ago with a senior trader who in passing commented that 'only dreamers buy options'. Although it was meant as a light-hearted comment, perhaps Table 11.2 suggests there is some merit in this view. The table shows that there is no single 'right' solution but it does force the investor to consider the risk-return payoff under a variety of different scenarios, only a small number of which return a profit.

11.3.2 Call Spread

A call spread involves the purchase of a low strike call and the sale of a higher strike call both with the same maturity. The premium paid on the low strike, long call option is higher than the income received on the higher strike, short call making this a debit strategy. To reflect this initial cost, the strategy is also sometimes referred to as a long call spread.

With the spot price of BBRY at $10.00 a '$10.50/$12.00 call spread' would cost $0.43 per share. The structure comprises:

- The purchase of a call at $10.50 at a cost of $0.83.
- The sale of a call at $12.00 that generates a premium of $0.40.

The constituent options and the associated 'at maturity' payoffs are shown in Fig. 11.6.

Suppose that at maturity the stock price has risen to $12.50. The long call option pays the investor $2 while the short call option loses $0.50. The investor will have made a profit of $1.07 ($1.50 − $0.43), which is a 248 % return on their investment.

There are a few points that are worth mentioning about this structure:

- The maximum loss is equal to the premium paid ($0.43 per share), while the maximum profit is $1.07.
- Although this strategy is most commonly referred to as a call spread it is perhaps more accurate to refer to it as a bull spread, that is, the greatest profit is made when prices rise.
- A bull spread can also be constructed using put options. The purchase of a put at $10.50 and the sale of a put at $12.00 would generate the same at expiry profile. However, the risk-return payoff is slightly different; using puts the maximum profit is equal to the premium income of $1.06 (less than the call structure) while the maximum loss is $0.44 (greater than the call structure).

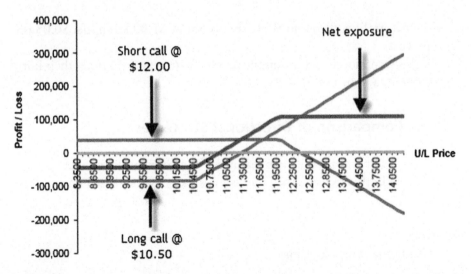

Fig. 11.6 At expiry payoff of a call spread. Position is based on a notional of 100,000 shares (*Source*: author)

- Creating a bull spread using puts is not, however, a put spread. Put spreads are a bearish strategy that involves the purchase of a high strike (i.e. ITM) put and the sale of a low strike (i.e. OTM) put at a net cost.[5]

11.3.3 1 × 2 Call Spread[6]

This strategy is an extension of the call spread introduced in the previous section. Based on the market data for BBRY it can be constructed as follows:

- Purchase of a call struck at $10.50 (premium cost $0.83/share)
- Sale of two calls struck at $12.00 (total premium income $0.80/share)

So it is simply a call spread with a second call added at the higher strike. The sale of the second call option at the higher strike reduces the net outlay to $0.03/share.

Diagrammatically the 'at expiry' payoff of the option is shown in Fig. 11.7.

Suppose that at maturity BBRY's share price has increased to $12.50. The profit and loss on the different components are as follows:

- Long call option shows a profit of $2.00/share ($12.50 − $10.50).
- The short call options show a loss of $1.00/share (($12.00 − $12.50) × 2).

The net profit is therefore $0.97 (net profit of $1.00 less initial $0.03 premium cost).

In this scenario, the return on the investor's strategy is 32 times their initial investment, a return of 3133 %.

11.3.4 Comparison of Directional Strategies

Table 11.3 summarizes the main features of the different directional strategies considered in this section. The table assesses the strategies based on a number of criteria:

- Cost
- Maximum payout at expiry

---

[5] It follows that a bear spread could also be created using calls, which would generate premium income but would have a different risk–return profile.
[6] This strategy is sometimes referred to as a call ratio spread.

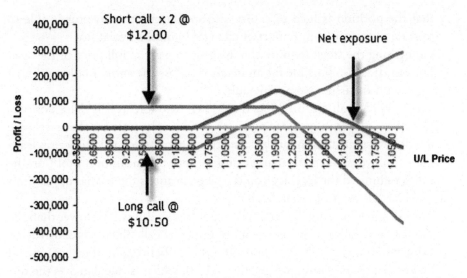

Fig. 11.7 At expiry payoff of a 1 × 2 call spread. Position is based on a notional of 100,000 shares for the long call position and 200,000 shares for the short call position (*Source*: author)

- Maximum loss
- Leverage. In this context leverage is defined as the maximum possible 'at expiry' profit divided by the initial option premium
- View on the market

So what are the main conclusions to be drawn from Table 11.3?

- In one sense the purchase of the stock is the only 'pure' directional trade as the remaining strategies have some exposure to movements in implied volatility. However, all of our examples in this section are based on the notion

Table 11.3 Comparison of directional strategies

Strategy	Cost	Maximum payout	Maximum loss	Leverage	View on market?
Long stock	$10.00	Unlimited	$10.00	None	Rise in market
Call struck @ $10.50	$0.83	Unlimited	$0.83	Potentially very high	Delta and vega positive
Call spread ($10.50/$12.00	$0.43	$1.50	$0.43	3.48	Slightly delta positive but vega neutral
1 × 2 call spread ($10.50/$12.00)	$0.03	$1.50	Unlimited	50	Slightly delta negative but vega neutral

that the position is held to expiry and so assumes the investor is able to tolerate the revaluation impact of changes in implied volatility.

- Going long the stock requires the investor to pay the full price of the asset upfront. It is also possible for an investor to lose the entire market value of the asset if the issuer were to default.

- A long OTM call option offers directional exposure as it is delta positive. However, it is also vega positive so it would be plausible for the asset price to fall by a small amount at the same time that implied volatility rises leading to an overall mark-to-market profit. Since the maximum profit on the call is unlimited the leverage could be significant as there is no upper limit to which the asset price could rise.

- The call spread is initially delta positive although this will be lower than the single OTM call strategy as a result of the short call. Since it is constructed using both long and short call positions the initial vega on the position will be low. The maximum gross profit is $1.50, which is calculated as the difference between the two option strikes. The long call at $10.50 is the lowest price at which the investor can buy the asset while the strike of the short call—$12.00—is the highest price at which he will be required to take delivery. This returns a leverage value of 3.48 ($1.50/$0.43).

- The 1 × 2 call spread has a lower overall premium and offers a greater degree of leverage. The maximum payout (as opposed to net profit) on the strategy is achieved at a price of $12.00 which occurs at the strike of the two sold call options. At this expiry price the investor will receive a $1.50 payoff from the single long call but will not be required to make any payments under the short call positions as they are not exercised. This returns a leverage value of 50 ($1.50/$0.03). Although the leverage value is very attractive, there is considerable downside risk. As Fig. 11.7 shows an increase in prices could lead to unlimited losses. Tompkins (1994) describes this type of transaction as a 'leaning volatility trade'. Initially the position is slightly delta negative reflecting the fact that it will lose money from an increase in prices. It is also slightly vega negative, by virtue of the two sold options. So it begs the question as to whether this is really a directional trade. In one sense yes because the maximum profit is made when prices rise a little; however, a substantial rise in prices would result in significant losses. On the other hand, a significant fall in prices would result in losses equal to the initial premium paid.

So which strategy is appropriate? It depends! There is no single right answer and the investor is faced with having to make a judgement call based on a number of factors that could include the following:

- Views on the likely share price at maturity, which may be driven by fundamental issues.
- How certain are they of their view? If they are very certain then perhaps the purchase of a share would be more appropriate than an option-based strategy.
- Does the investor think there is limited upside in the price movements? If they were bullish but felt strongly there was limited upside perhaps this may make a 1 × 2 call spread attractive.
- Does the investor believe that volatility is fairly valued? Is the investor allowed to sell options? If the investor felt that implied volatility was overvalued, then it may be appropriate to be a seller rather than a buyer of an option. For example, the sale of a put may be attractive if the investor believes a rise in the market may be associated with a fall in implied volatility.

So perhaps the conclusion is that an investor should always think in terms of scenarios. Sometimes a strategy will make money while other times it will lose; sometimes a strategy works well but in other circumstances it will not!

11.4 Range-Bound Versus Volatile Views

The examples in this section are again based again on BBRY and use the same market values presented in Sect. 11.3. The underlying scenario is based on the idea that the market is perhaps split on the future prospects for the company; ongoing poor earnings may trigger another fall in the price of the share but positive news may lead to a rally. Either way movements in the stock price are expected to be significant. It is also assumed that the investor considers implied volatility to be fairly valued.

This section considers two popular strategies that can be used to express views on whether an asset will trade inside or outside a particular range of values. These are also sometimes referred to as 'volatility' trades.

11.4.1 Straddles

A long straddle is a combination position that comprises of a purchase of a call and a put with the same strike and maturity. These could be constructed in a variety of different ways:

- ATM spot
- ATM forward
- Delta neutral

An ATM spot straddle would require that the options be struck at the pre-vailing spot price of $10.00. The call would be priced at $1.04/share, while the put would cost $1.01/share. Since the investor is buying both options this results in a net cost of $2.05. The ATM forward structure returns a premium of $1.03/share for both options by virtue of the principles of put call parity.

However, if either of these positions were established as suggested they would both possess a small initial directional exposure. The ATM spot position has a net delta of 11 %, while the ATM forward position has a net delta of 10 %. Some traders may decide to select the strikes such that the position is initially delta neutral. Using the market data for BBRY this can be achieved by setting the option strikes equal to $10.36. Neither option is ATM on either a spot or forward basis but both will have an option delta of 50 %—positive for the call and negative for the put. This also highlights that an ATM will not always trade with a delta of 50 %, which is a common misconception. The delta-neutral long straddle position is illustrated in Fig. 11.8.

This strategy will tend to perform well when implied volatility is relatively low with respect to expected market movements. So if the investor did believe that implied volatility was a measure of future realized volatility but had a

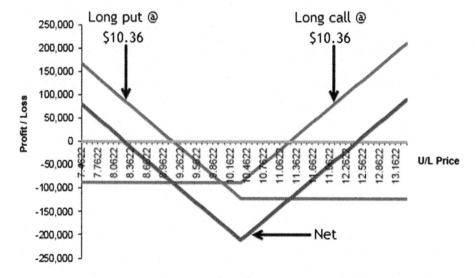

Fig. 11.8 At expiry delta-neutral long straddle position. Position is based on a notional of 100,000 shares per leg (*Source*: author)

view that the market was underestimating expected market movements, this strategy may be appropriate.

The cost of the 3-month long delta-neutral straddle is $2.10/share and so this means that the investor must believe that BBRY's share price movements will be greater than the strike plus or minus the net premium cost, that is, less than $8.26 or greater than $12.46. If the market does not move, then the passage of time (i.e. the theta effect) will reduce the value of the option. Indeed, the maximum loss of $210,000 will be realized at expiry if the underlying share price has not moved.

11.4.2 Strangle

A strangle position is a less expensive way of expressing a similar view on an asset's future realized volatility but for it to be profitable the asset price will have to move by a significant amount. There are a number of ways in which the strategy could be defined but a common way is to structure the trade according to each option's delta. So a '25 delta strangle' is constructed such that the strike of each option equates to a delta of 25. Based on the market data already presented the respective strikes would be as follows:

- Long call struck at $12.34, premium $0.34/share
- Long put struck at $8.71, premium $0.44/share
- Net premium cost = $0.78/share

The long strangle is shown in Fig. 11.9.

For this position to be profitable the share price would have to move beyond the two respective strikes by the amount of the initial premium.

- Breakeven for the long put option: $8.71 minus premium of $0.78 = $7.93.
- Breakeven for the long call option: $12.34 plus the premium of $0.78 = $13.12.
- Similar to the straddle the passage of time (i.e. the theta effect) will result in the investor losing both premiums if the share price does not move.

11.4.3 Comparison of Volatility Strategies

As with most option strategies there is only a right answer with the benefit of hindsight. The straddles will pay the investor more if the view is right but suffer from significant time decay if the view is wrong. The strangle will also

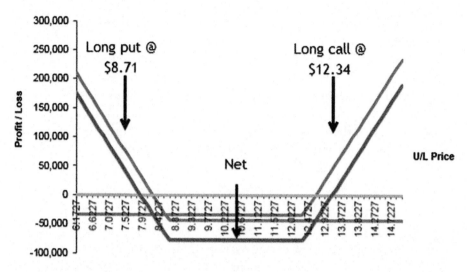

Fig. 11.9 Long strangle. Position is based on a notional of 100,000 shares per leg (*Source*: author)

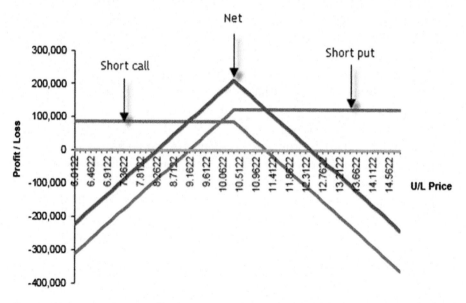

Fig. 11.10 At expiry payoff of delta-neutral short straddle. Sell a call and a put with the strikes set such that the net delta is zero. Based on a notional amount of 100,000 shares per leg (*Source*: author)

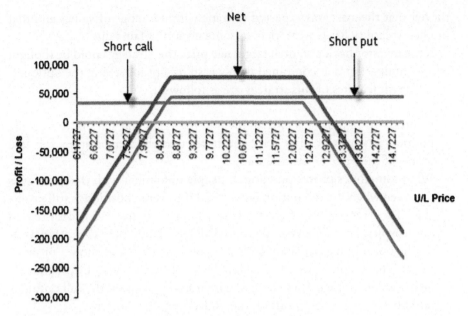

Fig. 11.11 At expiry payoff of 25 delta short strangle. The strike of each option is set at a level that corresponds to a delta value of 25. Based on an option notional of 100,000 shares per leg (*Source*: author)

suffer from time decay but to a lesser extent as the premium is lower. However, it will require a more significant move in the underlying asset price for the strangle to be profitable.

Although this section focused on expected volatile movements in the share price, the same trades can be used to express range-bound views. These short positions are shown in Fig. 11.10 (short straddle) and Fig. 11.11 (short strangle) and are based on the same market factors and strikes as the equivalent long position.

11.5 Yield Enhancement Strategies

11.5.1 Covered Calls/Call Overwriting

A covered call consists of a long position in an underlying asset combined with the sale of an OTM call option (Fig. 11.2). Using the market data for BBRY and a strike of $11.00 for the option position the strategy earns the investor $0.66 premium on the short call position. In essence the strategy is based on the idea that the short call option will not be exercised allowing the investor to keep the premium. So this strategy may be appropriate if the investor felt that the asset was expected to trade within a range of values and that implied volatility levels were 'rich' to some notion of fair value.

If the investor has a potential target sale price this strategy could be thought of as a 'limit sell order' combined with a cash receipt for selling the option.

The main features of this strategy are as follows:

- Contrary to popular belief that 'owning the share and sell options on the position has no risk', Fig. 11.2 illustrates that the net position will lose money if the price of the asset falls.
- What sometimes proves puzzling to people unfamiliar with this strategy is that even when the call option is exercised the overall position is still profitable. The easy way to grasp this is to assume that the call is cash-settled upon expiry. So if the expiry price of BBRY is $12.00 then the cash payout on the option on a per share basis is $1.00 but the shares show a profit of $2.00. The net profit would therefore be $1.66/share when the premium is included. So as the price goes up the increased payout on the call option is offset by an increasing profit on the underlying shareholding.
- The point at which the overall strategy loses money is equal to the market price of the asset less the initial premium. In this case the net position loses money from a price of $9.34 ($10.00 − $0.66).
- There is a cross-over point where the net position becomes less attractive than holding the underlying share. This is where the short call option

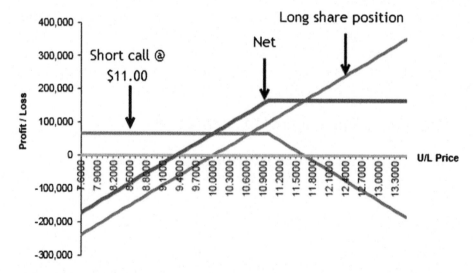

Fig. 11.12 Covered call. Investor is long the share and short an OTM call option. Example is based on a notional position of 100,000 shares (*Source*: author)

breaks even and is equal to the strike price plus the premium, that is, $11.66.

- Between $9.34 and $11.66 the transaction outperforms a holding in the underlying share. Indeed, it could be argued that if the share price is less than $9.34 the net position still outperforms as it loses less than an outright position in the asset (Fig. 11.12).

11.5.2 Call Spread Overwriting

If the investor's performance is benchmarked to an index, then if the markets were to rally significantly a covered call strategy would result in relative underperformance. This can be managed by the additional purchase of an OTM call. Figure 11.13 shows this strategy which is constructed by adding a long OTM call struck at $12.00. This additional option costs $0.44/share reducing the initial net income to $0.26/share.

Figure 11.13 shows that as the price moves beyond the strike of the long call option the position will rise in value in parallel with the underlying market. However, it still underperforms by the amount equal to the difference between the two option strikes plus the initial premium. So if at expiry the price of BBRY is $13.00 the profit from just holding a share would be $3.00. However, the combined call spread overwriting position will show a profit of $2.26, which is an underperformance of $0.74. This $0.74 can be decomposed into the net of

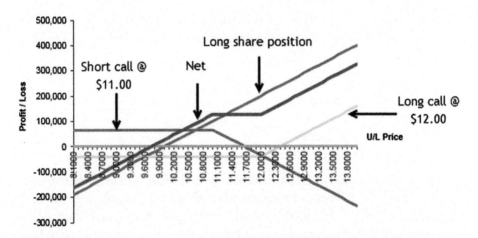

Fig. 11.13 Call spread overwriting. Example is based on a notional position of 100,000 shares (*Source*: author)

- A loss of $2.00 on the short call
- A gain of $1.00 on the long call
- The receipt of the initial premium $0.26

11.5.3 Put Selling

Another strategy used by investors is to sell put options on stocks they would happily buy at a relatively low price. Suppose that an investor is bullish on BBRY but is looking to acquire the share during a dip in its price. The investor decides to sell a put option with a strike of $9.00 to earn $0.55/share. If the share price falls below the strike the option is exercised against the investor who takes delivery of the share at a net cost of $8.45, that is, the $9.00 strike less the $0.55 cent premium received. However, this strategy is fundamentally bullish as the short put is delta positive and would show a profit if the underlying price were to rise.

It is a form of yield enhancement as this strategy could be viewed as a 'limit buy order' combined with a cash receipt for selling the put option.

11.6 Outperformance Strategies

Outperformance strategies focus on the relative performance of one share with respect to another. Motivations for these trades could be based on the following:

- *Fundamental views*—here the investor's focus is how the company is performing relative to the current phase of the business cycle. Popular trades may include

    - large versus small capitalized companies;
    - assets that are designated as 'value' against those seen as 'growth' shares;
    - index versus Index;
    - sector versus sector trades.

- *Quantitative views*—here the investor's initial focus is to identify two assets that are linked from a fundamental analysis perspective (e.g. the same industry sector). The analyst would then apply some quantitative technique to identify potential value. One possible approach would be to identify a spread between the two (e.g. price or volatility) and then base their trading decisions on deviations from the mean value.

Table 11.4 Market data for BBRY and APPL

	BBRY	APPL
Share price	$10	$128
Dividend yield	0 %	1.48 %
1-year forward price	$10.10	$127.64
1-year 50 call delta vol	48 %	28 %
1-year normalized delta skew	9 %	6.5 %
Correlation (30-day rolling correlation for 12-month period)	0.21	0.21

In this section we will illustrate a possible approach using two assets, BBRY and Apple (APPL). The market data used in the examples is shown in Table 11.4.

11.6.1 Option Ratios

Option ratios comprise of a long and short position of the same option type for the same maturity but in different assets.

Call ratios

- Buy a call option on asset A
- Sell a call option on asset B

Put ratios

- Buy a put option on asset A
- Sell a put option on asset B

The key driver behind the transaction is an expectation that the implied volatility differential between the two shares will converge. Using the data in Table 11.4 the volatility differential for BBRY and APPL is 20 % for the 50 delta call options. The trade involves buying optionality on the lower volatility share and selling optionality on the higher volatility share.

There are a number of ways in which the strike rate could be chosen:

- ATM spot.
- ATM forward.
- The same degree of 'moneyness', for example, both strikes are set at the same percentage as their spot price—say, 105 %.

- Equivalent delta values, for example, both options are traded with a strike that corresponds to the same delta—say, 40 %. This means that the positions will have the same initial exposure to changes in their respective underlying price.

There are also different approaches to the choice of notional amount:

- Equal notional amounts such that the number of options × contract size × spot price is the same for both legs.
- Volatility-weighted notionals, for example, since BBRY is more volatile than APPL then trade 1.71 times (48 %/28 %) more of APPL than BBRY.
- Notional amounts set at a level that generates a net premium of zero.

To illustrate these principles, consider the following hypothetical example:

- Buy call options on APPL struck at a 40 delta ($141.69). Premium cost per share is $8.81.
- Sell call options on BBRY struck at 40 delta ($12.80). Premium income per share is $1.07.

In this case although APPL is trading with a lower implied volatility, a trade based on the same number of shares would result in a net outflow of $7.74/share ($8.81 − $1.07). In order to structure a zero premium trade, the investor would need to decide upon an appropriate trade size for one of the assets and weight the other accordingly. Suppose that the investor decided that the appropriate size for the trade was 300,000 BBRY options,[7] which would generate an initial net premium of $321,000. To make this structure zero premium the investor would need to buy 36,436 (rounded) APPL options.

So why do this trade? The main motivation is that the investor is hoping that the implied volatility of BBRY will fall relative to APPL such that the position could be unwound at a profit, all other things being equal. However, the strategy is not without risk:

- The short call could suffer from losses if BBRY's share price increased significantly. This potential loss could be managed by the purchase of an extra OTM call.

---

[7] Assume that 1 option = 1 share.

- If both share prices fell and the position is held to maturity both options would expire OTM and so the investor would not make any money.
- Chapter 6 illustrated that there is typically an inverse relationship between the levels of implied volatility and asset prices. So a fall in BBRY's volatility could be associated with a rise in the price, which would make the short call position less profitable. The same could also be said of APPL—an increase in implied volatility will increase the value of the call, but this could be offset by a possible fall in the share price.
- Recall from Chap. 4 the inverse relationship between call option premiums and dividends. If BBRY were to pay a dividend during the life of the transaction the short call would lose value resulting in a profit.

11.6.2 Risk Reversals

A risk reversal strategy is designed to profit from movements in an option's volatility skew and involves the purchase of an OTM call, which is financed by the sale of an OTM put.

Table 11.4 shows the normalized skew of both assets. This concept was introduced in Chap. 6 but the formula is repeated here for ease of reference:

$$\frac{\left(\text{Volatility of 25 delta put} - \text{Volatility of 50 delta put}\right)}{\text{Volatility of 50 delta put}}$$

$$\text{Minus} \tag{11.5}$$

$$\frac{\left(\text{Volatility of 25 delta call} - \text{Volatility of 50 delta call}\right)}{\text{Volatility of 50 delta call}}$$

At a very simple level the higher the normalized skew the more the asset is 'skewed to the downside', that is, OTM low strike puts are trading with higher implied volatilities than OTM high strike calls.

Suppose that an investor believes that BBRY's share price is likely to increase and observes the following 12-month implied volatility values in the market:

- 25 delta put struck at $8.17. Implied volatility 50 %, premium of $0.98/share
- 25 delta call struck at $15.48. Implied volatility 47 % premium of $0.57/share

The investor buys the 25 delta call option and finances it by selling the 25 delta put option to create a 'long' or 'bullish' risk reversal position. When the position is structured in this way it will have a net positive delta exposure of 50 %. Since the investor is trying to make money from movements in volatility, they may possibly decide to make the position delta neutral by borrowing and short selling the underlying asset.

The trader is looking to profit from an anticipated increase in the share price, so if he were to pre-emptively buy an OTM call and sell an OTM put, he would make money if the underlying price were to move as expected. Although this suggests a directional view one of the main motivations for this trade is based on expected changes of implied volatility. The increase in demand for OTM calls should in turn lead to an increase in implied volatility and, all other things being equal, an increase in their value. The selling pressure on the OTM puts would lead to a fall in both its implied volatility and premium which would also result in a profit.

The example just illustrated was based on equal notional amounts with the options struck at the same delta level. It is also common for the trade to be structured to be zero premium. So based on the figures for BBRY and assuming the investor is happy with the 25 delta strike for the call option, the strike on the short put would need to be set at a lower level of $7.05 for the position to return a zero premium.

Suppose that after 6 months the investor's view does materialize such that the share price has risen to $12.00. Assume the following values are now observed in the market:

- Put struck at $8.17. Implied volatility 49 %, premium = $0.22/share.
- Call struck at $15.48. Implied volatility 48 %, premium = $0.62/share.

So if the investor were now to unwind the position, they would make $0.05/share on the long calls and $0.76/share on the short puts to return a net profit of $0.81/share.

So when the position was first established, the market displayed a 'negative skew' but after 6 months, it is now relatively flatter. This is shown in Fig. 11.14.

From an outperformance perspective, if the investor believed that APPL's share price might decline and that this would be associated with an increase in the skew to the downside, then at the same time they could enter into a short risk reversal position:

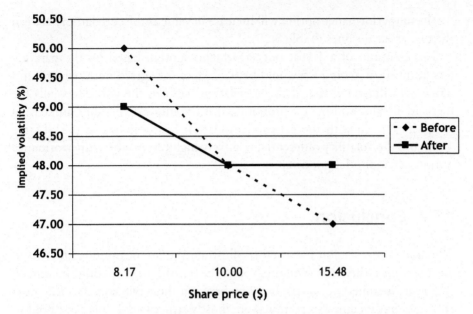

Fig. 11.14 Evolution of volatility skew for BBRY. Hashed line shows the initial volatility values; unbroken line shows final values (*Source*: author, Barclays Live)

- Buy an OTM put (i.e. low strike put).
- Sell an OTM call (i.e. high strike call).

So the outperformance of BBRY's share price over that of APPL is reflected by a change in their respective skews:

- BBRY's skew is less negative (i.e. flatter).
- APPL's skew is more negative (i.e. steeper to the downside).

11.6.3 Outperformance Options

Outperformance options were considered in detail in Sect. 8.4. Suppose an investor believes asset A (BBRY) will outperform asset B (APPL) over some given time period. Equation 11.6 shows the expiry payoff at a future time period, t, of an outperformance asset written on the two assets.

$$\text{Notional amount} \times MAX\left(\frac{\text{Asset price}_{A,t}}{\text{Asset price}_{A,0}} - \frac{\text{Asset price}_{B,t}}{\text{Asset price}_{B,0}}, 0\right) \quad (11.6)$$

The outperformance option will increase in value as the correlation between the two assets declines (Table 8.10).

The premium of a 1-year outperformance option based on the parameters outlined in Table 11.3 would be 0.24 % of the agreed notional amount. Table 8.11 illustrates that if the correlation between the two assets falls the increase in value will be less pronounced if the implied volatility differential is significant. So with the existing correlation relatively low at 0.21 (Table 11.3) and the volatility differential relatively high (20 %) the outperformance option may not offer good value.

11.7 Conclusion

The aim of this section has been to illustrate the use of options more from an investing rather than a trading perspective. Although it could be argued that there is sometimes a very fine line between these two concepts the main strategies outlined in this section were mostly structured as 'buy and hold to maturity' positions. More 'view driven' strategies involving correlation and volatility are considered in Chaps. 14 and 15.

12

Structured Equity Products

12.1 Introduction

Structured equity products have been a feature of the equity markets for many years. But what is a structured product? In general terms, a structured product is an investment whose risk-return profile cannot be easily replicated by the end investor. Broadly speaking there are two ways of structuring this type of instrument. Some can be 'engineered' by combining different instruments; for example, a basic capital protected note can be replicated by a zero coupon deposit and a long call option. On the other hand, some so-called exotic structured products are designed with a specific investor payout in mind and the payoffs are modelled using a Monte Carlo simulation.

Structured products have been well documented over the last few years and so this chapter covers a specific number of topics. These include the following:

- Examples of the most popular types of note
- An intuitive explanation of how the products are structured
- The residual risks faced by the structuring banks

By focusing on the residual risk for the structuring banks it is possible to understand the source of the different market flows illustrated originally in Fig. 6.3. The main conclusion of this chapter is that from a risk-management perspective, the structured product business leaves a bank with

© The Author(s) 2017

N. Schofield, *Equity Derivatives*, DOI 10.1057/978-0-230-39107-9_12

- short volatility;
- long dividend risk;
- short correlation.

As a result of these exposures, banks have then developed products or strategies in an attempt to mitigate the risk, for example, dividend swaps or dispersion trading.

12.2 Capital Protected Notes

Introduction
The earliest incarnation of structured notes offered investors a payoff based on the performance of a designated index in addition to the protection of their capital. These notes were often casually referred to as being capital 'guaranteed', but in reality this was not the case. These instruments are liabilities of the issuing entity and are often structured so that the investor is an unsecured creditor in the event of bankruptcy. This means that not only does the investor have exposure to the movement in the index, but they also must consider the creditworthiness of the issuer.

Example Termsheet
To illustrate the payoff of these notes, consider the following hypothetical structure.

Issuer:	Bank
Issue size:	$10,000,000
Note amount:	$1000 per note
Price per note:	100 %
Tenor:	4 years
Principal protection:	100 %
Interest:	None
Underlying index:	S&P 500
Participation rate:	100 %
Initial index value:	2000
Payment at maturity:	(a) If the final index value is greater than the initial index value, the investor earns $1000 + supplemental return amount.
	(b) If the final index value is less than or equal to the initial index value, the investor receives back $1000.
Supplemental return:	$1000 × participation rate × index percent change
Index percent change:	(final index value − initial index value)/initial index value

Table 12.1 Potential 'at maturity' payoffs from a capital protected structured note

Final index value	Index percent change	Payment at maturity
1800	−10.00	$1000
1900	−5.00	$1000
2000	0.00	$1000
2100	5.00	$1050
2200	10.00	$1100
2300	15.00	$1150

Investor's Return

Table 12.1 shows the amount an investor would receive based on different index values at the note's maturity based on a single note holding of $1000.

Structuring Principles

When structuring the capital protected note, there are two key themes:

- How will the structuring bank ensure there are sufficient funds available for the capital protection?
- How is the upside participation rate to be engineered?

To illustrate both of these issues, the following market values are assumed:

S&P 500 Index level:	2000
Tenor:	4 years
Funding rates:	1.00 %
Dividend yield:	2.00 %
Index implied volatility:	20 %

The capital protection is achieved by placing a proportion of the investor's initial funds on deposit such that it will accrue in value over the term of the note to reach $1000 by the maturity. Given the parameters stated above, this would require the structuring bank to deposit the present value of $1000:

$$\frac{\$1,000}{(1+0.01)^4}$$
$$\frac{\$1,000}{1.0406} = \$961$$

(12.1)

In the most basic structure, the investor's upside return is structured using a long call option that is struck ATM spot. This option is purchased using the balance of the investor's proceeds once sufficient funds have been allocated to the deposit—$39 in this case. The cost of an ATM spot option in this example costs 262 index points (rounded) but this needs to be converted into a cash equivalent. This is done by expressing the premium as a percentage of the strike, which returns a value of 13.1 %.[1] This represents the percentage of the amount invested in the note that it would cost to buy an option that would offer 100 % participation in the index. Since the cost of 1 certificate is $1000 the cost of an option with a notional amount of $1000 that offers 100 % participation would be $131. However, in our example this presents the structurer with a problem as they only have $39 available meaning they can only afford 30 % of the option; or put another way they could afford one option with a notional amount of $300 that offers 100 % upside.

Since a 30 % upside would not be particularly attractive to an investor the structurer has a number of techniques at his disposal to 're-engineer' the note.

The first technique would be to *alter the initial level of the index from which the performance is measured*, that is, the strike rate of the underlying call option. Although in our example the strike is ATM spot, the option is European in style and as such a BSM framework would value the option relative to the forward price. So although the option is ATM spot it is OTM on a forward basis,[2] which works in the investor's favour as the chosen strike cheapens the option. Let us say that the structurer decides to move the strike to a level of 2100, which returns a lower premium of 228 index points (10.86 % of the strike or $109). With $39 available to buy the option, the participation rate is now 36 %.

The next technique is to *increase the maturity of the transaction*, which will also have an impact on the amount of cash needed to generate the degree of capital protection. For ease of illustration we will assume that the proposed maturity is extended by one year and that 5-year interest rates are 1.5 %. This means that the bank needs to deposit only $929 (rounded) to generate $1000 in 5 years' time. However, although this releases a greater amount of cash to spend on the option two factors now work against the structurer. The option is now more expensive as it is longer-dated and 5-year interest rates are higher than 4-year rates. This increases the option premium to 268 index points (13.76 % of the 2100 strike). However, by a quirk of financial mathematics this is not all bad news—the amount of money required for the deposit has fallen by a greater amount than the increased cost of the option. This means that the participation rate will have increased as a result of the increase in the note's maturity. The components of the bond are as follows:

---

[1] See the appendix to this chapter for an explanation of this approach.
[2] The forward index level is $2,000 \times \exp^{(0.01-0.02)\times4} = 1,921.57$

- 5-year note struck 5 % OTM
- $1000 − $929 = $71 for purchase of option
- Index call option premium 12.76 % of the strike, that is, $128
- Participation rate = 55 %

Another technique that could be used is to *change the degree of capital protection offered by the note*. Suppose that instead of offering 100 % capital protection the structurer offers only 90 %. Based on the 5-year maturity this would mean that the structurer would only need to deposit $836.

$$\frac{\$900}{(1+0.015)^5}$$
$$\frac{\$900}{1.077} = \$836 \tag{12.2}$$

This now frees $164 worth of funds to buy the 5 % OTM call, which for a 100 % participation would only cost $128. However, the lower degree of capital protection creates a problem. If the note ends up OTM at maturity, that is, less than the strike of 2100 index points the investor will only receive back 90 % of their investment. So if the market does not move from its initial value the investor would still lose 10 %. In order to offer such a payout the issuer could structure the note with two options such that the investor was

- Long an 'up and out' barrier call option with a strike set at 90 % of the initial spot price (1800) but which knocks out at a level of 105 % of the index (2100). The cost of this option is 0.44 index points.
- Long an 'up and in' barrier call option with a strike set at 105 % of the initial spot price (2100) and also knocks in at 105 % (2100). The cost of this option is 268 index points.

The combination of options will result in the following payoffs, which are also summarized in Table 12.2:

- If the market ends up at less than 90 % of the original spot value
  - both options expire worthless;
  - the investor receives back the capital protected amount of $900.
- If the market ends up between 90–105 % of the original spot value
  - the 'up and out' option will pay out a return;

- the 'up and in' option is not activated;
- the investor receives back the capital protected amount.

- If the market ends up greater than 105 % of the initial spot price
  - the 'up and out' option is knocked out;
  - the 'up and in' pays the investor the associated return;
  - the investor receives back the capital protected amount.

Table 12.2 Payoff from structured note assuming 90 % capital protection and two barrier options

Index level at maturity	Payout from 'up and out' call option	Payout from 'up and in' call option
1800	No	No
1900	Yes	No
2000	Yes	No
2100	No	Yes
2200	No	Yes
2300	No	Yes

The combined cost of the two options is therefore 268.44 index points which is 12.78 % of the strike. So under these new conditions the structured product components are as follows:

- 5-year maturity
- Strike 5 % OTM
- Two barrier options to generate the upside return
- 90 % capital protection requiring an initial deposit of $836
- $164 available to buy the two options, which will cost $128.

As a result, the participation rate for the note is now 128 %.

There are also a number of other techniques that the bank could use to improve the participation rate:

- *Select an index with a higher dividend yield*—an increase in the dividend yield reduces the cost of a long call option increasing the participation rate.
- *Pick an index that trades with lower volatility*—the lower the volatility the lower the cost of the call option, the higher the participation rate.
- *Cap the investor's upside return*—if the structurer were to include a short investor call option at a higher strike this would generate more proceeds for the bank to improve the participation rate.

- *Remove the capital protection at very low strikes*—here the structure would include a low strike short investor put. This means that from the strike of this option the note would no longer offer any capital protection. However, the short put would generate funds to improve the upside participation.
- *Include some form of averaging into the payout process*—here the payout on the upside call option is based on the average performance of the index over a pre-defined period; say the last 6 months' worth of observations. The payoff of an average rate call option is:

$$\text{MAX}\,(\text{Average spot rate} - \text{strike}, 0)$$

In some early forms of structured products this feature was marketed to investors on the basis that their final payout would be protected if the market had been rising over the life of the note but suddenly experienced a sharp decline. Of course this works both ways—the investor would not be able to benefit from a sharp rise in price! From a pricing perspective this type of average rate option is cheaper than a non-averaging equivalent. This is because the volatility of this type of option is the volatility of an average price series, which will be lower than the volatility of a non-averaged equivalent. This cheapens the option increasing the participation rate.

- *Embed a correlation-dependent option into the structure*—instead of using a vanilla call option to generate the investor's upside, the structurer could use a correlation-dependent call option. For example, the payoff could reference a basket of indices, which again would cheapen the option and make the participation rate more attractive.[3]
- *Sell the note above par*—it is also possible for the structurer to sell the note for more than its par value. So for example, the note could cost the investor 103 % of par (i.e. $1030 per note) from which the structuring bank would charge fees of, say, 2 % of par ($20 per note) leaving them with proceeds of 101 % ($1010). However, all of the upside returns would be based on a par value of $1000.

Table 12.3 summarizes the impact that some of the preceding techniques has on determining the participation rate.

---

[3] See Sect. 8.2

Table 12.3 Factors that impact the participation rate of a capital protected note

Change in factor	Impact on option premium	Amount of cash required for deposit	Participation rate
Higher strike	⇩	–	⇧
Higher interest rates	⇧	⇩ ⇩	⇧
Higher dividend yields	⇩	–	⇧
Longer time to maturity	⇧	⇩ ⇩	⇧
Lower implied volatility	⇩	–	⇧

Risks to the Investor

The capital protected note offers unlimited upside potential unless the instrument is structured with a cap to limit the investor's participation above a certain strike rate. The downside risk is generally limited as the note offers full principal protection. As was pointed out earlier, it is possible for the structurer to create a note which only offers capital protection to a particular index level.

There could also be an opportunity cost of investing in the note. If the market were to fall the investor will have lost use of their funds for the period. Typically, the capital protected note does not pay any interim coupon and so in a relatively high interest rate environment this 'loss' could be significant. In the same vein the structured note investor does not receive any dividends. So if the investor were to buy a portfolio of shares referencing the same index they would earn both capital appreciation and dividend payments so arguably a participation rate of 100 % would be less efficient than holding a portfolio of shares. Admittedly, this does ignore any fees that the cash investor would need to pay when holding the portfolio of shares.

Risks to the Structuring Bank

Focusing primarily on the option that generates the investor's upside return the bank is short a call option whose primary risks are as follows:

- Short market direction (delta)
- Short implied volatility (vega)

- Long dividend risk (phi)
- Short interest rate risk (rho)

12.3 Yield Enhanced Structures

Introduction

A reverse convertible is an enhanced yield structure that can be decomposed into two individual products. From the investor's perspective they are the following:

- Long an interest bearing deposit
- Short a put option on a 'blue chip' share

Example Termsheet

To illustrate the concepts, consider the following termsheet:

Issuer:	Bank
Coupon:	13.6 % p.a. payable at maturity
Maturity:	12 months
Currency:	USD
Underlying asset:	Hewlett Packard (HP)
Issue price:	100 %
Initial investment:	USD 1000
Redemption:	(a) If at maturity the share price is equal to or less than $34.00 the investor will receive the coupon plus the stock redemption amount. (b) If the share price is greater than $34.00 the investor receives the coupon plus their initial investment.
Stock redemption amount:	29.41 shares for each $1000 principal invested, which is equal to $1000 divided by the initial share price.

Assume that at the time of issue the following market conditions existed:

12-month USD LIBOR:	0.75 %
HP dividend yield:	1.98 %
HP share price:	$34.00
HP implied volatility:	31 %

To understand how this structure is engineered consider the payoff at maturity. Initially, the investor pays $1000 to the issuer, which is placed on deposit to earn interest at the prevailing market rate. If at maturity the share price has fallen the investor receives the coupon but does not receive back their initial investment. Instead they receive a fixed number of shares as they are short a physically-settled put option. A fall in the price of the share makes the option ITM from the structuring bank's perspective. The bank exercises the option and delivers a fixed number of shares to the client as determined by the initial strike price. The investor's initial $1000 investment is retained by the bank and is used to pay for these shares.

If the share price is greater than the initial spot price of $34.00, the investor receives the coupon as well as their initial cash investment. This is because the put option is OTM and so is not exercised by the bank. The investor therefore receives back their initial investment as well as the coupon.

Investor's Return
The investor's returns at maturity are considered in Table 12.4.

The return on the reverse convertible when the share price increases beyond the strike of the put is equal to the coupon. When the share price falls the return is the loss on the share position offset by the receipt of the coupon. With interest rates at 0.75 % a coupon of 13.60 % represents a significantly enhanced yield. This enhanced yield comprises of interest on the investor's initial investment plus the premium on the short put position.

Structuring Principles
The 'fair value' of the reverse convertible's coupon should simply be the sum of the component parts.

The fair price of a 12-month ATM spot option on HP given the market conditions highlighted above is $4.34 per share or 12.76 % of the strike price. Another way of expressing this is to recognize that the investor is receiv-

Table 12.4 At maturity returns for reverse convertible investor

HP share price	Outcome	Return on reverse convertible (%)
$26.00	Fixed number of shares + coupon	−9.93
$30.00	Fixed number of shares + coupon	+1.83
$34.00	Fixed number of shares + coupon	13.60
$38.00	Principal + coupon	13.60
$42.00	Principal + coupon	13.60

ing $4.34 for each of the 29.41 shares embedded within the structure. This returns the investor $127.64, which is 12.76 % of his initial $1000 investment. However, the option premium is not received by the investor until maturity and so needs to be future valued at prevailing market rates.

$$\$4.34 \times (1.0075) = \$4.37 \qquad (12.3)$$

Based on the holding of 29.41 shares the total premium in cash terms would be $128.52. The investor's $1000 investment is also placed on deposit to earn 0.75 % returning interest of $7.5.[4] Taking both the interest on the deposit and the premium on the option together suggests that the proceeds at maturity will be $136.02. This represents an interest rate of 13.6 % per annum.[5]

Another popular way of structuring reverse convertibles is for the short put to be a 'down and in' barrier option. Consider the same HP reverse convertible but this time with a change to the redemption feature:

Trigger level: 80 % of the initial share price (i.e. $27.20)
Redemption: *(1) If the trigger level trades*
      If at maturity the share price is equal to or less than $34.00, the
      investor will receive the coupon plus the stock redemption amount.
      If at maturity the share price is greater than $34.00, the investor
      receives the coupon plus their initial investment.
      (2) If the trigger level does not trade
      The investor receives the coupon plus their initial investment.

This additional feature could be seen as a benefit to the investor as it affords them an extra level of downside protection.

As is common with all barrier options the premium will be lower than that of a non-barrier equivalent. In this case the barrier option will be valued at $4.07 per share, resulting in a lower coupon of 12.81 %. Table 12.5 shows the return on a 'vanilla' reverse convertible against an equivalent structure which is structured with a knock in put.

Table 12.5 illustrates that the return on the vanilla structure is greater if the share price were to remain stable or rise. If the share price falls, the structure with the barrier option will outperform but only if the barrier is not activated. If the barrier is activated the lower premium on the knock in option does not generate as much premium and so the losses are higher than the vanilla equivalent, that is, the barrier structure underperforms.

---

[4] An actual/actual day count has been assumed.
[5] The example has ignored the structuring bank's fees.

Table 12.5 Return on a 'vanilla' reverse convertible vs. reverse convertible with a knock in put

HP share price	Return on vanilla reverse convertible (%)	Reverse convertible with barrier	
		Barrier not activated (%)	Barrier activated (%)
$26.00	−9.93	N.A.	−10.72
$30.00	1.84	12.81	1.05
$34.00	13.60	12.81	12.81
$38.00	13.60	12.81	12.81
$42.00	13.60	12.81	12.81

Table 12.6 Comparison of the returns on a vanilla reverse convertible with a deposit and a holding in the physical share. The return on the cash shareholding is calculated as the change in the share price to which the dividend yield is added

HP share price	Return on vanilla reverse convertible (%)	Return on 12-month deposit (%)	Return on cash shareholding (%)
$26.00	−9.93	0.75	−21.55
$30.00	+1.84	0.75	−9.78
$34.00	13.60	0.75	1.98
$38.00	13.60	0.75	13.74
$42.00	13.60	0.75	25.51

Risks to the Investor

At a very simple level these structures would be very attractive when both interest rates and implied volatility are elevated.

But one way in which the risks to the investor could be considered would be to compare the vanilla reverse convertible with two alternatives:

- Placing $1000 on deposit for 12 months (on an actual/actual day basis),
- Investing $1000 in HP shares at an initial price of $34.00.

These alternatives are considered in Table 12.6.

Table 12.6 shows that if the share price were to fall substantially then the deposit would be the best scenario. A steep rise in the share price would suggest that going long the share would return the greatest amount. The reverse convertible tends to be the superior option when the share price trades in a relatively narrow price range.

Risks to the Structuring Bank
The risks to the bank from their long put position are as follows:

- Short market direction (delta)
- Long implied volatility (vega)
- Long dividend risk (phi)
- Short interest rate risk (rho)

Another of the risks faced by the structuring bank where the reverse convertible has an embedded reverse barrier relates to the management of the delta exposure as the instrument approaches maturity.[6] The bank is long a 'down and in' put option whose initial delta value is −47 %. The associated delta hedge would require the trader to buy the underlying share. However, suppose that with one week prior to maturity HP's share price has fallen to $28.00. At this point the delta on the embedded option will be −353 %. If the barrier was now touched, the option would become European in style but cannot have a delta greater than −100 %. This would mean that the trader would be overhedged and so would have to unwind part of the position. Since the underlying market is now falling this would result in a loss. One of the ways in which this risk could be managed would be to price and risk manage a position with a barrier set at a lower level—say 77 %. This would result in a lower premium for the investor whose transaction confirmation would state that the barrier would be activated at 80 %.

12.4 Income Structures

Introduction
An autocallable note is a yield-enhanced interest bearing structure that will be 'automatically callable' if certain market conditions occur. A precise definition of an autocallable is difficult as a variety of permutations have been issued. Arguably, they are characterized by the following features:

- They are regarded as a yield-enhanced investment.
- They will pay the investor a coupon which will be contingent on the level of the underlying.

---

[6] See Sect. 7.2.4.3.

- They tend to perform well in neutral or bearish market conditions.
- The note will automatically terminate under pre-specified market conditions.
- They will offer some element of capital protection.
- They are designed as a 'hold to maturity' structure.

Example Termsheet

Consider the following hypothetical autocallable which references the Russell 2000 Index, which measures the performance of the small-cap segment of the US equity universe.

Issuer:	Bank
Principal amount:	$1000
Underlying asset:	Performance of the Russell 2000 Index
Maturity:	2 years
Coupon frequency:	Quarterly, if the notes have not been redeemed early
Conditional coupon:	6.00 % p.a. (1.50 % per quarter) as long as underlying asset is trading at or above the coupon barrier level
Reference swap level:	1 %
Coupon barrier level:	70 % of the initial level of the underlying
Early redemption:	Autocallable quarterly
Early redemption condition:	Note will terminate if the level of the underlying asset is at or above its initial level
Early redemption amount	100 %
Barrier level	70 % of the initial underlying price
Maturity redemption	1. *Closing level of the underlying is at or above 70 % of its initial value*
	The investor receives 100 % of the principal amount of the notes.
	2. *Closing level of the underlying is below 70 % of its initial level*
	The investor is exposed to the negative performance of the underlying with a possible loss of 100 % of the principal invested. The repayment amount is determined according to the following formula:

$$100\% - \max\left[\frac{\text{Index}_0 - \text{Index}_T}{\text{Index}_0}, 0\right]$$

Where:
Index$_0$ = initial value of index
Index$_T$ = final value of index

Investor's Return

The termsheet indicates there are two primary sources of return for the investor. The first is the payment of a conditional quarterly coupon of 1.5 %, that is, $15.00 per note. For the investor to receive this payment the index needs to be trading above 70 % of its original value on the designated observation date at the end of each quarter. If the index exceeds its initial value, the investor will receive their coupon for that period but the note will be automatically called by the issuing bank. As a result, no further coupon payments will be made but the investor will receive back 100 % of their investment.

The second source of the investor's return is the original investment that they will receive at the note's final maturity. As long as the index is above the pre-determined barrier level of 70 % the investor will receive back 100 % of their investment. However, below this level the investor's principal is at risk. So if the index falls by 40 % from its initial level then the investor will only receive back 60 % of their initial investment. Although the autocallable is modelled using a Monte Carlo process, the note can be thought of as being comprised of the following:

- The investors' initial proceeds
- A long position in a strip of contingent digital options that generate the investors' coupon payments
- A short investor 'up and out' barrier option which helps finance the purchase of the digital options

Structuring Principles

Coupon payments—from the investor's perspective the coupon payments are generated by a long position in a strip of contingent digital call options, each with a different maturity. In the example termsheet where the coupon is paid quarterly over a 2-year period, this would imply a total of eight options. The strike of the digital is set at 70 % of the market with the payoff set equal to the stated coupon amount, which would be $15.00 in our example. The coupons are contingent in that if the note is subject to early redemption the remaining digital options will automatically terminate. This knock out feature of the barrier is only monitored on the date of each coupon payment. Suppose that at the end of the 4th quarter the underlying index closes at 102 % of its initial value. The investor receives their 4th coupon of $15.00 but the remaining four digital options are knocked out. There will be no subsequent coupon payments and the note will be subject to the early redemption terms.

Early redemption feature—to finance the early termination payment the note is structured with an 'up and out' put option with a strike of 0 % but a knock out barrier set at 100 % of the initial market level with a rebate set equal to 100 % of the notional. If the put option is structured with a 0 % strike the seller will never have to make any payout to the holder. This would suggest that this option is worthless but the fact that the seller may have to pay a rebate means the option will incur a premium cost. Since the option is designed to repay the investor's principal they are long the option. The barrier on this option is only monitored on each payment date.

The 'at maturity' redemption proceeds—these funds are generated by changing the terms of the 'up and out' put used to generate the early redemption proceeds. On the redemption date the barrier is not 100 % but 0 %, so since the option has a 100 % rebate the investor's principal will be returned in full.

'Soft' capital protection—so far the investor has paid the initial price of the note which is used to buy a strip of digital option as well a long 'up and out' barrier put. Since the combined cost of these two option positions may exceed these proceeds, the investor will need to sell some form of optionality. This is in the form of a 'down and in' put with the following features:

Strike: 100 % of the initial index price
Downside knock in: 70 % of the initial index price
Upside knock out: 100 % of the initial index price. Barrier is only monitored on each coupon payment date

As a result, the investor's principal is at risk below a closing index level equal to 70 % of the initial price.

Risks to the Investor

To get a sense of how all of the options embedded within the autocallable combine, and the risks that they pose to the investor, consider two scenarios at different points in time and under different market conditions.

Scenario #1—4th coupon payment date. Market is at 101 % of its initial value.

- The early redemption 'up and out' put is activated and the investor is paid 100 % of their principal courtesy of the option's rebate feature.
- Since the note has survived to the end of the first year, the investor will have received four coupons.

- The remaining four digital options are knocked out.
- The 'down and in' put option is also knocked out.

Scenario #2—8th coupon payment date. Market is at 60 % of its initial value.

- Since the note has survived to its final maturity, the investor will have already received seven coupons. But since the closing index value is below the coupon barrier level, they will not receive the final coupon.
- Since the note has survived to maturity, the barrier on the 'up and out' put option will be 0 % which means it will be knocked out with the investor being paid 100 % of their principal courtesy of the option's rebate feature.
- However, the 'down and in' option is now knocked in and since the investor is short this option their final proceeds are reduced by 40 %.

Risks to the Structuring Bank
From the structuring bank's perspective, they are as follows:

- Short a strip of digital call options
- Short an 'up and out' put option
- Long a 'down and in' put option

The risks of the autocallable and how this has an impact on the overall flows within the equity derivatives market are considered in more detail in Sect. 12.7.

12.5 Volatility Structures

Introduction
A 'twin win' structure pays a return whether the value of the underlying (typically an index) moves up or down, as long as it stays above a specified barrier level. This is in effect a 'long volatility' position from the perspective of the investor and in some ways resembles the long straddle position illustrated in Fig. 11.8.

Example Termsheet

Issuer:	Bank
Underlying index:	S&P 500
Notional amount per certificate:	$1000
Maturity:	3 years
Knock out event:	A knock out event will occur if at anytime during the life of the structure the index hits 50 % of its initial value.
Final redemption amount:	At maturity each certificate will be redeemed in cash.

1. If no knock event has occurred

$$\text{Notional} \times \left[100\% + ABS \left(\frac{\text{Index}_{Final} - \text{Index}_{Initial}}{\text{Index}_{Initial}} \right) \right]$$

Where:

ABS = Absolute value

2. If a knock out event has occurred

$$\text{Notional} \times \frac{\text{Index}_{Final}}{\text{Index}_{Initial}}$$

The 'twin win' structure has a barrier set at 50 % of the initial index level, which, if breached, converts the instrument into to a long position in the underlying.

Investor's Return

Table 12.7 illustrates the investor's redemption payout for a variety of index values assuming that the barrier has or has not been breached.

The payoff illustrates that as long as the 50 % barrier is not hit the investor will enjoy a return irrespective of any directional move of the market. However, if the barrier is hit then the payoff is linear and moves in line with the market, resulting in a long position. Another consequence of the knock event is that the investor's principal is no longer protected. This payoff is shown diagrammatically in Fig. 12.1.

Table 12.7 Expiry payout from Twin Win structured note

Change in index value (%)	Barrier breached?	Investor's payout	Barrier breached?	Investor's payout
40	No	$1400	Yes	$1400
20	No	$1200	Yes	$1200
0	No	$1000	Yes	$1000
−20	No	$1200	Yes	$800
−40	No	$1400	Yes	$600

Table 12.8 Potential investor returns on hybrid security

Final value for SPX	Final value for CPI	SPX performance (%)	CPI performance (%)	Basket return (%)	Payment at maturity
2500	256.3	+25	+10	+17.5	$1175
2500	209.7	+25	−10	+7.5	$1075
1500	256.3	−25	+10	−7.5	$1000
1500	209.7	−25	−10	−17.5	$1000

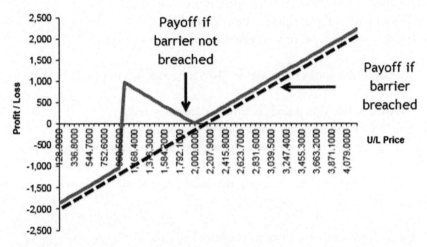

Fig. 12.1 Payoff from a 'twin win' structured note. Solid line shows the payoff if the barrier is not breached. Dotted line shows the payoff if the barrier is breached; this payoff is shown as being slightly offset for ease of illustration (*Source*: author)

Structuring Principles

Different banks issue the twin win with slightly different variations but the transaction highlighted on the previous termsheet can be decomposed into a number of options. From the investor's perspective they are:

- Long an ATM spot 'down and out' barrier call option. Barrier is set at 50 % of the initial spot price.
- Long an ATM spot 'down and out' barrier put option. Barrier is set at 50 % of the initial spot price.
- Long an ATM spot 'down and in call'. Barrier is set at 50 % of the initial spot price.

- Short an ATM spot 'down and in put'. Barrier is set at 50 % of the initial spot price.

To illustrate how these options combine consider three scenarios from Table 12.7.

Scenario #1—index increases by 40 %; barrier has not been breached

- Neither of the 'down and in' options are activated.
- 'Down and out' put option expires worthless.
- 'Down and out' call option generates the investor's return.

Scenario #2—index decreases by 40 %; barrier has not been breached

- Neither of the 'down and in' options are activated.
- The 'down and out' call option expires worthless.
- The 'down and out' put option generates the investor's return.

Scenario #3—index increases or decreases by 40 %; barrier has been breached

- Both 'down and out' options are knocked out.
- Both 'down and in' options are knocked in. So by the principles of put call parity the resulting position is a synthetic long position in the underlying struck at the initial level of the index.

Risks to the Investor

The most favourable return to the investor would be when the market displays an element of realized volatility that does not result in the barrier being triggered. So if the market is going to be volatile the hope is that this will be to the upside. If the barrier level is hit and the market does not recover the investor is left with a long position which is now substantially below the initial value of the index. The index would now have to double in value for the investor to break even.

Risks to the Structuring Bank

From the bank's perspective the position is initially delta negative overall. This is by virtue of the short 'down and out' call and the long 'down and in' put. The net combination of the four barrier options also leaves the bank long vega.

12.6 Hybrid Structures

Introduction

Hybrid structures allow investors to take exposure to more than one asset within a single structure using, for example, a basket option. Strictly speaking to be classified as a hybrid, the underlying assets should be from different asset classes. Chapter 8 considered a number of correlation-dependent structures but focused only on examples where the underlying assets were just equity. It would be perfectly feasible to have a basket option where the payoff was linked to, say, equities and commodities—or as many different asset classes as the investor desired.

Example Termsheet

Issuer:	Bank
Maturity:	6 years
Currency:	USD
Underlying assets:	*Equity*: S&P 500 index (SPX)
	Inflation: US Consumer Price Index (CPI)
Initial SPX level:	2000
Initial CPI level:	233.0
Nominal value:	$1000
Payment at maturity:	$1000 plus the additional amount
Additional amount:	This will be equal to the greater of (a) zero and (b) $1000 × basket return × participation rate
Basket return:	(final basket level – initial basket level)/initial basket level
Initial basket level:	100
Final basket level:	100 × [1 + (CPI percentage return × 50 %) + (S&P 500 percentage return × 50 %)]
Participation rate:	100 %

Investor's Return

To illustrate the possible returns at maturity, consider the following scenarios:

To illustrate how the maturity payment is calculated consider the first scenario.

The final basket level is:

$$100 \times [1 + (0.10 \times 0.5) + (0.25 \times 0.5) = 100 \times 1.175 = 117.50 \qquad (12.4)$$

The basket return is:

$$(117.50 - 100.00)/100.00 = 17.5\% \qquad (12.5)$$

The additional amount paid to the investor is therefore:

$$\$1,000 \times 17.5\% \times 100\% = \$175 \qquad (12.6)$$

The total amount paid to the investor is therefore:

$$\$1,000 + \$175 = \$1,175 \qquad (12.7)$$

Structuring Principles

In many ways the principles used to structure this note are very similar to those highlighted in Sect. 12.2. The structuring bank will take the investor's initial proceeds and place a proportion of the funds on deposit to generate the $1000 principal at maturity. The balance of the proceeds is used to buy a basket call option. The basket is an option on two equally weighted underlying assets.

Risks to the Investor

The most favourable outcome to the investor would occur if both inflation and the underlying economic index were to increase over the life of the note. The potential upside of the note is unlimited.

However, there are two main risks to the investor:

- They have exposure to the issuer's credit risk.
- If the basket performance is negative, they will only receive back the initial amount invested without any interest.

Risks to the Structuring Bank

The risks highlighted in this section were also covered in the analysis of basket options in Sect. 8.2. One of the key risks associated with the basket option is the structuring bank's exposure to correlation. An increase in correlation between the assets will lead to an increase in the value of the embedded call and therefore lead to an increased payout. Since the bank is short the basket call option they are short correlation.

12.7 Structured Product Risk Management

12.7.1 Introduction: Autocallable Market Risks

> It's like musical chairs. Everyone's happy when the market goes up, products knock out and you get new money all the time, but when the music stops some dealers find themselves in real trouble. Risk (2015b)

To illustrate the wider impact that structured products have on the equity derivative market, it is instructive to consider how the risks associated with autocallable notes are managed. For example, losses relating to the selling and risk managing of autocallables were reported at $500 m in 2012 and $300 m in 2015 (Risk 2015a, b).

The financial crisis of 2008 led to a period of sustained low interest rates, which led to lower issuance of capital protected notes. This was because the proceeds available to buy the embedded option were relatively low and so the participation rates were relatively unattractive. Instead there was a substantial increase in demand for yield-enhanced structures with autocallables being particularly popular in Europe and Japan.

Anecdotally, autocallables tended to be issued with maturities of 4 to 6 years with an expectation they would be knocked out after a year as a result of rising markets. However, during the initial phase of the financial crisis markets fell sharply increasing the maturity of autocallables. So the longer maturities resulted in an increased hedging requirement.

This section will cover the risk posed by the options embedded within the autocallable's options. From the structuring bank's perspective, they have two main positions:

- Short a strip of digital call options
- Long a 'down and in' put option

12.7.2 Market Risk Associated with Digital Options

The market risk associated with digital options was covered in Chap. 7. However, the associated risk management techniques warrant further investigation. Figure 12.2 shows the payoff of a stylized digital call option on a nameless asset with a strike of 105 and a payoff of 5 units. This digital payoff can be partially replicated by executing a call spread (see Sect. 11.3.3). So when structuring a digital the bank will have a contractual fixed payout but will record and risk manage a call spread.

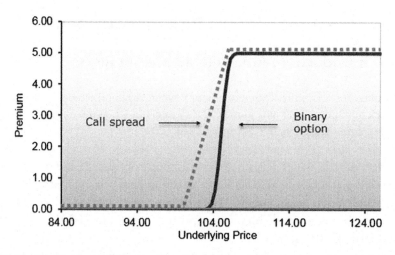

Fig. 12.2 Replicating a binary call option with a call spread (*Source*: author)

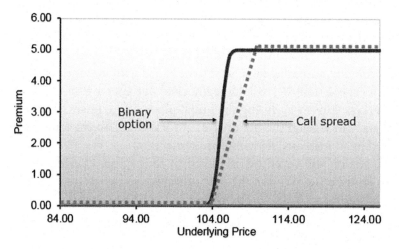

Fig. 12.3 Binary option hedged with call spread (*Source*: author)

Notice in Fig. 12.2 that the lower strike of the call spread is placed below the strike of the binary option. So if the underlying price rises the bank's call spread hedge would pay out before any contractual payment is due under the terms of the binary option. If the call spread had been structured so that the lower strike call had been set equal to the strike of the binary the bank would run the risk that the underlying price could just hit the strike and go no further. This would result in an immediate full payout on the contractual digital payment while the call spread hedge would not provide an offsetting profit (Fig. 12.3).

If the trader decides to use the call spread to hedge the digital exposure the next choice they are faced with is the choice of strikes. If they executed the call spread with strikes of 100/105 then the trader would need to buy one lower strike call and sell one higher strike call to construct the hedge. So if the price were to rise beyond the upper strike the gross profit on the call spread would be 5 units.[7,8] If the underlying asset ends up at less than 105, the trader does not need to pay out on the binary but will collect on the hedge. If the trader picked a narrower range of strikes such as 102.5/105 then the notional on the call spread would need to double in order to generate the 5-unit payment.

Because the call spread consists of bought and sold call options, then from a risk-management perspective, there is an element of netting that minimizes the relevant exposures:

Delta: long call is delta positive, short call is delta negative.

Vega: long call is vega positive, short call is vega negative.

12.7.3 Market Risk Associated with 'down and in' Put Option

The second major component of the autocallable structure is a 'down and in' put option which is sold by the investor to the bank to finance the coupon payments. The market risk profile of a stylized long 'down and in' put is shown in the upper panel of Fig. 12.4. The main parameters used to value this option are:

Strike:	100
Spot:	100
Barrier:	60
Maturity:	1 year
Implied volatility:	20 %

12.7.3.1 Delta Risk

The structuring bank is long the put option and as such is short delta which means that as the market falls the trader will need to buy the underlying asset

---

[7] This is because the 100 strike represents the level at which the asset is bought while 105 is the level at which the asset is sold.

[8] The hedge is not costless which in this example would require the payment of a 2 unit premium.

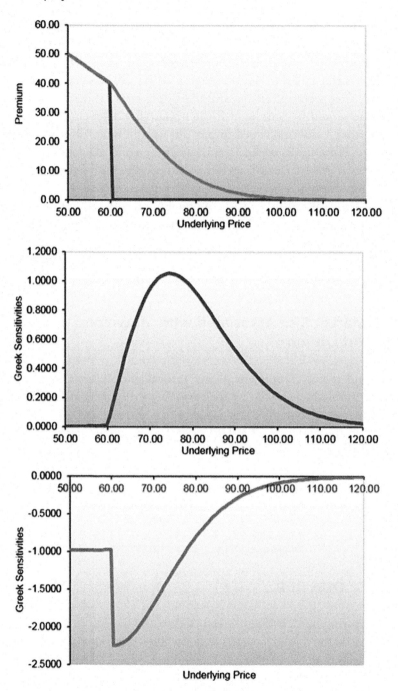

Fig. 12.4 Payoff and risk management profiles for 'down and in' put option. Upper panel shows at and pre-expiry payoff; middle panel is the vega profile while lowest panel is the delta profile (*Source*: author)

in order to maintain delta neutrality. In the Japanese and European auto-callable markets, traders hedged their exposure by buying short-term index futures. These were preferred to longer-dated forwards which were perceived as being relatively illiquid. Since there was significant note issuance, traders needed to buy large amounts of index futures which in turn resulted in negative implied equity repo rates.

Recall that a forward price represents the net financing cost of holding a spot position for a given period of time.[9] 'No arbitrage' conditions state that the forward price is the spot price plus financing costs minus gross dividends. However, banks will often adjust their quoted forward prices to take account of the following:

- Equity repo rates (i.e. stock borrowing costs)
- Bid-offer spreads
- Transaction taxes
- Dividend taxation
- Balance sheet costs

So while spot prices, interest rates and gross dividends are directly observable the other adjusting items will vary significantly and are often aggregated into a single term referred to as 'the implied equity repo rate'. To illustrate this, suppose an asset is trading at a price of 100, interest rates are 1 %, dividend yields are 2 % and implied repo is 0.25 %. The 12-month forward price would be[10]:

Forward price =
Spot price + financing – dividend yield – implied equity repo rate   (12.8)

$$98.75 = 100 + 1 - 2 - 0.25 \qquad (12.9)$$

Suppose that there is a sudden increase in the demand for the forward pushing the price to 99.50 but the spot price, interest rate and dividend yields remain unchanged. The forward price is therefore:

$$99.50 = 100 + 1 - 2 + 0.5 \qquad (12.10)$$

---

[9] See Chaps. 4 and 9.
[10] Calculation assumes an actual/actual day count convention.

This means that implied repo rate backed out of the observed market values is −0.50 %. The trading of implied repo rates using total return swaps was covered in Sect. 10.5.3.

12.7.3.2   Dividend Risk

Section 4.6.5 established that a long put option has a long dividend exposure. As a result of the autocallable positions written by the banks they needed to take on an offsetting short position in order to mitigate the risk. One of the popular ways to do this was to sell dividend futures.[11] However, the volumes sold by the banks caused longer-dated dividend futures to trade below what was considered to be their fundamental value.

12.7.3.3   Vega Exposures

The middle panel of Fig. 12.4 shows that a long 'down and in' put option results in a long vega exposure. In an ideal world the bank would seek to offset the exposure with another counterparty by selling volatility.

Notice from Fig. 12.4 that if the underlying market were to fall towards the barrier the option's vega exposure initially increases. This means that a 1 % change in implied volatility at lower spot prices is more significant than at higher prices. So when the spot price is 100 a 1 % change in implied volatility will cause the premium to change by 0.21 index points but at a spot price of 74 the same change in implied volatility causes the premium to move by 1.05 index points. This effect is termed negative vanna and was introduced in Sect. 5.9.2. As equity markets fell in the aftermath of the financial crisis, this negative vanna exposure would occasionally trigger bank risk management limits requiring autocallable hedgers to sell volatility. This resulted in an element of positive correlation between the level of the cash market and implied volatility.

Figure 12.5 shows two incidents where this occurred: October 2014 and the second quarter of 2015. However, in both Japan and Europe an imbalance had emerged between the demand for and supply of volatility. As a result of the popularity of autocallables with retail investors this segment had in effect become the main source of volatility supply. So when there was a need for the banks to reduce their volatility exposures there was not an immediate and obvious source of demand. This was exacerbated by the fact that institutional

---

[11] Dividend futures are covered in Chap. 13.

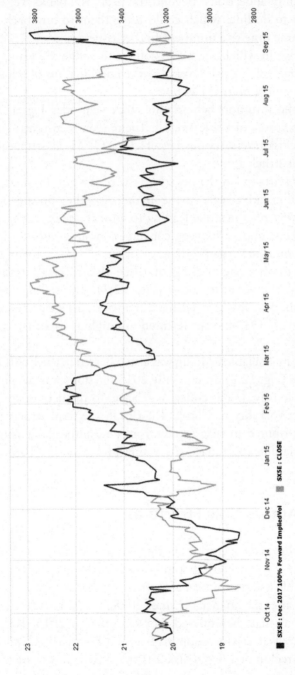

Fig. 12.5 Level of EURO STOXX 50 (SX5E) vs. 2-year implied volatility. September 2014–September 2015 (Source: Barclays Live)

investor demand for downside put options had fallen as these participants had reduced their equity allocations. Beyond the peak, the banks' vega exposure would now start to decline, which could force them to buy back volatility, possibly at the same time as a number of other issuers.

One of the ways in which the banks sought to hedge the vanna exposure was to use risk reversals. A risk reversal is the combination of a long (short) OTM call and a short (long) OTM put.

To illustrate the intuition behind this tactic, consider Fig. 12.6, which shows the vega exposure of a risk reversal. The market is currently assumed to be at 100 and the risk reversal comprises of a long OTM call struck at 110 and a short OTM put struck at 90.

As the market starts to fall the negative vega of the put dominates and the position is overall negative vega. As the market rises the opposite occurs; the long call moves towards the strike leading to an increase in its vega. The put option moves OTM and so its vega converges towards zero. So in a rising market the position is net vega positive.

However, in Europe the trading of these risk reversals resulted in a significant fall in the volatility skew (Fig. 12.7). The selling pressure on OTM puts resulted in lower volatility for lower strike options while the buying pressure on OTM calls resulted in higher volatility for higher strike options.

The impact of autocallable hedging was also reflected in the EURO STOXX 50 term structure (Fig. 12.8). In mid-July 2015 the slope was steeply inverted at the short end mostly due to concerns relating to the debt crisis in Greece and stock market volatility in China. The dip in the term structure beyond this point was attributed to vega supply from new autocallable issuance and the selling of volatility to manage the vanna impact of the banks' existing inventories.

12.7.4 Asian Autocallable Structures

If by this point the reader's head is starting to spin, then let me throw more fuel onto the fire by considering some of the hedging problems faced by Korean autocallable issuers. Autocallable structures became very popular with Korean investors after the financial crisis of 2008 mainly due to the significant yield enhancement that they offered. For example, in 2015, Korean auto-callable structures were paying coupons between 8 and 10 % when interest rates were in the region of 1.5 % (Risk 2015b). Sharp falls in the Hang Seng

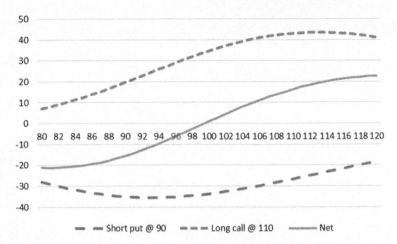

Fig. 12.6 Vega profile of a risk reversal. In this example the risk reversal comprises of the sale of a short put struck at 90 and the purchase of a long call at 110. Vega is measured on the Y axis in terms of ticks, that is, the minimum price movement of the underlying asset (*Source:* author)

China Enterprises Index (HSCEI) resulted in estimated losses of $300 m (Risk 2016b).

These Korean autocallables typically included a 'worst of' option which would often include the HSCEI as one of its components. This index references Chinese shares that are listed on the Hong Kong Stock Exchange. In 2015, the index suffered a 40 % decline in value which led to significant losses for autocallable issuers, believed to be in the region of $300 m (Risk 2015b). The losses were incurred due to the complexity of the issuers' required hedging strategies. Section 12.7.3.1 suggested that the main technique used by banks to hedge the autocallable delta risk was to buy index futures. However, the Hong Kong Stock Exchange had position limits in place which meant that some traders were unable to execute sufficient futures as their delta exposure increased. As a result some traders decided to use call spreads as a proxy hedge (Risk 2015b).[12]

The existence of the 'worst of' option would typically alter the payoff of the 'down and in' put option payoff. Recall that this option is sold by the investors to generate cash to fund the digital options. However, if activated it would impact the investors' maturity payoff. So if the final level of either

---

[12] Call spreads are explained in Sect. 11.3.2.

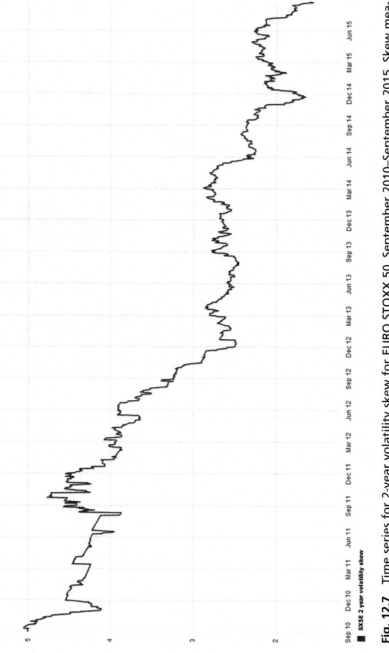

Fig. 12.7 Time series for 2-year volatility skew for EURO STOXX 50. September 2010–September 2015. Skew measured as the volatility of an option struck at 90 % of spot minus the volatility of an option struck at 110 % of spot (*Source*: Barclays Live)

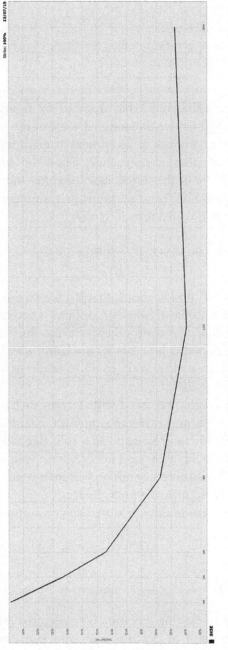

Fig. 12.8 Volatility Term structure of EURO STOXX 50. July 13th 2015 (*Source:* Barclays Live)

reference index is less than the 'down and in' barrier then the investor will receive:

> Nominal value of certificate +
> (Nominal value of certificate × the percentage change of the
> worst performing reference index)

So if at maturity neither index has declined by more than the barrier amount the investor will receive the nominal value of the security. But investors would lose some or all of their investment at maturity if there has been a decline in the level of either reference index below the barrier. Suppose that the barrier is set at 70 % of the initial value of either index. If the nominal value of the certificate is $1000 and the worst performing index falls by 50 % of its initial value, then the investor will receive

$$\$1,000 + (\$1,000 \times -50\%) = \$500$$

The use of a 'worst of' option means that the banks also have an exposure to correlation. The risk profile of 'worst of' options is covered in Sect. 8.3 and since the banks were short the option they were also short correlation. When the Chinese market crashed in June 2015, correlation with indices such as the EURO STOXX 50 increased from 55 to 80 % resulting in mark-to-market losses for the banks (Risk 2015b).

The Korean issuers were also faced with foreign exchange rate risk. The notes were issued to investors in Korean won but the underlying hedges were typically denominated in Hong Kong dollars. To hedge this optionality many traders attempted to buy Hong Kong Dollar/Korean won volatility but since this was a relatively illiquid currency option pair many traders preferred to use US dollar/Korean won options as a proxy hedge.

Given such hedging complexity, it is perhaps no surprise that losses were incurred.

12.8 Summary

There is a large body of existing literature on structured products and it was not the author's intention to describe each and every available variation. However, a book on equity derivatives would not be complete without some degree of coverage of this topic. Consequently, there were a number of objectives this chapter sought to address:

- What are the different types of equity structured product?
- How do the different products work?
- How are the different products engineered?
- What are the risks to the investor?
- What are the risks to the structuring bank?

One of the themes that permeates the book is the way in which the different components of the equity derivative market are linked. The final section of the chapter illustrates how the demand for yield-enhanced structures such as autocallables can impact a number of other market segments such as equity futures, implied equity repo rates, equity volatility and the market for traded dividends.

12.9 Appendix[13]

Section 12.2 introduced a shortcut technique to convert an OTC index option premium into a monetary equivalent without the use of a cash multiplier. The premium in index points is divided by the strike price which is then multiplied by the certificate's notional amount to determine the cash equivalent and the associated participation rate. The purpose of this appendix is to illustrate the logic behind this approach.

Listed index options make a payoff that is calculated by applying a cash multiplier to the option payoff which is expressed in index points; equally the cash value of the option premium is calculated by multiplying the option price in index points by the cash multiplier. To understand how this logic could be applied to an OTC option, assume, without loss of generality, that this cash multiplier is $1. In the base case scenario in Sect. 12.2, if the option costs 262 points it would cost $262 to buy an option that would pay $1 for every point that the index finishes above the strike. The investor invests $1000 in the note, but $960.98 of this is needed to fund the capital protected amount, leaving just $39.02 to purchase the option that will fund the supplemental payoff. This will allow the bank to buy 0.1489 (calculated as $39.02/$262) of an option that would pay $1 per index point above the strike, so the payoff

---

[13] Many thanks to David Oakes for his significant contribution to this appendix.

that the investor will receive on the option will be just $0.1489 for each point that the index finishes above the strike.

Suppose that the index finishes at 2100. This is a percentage gain of 5 % above the strike (calculated as (2100 − 2000)/2000). The supplemental payoff the investor receives from exercising the option, however, will be $14.89 (calculated as (2100 − 2000) x $0.1489). Since the supplemental payoff is:

$1,000 × participation rate × percentage increase in index relative to the strike

This can be rearranged to solve for the participation rate:

Participation rate =
supplemental payoff / ($1,000 × percentage increase in index relative
to the strike)

Inserting the relevant values gives:

$$\$14.89 \, / \left(\$1,000 \times 0.05\right) = \$14.89 \, / \, \$50 = 29.79\%$$

Now consider the case where the strike is increased to 2100. This reduces the option price to 228 points, so it now costs $228 to buy an option that will pay the investor $1 for every point by which the index finishes above the strike. The capital protection costs the same as in the base case, so the bank will still have only $39.02 to buy the option. This means that the bank can buy 0.1711 (calculated as $39.02/$228) of an option that would pay $1 for every point that the index finishes above the strike. Put another way, the investor will receive $0.1711 for every point by which the index finishes above the strike.

To facilitate comparison between the two cases, suppose that the index finishes at 2205. This index level is 5 % above the strike price of 2100 (calculated as (2205 − 2100)/2100). If the index finishes at this level, the investor will receive a payoff of $17.97 (calculated as (2,205−2,100) × $0.1711). Using the same formula as in the base case, we can calculate the participation rate as:

Participation rate =
supplemental payoff / ($1,000 × percentage increase in index relative
to the strike)

Inserting the relevant figures returns the following participation rate:

$$\$17.97 / (\$1000 \times 0.05) = \$17.95 / \$50 = 35.94\%$$

Using a 'percentage of spot' shortcut, the participation rate can be calculated as: participation rate = (nominal amount – amount required for capital protection)/((option premium/spot index level × nominal amount)).

For the base case, this gives participation rate as:

$$(\$1000 - \$960.98) / ((262 / 2000) \times \$1000) = 29.79\%$$

Using the 'percentage of strike' shortcut, the answer is the same because the spot and the strike are the same. But consider what happens if the strike is increased to 2100. The 'percent of spot' shortcut now gives the participation rate as: participation rate = (nominal amount – amount required for capital protection)/((option premium/spot index level) × nominal amount).

Inserting the relevant figures returns a value of:

$$(\$1000 - \$960.98)/(228/2000) \times \$1000) = 34.23 \%$$

which is the wrong answer! If, instead, the 'percent of strike' shortcut is used, the participation rate is: participation rate = nominal amount – amount required for capital protection)/(option premium/strike index level × nominal amount).

Using the relevant market data returns:

$$(\$1000 - \$960.98) / ((228 / 2100) \times \$1000) = 35.94\%$$

which is the right answer.

13

Traded Dividends

13.1 Introduction

The focus of this chapter is traded dividend risk, which is defined as the risk to an equity derivatives position from a change in dividends paid by a corporate entity.

The first section contains a quick recap of the sources of traded dividend risk identified in previous chapters. The chapter then considers the different products that have been developed to mitigate the risk. The chapter concludes by outlining a 'relative value' approach to expressing views on how dividends are expected to evolve.

13.2 Sources of Traded Dividend Risk

The topic of derivative dividend risk has already been addressed in previous chapters. This section contains a brief recap of the main topics and the associated references.

Futures
The dividend risk of a futures position was covered in Sects. 4.3.1 and 9.2. Table 9.1 illustrated the inverse relationship between dividends and forward prices, all other things being equal.

© The Author(s) 2017
N. Schofield, *Equity Derivatives*, DOI 10.1057/978-0-230-39107-9_13

Swaps

The impact of dividends on the price of equity swaps was covered in Sect. 4.4. An equity swap price was defined as the fixed spread to the LIBOR leg of the transaction. A swap whose equity return leg does not include dividends will trade at a lower 'price' than an equivalent position which does pay dividends. Theoretically, a swap whose equity return leg does include dividends will pay LIBOR 'flat', whereas a swap with no dividends will trade at LIBOR minus a spread.

Options

An option's dividend risk was covered in Sect. 4.6.5. For a call option the relationship is inverse; an increase in dividends reduces the value of a call option. For a put option an increase in dividends increases the value of the option.

Structured Products

Structured products were analysed in Chap. 12 and among the products discussed were the following:

*   *Capital protected notes*—where the structuring bank is short a call option on an index.
*   *Yield enhanced structures (e.g. reverse convertibles)*—the structuring bank is long a put option on a single stock.
*   *Autocallable structures*—the bank is long a 'down and in' barrier put option.

As a result of these short call/long put exposures, banks tend to be long dividend risk. Consequently, banks suffered losses after the financial crisis as many companies cut back their dividends as a result of falling profitability.

Section 12.7.3.2 highlighted that autocallable hedging had resulted in the sale of dividend futures by structuring banks. This selling pressure resulted in a downward sloping term structure that caused dividend futures to trade below their fundamental value.

13.3 Dividends as an Asset Class

Prior to the emergence of a traded dividend market, the only way to isolate the dividend exposure of an instrument would be to trade a product whose value was partially determined by dividends and then hedge away all of the other residual risks. OTC dividend swaps were created in the late 1990s, while listed dividend futures followed in 2008 with listed options being introduced in 2010. The market was initially dominated by hedge funds and proprietary trading desks but is now seen as an asset class in its own right as more investors have become comfortable with the various products.

Having a suite of products that reference dividends directly has a number of advantages:

- Investors can gain direct exposure to future dividends either of a single stock or an equity index.
- Investors can isolate the dividend component of a stock or index without any associated price risk.
- The products can be used to hedge dividend risk that arises in other parts of the business (e.g. structured products).
- Dividends can be a good source of portfolio diversification as they tend to display low correlation with other asset classes such as fixed income.

13.4 Dividend Futures

Eurex is one of the exchanges which quotes index dividend futures and launched its EURO STOXX 50 index dividend future in June 2008. Since then the exchange's offering has widened to include more indices as well as futures on a limited number of single stock names.

Table 13.1 outlines the contract specification for the index dividend future that references the EURO STOXX 50.

The Eurex futures contract covers a 12-month period and matures on the 3rd Friday of each December. The calculation to determine the qualifying dividends is performed daily, excluding the previous year's 3rd Friday in December up to

Table 13.1 Eurex EURO STOXX 50 Index futures contract specification

Reference equity index	EURO STOXX 50 Index
Underlying dividend points calculation	EURO STOXX 50 dividend point (DP)
Contract value	EUR 100 per index dividend point
Price quotation	In points with one decimal place
Minimum price change	0.1 index points, equivalent to a value of EUR 10
Settlement	Contract is cash-settled
Contract month	The ten nearest successive annual contracts of the December cycle

Source: Eurex

and including the 3rd Friday in December of the settlement year. The majority of companies within the EURO STOXX 50 index pay annual dividends usually between May and July which is often referred to as 'dividend season'.

Although the future takes its value from dividend payments, the unit of trading is called an index dividend point. The index dividend point is determined using a two-stage process.

Firstly, on a daily basis the exchange calculates an 'Index dividend amount' (DA) for each share that pays a qualifying dividend.[1]

$$\text{Index dividend amount, DA}_t = \sum_{i=1}^{n} d_{i,t} \times s_{i,t} \times ff_{i,t} \times cf_{i,t} \qquad (13.1)$$

t = day on which the amount is calculated
n = number of companies in the index
i = individual constituent share
d = the cash dividends paid on the day of calculation by the constituent share. The day the share goes ex-dividend is deemed to be the payment date
s = the number of shares outstanding on the calculation date for the constituent share
ff = the free float factor of the constituent company on the calculation date
cf = weighting capitalization factor of the constituent company on the calculation date.

The free float factor (ff) is the proportion of shares that are considered to be tradable within the market place for a given stock. For example, the index rules of the UK FTSE index family state: 'Each FTSE constituent weighting is adjusted to reflect restricted shareholdings and foreign ownership to ensure an accurate representation of investable market capitalization'.[2] So if 20 % of a share is known to be closely held and not freely available, then the market capitalization of the share is multiplied by 0.8 before compiling the index.

The weighting capitalization factor (cf): 'limits the maximum weighting for a stock…. The weighting cap factors are used to achieve a diversification and avoid a dominance of a single stock, region, country or sector in an index. Depending on the objective of the index different maximum weights are sets.

---

[1] Stock dividends are included at their cash equivalent value but special dividends and share buybacks are excluded.
[2] www.ftse.com. An example of a restricted shareholding could be when a quoted company is partially state-owned.

Blue-chip indices are capped at 10 % per component while some benchmark indices have a capping at 20 %.'[3]

So by way of example, suppose that on a particular calculation date one of the constituent shares goes 'ex-div'. The ex-dividend date means that anyone buying the share on or after this date will not be eligible to receive the dividend. The announced gross dividend is €2.00 per share; the issuer has 100 million shares outstanding and has a free float factor of 0.80. If there is no weighting capitalization factor, then the index dividend amount is €160 m (€2.00 ×100 m × 0.8).

The second step in the process is to convert the index DA into an index dividend point (DP). This is done by dividing the index DA by the index divisor. The formula is:

$$\text{Final index dividend points}\left(\text{DP}_t\right) = \frac{\text{DA}_t}{\text{D}_t} \tag{13.2}$$

Where D_t = official index divisor as calculated and published by the index provider at time t.

Index divisors were explained in Sect. 1.2.3 and are published by the exchange providers on a daily basis. The divisor ensures the continuity of the index when shares come into or out of the index or when certain corporate actions occur such as initial public offerings (IPOs). Using the same figures outlined in the calculation of the index dividend amount, suppose the index divisor was €100 m and there were no other payments on that day. This would mean that the index dividend point of the particular company's dividend payment would be 1.6 (€160 m/€100 m).

For those contracts that go to full maturity, the final settlement amount is based on the summation of the calculated index dividend points for each day during the contract period.

$$\text{Index dividend value} = \sum_{t=1}^{T} \text{DP}_t \tag{13.3}$$

Where:
T = Number of days in contract period

---

[3] www.stoxx.com.

Table 13.2 EURO STOXX 50 Index dividend futures. Quotation is dividend index points equivalent

Expiry	Price
DEC 2015	114.80
DEC 2016	117.10
DEC 2017	115.40
DEC 2018	113.0
DEC 2019	110.50
DEC 2020	107.70
DEC 2021	105.30
DEC 2022	102.60
DEC 2023	100.30
DEC 2024	98.80

Source: Eurex

Table 13.3 Barclays Bank dividend futures. Quotation is on a dividend per share basis

Expiry	Price
DEC 2015	7.00
DEC 2016	7.00
DEC 2017	8.00
DEC 2018	8.00
DEC 2019	8.00

Source: Eurex

As of the time of writing, dividend futures on the EURO STOXX 50 index were trading at the levels shown in Table 13.2.

One of the reasons why the Eurex dividend futures prices decline with respect to time has been partially attributed to bank hedging of structured products such as autocallables.[4] Another explanation (Risk 2016a) suggests that the term structure is downward sloping because of the perceived risk of negative dividend surprises.

Eurex also quotes single-stock dividends and Table 13.3 shows the quotes for Barclays Bank. There are fewer maturities quoted and the open interest in the contracts generally only exists in the first two maturities. By comparison the EURO STOXX index futures had open interest in all of the maturities.

13.5 Dividend Swaps

13.5.1 Features of Dividend Swaps

Like any form of swap contract the dividend variant will involve the exchange of cash flows, typically characterized as 'fixed vs. floating'. Dividend swaps

[4] See Sect. 12.7.3.2.

allow investors to take a view on the cumulative dividends that are expected to be paid by the constituents of an index or just a single stock over a pre-agreed period.

The key characteristics of dividend swaps are as follows:

- *Trade date*—the day on which the transaction is executed.
- *The underlying*—this could be a single stock, an index or a basket of stocks.
- *Notional amount*—for single-stock swaps the notional is expressed in terms of the number of shares. An index swap notional is quoted as a cash exposure amount per index point ('notional per point').
- *Valuation period*—swaps will reference dividends paid in a particular year. So it would be possible for an investor to enter into a deal in, say, August, which will reference dividends paid in the following calendar year. The valuation period is the time during which the dividends will qualify for inclusion in the swap. 'End of year' maturities are the most common type of structure.
- *Fixed rate*—this is the 'price' of the swap and is the rate that ensures that initially the net present value of the structure is zero, that is, the rate that ensures that the swap is initially considered to be an equitable exchange of cash flows.
- *Floating rate*—this cash flow comprises of the actual dividends paid by the underlying.
- *Payment date*—the date on which the cash flows will be exchanged. Typically, dividend swaps are 'zero coupon' in style, with all of the cash flows being paid at maturity. If structured in this way, it means that the product is actually a forward. It is possible for the swap to cover multiple years and in this case it is likely that the cash flows will be settled on an annual basis. Under the terms of the swap the maturity payout will be:

$$\text{Notional amount} \times (\text{Realized dividends} - \text{Market implied dividends})$$

A generic example of a dividend swap is outlined in Fig. 13.1.

A 'payer' swap is where an entity will pay the fixed rate, which in Fig. 13.1 would be the investor. Conversely, the bank would be regarded as the 'receiver'. The investor could also be described as being 'long' the swap or 'buying' the swap; the bank would be 'short' or be a 'seller'.

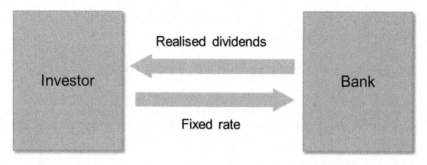

Fig. 13.1   Cash flows on a generic dividend swap (*Source*: author)

13.5.2 Quotation Conventions

Table 13.4 illustrates how a hypothetical index dividend swap could be quoted by the market.

Table 13.4 is sometimes referred to as a trader's 'daily run'; it is a series of prices quoted on a single day for swaps of different maturities. The swaps are quoted on a bid and offer ('ask') basis and are for specific future annual valuation periods. The year-on-year column measures the percentage change from the mid-price in the previous year to the mid-price in the current year. I/B/E/S is the Institutional Brokers' Estimate System which gathers estimates of expected dividend payments from a large number of market participants. These could be used by the trader to determine if the swap is trading in line with fundamental dividend valuations.

Single-stock swaps are quoted in currency units per share. For example, a 1-year single-stock dividend swap for BNPP might be quoted on a bid-offer basis as, say, €1.07–€1.47.

Table 13.4   Index dividend price quotes

Maturity	Bid	Ask ('offer')	Year on year	I/B/E/S
1	213.5	219.5	10.1 %	214.0
2	235.0	243.0	10.4 %	232.5
3	250.0	259.0	6.5 %	249.5
4	260.0	270.0	4.1 %	269.1
5	267.5	277.5	2.8 %	
6	273.5	284.5	2.4 %	
7	279.0	291.0	2.2 %	

Source: Author

13.5.3 Example Transaction

To place the product into some context, consider the following hypothetical term sheet.

Swap seller	Investment bank
Swap buyer	Client
Trade date	August 2016
Maturity	December 2017
Underlying index	Nikkei 225
Notional per point	YEN 800,000
Valuation period	Start date: 31st December 2016 (excluded from calculation) End date: 31st December 2017 (included in calculation)
Fixed strike	129 dividend points
Payment date	5th April 2018
Fixed amount	For each period an amount paid on the payment date by the swap buyer and defined as the: Fixed strike × notional per point
Floating amount	For each period an amount on the payment date by the swap seller and defined as the: Dividend amount × notional per point
Qualifying dividends	100 % of the gross cash dividend. Dividends are considered to be paid on the date they are declared ex-dividend
Dividend amount	For each period an amount defined as:

$$\sum_t \sum_i \frac{n_{i,t} \times d_{i,t}}{D_t}$$

Where:

t = each weekday in the dividend period

i = each share that is a constituent of the index

$d_{i,t}$ = a qualifying dividend paid at period 't' on share 'i'. If no dividend is paid an amount equal to zero

$n_{i,t}$ = the number of shares of the constituent stock in the index when a dividend is paid

D_t = the index divisor at period 't'

To illustrate the cash flows on the above swap, suppose that at maturity the constituent stocks of the Nikkei 225 have paid dividends equal to 140 index points.

The buyer/payer of fixed/long participant is obligated to pay:

$$\text{YEN } 800,000 \times 129 = \text{YEN } 103,200,000$$

The seller/payer of floating/short participant is obligated to pay:

$$YEN\ 800,000 \times 140 = YEN\ 112,000,000$$

Since the payments coincide there will be a net payment by the seller of YEN 8,800,000.

In this case the dividends realized by the index constituents were greater than the fixed rate.

13.5.4 Early Termination

Similar to all derivatives, dividend swaps can be unwound prior to maturity either by mutual agreement with the original counterparty or by taking an offsetting position with another entity.

Suppose that an investor had taken a long swap position in 2017 EURO STOXX dividends at a level of 115 index points with an associated notional of €100,000 per index point. After executing the deal but prior to the start of the valuation period, the fixed rate for contracts of the same maturity increase to 120 index points so the investor decides to close out the position. The first option would be to approach the original counterparty and mutually agree to terminate the deal with a payment to the participant for whom the transaction is ITM—in this case, the investor. The two parties would then agree a 'tear up' payment which would be the difference between the original fixed rate of 115 and the new level of 120. Based on the notional of €100,000 per index point this would result in a payment of €500,000. However, this payment would need to be present valued back to the early termination date as all cash flows on the swap were originally scheduled to be paid at the end of 2017.

If the early termination takes place within the valuation period, the participants would need to take account of any dividends paid as well as the prevailing fixed rate for dividend swaps with the same residual time to maturity.[5]

---

[5] An example of a similar type of calculation is shown for variance swaps in Sect. 14.6.1.3.

13.5.5 Novation

Another possibility that allows for early termination is the concept of novation— 'new for old'. Suppose that an investor has entered into a dividend swap where they have agreed to pay a fixed price of 110 index points with a bank counter-party ('A'). Shortly after executing the trade the investor sees the same swap being quoted in the market at a price of 115 index points by bank B. The investor approaches both bank A and B requesting a novation of the swap. Assuming that both banks agree the investor steps out of the transaction with all their rights and responsibilities being transferred to bank B. Bank A now faces bank B directly.

Since the fixed rate has increased, the swap is now ITM from the investor's perspective. So as part of the agreement bank B will make a payment to the investor equal to the deal's mark to market.

Novation could be attractive if the investor wanted to realize the profit on the transaction or if the credit risk associated with their original counterparty increased beyond their degree of comfort.

13.5.6 Dividend Swap Risk

There are a number of risks that are associated with dividend swaps. Some of the key risks include the following:

- Expected dividends may not be realized.
- The entity that is short the swap (i.e. payer of floating) is faced with a potentially unlimited payout as there is no upside to the amount of dividends that could be paid.
- There may be a lack of secondary market liquidity if the investor seeks to unwind the position prior to maturity.
- The swap counterparty could default prior to maturity.

13.5.7 Hedging Applications of Dividend Swaps

One of the popular motivations for using swaps relates to the notion of risk transformation. Some examples include the following:

- Asset managers who are long high dividend yielding stocks may wish to lock into an attractive rate by swapping into fixed.
- Convertible bond holders are short dividends and so may choose to hedge this exposure by entering into a long dividend swap position.

- Option traders who have a dividend exposure by virtue of their trading positions.
- Structured products that have an embedded dividend exposure.

13.5.8 Principles of Index Dividend Swap Valuation

There are a number of different approaches that can be used to value index swaps. If dividend swaps are structured to be zero coupon in style they are in effect forwards and as such should trade in line with similar products.

13.5.8.1   Forward Pricing

Recall from Sect. 9.2 the 'no arbitrage' pricing principles of a forward contract. That is:

$$\text{Forward price} = \text{Spot price} + \text{Funding cost} - \text{Equity repo} - \text{Dividends}$$

For any given calendar year, the funding cost can be observed from the interest rate swap market. The equity repo rate can be observed from the total return swap market.[6]

The forward price relationship could also be stated as follows:

$$\text{Forward price} = \left(\text{Spot price} - \text{PV of implied dividends}\right)$$
$$\times \left[\left(1 + \text{LIBOR} - \text{repo}\right)^{\text{time to maturity}} \right] \qquad (13.4)$$

Where PV is the present value.
Rearranging the formula gives:

$$\text{Implied dividend} = \text{FV} \times \left(\text{Spot} - \frac{\text{Forward}}{\left(1 + \text{Interest rate} - \text{repo}\right)^{\text{time to maturity}}} \right) \qquad (13.5)$$

Where FV is the future value. To illustrate the concept, consider the following worked example.

---

[6] In Sect. 10.2 it was shown that the spread to LIBOR on the floating leg of an equity swap should trade in line with the securities lending market.

Nikkei spot value: 20,000.00
12-month forward price: 19,500.35
1-year interest rate   1.00 %
  swap:
1-year total return swap: TIBOR—1 basis point

$$\text{Implied dividend} = 1.01 \times \left(20,000 - \frac{19,500.35}{(1.0099)} \right) = 697.72 \qquad (13.6)$$

The implied dividends for the present calendar year are therefore 698 index points. Based on the spot market value of 20,000 index points this returns a dividend yield of 3.49 %.

13.5.8.2   Extracting Implied Dividends from Options

One of the most powerful and underrated concepts in option theory is put call parity. The concept was first introduced in Sect. 4.7. Put call parity ensures that the option and cash markets are aligned from a valuation perspective. For equity options the relationship is:

$$C - P = S \times e^{-qt} - K \times e^{-rt} \qquad (13.7)$$

Where:
C = price of a call option
P = price of a put option
S = Spot rate
e = exponential function (e.g. 2.71828)
K = Strike price
q = dividend yield
r = funding costs
t = time to expiry

The formula can be rearranged to solve for the dividend implied by the observed option prices.

So using the values from the Nikkei example in the previous section a BSM option valuation framework would generate an ATM premium of 1920.88 index points based on an implied volatility of 25 %.

Nikkei spot value	20,000.00
12-month forward price	19,500.35
1-year interest rate swap	1 %
Implied volatility	25 %
ATM option premium	1920.68

Using put call parity (Eq. 13.7) and solving for the implied dividend returns a value of 3.53 %, which is within 4 basis points of the 'forward price' technique.

13.5.8.3   Bottom Up Approach

Strictly speaking a forward is not a forecast. Anecdotally, some participants will still view forwards as the 'market's best guess of future spot rates'. Risk (2016a) argues that dividend futures are priced from forecasts and so can be susceptible to changes in expectations. Participants also use fundamental analysis to determine the fair value of a future. This technique would essentially be an extension of the valuation principles introduced in Chap. 2. So it would be possible to develop a model that included dividend policies and payout ratios which would form the basis of the forecast. This could be incorporated into a simple model as follows:

- An investor could make an estimate of the cumulative dividend per share a company is expected to pay in during a year.
- This figure is then multiplied by the number of free float shares within the index.
- The result of the second step is then divided by index divisor to return the dividends in index points.

$$\text{Cumulative dividends in index points} = \frac{\text{Cumulative dividend per share} \times \text{Free float shares in index}}{\text{Index divisor}}$$

13.5.9 Pull to Realized

The 'pull to realized' effect[7] describes the process whereby the prices of dividend swaps or futures tend to converge with realized dividends. To illustrate

---

[7] Sometimes referred to as 'pull to par'.

this concept, suppose there is an index where the constituents pay a single annual dividend at the end of the first half of a particular year based on quarterly earnings announcements in the previous calendar year. After the third quarter's earnings announcement, an investor would be fairly confident of the company's annual earnings and the expected dividend to be paid in the subsequent year. This will be reflected in dividend swap/futures prices which will converge towards these realized values.

This example also indicates that the payout for a dividend swap/future that settles in December of a particular year will be known with reasonable certainty by the time the companies have announced their dividends 6 months earlier.

The concept of 'pull to realized' is illustrated in Fig. 13.2. The solid line shows the evolution of the 2014 EUREX STOXX index dividend future over its last few months of existence. The contract traded within a relatively narrow range compared to the 2015 maturity as the majority of constituents had paid dividends for that year. However, in late October one of the constituents announced an extraordinary qualifying dividend that caused the price of the 2014 contract to increase accordingly. The chart also shows how the price of the 2015 contract also displayed a similar characteristic.

One popular technique used in the futures market to exploit this characteristic is to systematically roll futures positions. This strategy has been termed a 'risk premia' trade as it represents an excess return that an investor can earn if they are willing to assume some identified risk. Figure 13.2 shows that the pull to realized tends to peak around March to April of a particular year and so an investor could go long a futures contract and profit from the fact that the pull to realized effect will cause it to rise in value. As the value of this future starts to plateau, the investor would then be able to sell at a profit and instantaneously buy the next-dated contract which if the term structure is downward sloping will be trading at a lower price. This type of 'sell high, buy low' rolling strategy is well documented in the commodities market and as long as the curve remains inverted should generate for the investor a 'roll yield'.[8]

13.6 Dividend Options

OTC dividend options referencing the EURO STOXX 50 (SX5E) emerged in 2007 but exchange-traded variants were first listed in 2010. The contract specification of the dividend option listed on EUREX is shown in Table 13.5.

---

[8] This strategy is also very popular in the commodity markets. See Schofield (2008).

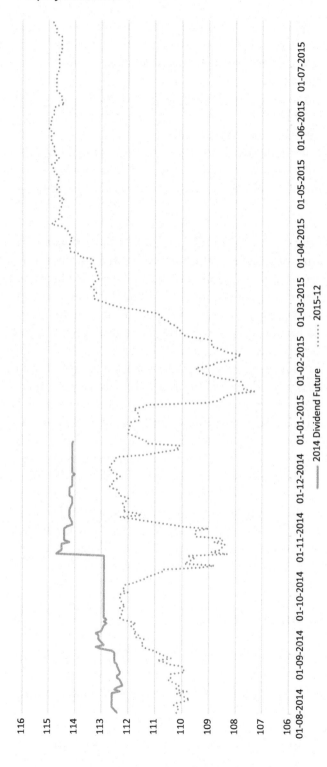

Fig. 13.2 Evolution of EURO STOXX dividend futures; 2014 and 2015 maturities. Data covers period July 2014–July 2015 (*Source:* Eurex, author)

Table 13.5 Contract specification for dividend options on SX5E

Underlying asset	EURO STOXX 50 index dividend futures
Contract value	EUR 100 per index point of the underlying
Settlement	Cash settlement
Price quotation	Index points to two decimal places
Minimum price change	0.01 points equivalent to a value of EUR 1 per contract
Contract months	Up to 119 months. Options are available on the ten nearest successive annual EURO STOXX 50 index dividend futures contract of the December cycle
Final settlement date	The third Friday of each December expiration month
Daily settlement price	Established by Eurex; price determined through the Black 1976 model
Final settlement price	Based on the final value of the underlying index for the relevant contract period. Determining is the cumulative total of the relevant gross dividends declared and paid by the individual constituents of the underlying index as calculated in the form of index points
Style	European
Option premium	Payable on trade date + 1

Source: Eurex

Within a particular maturity there would also be a range of strikes available. So taking the December 2015 as an example, at the time of writing, the future was trading at 114.0 and the range of strikes for calls on the future varied from 40 to 150 index points. So if in July 2015 an investor bought a call on a December 2015 index dividend future they would have a 6-month option which would be cash-settled against the final price of the underlying future at expiry.

13.6.1 Dividend Option Valuation

One of the ways to approach the valuation of dividend options is to use the Black model for options on futures. This model is used extensively in the interest rate options market for valuing caps, floors and swaptions and is also used in commodity markets where many options reference an underlying future. In a BSM model an analyst would typically input the spot price of the asset into the model, which combined with the 'carry' parameters (e.g. interest rates, dividend yields and equity repo rates) would generate the implied forward price. Based on the implied forward the model would then calculate the option's fair value. One of the main attractions of the Black model is its simplicity as the spot and net carry parameters are replaced with the observed forward or futures price. This would mean that the parameters required to price an option on a dividend future would be as follows:

- Price of dividend future,
- Strike,
- Option's time to maturity,
- Implied volatility of dividend future.

13.6.2 Characteristics of Implied Dividend Volatility

Figure 13.3 illustrates the volatility skew of options written on the 2018 dividend future at three different points in time. As a point of reference the volatility skew for 2-year options on the underlying EURO STOXX index on the 1st July 2015 was trading well above these levels:

90 %	21.9 %
100 %	20.7 %
110 %	19.8 %

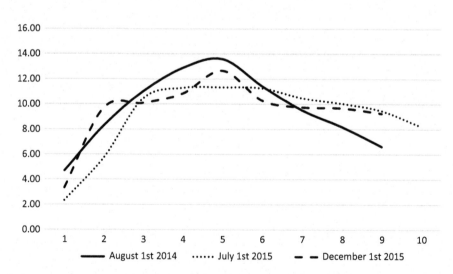

Fig. 13.3 Implied volatility skew for options written on the December 2018 SX5E dividend future at three different points in time. X axis is the strike price as a percentage of the underlying price (*Source*: Eurex, author)

   Similar to other option markets, dividend options also display a term structure of implied volatility (Fig. 13.4).
   Again to put this into some context the term structure for options of different maturities on the underlying equity index (SX5E) on 1 July 2015 was
upward sloping and the constituent values were trading above the levels seen
on the dividend market:

1 month:	12.6 %
2 month:	13.3 %
3 month:	14.0 %
6 month:	15.1 %
12 month:	16.6 %
24 month:	18.2 %

   As was noted in Sect. 6.4.1.5, implied volatility term structures normally
slope upwards unless the market is under stress when they tend to invert.
However, for dividend futures the term structure displays a 'humped' shape
with implied volatilities rising towards the 5-year maturity before declining. Since implied volatility is a measure of risk it could be argued that the
'hump' represents the greatest degree of uncertainty with respect to future
dividends. The decline in longer-dated volatility may be symptomatic of
the fact that the market expects dividends to revert to some long-term
average.

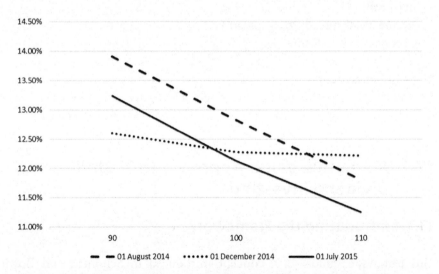

Fig. 13.4 Term structure of implied volatility for options on SX5E dividend futures
at three different points in time (*Source*: Eurex, author)

13.6.3 Applications

In some respects, the applications for dividend options are similar to those outlined in Chap. 11. As a quick recap the applications were categorized into the following themes:

- Portfolio downside protection
- Directional views
- Range-bound or volatility strategies
- Yield enhancement
- Outperformance strategies

Without wishing to repeat the content of that chapter, the following provides some dividend specific examples.

Portfolio Downside Protection
Within this category, the motivation would be to protect the value of some long dividend exposure perhaps by the purchase of a put option.

'View Driven'
These strategies could be structured to express a view on, say, the growth of dividends. For example, an investor could

- buy a call;
- execute a call spread ('bull spread');
- execute a '1x2' call spread.

Yield Enhancement
A popular strategy is for an investor to sell OTM puts. This might make sense if the investor considered the skew was to be 'too steep' to the downside.

13.7 A Relative Value Approach to Traded Dividend Investing

13.7.1 Introducing the Framework

This technique builds on a concept introduced in Schofield and Bowler (2011). Traditionally, relative value is often thought of in its literal sense, that is, one asset cheap or rich relative to another. With respect to dividends this might include the following types of strategy:

- Index versus Index (e.g. FTSE 100 dividends vs. S&P 500 dividends).
- Single stock versus Single stock (e.g. Apple vs. Amazon).

The alternative approach to relative value poses a different question: *what is the optimal way in which a particular view of the market can be expressed?* The approach is based on the notion that formal mathematical relationships exist between the different components of a traded market as shown in Fig. 13.5. For example, a spot and forward price are linked by the net carry on the underlying asset.

Suppose that an investor believed that 5-year dividend futures will rise over the next 3 months. What would be the optimal trade to express this view? There are a number of possibilities:

- Buy the dividend future.
- Put on a steepener (i.e. buy the 5-year, sell a shorter-dated contract).
- Put on a 'fly spread (i.e. sell the 3-year, buy the 5-year, sell the 10-year).
- Put on a cross market trade (buy 5-year EUREX dividend future, sell 5-year FTSE dividend future).
- Buy calls on the dividend future.
- Sell puts on the dividend future.

The strategy will depend on the investor's internal constraints as well as the relative value of the individual assets within the strategy. The optimal strategy will generally be the one that has the highest reward to risk payoff given the constraints that that investor faces. Arguably it is not about 'low' or 'high' risk strategies but ones that represent 'good quality' risks relative to the return that they offer. It is possible to have a low risk trade which is sub-optimal because it has a low prospective return.

To illustrate the approach, suppose that an investor is trying to identify if the slope of a curve is trading at fair value. To increase the probability of making money and reducing the probability of making losses an investor would

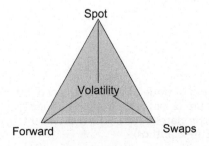

Fig. 13.5   The relative value (RV) triangle (*Source*: Author)

want to put on a steepener when the term structure is 'too flat' or to put on a flattener when the curve is 'too steep'. Such trade opportunities can be identified by using an additional measure such as the absolute level of the market. One possible approach would be to

- create a scattergraph of the slope of the dividend future term structure versus the level of the futures market;
- plot a line of 'best fit' with points on this line being considered as 'fair value';
- assess whether the current market is significantly away from the 'best fit' line.

This approach suggests that an investor does not need a theory of how term structures are determined; the only thing that is important is how they move in practice. An example is shown in Fig. 13.6.

Figure 13.6 suggests that if the latest observation sat beneath the line of best fit it would suggest that the slope is too steeply negative for a given level of dividends. If the investor expected the value of the slope to increase towards

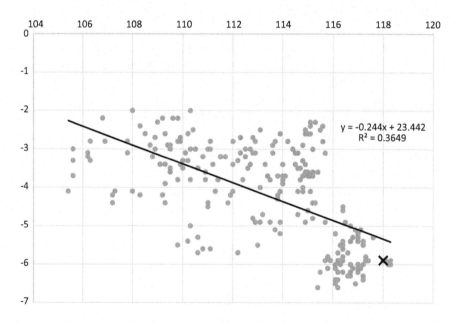

Fig. 13.6 Scatter graph of slope of 2020–2018 dividend futures slope (*y* axis) versus 2016 dividend future (*x* axis). The slope is defined as the long-dated dividend future minus the shorter-dated future. The most recent observation is highlighted with an 'X' (*Source*: Eurex, author)

zero, this would require the longer-dated contract to rise or the shorter-dated contract to fall (or some combination thereof).

13.7.2 Applying the RV Triangle: Individual Products

The following sections consider the different ways in which an investor could express a view that dividends are likely to increase by using individual products.

13.7.2.1   Cash Markets

The traditional way of taking exposure to dividends would be to simply buy the underlying share. Dividends tend to be somewhat 'sticky' in that issuers do not always cut dividends unless there is a significant downturn in the company's economic fortunes. The major downside of this strategy is that the position also has an exposure to the movement in the share price and so cannot be considered to be a 'pure' dividend strategy.

13.7.2.2   Dividend Futures and Swaps

Dividend futures and dividend swaps are essentially different sides of the same coin and so where the terms are identical, a trader's quote for both instruments should theoretically be identical. The main difference between the products is the counterparty risk, which would have to be reflected in the price. Any exchange-traded derivative would be subject to the margining process of the clearing house attached to the exchange and so the credit risk is mitigated. However, bilateral OTC transactions will often be subject to collateralization and margining which will have a similar effect. Consequently, which particular product a client chooses to use would be a function of any internal restrictions, systems limitations or the degree of comfort with a particular instrument.

Outright Strategies
Section 13.4 showed that dividend futures offer an investor an exposure to dividends without the need to incur any underlying price risk. Suppose that an investor observed the EURO STOXX 2017 dividend future trading at 114.50 index points and considered the contract to be undervalued; they may choose to simply go long the futures. Equally, an investor who thought that dividends were overvalued would go short the future.

Slope Trades

As with any product that displays a term structure it is possible to express views on how this is expected to evolve. Consider Fig. 13.7 which displays the term structure of EUREX dividend futures 12 months apart. It confirms the observation that generally speaking European dividend futures display downward sloping term structures, which at the time was attributed to the hedging of autocallable structured products (see Sect. 12.7.3).

One of the ways to exploit the inverted term structure is by systematically rolling futures. This strategy was discussed in Sect. 13.5.9.

Figure 13.8 shows the relationship between the slope of the term structure versus the absolute level of the market over time and indicates that as the absolute value of dividends increases the term structure becomes increasingly negative.

In a slope trade an investor would take offsetting positions in dividend futures. Suppose that an investor saw the following prices trading in the market:

- 2017 dividend future 114.50
- 2019 dividend future 108.90

The trader's analysis suggests that even though it is numerically greater, the 2017 contract is 'cheap' relative to the 2019 contract, that is, the spread between the two contracts is lower than he would expect. This could be as

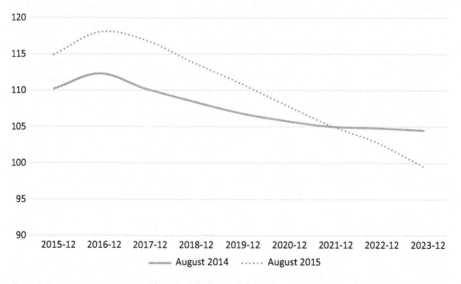

Fig. 13.7 Term structure of Eurex dividend futures at two different points in time (*Source*: Eurex, author)

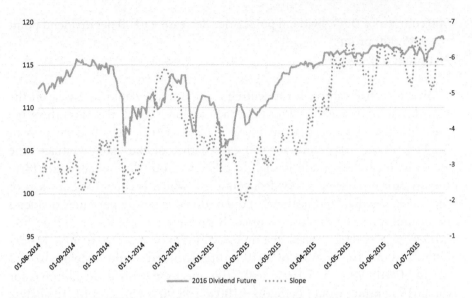

Fig. 13.8 Slope of term dividend future term structure (2020–2018; dotted line) versus the level of the market (2016 dividend future). Slope of term structure is the 2020 dividend future less the 2018 dividend future and is read off the left hand scale which is inverted (*Source*: Eurex, author)

a result of some fundamental analysis or simply because they feel that the current level is trading in a high percentile range relative to historical observations. A steepening trade would require the investor to go long the 2017 contract and short the 2019 maturity. The position would show a profit if the price of the 2017 contract increased relative to the 2019 contract. The position can be constructed by selecting notional amounts that are equal to each other, so the trader could go long 500 of the 2017 contracts and short 500 of the 2019 contracts. Assume that shortly after putting on the trade the spread widens with the following market prices being observed.

2017 dividend future	115.00
2019 dividend future	108.00

The investor's profit or loss will be as follows:

Long 2017 maturity
500 contracts × 0.50 dividend point price increase × €100 per dividend point
    = €25,000 profit
Short 2019 maturity

500 contracts × 0.90 dividend point price decrease × €100 per dividend point
   = €45,000 profit
Net profit = €70,000

An alternative motive for executing a slope trade would be based on the growth rate of dividends rather than the absolute spread. Based on the same previous data suppose that an investor believes that the dividend growth implied by the 2017 contract will exceed that of the 2019 contract. The construction of this trade is slightly different from the spread trade. Here the investor establishes a 'dividend notional' which is equal for both legs of the trade. The dividend notional is the notional exposure per index dividend point multiplied by the future's price. If the investor decides to go long 500 2017 contracts that equates to a dividend notional of 500 × €100 × 114.50 = €5,725,000. The number of 2019 futures required would therefore be 500 × 114.50/108.90 = 526 (rounded). This means the dividend notional for the 2019 contract would be 526 × €100 × 108.90 = €5,728,140. To analyse the profit or loss on the trade suppose that 2017 future increases by 1 % to 115.65 with the same percentage increase being observed on the 2019 position, that is, the 2019 contract moves to 109.99. The profit or loss on the position is therefore:

Long 2017 position
500 contracts × (115.65−114.50) × €100 = €57,500 profit
Short 2019 position
526 contracts × (109.99−108.90) × €100 = €57,334 loss

Since the contracts have experienced the same percentage change in dividends the position has virtually broken even.[9]

13.7.2.3   Dividend Options

Generic option strategies were covered in Chap. 11. Another possibility would be to apply the principles of put call parity which illustrated that options and the underlying asset could be combined in different ways to create a synthetic position. So an investor could buy a dividend call and sell a dividend put (same strike and maturity) and the position would be equivalent to be long the underlying dividend future.

---

[9] It is not exact due to rounding of the notional amount.

13.7.3 Applying the RV Triangle: Relationships Between Products

13.7.3.1 Cash Versus Futures/Swap

This strategy looks at combining the two products linked by the right hand side of the RV triangle in Fig. 13.5. Since dividend futures and swaps are economically equivalent it could also apply to the left hand side of the matrix. This relationship can be traded by using the exchange for physical (EFP) market which was covered in Sect. 9.7.

Recall that the difference between the spot and forward price of any financial asset comprises of the carry components:

Forward price = Spot price + LIBOR − Equity repo − Implied dividends

If an investor wanted to take exposure to a rise in the level of implied dividends, they would need to have a short forward position and be long the stock. This is sometimes referred to as 'selling the EFP'. If implied dividends increase in value, the forward would decline all other things being equal and result in a profit for the investor. However, the position is not a pure dividend exposure as there is a residual exposure to the remaining carry components, that is, LIBOR and equity repo rates.

13.7.3.2 Trading the Dividend Yield

A share's dividend yield is calculated as the historic divided by the current share price. However, many professionals will be interested in the prospective dividend yield; that is, expected dividends divided by the current share price. In this example the prospective dividends are taken to be those implied by the dividend swap market. In terms of where this would fit on the RV triangle it could initially be thought of as a trade that attempts to profit from the movement between dividend swap prices and spot equity prices. To go long the dividend yield an investor needs to take opposing positions in dividends and the underlying index. Since it is somewhat cumbersome to trade the individual components of the index, a near-dated index futures position is used as a proxy.

- *Long the dividend yield*: Long dividends, short the index
- *Short the dividend yield*: Short dividends, long the index

Suppose that in mid-2015 an investor considers the 2018 dividend yield to be 'too low' and so they decide to construct a long dividend yield trade with an exposure of €5,000,000:

- Long 2018 dividend swap @ 112.70 index points

Assuming a desired exposure of €5,000,000 this suggests a notional amount of €44,365 per index point (€5,000,000/112.70)

- Short September 2015 EURO STOXX 50 Index future @ 3672 index points

The EURO STOXX index futures contract trades with a fixed multiplier of €10, which means that the trader would need to execute 136 contracts to ensure that the exposure matches that of the dividend swap (3672 × €10 × 136 = €4,993,920).

These figures suggest that the initial dividend yield was 3.07 % (112.70/3672). The trader decides to close the position 1 month later when the dividend swap has increased to 113.50 and the index future has fallen to 3590 implying a dividend yield of 3.16 %. The profit and loss on the trade are as follows:

Index futures:
136 futures × (3672−3590) × €10 = €111,520 profit
Dividend swap:
€44,365 × (113.50−112.70) = €35,492 profit

The total profit on the trade is therefore €147,012.

13.7.4 Other Relative Value Trades

13.7.4.1   Dividends Versus Interest Rates

In general terms there is a fundamental relationship between interest rates and dividend yields. Increasing interest rates could be interpreted as a sign that the economy is expanding and a possible response would be for the Central Bank to increase interest rates to avoid excessive inflation. In this growth scenario one would expect an increase in dividend yields. A lowering of interest rates which could represent an attempt to stimulate a faltering economy could be associated with falling dividend yields. So all other things being equal there would be a positive relationship between interest rates and dividends. The rationale for the trade is explained in Barclays Capital (2010):

> As dividend swaps normally trade cheap compared with realized dividends, this cheapness can be extracted by putting on a relative value pair trade of long dividend yield short interest rates. Shorting interest rates can be thought of as hedging interest rate risk (in the same way as trading dividend yields rather than dividends hedges equity market risk). By trading dividend yield against interest rate swaps, the investor is exposed to the "pure" cheapness of dividends and has hedged the equity and interest rate risk of a naked long dividend trade.

Suppose that an investor believes that forward dividend yields for a given maturity (i.e. 1-year dividend yields, 3 years forward) are trading cheap to some notion of fair value. The investor structures the following position:

Long dividend yield

- Buy the dividend future that they believe is undervalued
- Sell an index future

Short interest rates

- Enter into a forward starting interest rate, whose maturity matches that of the dividend swap. The interest rate swap would be a proxy for 'interest rates'. The investor would receive fixed, pay LIBOR.

The notional amounts of the trade can be constructed in various ways. The dividend yield leg could be constructed in the same way that was outlined in Sect. 13.7.3.2. The interest rate swap notional could be constructed such that the change in the value of the swap would match the change in the value of the dividend yield position. One approach suggested by Barclays Capital (2010) would be to set the transaction sizes such that the profit and loss on the dividend yield position for a 1 % change in dividend yields would be equal to the profit and loss on the interest rate swap from a 1 % increase in interest rates. At first glance this may seem an odd choice as it suggests that the profit from an anticipated increase in dividend yields would be offset by an equal loss on the swap. However, recall that the motive was that the dividend yields were considered to be undervalued and so the movement in dividend yields would be greater than any change in interest rates. A slightly different approach based on fixed income market conventions would be to calculate the notional amounts based on a 1 basis point change in both dividend yields and interest rates. This is because the market to market of an interest rate swap is non-linear for significant changes in interest rates and displays an element of convexity.

Recall the dividend yield example from Sect. 13.7.3.2. The initial position was

Long dividend swap
€44,365 notional per dividend index point at a price of 112.70
Short index future
Sell 136 index futures at a price of 3672 index points and an index multiplier of €10

Taken together these implied a dividend yield of 3.07 %. Suppose that all other things being equal the implied dividend increases from 3.06 % to 3.07 % as a result of an increase in the implied dividends from 112.70 to 112.73. Assuming that the underlying index future remains the same, the profit and loss on the dividend yield position would be wholly accountable by the profit and loss on the dividend swap position:

$$(112.73 - 112.70) \times €44365 = €1330$$

The interest rate swap position was a 1-year swap about 2.5 years forward and must be traded with a notional such that a 1 basis point change in interest rates will result in a change in its mark to market of €1330. This is a well-established market risk measure in the fixed income market and is referred to as the DV01.[10] At the time of writing, an interest rate swap of this maturity had a DV01 of €99 per €1 mm notional,[11] so the requisite notional would be approximately €13,500,000 (€1330/€99 × €1 m, rounded).

13.7.4.2   Dividend Dispersion Trades

A strategy that involves trading index dividend futures against the constituent single-stock dividend futures is sometimes referred to casually as a 'dividend dispersion' trade. Strictly speaking this is not a 'true' dispersion trade as the transaction is not correlation-dependent. Since the sum of the dividends of

---

[10] The DV01 is the 'dollar value of a basis point'. It measures the change in the value of the swap for a 1 basis point change in swap rates. See Schofield and Bowler (2011) for more details.

[11] Figure obtained from Barclays Live.

the constituent shares of an index should equal the dividends implied by the index there is no correlation aspect to the trade. As such it has more in common with the index arbitrage trade that was discussed in Sect. 9.4. The motivation for the trade is based on the notion that index dividends trade cheap to fair value due to structured product hedging and as a result are trading out of line with the sum of the constituent dividends. The appropriate trade is to buy index dividends and sell single-stock dividends. However, the trade does have some risks (Barclays Capital 2010):

- The membership of the index could change.
- Dividends paid as stock are counted for single-stock swaps but may not be for index swaps.
- Lack of liquidity on index constituents may make the economics of the transaction unattractive.

13.7.4.3 High Versus Low Yielding Stock

A relatively simple RV position would be to go long dividend futures on companies that are expected to increase their dividend payout while going short companies that are expected to cut dividends. The same trade could be used to exploit expected dividend differences between indices.

13.7.4.4 Capital Structure Trades

Capital structure trades are long/short positions in different components of a company's capital structure. Suppose that an investor took a bearish view on the prospects of a particular company and decided to express this with the following trade:

- Selling default protection under the terms of a credit default swap[12] (CDS)
- Taking a short single-stock dividend swap position (i.e. receive the fixed implied dividends, pay the floating realized dividends)

This would make sense if the investor believed that the premium on the CDS was overvalued and that the dividend market did not reflect the same degree of pessimism.

---

[12] See Schofield and Bowler (2011) for more on Credit Default Swaps.

If the corporate were to suffer a 'credit event' then under the terms of the CDS, the investor would be required to make a payment to their counterparty. However, it is unlikely that the company would be in a position to pay any dividends so this would benefit the investor's dividend swap position. Since they are receiving the fixed rate and paying floating (i.e. the realized dividend) then the position would show a profit. So in theory the net cash flows received on the dividend swap could be used to finance the CDS payout.

If the corporate did not experience a credit event, then the trade may not necessarily lose money. The investor will receive a series of premium cash flows on the CDS, which could be used to finance the realized dividend cash flows on the swap.

13.8 Summary

The market for dividend derivatives largely evolved from banks' need to hedge their long dividend exposures that were associated with their structured product business.

Futures, swaps and options have evolved on an OTC and exchange-traded basis to meet this demand. These products offer a number of advantages:

- They provide an efficient hedge for single-stock or index dividend exposures.
- An investor can isolate exposure to dividends on a forward basis.
- They provide an opportunity to express a variety of views in a variety of ways on the level and growth rate of dividends.

14

Trading Volatility

14.1 Introduction

Volatility was introduced in Chap. 6 and topics covered included the following:

- Definitions
- Overview of trading strategies
- Characteristics
- Identifying value

Volatility is the annualized standard deviation of the log of the daily return of a stock or index price, whereas variance is the square of the standard deviation. However, this particular definition of volatility is sometimes referred to as 'realized' or 'historical', that is, it is a backward-looking measure that captures the magnitude of historical price movements. Implied volatility is a forward-looking measure of volatility—it is attempting to capture what the market expects the asset's actual volatility to be over some future time period.

This chapter contains more detail on how 'view-driven' variance and volatility strategies could be expressed.

14.2 Conventional Option Trades

In its simplest form trading volatility requires a trader to buy or sell options with an appropriate delta hedge in order to isolate the vega exposure. So if a trader believed that implied volatility was going to decrease,

© The Author(s) 2017   **417**

N. Schofield, *Equity Derivatives*, DOI 10.1057/978-0-230-39107-9_14

they could sell options (either calls or puts as both options will be vega negative) and trade the underlying in order to neutralize the delta exposure. Section 11.4 illustrated that volatility could also be traded by means of straddles and strangles. Although a delta-hedged vega position will be protected against small moves in the underlying asset, larger moves in spot could have an unwanted impact on the position's profit or loss; this is the 'gamma effect'.

The profit or loss that arises from the impact of gamma is a function of spot price movements. For example, gamma is greatest when the option is ATM; as spot moves away from this level gamma declines and so does the magnitude of delta-hedging profits and losses. This delta-gamma relationship is one of the reasons why there has been a move to 'purer' techniques of trading volatility, some of which are introduced in this chapter.

It is useful to categorize volatility trades into two main categories:

- *Gamma trades*—this type of transaction is used to express a view on how future realized volatility evolves relative to current implied volatility. Typically, the maturity of the option trade will correspond to the horizon over which the trader wishes to predict realized volatility.
- *Vega trades*—with this type of trade the investor will enter into a long-dated option trade with the intention of unwinding the position prior to expiry. The profitability of the trade will be a function of realized volatility up to the point that the trade is terminated as well as the future implied volatility from the unwind date to the original expiration.

14.3 Volatility Surface Trades

In Chap. 6 it was argued that the BSM assumption of constant volatility was a theoretical construct and that empirically volatility varied with respect to

- Option maturity, that is, it exhibits a term structure
- Strike

The combination of these two characteristics gives rise to what is referred to as the volatility surface. The existence of the surface offers a number of trading possibilities.

14.3.1 Trading the Slope of the Skew

In 'normal' circumstances the equity market is skewed to the downside. So volatilities for low strike OTM puts will be greater than the ATM volatility as well as higher strike, OTM calls (see Fig.6.10). The first type of 'surface' trade attempts to profit from a change in the observed slope of the skew. Here the slope is defined as the volatility difference between two options with different strikes but of the same maturity.

This also gives rise to some trading terminology that is worth defining. When measuring the skew, it is commonly calculated as the volatility for a 90 % strike option less the volatility for a 110 % option. If a trader 'sells the skew' or 'goes short the skew' then within an equity market context this is interpreted to mean that this differential will fall. Consequently, a trader will sell low strike OTM puts options and buy high strike OTM call options usually with the same maturity. Suppose that the volatility for a 90 % option is 20 %, while the market for a 110 % strike is trading at a level of 15 %; this would return an initial skew value of 5 %. If the 90 % volatility now fell to 18 % and the 110 % strike volatility increased to 16 %, the skew would be 2 %. If the trader had sold a 90 % put and bought a 110 % call, then all other things being equal the position would show a profit. 'Buying' or 'going long' the skew is a strategy where the trader buys low strike options and sells higher strike options, again with the same maturity.

So in summary:

Skew is believed to be too flat and is expected to steepen (i.e. implied volatility for low strike options will rise more than that of high strike options)

- Buy low strike options and sell high strike options.

These views could also be combined with a directional view of the market:

- *Bullish outlook on the market?* The trader should favour a bull spread using calls (buy low strike ITM call, sell high strike OTM call) or a bull spread using puts (buy low strike OTM put, sell high strike ITM put).
- *Bearish outlook on the market?* The trader may favour a collar buying an OTM put and financing it with the sale of an OTM call.

Skew is believed to be too steep and is expected to flatten (i.e. implied volatility for low strike options will fall more than that of the high strike options)

- Sell low strike options and buy high strike options.

As before the choice of trade may be influenced by expected market movements:

- *Bullish outlook on the market?* The trader may favour a collar buying an OTM call and financing it with the sale of an OTM put.
- *Bearish outlook on the market?* The trader should favour a bear spread using calls (sell low strike ITM call, buy high strike OTM call) or a bull spread using puts (sell low strike OTM put, buy high strike ITM put).

Risk reversals are a popular trade designed to express a view on the expected evolution of the skew and can be quoted for a variety of maturities and deltas, for example, '1 month 25 delta'. Risk reversal quotes represent the difference between two volatilities so a '25 delta risk reversal' is the volatility of a 25 delta call minus the volatility of a 25 delta put. An example of a risk reversal is shown in Fig. 14.1. Before the market moves the risk reversal is 4 % (18 % − 14 %); after the market moves it is 5 % (20 % − 15 %).

Risk reversals are quoted on a bid–offer basis so a trader quoting '0.3/0.5 puts over calls'[1] is first indicating that the price, in volatility terms, is higher for the puts than for the call with a similar delta. At the bid price, the market

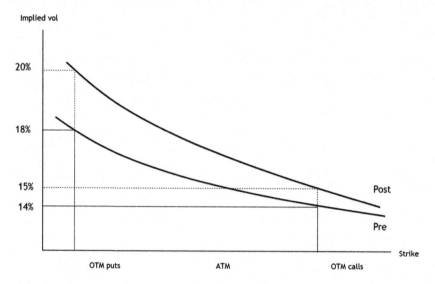

Fig. 14.1 Example of a risk reversal—equity market skew steepens (*Source*: author)

---

[1] This may be shortened sometimes to '0.3/0.5 puts over'.

maker would be willing to buy a put and sell a call by paying away 0.3 % in volatility terms. At the offer price, they would be willing to sell a put and buy a call and receive 0.5 % in volatility terms. Suppose that the market maker buys the risk reversal at his bid price. The participants will then agree the respective absolute volatilities. So the market maker will agree to buy the put of a given delta at a volatility of (say) 20.0 % and sell the call of an equivalent delta at a volatility of 19.7 %.

14.3.2 Trading the Curvature of the Skew

While a slope trade expresses a view on the volatility differential between two points, curvature trades are based on capturing the difference between three observations.

This curvature is measured using a 'butterfly spread' which is calculated as:

$$\frac{25 \text{ delta call volatility} + 25 \text{ delta put volatility}}{2} - \text{ATM volatility} \quad (14.1)$$

An example is shown in Fig. 14.2.

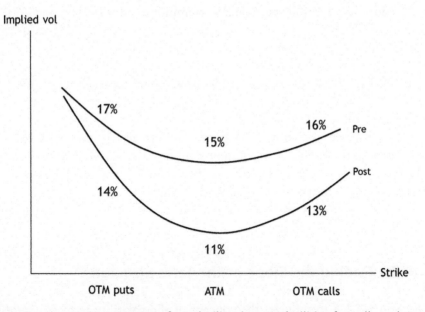

Fig. 14.2 Change in curvature of a volatility skew. Volatilities for calls and puts are assumed to be of equal delta value (e.g. 25 delta) (*Source*: author)

Using the values in Fig. 14.2 the butterfly spread is initially measured as:

$$(16\% + 17\%)/2 - 15\% = 1.5\%$$

Post the market move the spread is:

$$(13\% + 14\%)/2 - 11\% = 2.5\%$$

In this example the curve has fallen but its curvature has increased. The increased value of the spread indicates an increased degree of curvature. The most common way to trade an anticipated change in the curvature of the skew is by means of a butterfly trade. A butterfly position consists of

- Long a strangle and short a straddle or
- Short a strangle and long a straddle

Consider the following example referencing a nameless asset.

Long a strangle

- Buy an OTM call struck at 105 (premium payable 0.86)
- Buy an OTM put struck at 95 (premium payable 0.91)

Sell a straddle

- Sell an ATM call and put at 100 (total premium receivable 4.36)

Net premium receivable 2.59.

The net position is shown in Fig. 14.3 at both expiry and pre-expiry.

The position in Fig. 14.3 will show a profit if the OTM implied volatilities for the call and the put used to construct the long strangle increase and the ATM volatility for the short straddle decreases.

Butterfly spreads can be quoted on a bid–offer basis as shown in Table 14.1.

14.3.3 Trading the Slope of the Term Structure

Section 6.4.1.5 introduced the concept of the volatility term structure (see Figs. 6.17, 6.18 and 6.19). The term structure charts the relationship between

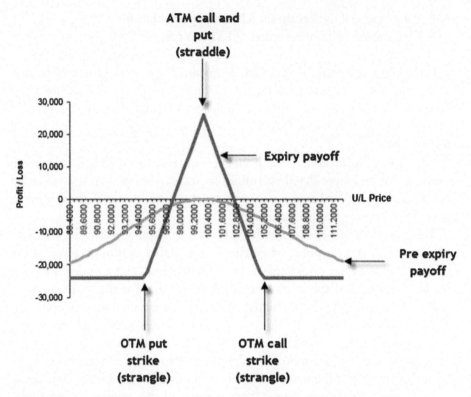

Fig. 14.3 Pre- and at expiry payoffs for a butterfly spread trade (*Source*: author)

Table 14.1 Quoting conventions for a butterfly spread from a market maker's perspective

	Bid Buy the spread	Offer Sell the spread
Strangle	Buy	Sell
Straddle	Sell	Buy
Premium	Receivable	Payable
Motivation	Expects more convex smile	Expects less convex smile

volatility and option maturity. Generally speaking, volatility term structures are upwards sloping unless the market is stressed, whereupon they will tend to slope downwards.

Calendar spreads can be used to express a view on how the slope of the curve could move. These trades would involve the purchase and sale of the same type of option but with different maturities. For example, if net carry is assumed to be zero for all maturities (i.e. spot equals forward),

- Buy a 1-year call option struck ATM at a price of 100.
- Sell a 6-month call option struck ATM at a price of 100.

If the term structure of volatility is upward sloping, the investor is buying a longer-dated option priced with a higher volatility and selling a less expensive shorter-dated option with a lower volatility. The combination of the different maturities and the different volatilities means a premium will be payable.

On a mark-to-market basis, if the term structure of volatility were to steepen, that is, longer-dated volatilities increase by more than shorter-dated volatilities, then all other things being equal the position will show a profit once the breakeven has been exceeded.

There is also another reason why this trade is popular. Consider the situation at the 6-month point when the shorter-dated option matures. If the price of the asset has not changed, then short-dated, short option position is not exercised and the seller retains the premium. For the first 6 months the time decay on the shorter-dated option that was sold would be relatively high. The trader has bought options with a relatively small time decay and sold options with a relatively high time decay and so has 'gone long the calendar spread' or 'bought the calendar spread'. The longer-dated, long option position is still open and has fallen in value but the rate of time decay at this point is relatively slow. Consequently, in this scenario these trades will show a profit. The profit or loss on the 12-month calendar spread trade after 6 months is shown in Fig. 14.4.

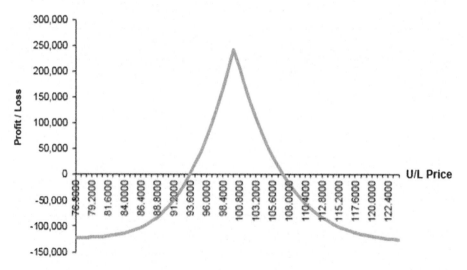

Fig. 14.4 Profit and loss on a 1-year calendar spread trade after 6 months (*Source:* author)

14.4 Range Trades

Two common range trades illustrated in Sect. 11.4 were straddles and strangles.

Another group of trades that are popular are referred to as 'range binaries'. There are a number of different possibilities:

- A *daily digital* is an option that pays out a fixed sum for every day that the option ends up ITM. This is constructed using a strip of sequential digital options, each with a maturity of one day.
- A *range accrual* extends the principles of the daily digital and is constructed using two digital options, each with a maturity of one day. The position includes a call and a put and can be structured such that the investor can earn a fixed payout each day based on the spot rate trading either inside or outside a range. The investor receives their payout at the maturity of the structure.
- A *double digital* is a structure that pays out a single fixed cash sum either if the spot rate touches one of two barriers, or if spot does not touch the barriers and trades within a range.

A double digital can be constructed using double barrier options. Consider the following long 'double digital no touch' structure, which pays out as long as the spot price does not touch 90 or 110.

Long a double barrier knock out call option

- Strike = 90
- Lower knock out barrier = 90
- Higher knock out barrier = 110

Long a double barrier knock out put option

- Strike = 110
- Lower knock out barrier = 90
- Higher knock out barrier = 110

The expiry payout to the investor is shown in Table 14.2 for a variety of different spot prices.

Table 14.2 Expiry payout from a 'double digital no touch option'

Spot price	Call option payoff	Put option payoff	Net investor payoff
85	0	0	0
90	0	0	0
95	5	15	20
100	10	10	20
105	15	5	20
110	0	0	0
115	0	0	0

Table 14.2 shows that the combination of the two barrier options will result in a digital-style payoff to the investor as long as spot trades within the 90–110 range.

14.5 Listed Volatility Contracts

14.5.1 The VIX®

In 1993 the Chicago Board Options Exchange (CBOE) introduced a volatility index called the VIX®, which is often referred to by the media as the 'fear index'.

The VIX® is an index value that reflects 30-day implied volatilities of near-term S&P 500 options with maturities ranging between 23 and 37 days in the future.

To get to grips with how the VIX® works it is important to understand how options on the S&P 500 are traded. Exchange-traded options on the S&P 500 come in two forms. Standard options expire on the 3rd Friday of each month and weekly options expire each Friday. Table 14.3 shows a number of exchange-traded S&P 500 options that were listed on the 2nd November of a particular year.

The calculation of the VIX® on 2nd November would be based on options maturing between 23 and 37 days in the future and so would take its value from the two weekly options maturing on the 27th November and 4th December. Having determined which options will be included in the calculation the next step is to calculate which strikes will be used. The VIX® methodology uses all OTM call and OTM put strikes with non-zero bid prices and so captures the extent of the volatility skew. The final step involves the derivation of a single composite implied volatility number for all of the options that are

Table 14.3 Determining which options will be included in the VIX® calculation

Expiry date	Type of option	Days to expiry
6th November	Weekly	4
13th November	Weekly	11
20th November	Standard	18
27th November	Weekly	25
4th December	Weekly	32
11th December	Weekly	39
18th December	Standard	46

referenced by the index. The generalized formula used to determine the VIX is given as Eq. 14.2.

$$\sigma^2 = \frac{2}{T}\sum_i \frac{\Delta K_i}{K_i^2} e^{RT} Q(K_i) - \frac{1}{T}\left[\frac{F}{K_0} - 1\right]^2 \qquad (14.2)$$

Where:
$\sigma = \text{VIX}/100$
T = time to expiration
F = Forward index level determined from index option prices
K_0 = First strike below forward index level
K_i = Strike price of the ith OTM option; a call is $K_i > K_0$ and a put if $K_i < K_0$
ΔK_i = interval between the strike prices; half the difference between the strike on either side of K_i
R = risk-free interest rate to expiration
$Q(K_i)$ = the midpoint of the bid–ask spread for an option with strike K_i

Interested readers are referred to the CBOE's website for a worked example of the VIX calculation.

14.5.2 VIX® Futures

Since the financial crisis interest in listed volatility contracts has increased significantly. The CBOE recorded that in 2006 the average daily volume for VIX® futures was 1731. By 2011 the number had increased to 47,744 and by mid-2015 had reached 207,718.

VIX® futures are based on forward 30-day implied volatilities. So a contract traded in March with a May expiry is a contract based on the 30-day implied volatility from the May expiry date.

A useful analogy is that the price of a VIX® futures contract is to the VIX® what a 30-day forward interest rate is to a 30-day spot interest rate. In the interest rate markets there is a well-defined relationship between spot and forward rate defined by 'no arbitrage' principles. So a 1-month rate, 1-month forward can be calculated from the 1- and 2-month spot interest rates.[2] However, for the VIX contract no such relationship exists. The VIX® future may have a value that could be lower, higher or equal to the spot VIX® depending on market sentiment in relation to the forward period.

Table 14.4 shows part of the contract specification for the monthly expiry VIX future.

Table 14.4 Contract specification for the VIX future

Contract name	CBOE Volatility Index future
Description	The CBOE Volatility Index—more commonly referred to as 'VIX'- is based on real-time prices of options on the S&P 500 Index, listed on the Chicago Board Options Exchange (Symbol: SPX), The VIX Index is calculated using SPX quotes generated during regular trading hours for SPX options. The VIX Index uses SPX options with more than 23 days and less than 37 days to expiration and then weights them to yield a constant, 30-day measure of the expected volatility of the S&P 500 Index
Units of quotation	Volatility (% per annum)
Minimum price movement	0.05 points equal to $50.00 per contract
Contract multiplier	The contract multiplier for each VIX futures contract is $1000. (a futures price of 15.73 has a monetary value of $15,733)
Final settlement date	The Wednesday that is 30 days prior to the 3rd Friday of the calendar month immediately following the month in which the contract expires
Final settlement value	The final settlement value for VIX futures shall be a Special Opening Quotation (SOQ) of VIX calculated from the sequence of opening prices of the options used to calculate the index on the settlement date
Delivery	Settlement of VIX futures contracts will result in the delivery of a cash settlement amount on the business day immediately following the Final Settlement Date. The cash settlement amount on the final settlement date shall be the final mark-to-market amount against the final settlement value of the VIX futures multiplied by $1000

Source: CBOE

[2] See Schofield and Bowler (2011).

Suppose that today is 1st October. Today's spot VIX® quotation is a composite value that reflects the implied volatilities embedded within options set to expire between 24th October and 5th November. However, a VIX® futures contract quoted on the same day but maturing the following April will measure the expected level of realized volatility from Wednesday 17th April (i.e. the future's expiry date) to 17th May.

The expiry of the VIX® is 30 days before the final settlement of an S&P 500 option. The final settlement price for the future is termed a 'special opening quotation' (SOQ) and is based on a single strip of OTM options. So in the April example cited above, which matures on the 17th of the month, the SOQ is based only on S&P 500 options that mature on 17th May. Since the future is settling against implied volatilities, only cash settlement is possible.

There are a number of ways in which an investor could use a VIX® future:

- *Trading the directionality of implied volatility*—if the trader believed that implied volatility was going to rise (or fall) they could buy (or sell) VIX® futures.
- *Implied volatility spreads*—the trader may wish to express a few on the spread between futures of different maturities; that is, on the slope of the VIX term structure.
- *Hedging market risk in a portfolio*—there is an inverse relationship between implied volatility and the level of an equity index. A short VIX future may be a proxy hedge for a long equity position.
- *Hedging option volatility exposures*—since the VIX references S&P 500 options it could be used to hedge the vega exposure of an index option position.

14.5.3 Options on the VIX®

Similar to VIX® futures, the volume of traded options on the VIX® have also experienced significant growth. In 2006, the average daily volume of VIX® option contracts were 23,491 but by the end of 2014, this had increased to 632,419. The main features of the VIX® option are shown in Table 14.5.

Although the options will settle against the spot VIX® at expiry, since they are European in style, the underlying is a forward value for the VIX® with the same residual maturity. The main factors impacting the option's value are as follows:

- The forward VIX price
- Strike price

Table 14.5 Contract specification for options on VIX® futures

Contract name	CBOE VIX options
Description	The CBOE Volatility Index—more commonly referred to as "VIX"—is an up-to-the-minute market estimate of expected volatility that is calculated by using real-time S&P 500®Index (SPX) option bid/ask quotes. The VIX is calculated using SPX quotes generated during regular trading hours for SPX options. The VIX uses SPX options with more than 23 days and less than 37 days to expiration and then weights them to yield a constant, 30-day measure of the expected volatility of the S&P 500 Index
Premium quotation	Volatility (% per annum); stated in points and fractions, one point equals $100
Contract multiplier	The contract multiplier is $100
Contract expirations	Up to 6-weekly expirations and up to 12 standard (monthly) expirations in VIX options may be listed
Exercise style	European
Final settlement date	The Wednesday that is 30 days prior to the 3rd Friday of the calendar month immediately following the month in which the contract expires
Settlement of option exercise	The exercise-settlement value for VIX options shall be a SOQ of VIX calculated from the sequence of opening prices of the options used to calculate the index on the settlement date.
	Exercise will result in delivery of cash on the business day following expiration. The exercise-settlement amount is equal to the difference between the exercise-settlement value and the exercise price of the option, multiplied by $100

Source: CBOE

- Time to maturity
- The volatility of the underlying, that is, the implied volatility of implied volatility.

An investor buys 100 November VIX call struck at say 20.00 and the final settlement price for the VIX for this expiration is determined to be 22.00. The settlement amount for the position would be:

$$\text{Settlement} = \text{number of contracts} \times \left(\$100 \times \left(\text{VIX settlement} - \text{strike}\right)\right)$$
$$\$20,000 = 100 \text{ contracts} \times \left(\$100 \times \left(22.00 - 20.00\right)\right)$$

These types of options can be used for a variety of different types of strategy similar to those considered in Chap. 11.

14.6 Trading Volatility Using Swaps

In Sect. 14.2 it was argued that trading volatility using options often gave rise to other exposures. For example, a trader may decide to express a view on vega but find that a particular trade results in a gamma exposure. As a result, the market has developed a number of structures designed to provide a cleaner method of isolating the desired exposure.

14.6.1 Variance and Volatility Swaps

14.6.1.1   Features

Variance swaps involve an exchange of cash flows based on how the variance of an underlying asset evolves relative to a pre-agreed fixed strike. However, they are often casually characterized as an instrument that can be used to express views on how implied volatility is expected to evolve relative to realized volatility. This is because the use of the term volatility is somewhat more intuitive than variance.

They are quoted on a bid–offer basis with the price relating to the 'strike' or fixed rate of the transaction which is expressed in implied volatility terms. So a quote might appear as follows:

Vega 000's	Bid	Offer	Vega 000's
100	16.00	16.50	100

At the bid price the market maker is willing to pay fixed (i.e. implied volatility) and receive floating (i.e. realized volatility). The vega 000's is variously referred to either as the 'vega notional' or 'volatility units' and relates to the approximate amount that a trader will gain or lose for every percentage point that realized volatility is different from the initial strike value. However, the settlement cash flows will be based on the realized variance of the underlying asset.

Suppose that the market maker believes that realized volatility will be greater than the current variance swap strike. They enter into a variance swap where they will pay fixed at 16.00 %. If realized volatility is, say, 17.55 % then they will receive approximately 1.55 times $100,000, that is, $155,000. A more formal calculation of the settlement cash flow is shown later in the section.

Consider the following hypothetical termsheet:

Seller:	Bank A; receives the strike, pays realized volatility
Buyer:	Bank B; receives realized volatility, pays the strike
Maturity:	6 months
Volatility units:	USD 100,000 per point
Variance units:	3125 (equal to volatility units/(2 × strike))
Underlying index:	S&P 500
Volatility strike:	16 %
Volatility payment:	Variance units × [(volatility)²–(strike)²]
	If the amount is positive, seller shall pay buyer. If the amount is negative, then buyer shall make a payment equal to the absolute amount to the seller.

$$\text{Volatility:} \qquad 100 \times \sqrt{\frac{252}{N} \times \sum_{i=1}^{n}\left[\ln\left(\frac{\text{Index}_i}{\text{Index}_{i-1}}\right)\right]^2}$$

Where:

252 = annualization factor, that is, number of business days in the year

N = number of observations, excluding the initial observation on trade date but including the observation on the maturity date.

Index$_i$ = The closing level of the underlying index i business days from the trade date

Some features are worth noting:

- The buyer of variance will profit from any increase in the volatility of the index above the swap strike, while a seller will profit from any decrease in volatility below the swap strike.
- By convention the calculation of realized volatility does not involve subtraction of the mean.[3]
- Although they are casually referred to as being a swap, since there is only one net settlement, economically they are forward contracts.
- When settling the cash flows, market convention is to scale volatility by a factor of 100. This means that 16 % is 16 rather than 0.16.
- The relationship between the volatility units ('vega notional') and the variance units is based on the notion that a trader will pick a desired vega exposure and then derive the appropriate number of variance units which is consistent with this view (Brask 2004). This is done by dividing the volatility units by 2 × volatility strike:

---

[3] The appendix to Chap. 6 shows the 'traditional' method of calculating a standard deviation (i.e. realized volatility).

$$\text{Payoff} = \text{Variance units} \times \left(\sigma^2_{\text{realized}} - \sigma^2_{\text{strike}} \right)$$

$$= \frac{\text{Volatility units}}{2 \times \sigma_{\text{strike}}} \times \left(\sigma_{\text{realized}} - \sigma_{\text{strike}} \right) \times \left(\sigma_{\text{realized}} + \sigma_{\text{strike}} \right)$$

$$= \text{Volatility units} \times \left(\sigma_{\text{realized}} - \sigma_{\text{strike}} \right) \times \frac{\sigma_{\text{realized}} + \sigma_{\text{strike}}}{2 \times \sigma_{\text{strike}}}$$

$$\cong \text{Volatility units} \times \left(\sigma_{\text{realized}} - \sigma_{\text{strike}} \right)$$

The swap is shown in Fig. 14.5.

The swaps will have a single payoff which will occur at the contract's maturity. Suppose that at maturity realized volatility in the above example is 17.55 %. The payoff on the swap is:

$$= 3{,}125 \times \left(17.55^2 - 16.00^2 \right)$$
$$= 3{,}125 \times \left(308 - 256 \right)$$
$$= \$162{,}500$$

Recall that the vega notional predicted a payment of $155,000.

A volatility swap will have similar characteristics to that of the variance swap but the payoff will be linear. So there will be an agreed vega notional which will be used to determine the magnitude of the cash flow settlement. So if the vega notional is $100,000, the fixed rate 16 % and realized volatility turns out to be 17.55 % the payout is:

$$\$100{,}000 \times \left(17.55 - 16.00 \right) = \$155{,}000$$

However, the downside of volatility swaps is that they are more difficult to hedge requiring a dynamically changing basket of variance swaps.

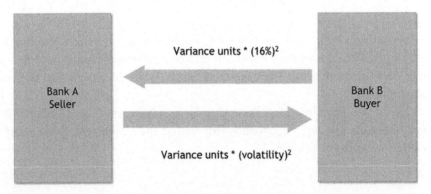

Fig. 14.5 Structure of a variance swap (*Source*: author)

Table 14.6 Payoff on a long variance swap position vs. long volatility swap position. Both positions assumed to have a vega notional $100,000 and strike of 16 %

Realized volatility %	Volatility swap settlement ($)	Variance swap settlement ($)
14	−200,000	−187,500
15	−100,000	−96,875
16	0	0
17	+100,000	103,125
18	+200,000	212,500

Table 14.6 shows different cash flow settlements for the variance swap illustrated in this section and the equivalent volatility swap. In both cases the vega notional is set at $100,000.

Table 14.6 also shows that for the buyer, their losses are capped as realized volatility cannot go below zero. So in this example the maximum losses for the buyer of this a variance swap would be:

$$3,125 \times 16^2 = \$800,000$$

But suppose that the trader had a short 12-month variance swap position on a single stock such as Morgan Stanley initiated in December 2007. Implied volatilities for the asset were trading in the region of 50 % but after the financial crisis, realized volatility increased significantly to reach 229 % by December 2008 (Fig. 14.6).

A variance swap struck at 50 % with a vega notional of $100,000, variance units of 1000 and realized volatility of 229 % would have resulted in a loss of:

$$
\begin{aligned}
&= 1,000 \times \left(229^2 - 50^2\right) \\
&= 1,000 \times \left(52,441 - 2,500\right) \\
&= \$49,941,000
\end{aligned}
$$

A volatility swap traded with the same values would have resulted in a loss of $17,900,000. Although perhaps an extreme example, it was one of the reasons why the market for single-stock variance swaps disappeared in the years that followed.

One of the ways in which these significant losses could be avoided would be to introduce a capped payout. This would mean that the calculation of realized volatility would be:

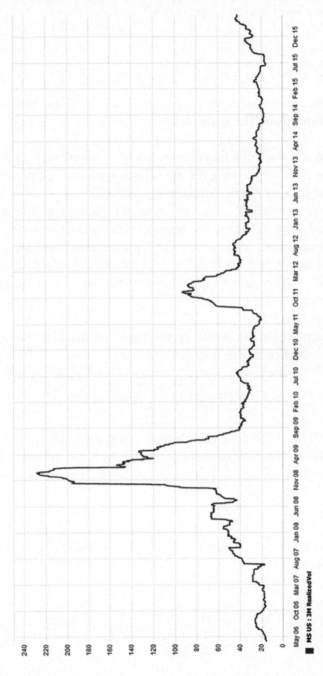

Fig. 14.6 Three-month realized volatility for Morgan Stanley. March 2006–March 2016 (*Source:* Barclays Live)

$$100 \times \text{MIN} \left[\text{Variance cap,} \sqrt{\frac{252}{N} \times \sum_{i=1}^{n} \left[\ln\left(\frac{\text{Index}_i}{\text{Index}_{i-1}} \right) \right]^2} \right] \quad (14.3)$$

Where the variance cap is typically defined as 2.5 × strike.

14.6.1.2   Valuation: The Intuition

The valuation of variance swaps is somewhat involved and so for purposes of space (and to avoid reinventing the wheel) readers interested in more detail than is offered here are referred to Allen et al. (2006).

The variance swap payoff shown in Table 14.6 displays positive convexity. As realized volatility increases, the buyer's profits accelerate but as realized volatility decreases their losses decelerate. This suggests that a long variance swap position means an investor is long the volatility of volatility. As a result of this convexity, variance swap quotes tend to be higher than the equivalent option volatility (see Fig. 14.7). Over the period highlighted the difference was on average 2.185 %.

A useful rule of thumb to determine the 'fair value' strike of a variance swap is (Bossu et al. 2006; Demeterfi et al. 1999)

$$K_{\text{VAR}} \approx \sigma_{\text{ATMF}} \sqrt{1 + 3T \times \text{skew}^2} \quad (14.4)$$

Where σ_{ATMF} is the ATM forward volatility, T is the maturity and skew is the slope of the skew. The slope of the skew is defined as the difference between the implied volatility of an option struck at 90 % and 100 %, all divided by 10.

So for values as of the 27th November 2015 and using 12-month maturities for the S&P 500, the ATM forward volatility was 17.58 %, while the 90–100 % forward skew differential was 3.40 %, and the estimate of the variance strike was:

$$K_{\text{VAR}} \approx 17.58 \times \sqrt{1 + 3 \times \left(\frac{3.4}{10} \right)^2} \quad (14.5)$$

$$K_{\text{VAR}} \approx 20.40$$

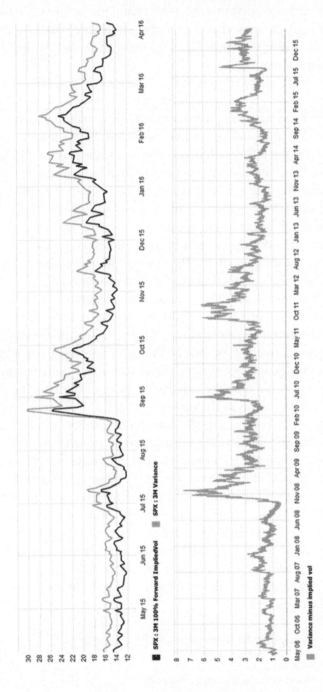

Fig. 14.7 Upper panel: 3-month ATM forward option implied volatility vs. 3-month variance swap prices. Lower panel: Variance swaps minus option implied volatility. Underlying asset is S&P 500. March 2006 to March 2016 (*Source*: Barclays Live)

The quoted 12-month variance swap rate for that day was 21.37 % but Bossu et al. (op. cit) note that this short-cut technique assumes a linear skew.

Bennett et al. (2012) argue that the variance swap quote trades in line with the 30 delta put. This is shown in Fig. 14.8 using the volatility of a 70 delta call as a close approximation.

A fundamental derivative valuation concept is that the price of any product is driven by the cost of hedging the underlying exposure. A variance swap market maker is faced with the prospect of having to make a non-linear payout and so logically the position should be hedged using instruments that have a similar exposure. Theoretically, a variance swap payout can be replicated by a portfolio of options with a continuum of strike prices.

To understand why this is so it is necessary to revisit the volatility trading strategy first presented in Sect. 5.2. The trading strategy involved the sale of a delta-hedged call option whose motivation was to capture a change in implied volatility. However, the position lost money as a result of realized volatility, that is, the gamma effect. The example was based on a short-term ATM option where the gamma impact was most pronounced.

Suppose an investor has sold 100 3-month call options on a nameless asset, which is trading at a spot price of $100 and is priced with 20 % implied volatility.[4] The premium on the option is $3.9679, the initial delta value is 0.5173 while gamma for a 1 % change in the underlying price is 0.0396. The initial delta hedge will require the trader to buy 52 units (rounded) of the underlying asset. Suppose that intraday the price of the asset increases by 1 % to $101. The premium on the option is now $4.5049, delta has moved to 0.5566 and gamma is now 0.0389. The option position will lose $53.70, while the delta-hedge gains $52.00, resulting in an overall loss of $1.70. To ensure they are delta neutral at a price of $101 the trader would need to be long 56 (rounded) units of the asset and so buys an extra 4 units at this higher price. If after rebalancing the hedge the price of the asset now retreats to its original level of $100, the trader would need to sell these recently acquired units to restore delta neutrality. As a result, their losses would be entirely explained by their delta-hedging activity as the profit and loss on the option would be zero. Overall they would incur a loss of $4.[5]

De Weert (2008) argues that the profit and loss on this transaction on a per unit basis can be calculated as:

$$\text{Change in the stock price} \times \text{change in delta} \qquad (14.6)$$

[4] Carry is assumed to be zero so spot and forward are identical.
[5] The trading is assumed to be intraday and so there is no theta effect.

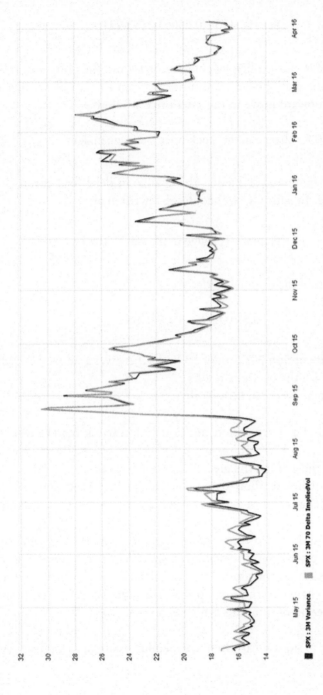

Fig. 14.8 Three-month variance vs. volatility for 30 delta put (70 delta call used as an approximation). Underlying index is S&P 500. March 2015 to March 2016 (*Source*: Barclays Live)

So substituting the values in the example,

$$\$1\times(0.5173-0.5566)=(\$3.93)$$

This is close to our explicit calculation of $4 and the difference is down to the fact that the delta hedge was rounded. From this it follows that the loss from just the upward move in the asset price would be:

$$0.5\times\text{change in the stock price}\times\text{change in delta} \qquad (14.7)$$

Recall that gamma is defined as the change in delta for a given change in the stock price. Equation (14.7) could be rewritten as:

$$0.5\times\text{gamma}\times(\text{change in the stock price})^2 \qquad (14.8)$$

So substituting the original values gives:

$$0.5\times0.0396\times1=0.0198$$

For the entire option position of 100 calls this gives a value of $1.98, which is consistent with the previous results.

From this analysis it can be seen that:

- Delta-hedging a short option position in a moving market will result in losses.
- The higher the gamma the greater the profit or loss.
- The profit or loss of short-dated delta-hedged ATM options will be very sensitive to changes in the underlying price, that is, realized volatility.

At first glance it would seem that this is a 'no win' strategy but recall that the trader will profit from the passage of time. So the next step is to incorporate this element into the profit and loss calculation. This is done initially by revisiting the 'change in the stock price' term. De Weert (op. cit) argues that over a small period of time this can be expressed as:

$$\text{Change in stock price} = \text{Implied volatility}\times\text{current spot price} \qquad (14.9)$$

Where the implied volatility figure has been scaled to reflect the appropriate time period.

Substituting 14.9 into Eq. 14.8 now gives the expected profit and loss on the delta-hedged position as:

$$0.5 \times \text{gamma} \times \text{implied volatility}^2 \times (\text{current stock price})^2 \qquad (14.10)$$

So substituting for our original figures[6] gives:

$$05 \times 00396 \times 10\% \wedge 2 \times 100 \wedge 2$$
$$05 \times 00396 \times 0.01 \times 10,000 = \$1.98$$

Which gives the same result as that suggested by Eq. 14.8.

Since the dealer has a trade-off between the profit and loss from delta-hedging and the passage of time (i.e. theta) then in theory:

$$0.5 \times \text{Gamma} \times \text{Implied volatility}^2 \times (\text{Current stock price})^2 + \text{Theta} = 0 \ (14.11)$$

Allen et al. (2006) argue that based on this relationship it follows that if delta-hedging is an option, the profit and loss for a single period is given by:

$$\frac{1}{2}\Gamma S^2 \times \left[\left(\frac{\Delta S}{S} \right)^2 - \sigma^2 \Delta t \right] \qquad (14.12)$$

Where σ^2 is the implied volatility of the underlying asset.
Which can be interpreted as:

$$0.5 \times \text{gamma} \times (\text{current stock price})^2 \times [(\text{return on the underlying})^2$$
$$-(\text{implied volatility of underlying})^2 \times \text{length of the time step}]$$

If the profits and losses for each single period are then summed, the final profit and loss will be:

---

[6] The implied volatility used to price the option was 20 % per annum. Since the option's maturity was 3 months this is scaled by dividing by the square root of the number of 3-month trading periods in a year, that is, the square root of 4 which is 2. Hence 20 % divided by 2 is 10 %.

$$\sum_{t=0}^{n} \gamma_t \left[r_t^2 - \sigma^2 \Delta t \right] \tag{14.13}$$

Where:

t is time,

r_t is the stock daily return at time t,

γ_t is the dollar gamma,

n is the number of trading days to expiry.

So what is the linkage with variance swaps? 'The main drawback of delta-hedged options as vehicles for trading (realized) volatility is that the dollar gamma,[7] which characterizes the exposure to (realized) volatility changes over time and with the level of the underlying. This means that the exposure to volatility is path-dependent ....To remove this path-dependency it is natural to look for a contract whose dollar gamma is constant both with the passage of time and with changes in the underlying.' (Allen et al. 2006). They go on to argue that such a contract can be created by delta-hedging a static portfolio of options across a continuum of strikes, each with a weight of $1/\text{strike}^2$. This would result in an exposure to realized volatility (squared) which is independent of the path of the underlying: 'a variance swap consists of this portfolio, bundled up with the necessary delta hedging'.

Therefore, the price of the variance swap should reflect the cost of this static portfolio of options.

14.6.1.3   Mark-to-Market

The calculation of a variance swap's mark-to-market is a relatively straightforward process and all that is needed is the realized variance since the start of the swap and the current variance strike for the residual time to maturity.

Consider the following swap written on a hypothetical equity index.

Initial maturity:	1 month (31 calendar days)
Initial strike:	10 %
Vega notional ('volatility units'):	$100,000
Variance notional:	5000
Revaluation point:	Close of business at end of second week (i.e. 12th calendar day of the month)
Variance swap quote to maturity:	9 %

---

[7] The dollar delta is the 'delta equivalent' value of the option, that is, notional × delta. The dollar gamma is the change in the dollar delta for a 1 % move in the underlying.

The generalized formula for calculating the variance swap profit and loss at time t of a variance swap with maturity T, per unit of variance notional is (Allen et al. (2006)):

$$= \frac{t}{T}\left(\sigma_{0,t}^2 - K_{0,T}^2\right) + \frac{T-t}{T}\left(K_{t,T}^2 - K_{0,T}^2\right) \tag{14.14}$$

$$= \frac{1}{T}\left[t\sigma_{0,t}^2 + (T-t)K_{t,T}^2\right] - K_{0,T}^2$$

Where:

$K_{s,t}$ = the strike for a variance swap at time s maturity at time t

$\sigma_{s,t}$ is the realized volatility between time s and time t

The first step is to calculate the realized volatility from the inception of the swap to the point of revaluation. This is done using the same formula originally introduced in the first variance swap termsheet but repeated here for convenience:

$$100 \times \sqrt{\frac{252}{N} \times \sum_{i=1}^{n}\left[\ln\left(\frac{\text{Index}_i}{\text{Index}_{i-1}}\right)\right]^2} \tag{14.15}$$

Where:

252 = annualization factor, that is, number of business days in the year

N = number of observations, excluding the initial observation on trade date but including the observation on the maturity date

Index_i = The closing level of the underlying index i business days from the trade date

The calculation of the realized variance and volatility is shown in Table 14.7.

Inserting the values into Eq. 14.14 gives

$$= \text{Variance notional} \times \frac{t}{T}\left(\sigma_{0,t}^2 - K_{0,T}^2\right) + \frac{T-t}{T}\left(K_{t,T}^2 - K_{0,T}^2\right)$$

$$= 3{,}571.4286 \times \left[\frac{12}{31}\left(9.08^2 - 10^2\right) + \frac{31-12}{31}\left(9^2 - 10^2\right)\right] \tag{14.16}$$

$$= 3{,}571.4286 \times \left[0.3871 \times (82.45 - 100) + 0.612903 \times (81 - 100)\right]$$

$$= 3{,}571.4286 \times \left[-6.79 - 11.65\right]$$

$$= \$65{,}857.14$$

Table 14.7 Calculation of realized volatility

Day	Index level	Log return	Log return squared
1	6356		
2	6375	0.002984842	8.90928E-06
3	6393	0.002819551	7.94987E-06
4	6337	−0.008798171	7.74078E-05
5	6277	−0.009513311	9.05031E-05
8	6305	0.00445081	1.98097E-05
9	6334	0.004588979	2.10587E-05
10	6329	−0.000789702	6.2363E-07
11	6278	−0.008090787	6.54608E-05
12	6268	−0.001594134	2.54126E-06
	Total		0.000294
	Annualized variance		0.008239 (i.e. Total × 252/9)
	Annualized volatility		9.08 %

This calculation produces an 'at maturity' mark to market. To calculate the mark to market as of time 't' the result of Eq. 14.16 would need to be present valued. Since volatility has declined since the start of the transaction the buyer would record a mark-to-market loss.

14.6.1.4 Applications

There are a number of general applications for variance swaps:

Expressing views on expected moves in variance:—in the introduction to this chapter a distinction was made between gamma and vega trades. Within a variance swap context these trades would be:

- Investor believes that future realized variance will be different from the initial implied variance. This is a gamma trade and so the investor will use the instrument to buy or sell realized volatility probably with an intention to hold the position until maturity.
- Investor believes that future implied variance will be either higher or lower than its current value. This is a vega trade where the investor will enter into a variance swap position with an expectation of unwinding the position at a profit.

Variance risk premium—perhaps the simplest way of using variance swaps is to express a view on the evolution of realized volatility relative to the initial variance strike. Similar to implied volatility there is the existence of the 'variance risk premium' (Fig. 14.9). This is the tendency for the variance swap

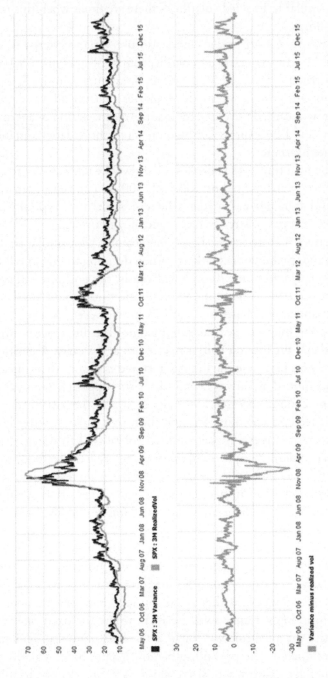

Fig. 14.9   Upper panel: 3-month variance swap quotes for the S&P 500 (in implied volatility terms) vs. realized volatility. Lower panel: Variance swap prices minus realized volatility. March 2006 to March 2016 (*Source:* Barclays Live)

strike expressed in volatility terms to be higher than realized volatility. Note, however, that similar to implied volatilities there are times when this relationship does not hold.

Term structure trades—A trader could also use variance swaps to express views on how the term structure of volatility may evolve. Figure 14.10 shows that the term structure for S&P 500 variance swap quotes in the first quarter of 2015 was upward sloping. In the third quarter concerns over the prospects for Chinese growth caused the curve to invert. An expectation of a term structure inversion could be expressed by going long, short-dated variance and short, long-dated variance.

Instead of being a time series, Fig. 14.11 shows the term structure of volatility for variance swaps quoted on the S&P 500 on two separate dates. The chart indicates that in 'normal' markets the term structure is typically upward sloping though in times of stress it has a tendency to invert.

Volatility term structure trades share some features with similar trades that are popular in the fixed income markets. When deciding to buy or sell a bond a trader will usually determine if, on a daily basis, the position will cost him money or generate cash. A bond trader would need to borrow funds to purchase the asset and so will have an ongoing cost; however, for every day that they hold the bond they will earn coupon income. The difference between the income earned and the interest paid is referred to as the carry. A position that carries positively is one where the income received is greater than the expense incurred. A position that carries negatively is the opposite; repo expense is greater than the coupon income. For variance swaps, the carry is defined as implied minus realized volatility. So a position that carries positively is one where the investor receives a higher implied volatility than they pay. Figure 14.7 shows that typically implied volatility is greater than realized, so being long variance (i.e. paying implied volatility and receiving realized volatility in a variance swap) will result in negative carry while being short variance will represent a situation of positive carry (i.e. receiving implied and paying realized in a variance swap).

Another term structure related concept is 'roll down' or 'slide'. This is the profit or loss that a trader will make from holding a position as a result of the passage of time, assuming the term structure does not change. This concept is analogous to that of an option. Suppose a trader enters into a 12-month long variance swap position where the fixed rate is 20 %. After 9 months the position will have a residual maturity of 3 months and will be revalued at the prevailing 3-month rate. Since volatility term structures generally exhibit a positive slope (see Fig. 14.8) the position will be revalued at a lower rate. This will mean that the buyer of variance

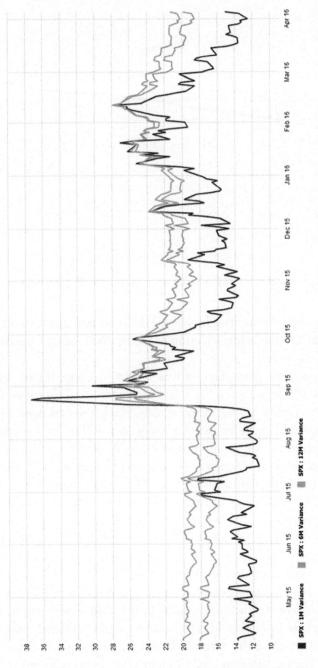

Fig. 14.10 Time series of S&P 500 variance swap strikes: 1 month, 6 months and 12 months. March 2015 to March 2016 (*Source:* Barclays Live)

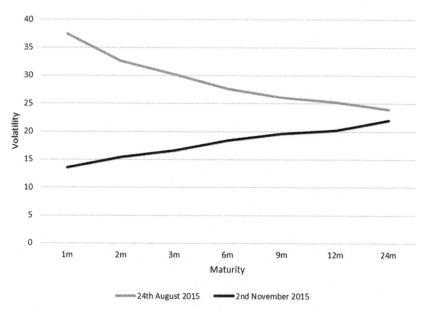

Fig. 14.11   Term structure of S&P 500 variance swap quotes (*Source*: Barclays Live)

will be faced with a potential loss. Roll down is not guaranteed but is a major consideration in trade selection as traders will look to 'optimize' this component.

Hedging a portfolio of equities—it was shown in Chap. 6 that one of the characteristics of implied volatility was that it tended to vary inversely with the level of the equity market. One possible hedge for an equity portfolio would be to go long an index variance swap so a decline in the value of the cash portfolio could be offset by a rise in value of the swap position.

Relative volatility movements—if a trader believed that the spread between the implied volatilities of two different markets was mis-valued then it would be possible to use variance swaps to express the view. Figure 14.12 shows the relationship between 3-month variance swap quotes for the S&P 500 and the EURO STOXX 50. If a trader believed that the volatility spread between the two indices was going to fall, then they could go long an S&P 500 variance swap and short an EURO STOXX 50 variance swap.

Cross asset class volatility—there is an intuitive link between the risk of a company defaulting, its stock price and volatility. As the perception of default increases the share price should decline and volatility should increase. This could suggest that an equity variance swap could be used to hedge a portfolio of bonds. The relationship could also be used to express views on equity and credit volatility. Figure 14.13 shows the implied volatility of 3-month

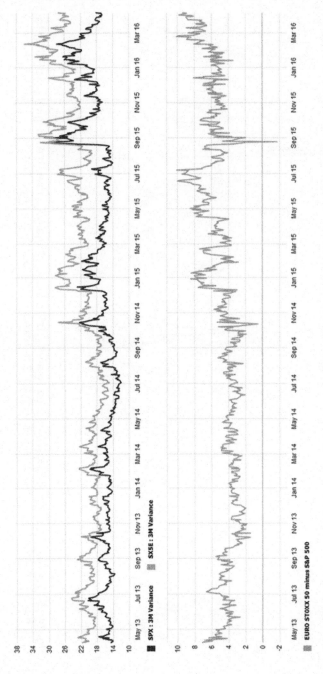

Fig. 14.12 Upper panel: 3-month variance swap quotes for EURO STOXX 50 vs. S&P 500. Lower panel: Bottom line shows the difference between the two values. March 2013 to March 2016 (*Source*: Barclays Live)

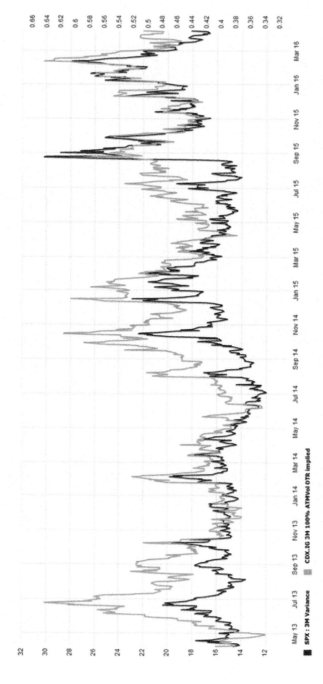

Fig. 14.13 Three-month ATMF S&P 500 implied volatility (left hand side) against 3-month ATM implied volatility for options on CDX index (right hand side). March 2013 to March 2016 (*Source:* Barclays Live)

S&P 500 options plotted against the 3-month implied volatility of options on the CDX credit default swap index. The expected evolution of the spread between the two measures could be exploited as a relative value trade.

14.6.2 Forward Variance Swaps

A forward variance swap allows an investor to express a view on the evolution of forward starting variance. Chapter 4 illustrated how forwards are constructed on the basis of 'no arbitrage' principles. This means that they are a breakeven number and so represent a value that an investor has to 'beat' in order to make money; they are not 'the market's best guess of future expected spot price'.

Similar to the interest rate market it is possible to create a synthetic forward position by the combination of two spot-starting structures. Consider the following combination:

- Long a 2-year variance swap
- Short a 1-year variance swap

This creates a position where an investor is long 1-year variance, 12 months forward. Brask (2005) points out though that this replication technique is not perfect as it will involve two cash flow settlements; one at the end of the first year and the other at the contract's maturity. As a result, the process does introduce some element of interest rate risk.

What would be the motivation for this trade? In 1 year's time the short-dated variance swap will have matured and the investor will be left with a 1-year position. If prevailing variance swap levels are greater than the initial implied forward breakeven the investor could close out the position at a profit. Another possibility is that the investor could leave the remaining position in place and let it run to expiry.

Suppose that 6-month variance swaps on the EURO STOXX 50 are trading at 22 %, while 12-month swaps are being quoted at 24 %. A trader believes that 6-month strikes in 6 months' time will be below the current implied forward and so decides to sell forward variance on a vega notional of €100,000.

The forward variance swap rate is calculated as:

$$F_{t,T} = \sqrt{\frac{T}{T-t} \times K_T^2 - \frac{t}{T-t} \times K_t^2}$$

$$= \sqrt{\frac{1}{1-0.5} \times 24^2 - \frac{0.5}{1-0.5} \times 22^2} \qquad (14.17)$$

$$= \sqrt{1{,}152 - 484}$$

$$= 25.85\%$$

Where:
$F_{t,T}$ = Forward variance swap strike
K_T = strike of the longer-dated variance swap with maturity T
K_t = strike of the shorter-dated variance swap with maturity t

This would equate to a forward starting variance notional of 1934.24 [i.e. €100,000/(2 × 25.85)]. This can be constructed from two spot-starting variance swaps with the following notional amounts:

• $t/(T\text{-}t)$ × forward variance notional for the short-dated swap but with a payment delayed until period T
• $T/(T\text{-}t)$ × forward variance notional for the long-dated swap

Using the values from the previous examples this gives:

$$\text{Short-dated swap} = 0.5 / (1-0.5) \times 1934.24 = 1934.24$$
$$\text{Long-dated swap} = 1 / (1-0.5) \times 1934.24 = 3868.48$$

Allen et al. (2006) point out that:

• The notional on the longer-dated swap will be greater than that of the short-dated swap.
• The total notional of the two spot-starting swaps will be greater than the notional on the forward.

14.6.3 Conditional Variance Swaps

A conditional variance swap allows an investor to take exposure to realized volatility within a pre-agreed range. If realized volatility trades outside of this range, then no profit or loss will accrue. The variance swap could be structured in such a way that the profit will only accrue when the underlying trades above a particular level ('up variance') or when it trades below a particular level ('down variance'). These levels are also sometimes casually referred to as 'barriers'. It would also be possible to have a transaction that will only accrue profit when the asset trades between two levels. The so-called barriers are usually expressed as a percentage of the current market price. Examples would be as follows:

- 90—up
- 105—down
- 85—115

These products have a number of features in common with a vanilla variance swap. They are as follows:

- Exchange of cash flows
- Fixed versus floating
- Vega and variance notional

However, the calculation of realized volatility will be different. Equation 14.18 shows how realized volatility is calculated for a conditional variance swap where the underlying needs to trade between two barriers for the accrual to occur.

$$100 \times \sqrt{\frac{252}{n} \times \sum_{i=1}^{n} \left[\ln\left(\frac{\text{Index}_i}{\text{Index}_{i-1}} \right) \delta_i \right]^2} \qquad (14.18)$$

Where:
n = number of days that the underlying closes within the specified trading range
δ_i = 1 if the price of the underlying trades between the barriers in period $i - 1$; 0 if otherwise

The actual payoff to the investor will also differ from that of a vanilla variance swap and be in the form of:

$$\text{Variance units} \times \left(\text{realized volatility}^2 - \text{vega strike}^2 \right) \times n / N \qquad (14.19)$$

Where:

n = the number of days that the index closes within the specified barriers

N = number of observations (excluding the initial observation on trade date but including the observation on the maturity date)

When $n = 0$ the swap's payoff will be zero but when $n = N$ then the payoff will be the same as a vanilla variance swap.

14.6.4 Corridor Variance Swaps

A corridor variance swap is closely related to the conditional variance swap. They are another way of expressing a range-bound view of volatility. As the name suggests the product will pay out based on the underlying trading above/below/within a pre-specified range. However, there are a few subtle differences. Firstly, when calculating the realized volatility every observation day is included within the calculation. This means that Eq. 14.18 would be slightly different for a corridor variance swap as the annualization factor of 252 would be divided by the total number of trading days (i.e. N) rather than the number of trading days the underlying was within a range (i.e. n). This means that when the underlying asset trades outside of the range they are deemed to have a zero return and so could result in very low values for the realized return calculation. Secondly, the payoff on the corridor variance swap is the same as a regular variance swap and is not pro-rated like the conditional variance swap:

$$\text{Variance units} \times \left(\text{realized volatility}^2 - \text{vega strike}^2\right) \qquad (14.20)$$

So in the case when all of the observations fall outside of the range, the realized volatility component of the payout will be equal to zero. This would mean that the payer of the strike would not receive an offsetting cash flow. In this case the payoff would be:

$$\text{Variance units} \times \text{vega strike}^2 \qquad (14.21)$$

However, this is not as dramatic as it first appears (BNP Paribas (2007)). Consider a variance swap struck at 15 % where realized volatility is measured as 0. The investor will make a loss of 225 variance units (i.e.

15^2). This is the same as an equivalent variance swap that is struck at 25 % which realizes volatility of 20 % (i.e. $25^2 - 20^2 = 625 - 400 = 225$ variance units).

To illustrate the difference between the payoffs of the different types of variance swap consider the following 'at maturity' worked example:

Initial maturity:	1 month (31 calendar days)
Volatility strike:	15 %
Vega notional:	$100,000
Variance notional:	5000
Revaluation point:	Close of business at end of 2nd week
Barrier level:	Only values greater than 6300 will be included (conditional and corridor variance swaps only)

With respect to the vanilla variance swap, suppose that the following values are observed for the underlying index (Table 14.8):

Table 14.8 Calculation of realized variance for vanilla variance swap

	Index level	Log return	Log return squared
1	6356		
2	6375	0.00298484	8.90928E-06
3	6393	0.00281955	7.94987E-06
4	6337	−0.0087982	7.74078E-05
5	6277	−0.0095133	9.05031E-05
8	6305	0.00445081	1.98097E-05
9	6334	0.00458898	2.10587E-05
10	6329	−0.0007897	6.2363E-07
11	6278	−0.0080908	6.54608E-05
12	6268	−0.0015941	2.54126E-06
15	6146	−0.0196559	0.000386353
16	6118	−0.0045662	2.08503E-05
17	6178	0.00975935	9.52449E-05
18	6297	0.01907874	0.000363998
19	6275	−0.0034998	1.22489E-05
22	6295	0.00318218	1.01263E-05
23	6353	0.00917147	8.41159E-05
24	6364	0.00172997	2.99279E-06
25	6412	0.00751412	5.64621E-05
26	6383	−0.004533	2.05483E-05
29	6361	−0.0034526	1.19205E-05
30	6372	0.00172779	2.98527E-06
31	6371	−0.0001569	2.4633E-08
		Total	0.001362135

Vanilla variance swap payout

Step I—calculation of realized volatility

$$= 100 \times \sqrt{\frac{252}{22} \times 0.001362135}$$

$$= 12.49\%$$

Step II—payoff calculation

$$= 5{,}000 \times \left(15^2 - 12.49^2\right)$$
$$= 5{,}000 \times \left(225 - 156\right)$$
$$= \$345{,}000$$

In this example the seller of volatility will receive the payment.

In the conditional and corridor variance swap examples, it will be assumed that the squared returns are only included if the underlying index trades above 6300 on the previous day. As a result, the calculation of the realized volatility using the same data set as before is now different (Table 14.9).

Table 14.9 Calculation of realized volatility for conditional and corridor variance swaps. Squared returns are only included if the index trades above 6300 on the previous day

	Index level	Log return	Log return squared
1	6356		
2	6375	0.00298484	8.90928E-06
3	6393	0.00281955	7.94987E-06
4	6337	−0.0087982	7.74078E-05
5	6277	−0.0095133	9.05031E-05
8	6305	0.00445081	0
9	6334	0.00458898	2.10587E-05
10	6329	−0.0007897	6.2363E-07
11	6278	−0.0080908	6.54608E-05
12	6268	−0.0015941	0
15	6146	−0.0196559	0
16	6118	−0.0045662	0
17	6178	0.00975935	0
18	6297	0.01907874	0
19	6275	−0.0034998	0
22	6295	0.00318218	0
23	6353	0.00917147	0
24	6364	0.00172997	2.99279E-06
25	6412	0.00751412	5.64621E-05
26	6383	−0.004533	2.05483E-05
29	6361	−0.0034526	1.19205E-05
30	6372	0.00172779	2.98527E-06
31	6371	−0.0001569	2.4633E-08
		Total	0.000366847

Conditional variance swap payout
Step I—calculation of realized volatility

$$= 100 \times \sqrt{\frac{252}{14} \times 0.000366847}$$
$$= 8.13\%$$

Step II—payoff calculation

$$= 5,000 \times \left(15^2 - 8.13^2\right) \times 14 / 22$$
$$= 5,000 \times \left(225 - 6.10\right) \times 14 / 22$$
$$= \$505,591$$

Since realized volatility is lower than the vanilla variance swap example, the payout to the seller is greater.

Corridor variance swap payout
Step I—calculation of realized volatility

$$= 100 \times \sqrt{\frac{252}{22} \times 0.000366847}$$
$$= 6.48\%$$

Step II—payoff calculation

$$= 5,000 \times \left(15^2 - 6.48^2\right)$$
$$= 5,000 \times \left(225 - 41.99\right)$$
$$= \$915,050$$

Again the realized volatility is lower than the strike and so the seller of volatility will receive the payment.

14.6.5 Gamma Swaps

Gamma is an option trader's exposure to realized volatility. This exposure is greatest for short-dated ATM options and so is a function of the level of the underlying market. The realized volatility exposure of variance swaps (i.e. the gamma exposure) is not a function of the level of the market and so these products are thus said to have constant 'cash gamma' exposure.

A gamma swap allows a trader to express a view on realized volatility where the payout will be a function of the price level.

The payoff on a gamma swap is:

$$(\text{Gamma} - \text{Gamma strike}) \times \text{variance units}$$

Where gamma is defined as:

$$100 \times \sqrt{\frac{252}{N} \times \sum_{i=1}^{n} \left[\left(\ln\left(\frac{\text{Index}_i}{\text{Index}_{i-1}} \right) \right)^2 \times \frac{\text{Index}_i}{\text{Index}_0} \right]} \qquad (14.22)$$

Where:

252 = annualization factor, that is, number of business days in the year

N = number of observations, excluding the initial observation on trade date but including the observation on the maturity date

Index_i = The closing level of the underlying index i business days from the trade date

Index_0 = the closing level of the underlying index at the trade date

Bennett et al. (2012) argue: 'Should spot decline the payout of a gamma swap decreases. Conversely, if spot increases, the payout of a gamma swap increases.' They point out that:

- Gamma swaps do not need a cap because if the price of a stock falls substantially then its volatility will likely increase. Multiplying the payout by the ratio of the spot prices would reduce the payout.
- They can be used for dispersion trading as the trade does not need to be rebalanced.
- Gamma swaps can be a useful hedge for structured products where the volatility exposure falls as prices fall.

Gamma swaps are relatively illiquid products.

14.7 Options on Realized Variance

14.7.1 Features

With the development of swap products, which are arguably forwards on realized variance, it was perhaps inevitable that an option product would emerge. A call option gives the holder the right (but not the obligation) to buy realized variance, while a put option gives the holder the right (but not the obligation) to sell realized variance. The payoffs for call and put options on realized variance are:

$$\text{Call option} = V \times \text{MAX}\left(\sigma^2_{realized} - \sigma^2_{strike}, 0\right)$$

$$\text{Put option} = V \times \text{MAX}\left(\sigma^2_{strike} - \sigma^2_{realized}, 0\right)$$

$\sigma_{realized}$ = realized volatility
σ_{strike} = volatility strike
V = variance units

The variance units are calculated as the volatility units ('vega notional') divided by 2 × volatility strike of a variance swap with the same maturity. By convention the variance swap strike is used to determine the variance units regardless of the option's strike price. Realized volatility is calculated in the same way as a variance swap which means that the options are European in style as the payoff cannot be calculated until maturity.

Premiums can be quoted in two different ways. Suppose a call option is quoted with a strike of 12 % when the ATM level is 14 %. If the premium was quoted as 3.01 'vol points', then the cash payable is the premium multiplied by the vega notional. So if the vega notional was $100,000 the premium would be $301,000. The other method is to quote the premium in basis points per $1 of variance units. For the same option a premium of 84.4 basis points would yield the equivalent result:

$$\$100,000 / (2 \times 14) = 3,571.43$$
$$3,571.43 \times 84.28 = \$301,000$$

14.7.2 Applications

There are a number of possible usages for options which generally follow the main principles highlighted in Chap. 11.

Buying a call option
An investor could buy a call option as a possible directional strategy, that is, if they believed that realized variance was expected to increase. They could also

be used to hedge the losses that could be experienced if the investor is short variance by virtue of a swap position.

Buying a put option
Here the strategy will pay off if the investor expects lower realized volatility. This might be attractive if levels of volatility are elevated and the investor believes they will display an element of mean reversion.

Buying or selling straddles
If the investor believed that volatility was expected to become volatile, then they may choose to buy a straddle. If the investor expected stable volatility, they may decide to execute a short straddle.

14.8 Summary

This chapter developed a number of themes relating to variance and volatility that were initially introduced in Chap. 6.

The focus of this chapter was the different ways in which volatility could be traded and the chapter started with a recap of conventional option volatility strategies. Since the constant volatility assumption of the option valuation framework does not hold in practice this chapter outlined how the term structure and skew could be traded. One of the consequences of the great financial crash was the increased popularity of listed volatility products and the chapter reviewed the features of futures and options on the VIX®.

Although options have been the mainstay of volatility trading through the years, the use of swaps to trade this asset class has increased substantially. The chapter introduced the basic building blocks of variance and volatility swaps before analysing variants of the product such as conditional or corridor structures.

The chapter concluded with a review of options on realized variance.

15

Trading Correlation

15.1 Introduction

The initial coverage of covariance and correlation in Chap. 6 was designed to help readers successfully navigate the option materials that followed. However, the trading of covariance and correlation warrants a separate topic in itself.

As a brief recap, correlation and covariance are defined as follows:

- *Covariance* measures how two random variables behave in relation to each other, measuring the degree of linear association between the two variables. If the price of asset A generally rises (falls) at the same time that the price of asset B rises (falls), the covariance will be positive. If generally the price of asset A is associated with a fall in the price of asset B, the covariance will be negative.
- The degree of association between two variables can also be measured by converting the covariance into a *correlation coefficient*. This is a 'standardized covariance' measure whose values range from +1 to −1 and indicates the strength and direction of a linear relationship between two variables. The variable is often scaled by a factor of a 100 or shown as a percentage number, for example, +0.56, 56 or 56 %.

One of the easiest ways to grasp how correlation is traded can be seen from the correlation proxy formula introduced in Chap. 6. The formula is reproduced for ease of reference:

$$\text{Index volatility} \approx \sqrt{\text{correlation}} \times \text{average single stock volatility} \quad (15.1)$$

© The Author(s) 2017
N. Schofield, *Equity Derivatives*, DOI 10.1057/978-0-230-39107-9_15

So to isolate the correlation exposure a trader would need to take offsetting positions in index and single-stock volatility.

15.2 Sources of Correlation

One of the overall themes of the book is to analyse the relationships that exist between the different components of the equity derivatives market. The key diagram in this respect is Fig. 6.3, repeated here for convenience, which can be used to highlight some of the sources of equity market correlation.

One of the main principles of modern portfolio theory is that the volatility of a portfolio (e.g. an index) is less than the volatility of its component parts. This concept explains the relative positions of each curve and why in theory they should never cross; the closer the two curves the higher the correlation.

Most investment banks will typically have a short correlation exposure as a result of their particular business flows:

- *Vanilla option business*—Fig. 15.1 shows that a traditional form of market activity comes from institutional investors who buy OTM index put options and sell calls on individual stocks as a form of yield enhancement. The bank with whom the investor is trading will have the opposite exposure, namely they will be short index volatility and long single-stock volatility. This is a short correlation exposure.

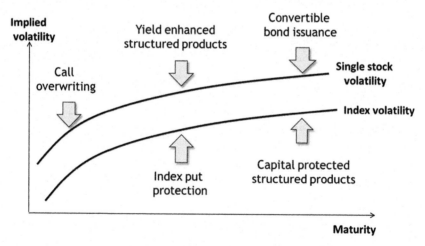

Fig. 15.1 Volatility flows for the equity derivatives market (*Source*: author)

- *Exotic options*—the correlation exposure of these products was considered in Chap. 8. The basket option often references a small number of underlying assets and given their bespoke nature they are relatively illiquid. So one possible hedging strategy is to offset the exposure with individual options on each of the underlying assets. The bespoke baskets are sold to investors leaving the bank short volatility. By buying options on the individual assets the volatility exposure is hedged away but again the banks are left with a short correlation position.
- *Structured products*—not unreasonably investors tend to 'hedge their bets' and so notes that have either an embedded basket or a 'worse of' option tend to be relatively popular products, which means the issuing bank will have a short correlation exposure.

15.3 Factors that Influence Correlation

Some of the factors that influence equity correlation are as follows:

- *Macroeconomic events*—when there is significant uncertainty (e.g. the financial crisis of 2008) equity markets are characterized by high volatility and high correlation (see Figs. 6.4, 6.26 and 6.27).
- *Increased use of equity index futures*—if the market experiences a significant increase in the use of index futures and index ETFs this could lead to an increase in correlation. Kolanovic (2010) points out that if investors buy index futures then through 'no arbitrage' relationships this should place upward pressure on individual shares. At the extreme, if all share trading comprised solely of index futures then the stock price movements would be 100 % correlated, that is, if everyone bought index futures all the stocks in the index would rise resulting in high positive correlation. He argues 'it is reasonable to expect that market correlations should be proportional to the prevalence of index products relative to stock volumes. Broad – index ETFs (such as S&P 500 ETFs) have a similar effect on market correlations.'
- *High frequency trading* (HFT)—Kolanovic (2010) highlights that HFT strategies might have an influence on correlation. For example, if the index future is believed to be trading cheap to fair value an index arbitrage strategy would buy the index and short sell the constituents. He argues: 'this trading activity will dampen the volatility of stocks and increase their correlation to the rest of the stocks within the index'.

15.4 Correlation Trading

15.4.1 Correlation-Dependent Exotics

A number of correlation-dependent exotics were covered in Chap. 8 and included the following:

- Basket options
- 'Best of' and 'worst of' structures
- Outperformance options
- Quanto options
- Composite options

15.4.2 Correlation Swaps

Arguably a swap is the simplest way to take exposure to correlation, although the product has traditionally suffered from a lack of liquidity. To illustrate the mechanics of the swap, consider the following hypothetical transaction used by a bank which is looking to buy correlation to hedge their 'natural' short correlation exposure.

Buyer of correlation:	Bank
Seller of correlation:	Hedge fund
Reference index:	EURO STOXX 50
Weighting of constituents:	Equal
Notional amount:	€10,000 per correlation point
Correlation strike (i.e. fixed rate):	60 points
Floating rate:	Pairwise realized correlation
Bank pays:	Correlation strike
Hedge fund pays:	Floating rate
Maturity:	1 year
Settlement date	At maturity

Diagrammatically the swap could be represented as per Fig. 15.2. The payout on the swap is:

$$\text{Notional amount} \times (\text{pairwise realized correlation} - \text{correlation strike})$$

If the investor has traded a correlation swap where the index constituents are deemed to be equally weighted, the formula required to calculate the pairwise realized correlation is given in Eq. 15.2.

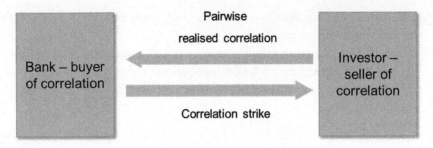

Fig. 15.2 Structure of correlation swap (*Source*: author)

$$\frac{2}{n(n-1)}\sum_{i>j}\rho_{i,j} \qquad (15.2)$$

For 'n' single stocks the number of correlation pairs is equal to $(n \times (n - 1))/2$. So for the EURO STOXX 50 this equals $(50 \times 49)/2 = 1225$ combinations.

However, if the trade investor has set up the trade based on the weight of the constituents within the index the formula used to calculate pairwise realized correlation is:

$$\frac{\sum_{i=1,j>1}^{n} w_i w_j \rho_{i,j}}{\sum_{i=1,j>1}^{n} w_i w_j} \qquad (15.3)$$

If at the maturity of the swap the realized correlation is calculated to be 67, that is, 0.67, the payoff would be:

€10,000 × (67 − 60) = €70,000 in favour of the correlation buyer

Note that similar to variance swaps the correlation measure is scaled by a factor of 100.

15.4.3 Basket Call Versus a Basket of Calls

Basket calls were introduced in Sect. 8.2 and the key points were as follows:

- The volatility of a portfolio (i.e. its risk) was lower than the volatility of its constituent components.[1]
- Basket option valuation requires an investor to make some assumption on the degree of expected correlation between the index constituents.
- A single option on a basket of shares was cheaper than a basket of individual options.
- A basket option is long correlation.

Since a basket option also results in an exposure to movements in the implied volatility of the basket constituents, the correlation can be isolated by taking an offsetting position with a number of individual options, that is, trade a basket call option against a basket of calls. This can be illustrated using the same assets introduced in Chap. 8, namely Chevron and ExxonMobil. The market factors used to derive a value for the various options are represented in Table 15.1.

Table 15.1 Initial market parameters for Chevron and ExxonMobil

Share	Share price	Dividend yield %	Financing costs %	3-month option volatility %	ATM spot vanilla option premium
Chevron	$110	3.6	0.25	16	$3.05
ExxonMobil	$90	2.8	0.25	15	$2.40
				Totals	$5.45

A 3-month equally weighted basket ATM call option on the two assets priced with a correlation of +0.5 returned a premium of $2.33.

The basket could be constructed in such a way that it is initially neutral to changes in implied volatility and will only change in value if there is a change in correlation. Suppose that the investor believes that the correlation between the two assets will decline and so decides to 'sell correlation'. A decline in correlation will reduce the volatility of a basket option so as a result he sells the basket and buys two call options.

The basket option is equally weighted and is comprised of 10,000 shares. The investor's pricing model suggests that a 1 % increase in the implied volatilities of both Chevron and ExxonMobil will result in an increase in the basket option premium from $2.33 to $2.50 leading to a change in the position's value of $1700.

---

[1] Unless all of the assets are perfectly positively correlated, which is unlikely.

To determine the notional amount of the two individual call options the investor needs to identify their vega exposures. The investor's pricing model suggests that for a 1 % increase in implied volatility a call on Chevron would increase in value by $0.22 while ExxonMobil would increase in value by $0.18. If the investor bought 5000 ExxonMobil calls and 5000 Chevron calls a 1 % increase in each of their implied volatilities would generate a profit and loss of $2000.[2] This is greater than the basket option's exposure to implied volatility.

An alternative would be to weight the hedge such that the position is initially vega neutral. For example, a notional of 3863 calls for Chevron and 4722 for ExxonMobil would generate a change in value of approximately $850 for each asset as a result of a 1 % change in volatility, exactly offsetting the profit and loss on the basket.

However, the trade will not be vega neutral for larger movements in the constituent volatilities. If implied volatilities increase by 5 % then the profit and loss would be:

Basket option

- Premium increases from $2.33 to $3.19; on a 10,000 share position this would result in a change in value of $8600.

Offsetting call options
Chevron

- Calls increase in value from $3.05 to $4.13; on a 3863 share position would result in a change in value of $4172.

ExxonMobil

- Calls increase in value from $2.40 to $3.47; a 4722 share position would result in a change in value of $5053.

The total change in the two offsetting calls is $9225 while the change in the value of the basket is $8600. This reflects the impact of correlation—that is, the volatility of a portfolio is less than the volatility of its constituents.

The basket will also have an exposure to the move of just one of the constituent implied volatilities. To illustrate this point, suppose that all other things being equal the implied volatility of Chevron increases by 1 %. The profit and loss on the position will be:

---

[2] (5000 shares × $0.22) + (5000 × $0.18).

Basket option

- Premium moves from $2.33 to $2.43; loss is 10,000 shares × $0.10 = $1000.

Offsetting calls

- No change in value for the ExxonMobil position.
- Chevron call premium moves from $3.05 to $3.37; profit is 3863 shares × $0.32 = $1236.

Overall there is a profit of $236 on the position.

If the trade is constructed to be neutral to small movements in the underlying implied volatilities, it will just about be premium neutral.

Option premium received on the basket

- 10,000 × $2.33 = $23,300

Option premium paid on offsetting call options

- Chevron: 3863 × $3.05 = $11,782
- ExxonMobil: 4722 × $2.40 = $11,333
- Total premium = $23,115

There is a small net premium receivable of $185 but the investor may decide to adjust the notionals to achieve a zero premium solution.

So in summary, the position will (all other things being equal)

- be neutral to small equal movements in the implied volatilities of the underlying assets but be exposed to larger changes in implied volatilities;
- have an exposure to the move of one of the constituent implied volatilities;
- benefit from a decrease in the implied correlation between the two assets.

15.4.4 Covariance Swaps

The exposures faced by institutions trading structures such as basket options led to the evolution of covariance swaps. To understand why, recall that the volatility of an equally weighted two-asset basket is calculated as:

$$\sigma_{basket} = \sqrt{\left(w^2_{x_1}\, \sigma^2_{x_1}\right) + \left(w^2_{x_2}\, \sigma^2_{x_2}\right) + 2 \times \left(w_{x_1}\, w_{x_2}\, \rho_{x_1 x_2}\, \sigma_{x_1}\, \sigma_{x_2}\right)} \qquad (15.4)$$

where :

$\sigma^2_{x_1}$ = Variance of asset 1

$\sigma^2_{x_2}$ = Variance of asset 2

$\rho_{x_1 x_2}$ = Correlation between asset 1 and asset 2

σ_{x_1} = Volatility of asset 1

σ_{x_2} = Volatility of asset 2

w_{x_1} = Proportion of asset 1

w_{x_2} = Proportion of asset 2

So the 'true' exposure of a basket option can be decomposed into two parts:

1. The variance of assets 1 and 2 (i.e. everything to the left hand side of the second '+' sign in Eq. 15.4)
2. The covariance exposure which is the product of everything to the right of the second '+' sign, namely:

   (a) The correlation between assets 1 and 2
   (b) The volatility of asset 1 × volatility of asset 2

Hedging the variance component can be achieved by buying volatility on the constituent components. The covariance component—correlation times the respective volatilities of the underlying assets—is more difficult to hedge. So from a dealer perspective the demand should actually be to buy covariance rather than correlation and this can be done in swap format. Consider the following hypothetical termsheet:

Buyer of covariance:	Bank
Seller of covariance:	Hedge fund
Reference indices:	EURO STOXX 50 and Nikkei 225
Currency:	EUR
Covariance strike (i.e. fixed rate):	4.00 %
Floating rate:	Realized covariance
Bank pays:	Covariance strike
Hedge fund pays:	Floating rate
Maturity:	1 year
Settlement date	At maturity

Similar to other swaps of this type the two parties would need to agree a notional that allows them to 'monetize' the change in the covariance.

Realized covariance is calculated as follows:

$$\frac{252 \times \sum_{t=1}^{n}\left(\ln\frac{P_t}{P_{t-20}}\right)\times\left(\ln\frac{Q_t}{Q_{t-20}}\right)}{\text{Expected OR} \times 20} \qquad (15.5)$$

Where:

t = the relevant observation day

n = number of observed returns, each measured over a 20-day period

Expected OR = the expected number of observation returns

P_t = Closing level of Nikkei 225

Q_t = closing level of EURO STOXX 50

From the bank's perspective they are:

- Long realized correlation between the two indices
- Long realized volatility of EURO STOXX 50
- Long realized volatility of Nikkei 225

These exposures can be seen by reworking the swap's payoff:

$$\begin{aligned}\text{Payout} &= \text{Covariance strike} - \text{Realized covariance} \\ \text{Payout} &= \text{Covariance strike} - \left(\rho_{SX5E,NKY} \times \sigma_{SX5E} \times \sigma_{NKY}\right)\end{aligned} \qquad (15.6)$$

From Eq. 15.6 it can be seen that:

- An increase in the volatility of the EURO STOXX 50 or the Nikkei 225 will increase the realized covariance.
- An increase in the correlation between the two indices will also result in an increase in realized covariance.
- Combining both of these elements it is possible to conclude that in this covariance swap the bank is buying both volatility and correlation.

A covariance swap would be marked to market in the same way as a variance swap. This technique was illustrated in Sect. 14.6.1.3.

15.4.5 Dispersion Trading

15.4.5.1   Definition

Dispersion trading is a strategy that allows a trader to express views about the expected evolution of the correlation that exists between the constituents of an index. Dispersion can be thought of as the 'scattering' or 'spreading widely' of data around some average value. It could be argued that dispersion and correlation are simply opposite sides of the same coin.

• Higher dispersion means lower correlation.
• Lower dispersion means higher correlation.

The structure of a dispersion trade can be seen from Eq. 15.1. Trading dispersion involves trading the volatilities of a basket of shares against the volatilities of the constituents with the aim of isolating the correlation exposure. In this sense it is basically a relative value trade.

15.4.5.2   Quoting Conventions

Dispersion trades can be quoted in two formats:

• *As the implied average pairwise correlation*—this measure of correlation is implied from the observed values of the index and constituent member volatilities. It is the output of Eq. 6.4 and can be approximated using formula 15.1. However, it is important to note that it is not the average of all of the individual pairwise implied correlations, as these are not observable.
• *As a difference in implied volatility*—this is expressed as weighted-average single-stock volatility minus index volatility. However, the correlation implied by a given spread is also a function of the absolute level of volatility. If index volatility is 28 % and single-stock volatility 30 %, the implied correlation is 0.87. If the values for the index and single-stock volatilities were 18 % and 20 % respectively, the implied correlation would be 0.81. It follows that for a higher level of volatility, a given correlation will result in a larger volatility spread and vice versa. For example, if the correlation between an index and its constituents is 0.5 and the volatilities are 28 % and 36 %, respectively, the same correlation value would apply if index volatility was 18 % and single-stock volatility was 25 %.

15.4.5.3   Choice of Instruments

A dispersion trade can be constructed by buying (or selling) volatility on the index against selling (or buying) volatility on the index constituents. These trades are summarized in Table 15.2.

Because of transaction costs traders will tend to favour indices with fewer constituents (e.g. EURO STOXX 50) but may choose to express the view by trading the volatility of a larger index such as the S&P 500 against a representative basket of constituents (e.g. the top 50 shares).

There are a number of different instruments that the trader could use to express a view on dispersion:

- *Vanilla options*—this is typically done using straddles or strangles. To sell correlation the trader would sell straddles/strangles on the index and buy straddles/strangles on the index constituents with their trade size based on their index weight. One of the benefits of using straddles/strangles is that they tend to be quoted with a higher level of implied volatility than variance swaps. This is because variance swaps tend to be more expensive to hedge, which has to be reflected in their price. Although options are typically very liquid the implementation of this strategy would require the position to be delta-hedged on an ongoing basis.
- *Variance swaps*—to short correlation using variance swaps the investor would sell index variance and buy single-stock variance. Typically, the notional of the single-stock trades are based on the constituents' weight within the index and their payouts would probably be capped. Variance swaps are usually hedged with a static portfolio of puts and calls struck along a continuum. Risk (2011) points out that before the financial crash traders would hedge using a limited number of strikes around the level of spot. However, upon the collapse of Lehman Brothers this hedge liquidity dried up with dealers losing "billions".
- *Volatility swaps*—for the buyer of correlation, these have the advantage of having lower losses than variance swaps if volatility on single name stocks increases significantly.
- *Correlation swaps*—these were considered in Sect. 15.4.2 and consist of a single payoff between a pre-agreed strike and realized correlation. The most

Table 15.2 Components of a dispersion trade		Sell correlation	Buy correlation
	Index	Sell volatility	Buy volatility
	Constituents	Buy volatility	Sell volatility

common convention is for the names to have equal weights. Although this offers a 'pure' exposure to correlation the instrument is relatively illiquid. This lack of liquidity and the difficulty in hedging this type of instrument has meant that the strikes for these instruments are lower than those achieved when trading correlation using variance swaps (Granger et al. 2005).

15.4.5.4   Dispersion Trade Weighting Techniques

If a variance swap is set up with equal vega notionals the position will still have an exposure to volatility. Suppose that an investor decides to execute the following short correlation trade:

- Sell index variance swap with a vega notional of $20,000 at a strike of 15.
- Buy single-stock variance swaps with a total vega notional of $20,000 at a strike of 25.

Based on the correlation proxy equation, these two components suggest an implied correlation of 36 %.

Suppose that average single-stock volatility increases by 1 % but correlation remains unchanged. Using the correlation proxy measure this means that index volatility will be 15.6 %.[3] So a 1 % increase in single-stock volatility will cause index volatility to increase by 0.6 %. Since the investor has executed a short correlation position the profit on the single-stock variance swap position will be greater than the loss on the index position, that is, the short correlation trade with equal vega notionals is vega positive.

To avoid this directional exposure to volatility the notionals would need to be adjusted to ensure that the trade is initially vega neutral. The vega exposure of a variance swap measures how the position's profit and loss will change if implied volatility were to move by 1 % point from its initial strike. So vega neutrality requires that the notional amounts be set at such a level that a 1 % change in volatility for the index and its constituents will not generate any profit or loss. This concept is also sometimes referred to as the 'crossed vega'.[4]

To illustrate how a vega neutral trade is set up, consider the following hypothetical transaction referencing the EURO STOXX 50 Table 15.3.

---

[3] SQRT (0.36) × 26 % = 15.6 %.

[4] Crossed vega is the amount of vega traded on both single stock and indexes. So $10 m of crossed vega at a portfolio level means that $10 m of vega on the single stocks is matched with $10 m vega on the index (Risk 2011).

Table 15.3 Term sheet for hypothetical dispersion trade

	Index variance swap leg	Single-stock variance swap legs
Buyer	Bank	Hedge fund
Seller	Hedge fund	Bank
Maturity	1 year	1 year
Volatility units (EUR per point)	126,229	Various, totalling 100,000
Variance units	3607	Various
Volatility strike	17.50 %	Various

Table 15.4 Structuring a variance swap dispersion trade on the EURO STOXX 50

Equity	Index weight	Volatility units (€ per point)	Variance units	Volatility strike	Weighted strike
ABN AMRO	2.20 %	2200	51	21.47	0.47
Aegon	0.90 %	900	16	27.94	0.25
Ahold	0.60 %	600	10	29.33	0.18
Telecom Italia	1.60 %	1600	38	21.02	0.34
Total	6.80 %	6800	178	19.15	1.30
Unilever	1.80 %	1800	46	19.36	0.35
Totals	100 %	100,000			22.09

The index variance swap leg consists of a single swap on the underlying index, whereas the single-stock leg is made up of 50 individual variance swaps each with a different notional amount, partial details of which are shown in Table 15.4. Notional amounts on the single-stock positions are determined as follows:

- The investor decides the total desired volatility exposure for the constituents (e.g. €100,000).
- The volatility units for each constituent are the product of this total desired exposure and the constituent weight within the index. For ABN AMRO the volatility units are €100,000 × 2.2 % = €2200.
- The variance units for each constituent are equal to the volatility units divided by (2 × strike). For ABN AMRO this would be €2200/(2 × 21.47) = 51.

The final stage is to determine the notional on the index trade to ensure vega neutrality. This is achieved by weighting the total desired volatility exposure for the single-stock leg by the ratio of the implied volatilities of each leg of the trade. For the index position the implied volatility used for this calculation is the variance swap strike, which in this case is 17.50 %. For the single-stock position, the implied volatility is calculated as the sum of the weighted strikes:

- The observed volatility strike is multiplied by the constituent's weight in the index. For ABN AMRO on Table 15.4, it is 0.47, that is, 21.47 × 2.2 %.
- These individual values are then summed (e.g. 22.09).

$$\text{Index Notional} = \text{Single stock notional} \times \sum \frac{\text{Weighted strike of constituents}}{\text{Volatility strike of index}}$$

$$= 100,000 \times \frac{22.09}{17.50}$$

$$= 126,229$$

The payoff on all of the swaps follows the normal variance swap conventions illustrated in Sect. 14.6.1.

There are two other points worthy of mention with respect to dispersion trading:

- 'Market disruption events' will impact the payoff of a variance swap as it will influence the calculation of the realized volatility. Typical examples of market disruption would be as follows:

  - Early closing of the market, for example, due to technological problems
  - Suspension of trading in a share
  - Insufficient liquidity or trading volumes
  - Conditions that impact an entity's ability to hedge an exposure

- Some trades also allow for the closing value of the share to be adjusted by the amount of a gross cash dividend when it is paid on an observation date.

15.4.5.5 Dispersion Options

A dispersion option can be linked to the performance of a bespoke basket of assets such as equity indices. Consider the following hypothetical termsheet:

Notional amount:	$1 m
Maturity:	1 year
Underlying indices:	S&P 500, EURO STOXX 50, Nikkei 225
Strike rate:	0.05 as a decimal or 5 %

Option payoff:

$$\mathrm{MAX}\left(\frac{1}{n}\sum_{i=1}^{n}\left|\frac{S_t^i}{S_0^i}-\mathrm{Basket}_{average}\right|-\mathrm{Strike},0\right)$$

$$\mathrm{Where:Basket}_{average}=\frac{1}{n}\sum_{i=1}^{n}\frac{S_t^i}{S_0^i}$$

S_t^i = Final level of index 'i'

S_0^i = Initial level of index 'i'

To illustrate how the option might pay off consider the following example:

The steps to calculate the option payoff are:

- The performance of each index was calculated over the option's maturity (fourth column of Table 15.5).
- These individual performances were then averaged to determine the 'basket average' (bottom figure of column four of Table 15.5).
- The absolute value of each index performance was then calculated with respect to the 'basket average' (5th column of Table 15.5).
- These absolute values were then averaged (bottom of 5th column of Table 15.5) and compared to the strike rate to determine the option's payoff. The payoff of the option is therefore:

$$\$1,000,000\times\mathrm{MAX}\left(0.08-0.05,0\right)=\$30,000$$

To get a sense of how the option's payoff will vary consider Table 15.6, which takes the same initial values but a different set of final values, which are more dispersed.

Table 15.5 Calculation of dispersion option payoff

Index	Initial level	Final level	Performance	Absolute value of difference
S&P 500	2000	1800	0.9	0.9–1.02 = 0.12
EUROSTOXX 50	3000	3150	1.05	1.05–1.02 = 0.03
Nikkei 225	16,000	17,600	1.10	1.10–1.02 = 0.08
		Basket average =	1.02	0.08

Table 15.6 Calculation of option payoff in a 'high' dispersion scenario

Index	Initial level	Final level	Performance	Absolute value of difference
S&P 500	2000	1600	0.8	0.8–1.02 = 0.22
EUROSTOXX 50	3000	3200	1.07	1.07–1.02 = 0.05
Nikkei 225	16,000	19,200	1.20	1.20–1.02 = 0.18
		Basket average =	1.02	0.15

In Table 15.6 although the 'basket average' is about the same as the first example,[5] the dispersion of values is greater. The payoff of the option is therefore:

$$\$1,000,000 \times MAX\left(0.15 - 0.05, 0\right) = \$100,000$$

So the key features of the dispersion option as shown here are as follows:

- The payoff will increase if realized correlation between the components falls (i.e. if dispersion increases).
- If implied volatilities are high this increases the possibility that the future realized performance will be more dispersed.

15.5 Summary

Chapter 6 looked at the characteristics and calculation of correlation and covariance. Chapter 8 analysed the mechanics of a number of correlation-dependent structures such as basket options. This chapter argued that correlation risk was a consequence of the investment banking business model. The main focus of this chapter was the different ways in which correlation and covariance could be hedged and traded. The products considered were as follows:

- Correlation swaps
- Basket calls versus a basket of calls
- Covariance swaps
- Dispersion trading using variance swaps
- Dispersion options.

[5] The results are not strictly speaking the exactly same as the average has been rounded to two decimal places.

Bibliography

Allen, P., Einchcomb, S., & Granger, N. (2006) *Variance swaps* JP Morgan research
    Bank for International Settlements (BIS) (2013) – *Triennial Central Bank survey*
Barclays Capital (2007) *Investing in dividend yield* Barclays Bank research
Barclays Capital (2010) *Dividend swaps and futures* Barclays Bank research
Barclays Capital (2016) *Equity Gilt Study* Barclays Bank research
Barclays Capital (2011) *Index dividend options primer* Barclays Bank research
Barclays Capital (2012) *GAAP matter 2012* Barclays Bank research
Bennett, C., & Gil, M. (2012) *Volatility trading* Santander
Blake, D. (1990) *Financial Market Analysis* McGraw Hill
BNP Paribas (2007) *Corridor variance swaps* BNP Paribas research
BNP Paribas (2005) *Volatility investing handbook* BNP Paribas research
Bossu, S., Strasser, E., & Guichard, R. (2005) *Just what you need to know about variance swaps* JP Morgan research
Bouzoubaa, M., & Osseiran, A. (2010) *Exotic options and hybrids* Wiley
Brask, A. (2004) *Variance swap primer* Barclays Capital Research
Brask, A. (2005) *Forward variance swap primer* Barclays Capital Research
Brask, A., Baror, E., Deb, A., & Tang, M. (2007) *Relative value vehicles and drivers* Barclays Capital
Citigroup (2008) *A jargon-busting guide to volatility surfaces and changes in implied volatility* Equity derivatives research
Combescot, P. (2013) *Recent changes in equity financing* Presentation to the Society of Actuaries
De Weert, F. (2006) *An introduction to options trading* Wiley
De Weert, F. (2008) *Exotic option trading* Wiley
Deb, A., & Brask, A. (2009) *Demystifying volatility skew* Barclays Capital
Demeterfi, K., Derman, E., Kamal, M., & Zou, J. (1999) *More than you ever wanted to know about volatility swaps* Goldman Sachs research

© The Author(s) 2017
N. Schofield, *Equity Derivatives*, DOI 10.1057/978-0-230-39107-9

Derman, E. (1992) *Outperformance options* Goldman Sachs

Galitz, L. (2013) *Handbook of financial engineering* third edition FT publishing

Gray, G., Cusatis, P.J., & Woolridge, J.R. (2004) *Streetsmart guide to valuing a stock* Second edition, McGraw Hill

Granger, N., & Allen, P. (2005) *Correlation vehicles* J.P. Morgan Chase

Groves, & Francis. (2011) *Exchange Traded funds* Harriman

Haug, E. (2007) *The complete guide to option pricing formulas* McGraw Hill

Hull, J.C. (2012) *Options, futures and other derivatives* Pearson

ICE futures Europe (2016) *Corporate actions policy*

Kani, I., Derman, E., & Kamal M. (1995) *Trading and hedging local volatility* Goldman Sachs research

Kani, I. Derman, E. Kamal, M (1996) *Trading and hedging local volatility* Goldman Sachs

Kay, J. (2009) *The long and the short of it* Erasmus Press

Kolanovic, M. (2010) *Why we have a correlation bubble* J.P. Morgan research

Magrabe, W. (1978) The value of an option to exchange one asset for another, Journal of Finance, 33 (March 1978)

Marroni, & Perdomo. (2014) *Pricing and Hedging Financial Derivatives* Wiley

Nashikkar, & Amrut. (2011) *Understanding OIS discounting* Barclays Capital

Natenberg, S. (1994) *Option pricing and volatility* McGraw Hill

Pinto, J.E., Henry, E., Robinson, T.R., & Stowe, J.D. (2010) *Equity asset valuation* Wiley

Rattray, S. (2000) *Assessing a fair level for implied volatility* Goldman Sachs

Risk Magazine (2011) *Dispersion tactics* Structured products, January

Risk Magazine (2013) *Inventory pressures* August

Risk Magazine (2015a) *Autocallable issuance upsets Euro Stoxx volatility market* August

Risk Magazine (2015b) *Korean crunch: how HSCEI fall hammered exotics desks* November

Risk Magazine (2015a) *Autocallable issuance upsets Euro Stoxx volatility market* August

Risk Magazine (2016a) *Dealers fear death of dividend risk premia strategy*

Risk Magazine (2016b) *Sliding HSCIE threatens fresh autocallable losses*

Schofield, N.C. (2008) *Commodity derivatives* Wiley Finance Series

Schofield, N.C., & Bowler, T. (2011) *Trading, the fixed income, inflation and credit markets: a relative value guide* Wiley Finance Series

Simmons, M. (2002) *Securities Operations* Wiley Finance Series

Tompkins, R. (1994) *Options explained²* Palgrave Macmillan

UBS (1999) *Options: the fundamentals* UBS

Vasan, P. (1998) *Foreign exchange options* Credit Suisse First Boston

Vause (2005) *Guide to analysing companies* The Economist

Viebig, Poddig, & Varmaz. (2008) *Equity valuation: models from leading investment banks* Wiley Finance Series

Watsham, T.J., & Parramore, K. (1997) *Quantitative methods in finance* Thomson

Index

Note: Page numbers followed by 'n' denote notes.

© The Author(s) 2017
N. Schofield, *Equity Derivatives*, DOI 10.1057/978-0-230-39107-9

Printed by Printforce, the Netherlands